RESEARCH IN
LABOR ECONOMICS

Volume 11 · 1990

LABOR ECONOMICS AND
PUBLIC POLICY

RESEARCH IN
LABOR ECONOMICS

A Research Annual

LABOR ECONOMICS AND PUBLIC POLICY

Guest Editors: LAURIE J. BASSI
Departments of Economics and Public Policy
Georgetown University

DAVID L. CRAWFORD
Econsult Corporation and
University of Pennsylvania

Series Editor: RONALD G. EHRENBERG
Irving M. Ives Professor of Industrial
and Labor Relations and Economics
Cornell University

VOLUME 11 · 1990

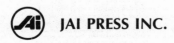 JAI PRESS INC.

Greenwich, Connecticut   London, England

CONTENTS

LIST OF CONTRIBUTORS

Laurie J. Bassi

Departments of Economics and
Public Policy
Georgetown University

Edward Berkowitz

Department of History
George Washington University

Monroe Berkowitz

Department of Economics
Rutgers University

John Bishop

Center for Advanced Human
Resource Studies
Cornell University

Rebecca M. Blank

Department of Economics and
School of Education and Policy
Northwestern University

Charles Brown

Institute for Social Research
University of Michigan and
National Bureau of Economic
Research

Richard V. Burkhauser

Department of Economics
Vanderbilt University

James C. Cox

Department of Economics
University of Arizona

David L. Crawford   Econsult Corporation and
                                     University of Pennsylvania

Daniel S. Hamermesh   Department of Economics
                                     Michigan State University

Harry J. Holzer   Department of Economics
                                     Michigan State University

Michael Horrigan   Bureau of Labor Statistics
                                     Washington, DC

Jonathan S. Leonard   School of Business
                                     University of California,
                                     Berkeley

Olivia S. Mitchell   Department of Labor Economics
                                     Cornell University and
                                     National Bureau of Economic
                                     Research

Ronald L. Oaxaca   Department of Economics
                                     University of Arizona

Donald O. Parsons   Department of Economics
                                     Ohio State University

John M. Quigley   Graduate School of
                                     Public Policy
                                     University of California,
                                     Berkeley

Joseph F. Quinn   Department of Economics
                                     Boston College

Eugene Smolensky   Graduate School of
                                     Public Policy
                                     University of California
                                     Berkeley

Stephen A. Woodbury   Michigan State University and
                                     W. E. Upjohn Institute

PREFACE

The papers in this volume were originally prepared as background papers for the Secretary of Labor's Commission on Workforce Quality and Labor Market Efficiency. Established in July 1988, this commission issued its final report, *Investing in People: A Strategy to Address America's Workforce Crisis,* on Labor Day 1989, and this report made numerous policy recommendations.

Laurie Bassi and David Crawford, the guest editors of Volume 11 of *Research in Labor Economics,* served, respectively, as deputy director and executive director of the commission. From the 49 background papers that were prepared, they have chosen 13 for inclusion in this [volume]. These papers provide critical summaries of the research in particular areas of labor economics, stress the policy relevance of the research findings, and indicate the areas in which future research might profitably be directed. The authors' own introductory essay summaries these papers, outlines the commission's final report, and stresses the areas in which they feel future research is needed.

Ronald G. Ehrenberg
Series Editor

LABOR ECONOMICS
AND PUBLIC POLICY

Laurie J. Bassi and David L. Crawford

The papers in this volume were originally prepared as background papers for the Commission on Workforce Quality and Labor Market Efficiency.[1] This independent, bipartisan commission was established in July 1988 by Ann McLaughlin, then the secretary of labor of the United States.[2] Without her vision and leadership, the commission and this volume would never have existed. In these and many other ways, she brought the labor economics research community back into the public policy debate. In recognition of her contributions and in appreciation of the opportunity she gave us, we dedicate this volume to Ann McLaughlin.

McLaughlin's charge to the commission was to

1. examine the roles and effectiveness of privately and publicly provided job training and education,
2. determine the best mechanisms to keep the education system and training providers continuously informed of the changing skill needs of employers and workers,
3. consider the problem of financing private investments in human capital and determine the best ways to access financial capital for that purpose,

---

Research in Labor Economics, Volume 11, pages 1–15.
Copyright © 1990 by JAI Press Inc.
All rights of reproduction in any form reserved.
ISBN: 1-555938-080-2

4. assess the appropriate roles of employers, unions, and government in retraining and relocating dislocated workers,
5. examine ways in which private and public job placement agencies can enhance the efficiency of the changing labor market of the future,
6. assess the need for greater flexibility of employers' policies to facilitate labor force entry,
7. evaluate the opportunities to enhance productivity through alterations of the employment arrangement such as innovative pay systems and benefit structures, employment security provisions, and worker involvement.

As the deputy and executive directors of the commission respectively, we were responsible for organizing the preparation of 49 background papers. We gratefully acknowledge the valuable contributions made by the commission staff at every stage of that process, including the original development of paper topics, the selection and supervision of authors, and the editing of preliminary drafts.[3] Authors were asked to summarize existing research in a particular area and to suggest specific recommendations for the commission's consideration. Most of the papers were written by outside experts, under contract with the department of labor; a few were written directly by the staff. The papers were originally published by the commission under the auspices of the department of labor, but it should be understood that opinions expressed are those of the authors and do not necessarily reflect the official position or policy of the commission or of the department of labor.[4]

Out of the 49 papers, we have selected the 13 that we believe will be of greatest interest to the readers of *Research in Labor Economics*. We regret that many excellent papers could not be included. All of the papers have been revised since their original publication, and we want to thank the authors for making those revisions quickly.

In the section that follows, we summarize the papers included in this volume, many of which were particularly influential in shaping the commissioners' deliberations and their ultimate recommendations. In Section II, we briefly outline the commission's final report. Section III outlines our thoughts on directions for future research, thoughts that grew out of our frustration when we found that we were unable to answer many of the commissioners' most important questions.

I. THE PAPERS IN THIS VOLUME

The first four papers in this volume address the education and training of both the future and current workforce. In "Incentives for Learning: Why American High School Students Compare So Poorly to Their Counterparts Overseas," John Bishop documents the startling differences between the level of achievement of students in the United States and that of students in other countries. He notes, for example, that by the end of high school, an average U.S. student is more than four grade level equivalents behind his Japanese counterpart in mathematics and science. Bishop presents some fairly compelling evidence indicating that this shortfall in achievement is, in large part, a result of the fact that U.S. high school students devote much less time and effort to the task of learning than do students in other societies. This shortfall in effort is, in turn, linked to an absence of financial incentives to learn while in school (particularly for students who do not plan to attend selective universities). Bishop suggests that the relationship between achievement in school and outcomes in the labor market ought to be strengthened. The notion of making credentials of high school achievement an integral component of the initial hiring process (particularly for those who do not attend college) is probably the most important. This is an idea that has already gained a considerable amount of interest, both in the business community and within the departments of labor and education. Within the next few years, we are likely to see demonstration projects that implement Bishop's ideas.

Donald Parsons, in "The Firm's Decision to Train," provides a critical review of models of employer-provided training, focusing on the distinction between the actual training activity and the financing of it. He outlines the conditions under which private markets generate an optimal amount of training, and then he proceeds to use those conditions to illustrate the circumstances under which markets will generate suboptimal levels of training. He suggests two policies for correcting market failure: The first would involve legal reform, designed to reduce the difficulties in creating enforceable apprenticeship contracts. The current legal environment can make it difficult for employers to recoup their investments in worker training. The second policy that Parsons suggests is to encourage the creation of multiemployer training cooperatives to provide workers with skills specific to an industry or a specific type of technology. Such cooperatives would reduce the disincentives for training that result from firms "raiding" one another's employees. Unfortunately, such arrangements could be illegal under our current laws. In order to encourage these cooperatives it may be necessary to amend those laws.

In the paper that follows, "Improving Efficiency in the Tax Treatment of Training and Educational Expenditures," John Quigley and Eugene Smolensky review the treatment of human capital investments in our personal and corporate income tax laws. They first discuss how different types of education and training receive more or less favorable treatment under the personal income tax code. They next turn their attention to a comparison of the corporate tax treatment of investments in human capital, physical capital, and research and development. After their review, they consider a variety of possible changes in the tax code and endorse two: (1) making all personal expenditures by employees immediately and fully deductible against the current wages and salaries of the employee, and

(2) combining corporate investments in research and development with human capital investments so that these two types of investments would be treated identically.

The paper by Charles Brown, "Empirical Evidence on Private Training," summarizes what we know about the distribution and intensity of employer-provided training. While in large part the results summarized in this paper indicate that the empirical findings are consistent with the predictions that emerge from the theoretical literature, the paper also reveals how little we actually know about training. This dearth of knowledge leads Brown to the conclusion that we should not consider pursuing policies to subsidize informal (on-the-job) training since monitoring such training is too difficult. He does, however, suggest several mechanisms for improving our knowledge of both the level and content of employer-provided training.

The next set of papers focuses on four groups that are of particular concern to policymakers: young men, part-time workers, older workers, and disabled individuals. In "Labor Force Participation and Employment among Young Men: Trends, Causes, and Policy Implications," Harry Holzer documents the decline in labor force participation rates among young men who are not enrolled in school. This decrease, which has been particularly pronounced among teenagers, high school dropouts, and young black men, seems to be unrelated to the business cycle. Holzer reviews the empirical literature, which points to a wide variety of factors contributing to this reduction in labor force participation among young men: The influx of women into the labor force, the shift in demand away from less educated workers, the slowdown in the rate of growth of productivity, industrial relocation, declining rates of unionization, lack of labor market information and "connections," Aid to Families with Dependent Children (AFDC), and high reservation wages all seem to be contributing factors. Holzer concludes that government-financed programs, linking employment, job training, and remedial classroom instruction should be expanded. He also suggests that wage subsidies for young and less-educated workers should be used during periods of slack in the labor market, and that these policies should be used on a regular basis for the most disadvantaged individuals.

In "Understanding Part-Time Work," Rebecca Blank reviews the evidence on both the trends in part-time work and the demographic composition of the part-time workforce. She summarizes the determinants of part-time vs. full-time work (both from workers' and firms' perspectives) and reviews the empirical literature on the part-time workforce. Part-time workers are 18% of all workers; 11% of all employed men and 27% of all employed women work part-time. These workers are a very heterogeneous group consisting largely of teenagers, women with young children, and workers over the age of 65. This diversity makes it difficult to sort out the policy concerns that are relevant to this group. While there are very substantial wage differentials between part-time and full-time workers, Blank points out that these differentials per se are not cause for concern. Other issues, however, may give rise to the need for public policy intervention. These issues include the dearth of part-time jobs that are career oriented, the need that many part-time workers have for fringe benefits, and the growth in the percentage of workers who report that they are involuntarily working part-time.

The papers by Richard Burkhauser and Joseph Quinn, "Economic Incentives and the Labor Force Participation of Older Workers," documents the steady decline that has taken place since 1970 in the labor force participation rates among men over the age of 55. For men over the age of 63, the decline began well before 1970. These steady, long-term declines give rise to public policy concerns. As the children of the baby boom approach the age of 50, we could well face prolonged labor shortages if current retirement patterns continue. Burkhauser and Quinn review the empirical literature, which can help us determine which policy options for increasing the labor force participation of older workers are likely to be most effective. They conclude that the single most promising policy is to promote the use of defined-contribution pension plans, rather than defined-benefit plans. They also suggest that a variety of policies are available to reduce either the tax burden of older workers who work part-time, or the cost to firms of hiring part-time older workers.

The next paper by Monroe and Edward Berkowitz, "Labor Force Participation among Disabled Persons," carefully reviews the institutional setting that affects the labor force participation of disabled individuals. The paper begins with a discussion of the difficulties involved in defining disability. They then review the evidence on the impact that the aging of the population is likely to have on the number of workers who are disabled. They move on to a review of the empirical literature, which has examined both the magnitude of the disincentive effects of a wide variety of disability programs and the efficacy of rehabilitation programs. They conclude with a variety of suggestions for improving the cost-effectiveness of the rehabilitation process.

The three papers that follow focus on recent trends in unemployment and on the effects of the unemployment insurance system. In their paper, "The Unemployment Experience of the Workforce," Jonathan Leonard and Michael Horrigan review the evidence on trends in unemployment over the past 20 years. In addition to presenting trends in overall unemployment rates over the course of the business cycle, they consider evidence on how the duration of unemployment has varied over time and across demographic and industry groups. They find that both the rate of unemployment (with the exception of the current recovery) and its duration have been trending upwards. They conclude that these upward trends cannot be accounted for by either the demographic or the industrial composition of the workforce. They find some evidence to suggest that jobs have become less stable and workers less mobile, and that the percentage of the unemployed who are job losers has increased. The conjunction of these factors suggests that reducing unemployment below its current level may be quite challenging.

The next paper by James Cox and Ronald Oaxaca, "Unemployment Insurance and Job Search," reviews the empirical studies of the effects of the unemployment insurance (UI) system on the duration of unemployment and the quality of job matches. Within both the literature on the recent UI experiments and the older nonexperimental literature, they report a consensus that the UI system does, indeed, increase the duration of unemployment for those workers who are eligible to receive benefits. There is no similar consensus, however, that the UI system improves the quality of the match between workers and employers. Cox and Oaxaca conclude that the lack of evidence on this latter point does not necessarily indicate that there are no such effects, but may instead be the result of data problems. They suggest that future UI research should focus on continued (longer-term) experimentation and on the impact of UI benefits on the quality of job matches for UI claimants.

The paper by Daniel Hamermesh, "Unemployment Insurance Financing, Short-Time Compensation, and Labor Demand," reviews both how the UI system is financed and the empirical evidence on the impact of the system, from the perspective of employers. Hamermesh first documents the "incomplete experience rating" of the system. Many firms that make substantial use of layoffs pay less into the UI system than their workers receive in UI benefits; other firms that use layoffs sparingly pay more than their workers receive in benefits. A large empirical literature indicates that this cross-subsidization between firms leads to larger employment fluctuations and more layoff unemployment. There is also some evidence that the incomplete experience rating of the UI system has resulted in the expansion of unstable industries and the contraction of stable industries. Finally, because the UI tax base is low (i.e., employers only pay a tax on employee's wages up to a specified ceiling), the UI system encourages firms to substitute high-wage workers for low-wage workers. These findings lead Hamermesh to suggest an increase in both the degree of experience rating and the wage ceiling on which employers' UI taxes are based.

The last two papers in the volume deal with various aspects of fringe benefits, which have become such an important percentage of total compensation. In "Current Developments in Employee Benefits," Stephen Woodbury reports that the trend toward ever-increasing employee benefits as a share of total compensation has now stopped. In large part, the cessation of this long-term trend seems to have been caused by a slowdown in the growth of legally required benefits and a reduction in marginal tax rates (which has reduced the incentive to shift compensation from wages to benefits). Nonetheless, the level and distribution of fringe benefits remain a policy issue. Woodbury outlines the arguments for and against increased taxation of voluntary fringe benefits, and reports on the estimated magnitude of the reductions in pension plans and health insurance that would result from such taxation. He concludes by suggesting that a tax cap should be placed on certain types of fringe benefits (especially health insurance) to help reduce both the oversupply of these benefits and the inequality of the income distribution.

Finally, in "The Effects of Mandating Benefits Packages," Olivia Mitchell identifies and quantifies (wherever possible) the labor market consequences of governmentally mandated employee benefits. She concludes that (1) while mandated benefits would, indeed, increase the availability and generosity of benefits to many workers who are now not covered, there would still be many individuals who would not be helped by mandated benefits, (2) the "costs" of mandating benefits would be a reduction in other (nonmandated) benefits, reduced hours of work and employment (particularly among those workers who are expensive to insure), and a possible reduction of output in the covered sectors, and (3) most of the proposals to mandate benefits exclude part-time and/or minimum wage workers and those in small firms—exactly the groups who are currently most likely not to be covered. She suggests that if benefits are, in fact, mandated, (a) a variable-cost format (based on hours of work) would reduce the adverse effects of the mandate, (b) mandates should be phased in gradually, and (c) an alternative system of providing benefits should be provided for those individuals who remain uncovered.

II. AN OVERVIEW OF THE COMMISSION'S REPORT

On Labor Day, 1989, the commission published its final report, titled *Investing in People: A Strategy to Address America's Workforce Crisis, Background Papers.*[5] By using the word *crisis* in the subtitle of the final report, the commission conveyed its sense of the urgency of increasing the productivity of the American workforce. In significant part, that sense was based on the projections of *Workforce 2000,* in our view the most influential report from the department of labor in at least two decades. That report predicted that demographic trends, technological change, and increased international competition would lead to shortages of skilled workers and surpluses of unskilled workers. Based on their own experiences, the commissioners believed that these threats were real and that they were already beginning to affect the American economy.

Many people, including most of the members of the press who covered the release of the report, have insisted on looking for a few "silver bullets," simple changes that would correct all or most of our workforce problems. In his letter of transmittal to Secretary Elizabeth Dole, Commission Chairman Richard Schubert wrote:

> At the beginning of the Commission's work, we hoped to identify two or three major initiatives that might produce immediate, significant improvements in workforce quality. We have since learned that there are no simple, easy solutions. Rather, we have identified a need for action on many fronts, action that will require the close cooperation of business, labor, and government at all levels.[6]

Consistent with this conclusion, the commission made 44 specific recommendations in its final report, recommendations directed to the secretary of labor, to other executive departments, to Congress, to business, to labor, and to the public.

The first chapter of the commission's report contains 14 recommendations concerning primary and secondary education. The first recommendation calls for the president to lead governors and others in the development of national educational goals and timetables. This recommendation has already been implemented through the "education summit" of late 1989, the president's 1990 State of the Union address, and subsequent activities.

In our view the most important recommendations in the first chapter are the two related to encouraging employers' use of high school transcripts and achievement test scores to evaluate young job applicants. These suggestions build on John Bishop's idea that students would be motivated to work harder in school if they knew that employers would reward their academic achievements. The Worklink project, recently begun by the American Business Conference, the National Alliance of Business, and the Educational Testing Service, is attempting to implement this idea by developing standardized credentials to be used in the screening of job applicants.

The second chapter presents recommendations regarding postsecondary investments in human capital. The first major theme of this chapter is the encouragement of employers' investments in their workers. The commission calls for new tax incentives for employer-provided training (discussed in the Quigley–Smolensky paper), the encouragement of multiemployer training cooperatives (discussed in the Parsons paper), and government support for the design and certification of employer-provided training. All of these suggestions are now being actively reviewed by the department of labor.

The second theme of the second chapter is the use of government programs to meet education and training needs that are unlikely to be met by the private sector. Toward that end, the commission recommended a more substantial commitment to adult basic education, a more intense focus of the Job Training Partnership Act (JTPA) on remedial education for the severely disadvantaged, more funding for JTPA and Job Corps, increased funding for education and training grants to high school graduates, and a cabinet level committee to coordinate human resource programs across executive departments. The Bush administration's proposed budget for 1991 calls for a 25% increase in the adult basic education program. Amendments to refocus JTPA were proposed by both Republicans and Democrats before the commission report was published. To our knowledge, there has been no movement on the other recommendations in this chapter.

After focusing in the first two chapters on ways to increase the skills of the American population, the commission turns its attention, in the third chapter, to ways in which existing skills can be used more effectively. First, to get more out of the skills of workers with family responsibilities, the commission recommends increased government support of dependent care. Suggestions include subsidy of community-based dependent care resource and referral agencies and increased subsidy of the child care expenses of low-income working parents. One specific idea endorsed by the commission—to make the existing child care tax credit refundable—has been rather quietly endorsed by the Bush administration, but the commission's basic suggestion to focus all subsidy on working parents who actually purchase child care services (as opposed to all parents) has been ignored.

Also in the third chapter, the commission suggests modifications of the Employment Service (ES), the UI system, and the immigration laws, all intended to improve the matching of workers and jobs. There are currently a number of efforts underway, both in the department of labor and Congess, that are consistent with the spirit of these recommendations. Finally, there is a call to use increased worker participation and innovative compensation arrangements to enhance worker productivity.

In the final chapter, the commissioners addressed issues of particular interest to the labor economics research community. In that chapter, they expressed their concern at the substantial reductions (since the mid-1970s) in funding for the data and research missions of the departments of education and labor. The commissioners call for increased funding and list several priorities for the use of those funds. With respect to data initiatives, they suggest the development of quick turnaround household surveys, support of longitudinal data bases, and pilot studies of new methods for (1) measuring labor turnover and labor shortages, (2) archiving UI records, and (3) matching data on establishments with data on employees of those establishments. As for the research agenda, the commission called for emphasis on "experimental evaluations of human resource programs, analysis of determinants of the labor market status of the economically disadvantaged, and collection and dissemination of information on best employment practices."[7] In the final section of this paper we present our own suggestions regarding the human resource research agenda.

Before ending our discussion of the commission report, we want to emphasize a final point of special importance. The commissioners were aware that some of their recommendations would involve significant costs. They were concerned about the federal budget deficit, but, at the same time, they were "convinced that, because today's skills deficit is so enormous, wisely chosen investments in human capital will yield substantial returns."[8] They called for more investment from states, communities, and the private sector and for a reallocation of federal human resource dollars. In perhaps its most newsworthy quote, this bipartisan commission went on to say that "there is likely, however, to be a clear and pressing need for a sustained increase in federal expenditure on human resource programs."[9] Their reason for coming to this conclusion was stated as follows: "We must not accept a workforce that is undereducated, undertrained and ill-equipped to compete in the twenty-first century."[10]

III.   THE HUMAN RESOURCE RESEARCH AGENDA

Quality, nonpartisan labor market research is the best foundation for labor market policy. Without it, policy will be based, at best, on intuition and, at worst, on special interests. Our work with the commission afforded us the opportunity to engage in a broad-based review of human resource research. As we reviewed academic and nonacademic research in a variety of disciplines, we were dismayed by the dearth of reliable research on many important questions.

This deficiency is in substantial part attributable to deep cuts in federal funds for human resource research. Since 1975, inflation-adjusted funding levels for research and evaluation in the department of labor have been cut by 52%, while inflation-adjusted funding levels in the department of education have been cut by 63%.[11] We believe, as did the commission, that it is essential that the departments of labor and education take the lead in addressing this problem by increasing their support of research.

It is also essential that these activities be carefully focused on the most pressing policy issues. In this section, we organize these issues into three categories: empirical questions about the workings of labor and human capital markets; questions regarding the design and efficacy of government human resource programs; and identification of "best practices" in private labor market innovations. The questions that are in need of answers are, by and large, empirical ones. That is not to say that there would not be substantial theoretical and methodological problems to solve along the way. In general, however, empirical (i.e., applied) research in labor economics has lagged far behind the theoretical developments. As a result, the research community's input into the policy-making process has been substantially diminished during the past decade.

Many of the specific ideas offered below were stimulated by informational needs that emerged during the deliberations of the commission. Other ideas have come from a variety of sources including background papers (some of which appear in this volume) prepared at the request of the commission and discussions with many experts both inside and outside government. While some research has already been done in many of the areas that we identify, more is clearly needed. Some of the questions we pose would be very difficult and/or expensive to answer. Even in cases where we see no clear way to answer a question, we have nonetheless posed the question in the hope that others may see promising approaches.

The development of public policies to address pressing human resource problems has been inhibited by a number of unresolved empirical questions regarding the workings of labor and human capital markets. We outline below some of the most important of these questions.

Labor force participation of black males   In general, what are the most important sources of the declining rates of labor force participation among black males? In particular, to what extent is this decline attributable to the suburbanization of jobs? What strategies appear to be most promising in reversing this decline? These questions can be best answered through statistical analysis of successive cross-sectional samples or panel data.

Access to postsecondary education   To what extent are able prospective students missing the opportunity of postsecondary education or training for want of financial resources? What impact would increased availability of student grants have on postsecondary enrollment of minority and non-minority students? Answering these questions will be difficult, but they are sufficiently important to deserve serious attention.

Transition from school to work   What are the costs of not having a structured school to work transition for the noncollege bound? Is it as inefficient as some observers suggest? Is job hopping an efficient way to develop human capital among youth? How much turnover is attributable to the nature of the jobs that young people hold as opposed to the characteristics of the young people themselves?

Labor shortages   Are there useful methods for measuring labor shortages? Could these methods be used to measure labor shortages by occupation and geographic region? How do labor shortages affect the employment prospects of economically disadvantaged individuals? Past efforts to address these questions have been largely unsuccessful, but their importance argues for continued attempts.

Employer-provided training   How much are employers currently investing in the skills of their workers? How are these investments distributed across industries, occupations, types of training, and firms of different sizes? Can we explain interfirm differences in training expenditures? Past attempts to address these questions have been seriously limited by the lack of relevant data. New data sources will have to be developed if we are to have any hope of progress. The first question to be asked, therefore, is how those data should be collected.

Another important focus for research is the effectiveness of government human resource programs. Policymakers need to know which programs work and why. Unfortunately, answering these questions is often expensive and time-consuming. For example, the process of evaluating JTPA is expected to take a total of six years (ending in 1992) and $20 million. This commitment to research, however, is entirely reasonable because the program spends over $3 billion each year.

One reason for the expense of the JTPA evaluation is the high cost of conducting experiments in which randomly selected individuals participate in a program and are then compared with individuals who were not exposed to the program. This experimental approach has provided most of what little we know about the effectiveness of training programs. Unfortunately, we know even less about the long-run effects of training programs because long-run experiments are particularly expensive and time-consuming.

Many of the specific questions that we raise below would be best answered through an experimental design. We recognize, however, that other questions cannot be answered through experimentation and must therefore rely on nonexperimental research designs.

The efficacy of JTPA programs   The critical question is, How does the impact of JTPA training vary with the level of intensity of the services and the characteristics of participants? Which measures of short-run gains could be used as predictors of long-run earnings gains? Which types of training are most effective in producing these gains? While JTPA experiments have been set up under Title II-A, they have ignored program impacts on in-school youth and dislocated workers. These groups should be incorporated into future experiments.

Labor market impacts of adult basic education   Do adult literacy programs have significant impacts on the earnings and employment of participants? What do these impacts imply about the rate of return to the investment in these programs? Do different types of programs or different types of participants realize different rates of return? Experimental comparisons of participants and nonparticipants would be the most promising approach to answering these questions.

Alternative Employment Service strategies   What are the most effective ways for state employment security agencies to carry out their missions? Which activities generate the largest net benefits? Careful interstate comparisons of labor market outcomes should provide insights into mechanisms that could improve the nationwide cost-effectiveness of the ES.

Incentives for student performance   What incentives are most effective in encouraging student effort and achievement? When firms ask for and receive the high school transcripts of students who apply for employment, do students expend additional effort to improve their grades and pursue more rigorous courses of study? Do occupational tests provide a useful vehicle for those high school students bound directly for work to communicate their skills and achievements to prospective employers? Do such tests produce incentives for students to work harder while in school? What, if any, are the undesirable effects of such tests? Such questions could probably best be answered through carefully designed pilot studies.

Providing parents with information on local child care options   Is adequate information readily available within most communities for parents to make well-informed child care decisions? Are private sector information services that market information on local child care options able to provide a socially optimal level of information? How effective are public/private partnerships in the provision of child care information? Careful evaluations of the costs and benefits of community-based child care information and referral services could begin to provide answers to these questions.

Case studies of program coordination   What are the costs and benefits of coordinating and/or integrating human resource programs such as JTPA, the ES, and UI? Under what circumstances is coordination most likely to happen and what circumstances make it least likely to happen? What have we learned about what works and what doesn't from the states that have been at the forefront of the effort to coordinate programs? Are additional incentives needed at the federal level to promote program coordination? What incentives would be most effective? A number of states and localities have been, or are in the process of, coordinating and/or merging their human resource programs. Case studies of these efforts would provide insights that are of use to policymakers at all levels of government.

The impacts of mandated benefits   What are the impacts of mandated benefits on both workers and firms? For example, how does mandated parental leave affect the employment and compensation of women? Careful statistical analysis of data from the states that have already implemented parental leave policies could yield valuable insights.

Strategies for targeting vocational rehabilitation   Which disabled individuals are likely to benefit most from vocational rehabilitation programs? The states provide a natural laboratory in which this question can be answered.

Strategies for enforcement of labor market regulations   Within each agency, which enforcement activities yield the greatest expected benefits? Are the enforcement energies of the department of labor allocated across regulatory activities in a fashion that reflects the relative importance of those activities? For example, how does the expected benefit of an additional OSHA inspection compare with that of an additional MSHA inspection? Alternatively, how does the expected net benefit of additional wage and hour enforcement activity compare to that of additional ERISA enforcement? These questions could be answered by careful measurement of costs and benefits of different DOL enforcement activities.

Yet another important focus for government research is the study of private labor market innovations. Government can collect information on which innovations work, which do not, and the conditions under which some work while others do not. When such information is disseminated, many parties will be able to learn from the successes and failures of a few. In some cases the department of labor may be able to encourage private parties to implement innovations in ways (e.g., controlled experiments) that facilitate measurement of the results of specific innovations. In general, the most important factors to be measured are so-called bottom-line effects on productivity, employees' incomes, and employers' profits.

Innovative methods for employee compensation   To what extent can innovative compensation arrangements (e.g., gain sharing, profit sharing, or employee ownership) lead to increased productivity? Does the success or failure of innovative compensation schemes depend crucially on the simultaneous introduction of mechanisms for worker participation? One way to address these questions is with careful before and after case studies of firms that adopt new compensation methods. Another promising avenue would be to encourage firms to set up controlled experiments in which innovations are initially limited to particular groups of employees.

Worker participation   To what extent can worker involvement in management decisions lead to increased productivity? Is worker participation more effective in the presence of incentive compensation arrangements? One way to address these questions is with careful before and after case studies of firms that adopt new compensation methods. Again, experimental methods hold promise.

Supportive work environments   What are the most effective ways to create work environments that facilitate employees' needs to balance the demands of work and family? What are the bottom-line effects of dependent care programs and flexibility programs on productivity, employee earnings, and profit? Case studies, statistical analyses, and experimental approaches could all yield useful insights.

Employer-provided training   What are the net benefits of employer-provided training from the employers' and employees' points of view? How do the returns to training vary across industries, occupations, and types of workers? Which training methods offer the highest rates of return? How does vendor-provided training compare to in-house training? Are some techniques more effective for small firms, while others are more effective for large firms? Answering these questions will be quite difficult. Initial inquiries will undoubtedly have to be based on a case study approach.

Business/education partnerships   What is the level of business involvement and how does it vary between urban, suburban, and rural areas? What are the impacts, both in the short and in the long run, of the business community's involvement in local school systems? Which types of business/education partnerships are most effective? For the past decade, the business community has been increasingly involved in the schools in many communities. This long-term, broad-based involvement creates a rich source of information on which case studies could be based.

NOTES

1. Laurie Bassi is an associate professor of economics and public policy at Georgetown University and former deputy director of the secretary of labor's Commission on Workforce Quality and Labor Market Efficiency. David Crawford is the president of Econsult Corporation, and adjunct associate professor of economics and management at the University of Pennsylvania, and the former executive director of the commission.

2. The members of the commission were Orley C. Ashenfelter, Morton Bahr, Gary S. Becker, Pat Choate, Constance E. Clayton, John L. Clendenin, William H. Kolberg, Jose I. Lozano, Gary E. MacDougal, Ethel Olson, Russell E. Palmer, Gloria M. Portela, Albert H. Quie, Isabel V. Sawhill, Richard F. Schubert (Chairman), Albert Shanker, John Sloan, Jr., Linda J. Wachner, Lynn R. Williams, and William J. Wilson.

3. The members of the commission staff were John R. Beverly III, Suzanne A. Brown, H. Peter Cappelli, John D. Carter, Amy B. Chasanov, Nancy Duhon, John P. Giraudo, Michael W. Horrigan, Nevzer G. Stacey, James F. Taylor, Tommy M. Tomlinson, and Nancy Zurich.

4. Papers were published in September 1989 in two volumes titled *Investing in People: A Strategy to Address America's Workforce Crisis, Background Papers*.

5. The report, published by the commission under the auspices of the Department of Labor, is available from the Superintendent of Documents, U.S. Government Printing Office, Washington, D.C. 20402, under stock number 029-000-00428-5.

6. Richard F. Schubert's transmittal letter to Secretary Dole, *Investing in People*, p. iii.

7. *Investing in People*, p. 37.

8. Ibid, p. 4.

9. Ibid.

10. Ibid.

11. Ibid., p. 36.

INCENTIVES FOR LEARNING:
WHY AMERICAN HIGH SCHOOL STUDENTS
COMPARE SO POORLY
TO THEIR COUNTERPARTS OVERSEAS

John Bishop

The scientific and mathematical competence of American high school students is generally recognized to be very low. The National Assessment of Educational Progress (NAEP) reports that only 7.5% of 17-year-old students can "integrate specialized scientific information" (NAEP, 1989, p. 56) and 6.4% "demonstrated the capacity to apply mathematical operations in a variety of problem setting" (NAEP, 1988b, p. 42).

There is a large gap between the science and math competence of young Americans and their counterparts overseas. In the 1960s, the low ranking of American high school students in such comparisons was attributed to the fact that the test was administered to a larger proportion of American than European and Japanese youth. This is no longer the case. Figures 1 to 4 plot the scores in algebra, biology, chemistry, and physics against the proportion of the 18-year-old population in the types of courses to which the international test was adminis-

Research in Labor Economics, Volume 11, pages 17–51.
Copyright © 1990 by JAI Press Inc.
All rights of reproduction in any form reserved.
ISBN: 1-555938-080-2

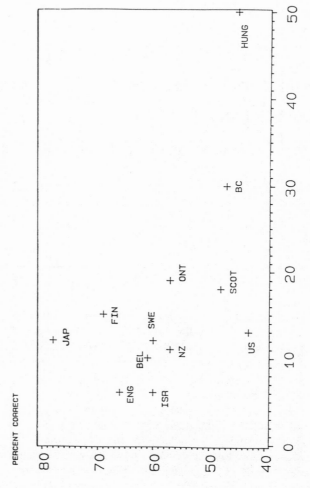

Figure 1. Algebra Results for 17-Year-Olds.

Figure 2. Biology Results for 18-Year-Olds.

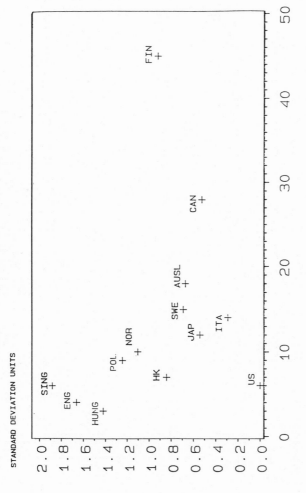

19

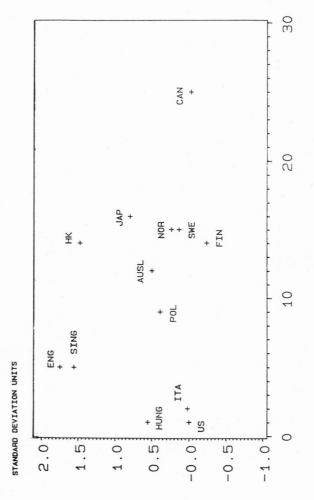

Figure 3. Chemistry Results for 18-Year-Olds.

Figure 4. Physics Results for 18-Year-Olds.

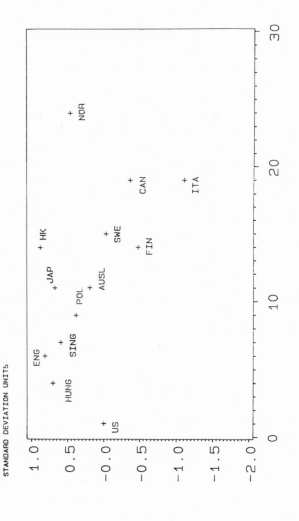

21

tered (IAEEA, 1987, 1988). In the Second International Math Study, the universe from which the American sample was drawn consisted of high school seniors taking a college preparatory math course. This group, which represents only 13% of American 17-year-olds, is roughly comparable to the 12% of Japanese youth who were in the sample frame and is considerably smaller than the 19% of youth in the Canadian province of Ontario and the 50% of Hungarians who were in college preparatory mathematics courses. In algebra, the mean score for this very select group of American students was about equal to the mean score of the much larger group of Hungarians and substantially below the Canadian achievement level (IAEEA, 1987).

The findings of the Second International Science Study are even more dismal. For example, the 25% of Canadian 18-year-olds taking chemistry know just as much chemistry as the very select 1% of American high school seniors taking their second chemistry course (most of whom are in "advanced placement"). The 28% taking biology know much more than the 6% of American 17- to 18-year-olds who are taking their second biology course (IAEEA, 1988).

The poor performance of American students is sometimes blamed on the nation's "diversity." Many affluent parents apparently believe that their children are doing acceptably by international standards. This is not the case. In Stevenson et al.'s (1986) study of fifth-grade math achievement, the best of the 20 classrooms sampled in Minneapolis was outstripped by every single classroom studied in Sendai, Japan, and by 19 of the 20 classrooms studied in Taipeh, Taiwan. The nation's top high school students rank far behind much less elite samples of students in other countries. In mathematics the gap between Japanese high school students and their white American counterparts is more than twice the size of the two to three grade level equivalent gap between blacks and whites in the United States (NAEP, 1988; IAEEA, 1987). The learning deficit is pervasive.

The costs in terms of competitiveness and living standards of these educational deficits is very large. Bishop (1989a) applied a growth accounting methodology to a related issue—the cost of the test score decline—and using conservative assumptions calculated the resulting reduction in GNP to be $86 billion in 1987, a reduction that was to projected to double in real terms by the year 2000. The test score decline between 1967 and 1980 was only 1.25 grade level equivalents on average across all academic subjects; the deficit with respect to Japan in math and science (the only two subjects for which there are recent international comparisons) is more than four U.S. grade level equivalents at the end of high school. Analyses of data from the National Longitudinal Study (NLS) youth cohort, the General Aptitude Test Battery (GATB) Revalidation Studies, and the military all indicate that mathematical competencies are better predictors of job performance and wages than verbal competencies in the great bulk of blue-collar and clerical jobs (Bishop, 1987b, 1988b). If this is the case and the deficit is not substantially made up in college, extrapolations from the test score decline study imply that the educational deficit could, ceteris paribus, produce a productivity differential of more than 10% between Japan and the United States.

This paper examines the causes of this learning deficit and then recommends policy measures for remedying the problems identified. Section I presents evidence that American students devote considerably less time and energy to learning in high school than their counterparts abroad. Section II attributes the differences in learning effort to differences across societies in the structure and magnitude of the rewards for academic achievement. It is demonstrated that the U.S. labor market underrewards learning achievements in high school and that the failure to signal learning achievements to employers is at the root of the American learning deficit. Section III sets forth a series of policy recommendations designed to improve student incentives to devote time and energy to learning and to strengthen parental incentives to demand that local schools be upgraded. Section IV discusses the likely impact of these reforms on the employment prospects of underrepresented minorities. It is argued that the learning response will be particularly large among minority youth, that improved signaling of academic achievement will stimulate an increase in affirmative action recruiting, and that minority youth will for the first time be able to compete for attractive primary labor market jobs on the basis of their achievements in high school.

I. APATHY: THE PROXIMATE CAUSE OF THE LEARNING DEFICIT

American high school students do poorly in international comparisons primarily because they devote much less time and energy to the task of learning. American students average nearly 20 absences a year; Japanese students only 3 a year (Berlin and Sum, 1988). School years are longer in Europe and Japan. Forty-five percent of Japanese junior high school students attend *juku,* private schools that provide tutoring in academic subjects (Leestma et al., 1987). Thomas Rohlen has estimated that Japanese high school graduates average the equivalent of four more years in a classroom and in studying than American graduates (PBS, 1989).

Observational studies of American classroom have found that time actively engaged in a learning activity is quite low. Studies have found that for reading and math instruction the average engagement rate is about 75% in typical middle-class schools (Fischer et al., 1978; Goodlad, 1983; Klein et al., 1979). Overall, Frederick et al. (1979) estimated 46.5% of the potential learning time was lost due to absence, lateness, and inattention.

In the High School and Beyond survey, students reported spending an average of 3.5 hours per week on homework (HSB, 1982). When homework is added to engaged time at school, the total time devoted to study, instruction, and practice is only 18–22 hours per week—between 15 and 20% of the student's waking hours during the school year. By way of comparison, the typical senior spent 10 hours per week in a part-time job and about 24 hours per week watching television (A. C. Neilsen, unpublished data). Thus, TV occupies as much time as learning. Students in other nations spend much less time watching TV: 60% less in Switzerland and 44% less in Canada (Organization of Economic Cooperation and Development, 1986: Table 18.1). Japanese fifth graders spend 32.6 hours a week involved in academic activities while American youngsters devote only 19.6 hours to their studies (Stevenson et al., 1986). Science and math deficits are particularly severe because most students do not take rigorous college preparatory courses in these subjects. The high school graduating class of 1982 took an average of only 0.43 credits of Algebra II, 0.31 credits of more advanced mathematics courses, 0.40 credits of chemistry, and 0.19 credits of physics (Meyer, 1989: Table A.2).

Even more important than the time devoted to learning is the intensity of the student's involvement in the process. At the completion of his study of American high schools, Theodore Sizer (1984) characterized students as, "all too often docile, compliant, and without initiative" (p. 54). John Goodlad (1983) described "a general picture of considerable passivity among students" (p. 113). The high school teachers surveyed by Goodlad ranked lack of student interest and lack of parental interest as the two most important problems in education.

The student's lack of interest makes it difficult for teachers to be demanding. Sizer's description of Ms. Shiffe's biology class illustrates what sometimes happens:

> She wanted the students to know these names. They did not want to know them and were not going to learn them. Apparently no outside threat—flunking, for example—affected the students. Shiffe did her thing, the students chattered on, even in the presence of a visitor. . . . Their common front of uninterest probably made examinations moot. Shiffe could not flunk them all, and, if their performance was uniformly shoddy, she would have to pass them all. Her desperation was as obvious as the students cruelty toward her. (Sizer, 1984, pp. 157–158)

Some teachers are able to overcome the obstacles and induce their students to undertake tough learning tasks. But for most, the student's lassitude is demoralizing. Teachers are assigned responsibility for setting high standards but we do not give them any of the tools that might be effective for inducing student observance of the academic goals of the classroom. They finally must rely on the force of their own personalities. All to often teachers compromise academic demands because the bulk of the class sees no need to accept them as reasonable and legitimate.

The Apathy of Parents and School Boards

The second major reason for the low levels of achievement by American students is parental and school board apathy. Japanese families allocate 10% of the family's after-tax income to educational expenses; American families only 2%. If American parents were truly dissatisfied with the performance of their local public schools, they would send their children to tuition-financed schools offering an enriched and rigorous curriculum and tutoring after school would be as common as it is in Japan. Most parents who send their children to private schools appear to be attracted by their stricter discipline and religious education, not more rigorous academics and better-qualified teachers. Private school students do not learn at an appreciably faster rate than public school students (Cain and Goldberger, 1983).

A comparative study of primary education in Taiwan, Japan and United States found that even though American children are far behind Taiwanese and Japanese children in mathematics capability, American mothers are much more pleased with the performance of their local schools than Taiwanese and Japanese mothers. When asked "How good a job would you say [your child]'s school is doing this year educating [him/her]," 91% of American mothers responded "excellent" or "good," while only 42% of Taiwanese and 39% of Japanese parents were this positive (Stevenson et al., 1986). Clearly, American parents hold their children and their schools to lower academic standards than Japanese and Taiwanese parents.

II. INCENTIVES: THE REAL CAUSE OF THE LEARNING DEFICIT

The fundamental cause of student and parental apathy is the absence of good signals of effort and learning in high school and a consequent lack of rewards for effort and learning. Signals of learning like years of schooling are handsomely rewarded. In 1987, 25- to 34-year-old male (female) college graduates working full-time full year earned 41 (48)% more than comparable high school graduates and high school graduates earned 21 (23)% more than high school dropouts. Schooling also reduces the risk of unemployment. These rewards have significant effects on student enrollment decisions. When the payoff to a college degree for white males fell in the early 1970s, the college attendance rates of white males fell substantially (Freeman, 1976). When the payoff to college rose again during the 1980s, rates of college attendance and graduation rose as well (Bishop, 1989b, Table 5). Years of schooling is only a partial measure of learning accomplishment, however.

In contrast to years spent in school, the effort devoted to learning in high school and the actual competencies developed in high school are generally not well signaled to colleges and employers. Consequently, while students are generously rewarded for staying in school, *the students who do not aspire to attend selective colleges benefit very little from working hard while in high school*. The lack of incentives for effort and learning accomplishment is a consequence of three phenomena:

1. The labor market fails to reward effort and achievement in high school.
2. The peer group actively discourages academic effort.
3. Admission to selective colleges is not based on an absolute or external standard of achievement in high school subjects. Rather, it is based, in part, on aptitude tests, which do not assess the high school curriculum, as well as measures of student performance such as class rank and grade point averages, which are defined relative to classmates' performances.

A. The Absence of Major Economic Rewards for Effort in High School

Students who plan to look for a job immediately after high school typically spend less time on their studies than those who plan to attend college. In large part, most see very little connection between how much they learn and their future success in the labor market. Less than a quarter of tenth graders believe that geometry, trigonometry, biology, chemistry, and physics are needed to qualify for their first-choice occupation (LSAY, 1988). Statistical studies of the youth labor market confirm students' skepticism about the benefits of taking tough courses and studying hard:

- Employers rank "reading, writing, math and reasoning ability" fifth on a list of six abilities they look for when hiring."
- For students seeking part-time employment while attending high school, grades and performance on academic achievement/aptitude tests have essentially no impact on labor market success. They have (1) no effect on the chances of finding work when one is seeking it during high school, and (2) no effect on the wage rate of the jobs obtained while in high school (Hotchkiss et al., 1982).
- For those who do not go to college full-time, high school grades and test scores had no effect on the wage rate of the jobs obtained immediately after high school in Kang and Bishop's (1984) analysis of High School and Beyond seniors and only a 1 to 4.7% increase in wages per standard deviation improvement in test scores and grade point average in Meyer's (1982) analysis of class of 1972 data. There was (1) a moderate effect on wage rates and earnings after four or five years [Gardner (1982) found an effect of 4.8% per standard deviation of achievement and Meyer (1982) found an effect of 4.3 to 6.0% per standard deviation of achievement], and (2) a small negative effect on the risk of unemployment immediately after high school (Kang and Bishop, 1984).
- Analysis of the youth cohort of the National Longitudinal Survey found that during the first ten years after leaving high school, young men received *no* rewards from the labor market for developing competence in science, language arts, and mathematical reasoning. The only competencies that were rewarded were speed in doing simple computations (something that

calculators do better than people) and technical competence (knowledge of mechanical principles, electronics, automobiles, and shop tools). For the non–college-bound female, there were small wage rate and earnings benefits to learning advanced mathematics but no benefits to developing competence in science or the technical arena (Bishop, 1988b).

The long delay before labor market rewards are received is important because most teenagers are shortsighted and liquidity constrained, so benefits promised for ten years in the future are likely to have little influence on their decisions.

Although to the employee the economic benefits of higher achievement are quite modest and do not appear until long after graduation, the benefits to the employer (and therefore, to national production) are immediately realized in higher productivity. Over the last 80 years, industrial psychologists have conducted hundreds of studies, involving hundreds of thousands of workers, on the relationship between productivity in particular jobs and various predictors of that productivity. They have found that scores on tests measuring competence in reading, mathematics, science, and problem solving are strongly related to productivity in almost all of the civilian jobs studied (Ghiselli, 1973; Hunter, 1983). Studies conducted by the military similarly find that scientific, technical, and mathematical reasoning competencies have large effects on both paper and pencil measures of job knowledge and hands-on measures of job performance (Hunter et al., 1985). Academic competencies increase productivity by more than they increase wage rates.[2] Apparently, when a non–college-bound students works hard in school and improves his or her competence in language arts, science, and mathematical reasoning, the youth's employer reaps much of the benefit. The youth is somewhat more likely to find a job, but not one with an appreciably higher wage.

B. Reasons for the Discrepancy between Wage Rates and Productivity on the Job

Why doesn't competition between employers result in much higher wages for those who achieve more in high school? The lack of objective information available to employers on applicant accomplishments, skills, and productivity explains much. Tests are available for measuring competency in reading, writing, mathematics, science, and problem solving, but Employment and Equal Opportunity Commission (EEOC) guidelines resulted in a drastic reduction in their use after 1971. A 1987 survey of a stratified random sample of small- and medium-sized employers who were members of the National Federation of Independent Business (NFIB) found that aptitude test scores had been obtained in only 2.9% of the hiring decisions studied (see note 1).

Other potential sources of information on effort and achievement in high school are transcripts and referrals from teachers who know the applicant. Both are underused. In the NFIB survey, transcripts had been obtained prior to the selection decision for only 14.2% of the high school graduates hired. If a student or graduate has given written permission for a transcript to be sent to an employer, the Federal Education Rights and Privacy Act obligates the school to respond. Many high schools are not, however, responding to such requests. Nationwide Insurance's national headquarters in Columbus, Ohio, for example, sent over 1200 requests (together with the necessary waivers by the applicant) to high schools in 1982 and received only 93 responses. The company reported that colleges were more responsive (interviews conducted by Kevin Hollenbeck in 1984). Most high schools have apparently designed their systems for responding to requests for transcripts around the needs of college-bound students rather than the students who seek jobs immediately after graduating.

There is an additional barrier to the use of high school transcripts in selecting new employees—when high schools do respond, it takes a great deal of time. For Nationwide Insurance the response almost invariably took more than two weeks. Given this time lag, if employers required transcripts prior to making hiring selections, a job offer could not be made until a month or so after an application had been received. Most jobs are filled much more rapidly than that. In the 1982 National Center for Research on Vocational Education (NCRVE) survey of small- and medium-sized employers, 84% of hiring selections were made in less than a month.

The only information about school experiences requested by most employers is years of schooling, diplomas and certificates obtained, and area of specialization. Only 15% of the NFIB employers asked applicants with 12 years of schooling to report their grade point average. The lack of questions about school performance on the job application does not reflect, however, an employer belief that school performance is a poor predictor of job performance. When employers have grade point average information, it has a major effect on the ratings employers assign to job applicants in policy-capturing experiments (Hollenbeck and Smith, 1984). The absence of questions about grades from most job applications probably reflects the low reliability of self-reported data, the difficulties of verifying it, and the fear of EEO challenges to such questions.

Hiring on the basis of recommendations by high school teachers is also uncommon. In the NFIB survey, when a high school graduate was hired, the new hire had been referred or recommended by vocational teachers only in 5.2% of the cases and by someone else in the high school in only 2.7% of the cases.

Clearly, hiring selections and starting wage rates often do not reflect the competencies and abilities students have developed in school. Instead, hiring decisions are based on easily observable characteristics (such as years of schooling and field of study) that serve as signals for the competencies the employer cannot observe directly. A study of how individual wage rates varied with initial job performance found that when people hired for the same or very similar jobs are compared, someone who is 20% more productive than average is typically paid only 1.6% more. After a year at a firm, better producers received only a 4%

higher wage at nonunion firms with about 20 employees, and they had no wage advantage at unionized establishments with more than 100 employees or at nonunion establishments with more than 400 employees (Bishop, 1987a).

Employers have good reasons for not varying the wage rates of their employees in proportion to their perceived job performance. All feasible measures of individual productivity are unreliable and unstable. In most cases measurement must be subjective. Risk-averse workers are reluctant to accept jobs in which the judgment of one supervisor can result in a large wage decline in the second year on the job (Hashimoto and Yu, 1980; Stiglitz, 1974). Most productivity differentials are specific to the firm, and this reduces the risk that not paying a particularly productive worker a comparably higher salary will result in him going elsewhere (Bishop, 1987a). Pay that is highly contingent on performance can also weaken cooperation and generate incentives to sabotage others (Lazear, 1986). Finally, in unionized settings, the union's opposition to merit pay will often be decisive.

Despite their higher productivity, *young workers who have achieved in high school do not receive appreciably higher wage rates after high school.* The student who works hard must wait many years to reap rewards, and even then the magnitude of the wage and earnings effect—a 1 to 2% increase in earnings per grade level equivalent on achievement tests—is hardly much of an incentive. It is considerably smaller than the actual gain in productivity that results.

C. The Zero-Sum Nature of Academic Competition in High School

The second root cause of high school students' poor motivation is peer pressure against studying hard (Covington and Beery, 1976; Thomas, 1980). No adolescent wants to be considered a "nerd, a brain geek, a grade grubber, or a brownnoser," yet that is what happens to students who study hard and are seen to be achieving academically. The norm is, "It's OK to be smart, but not OK to study hard." This phenomenon is caused in part by the way we assess and measure learning. If learning were defined relative to an objective outside standard, peers would not have a personal interest in persuading other students to put little effort into studying. Since, however, the school's signals of achievement assess performance relative to fellow students through grades and class rank, peers have a personal interest in persuading each other not to study and that is why peer pressure takes on the character it does.[3]

In nonacademic activities such as Boy Scouts, the school newspaper, the dramatics club, working at McDonald's and in team sports, peer pressure is, by contrast, supportive of effort and excellence. In these activities, young people are generally part of a team where individual efforts are visible and appreciated by teammates and/or by the school as a whole. Competition and rivalry are not absent, but they are offset by shared goals, shared successes, and external measures of achievement (i.e., satisfied customers or winning the game).

The second reason for peer norms against studying is that most students perceive the chance of receiving recognition for an academic achievement to be so slim they have given up trying. At most high school awards ceremonies, the academic recognition goes to only a few—those at the very top of the class. By ninth grade, most students are already so far behind the leaders that they believe they have no chance of being perceived as academically successful. Their reaction is often to dismiss the students who take learning seriously and to honor other forms of achievement—athletics, dating, holding their liquor, and being "cool"—which offer them better chances of success.

D.   Incentives to Upgrade Local Schools

The lack of external standards for judging academic achievement and the resulting zero sum nature of academic competition in the school also influences parents, school boards, and local school administrators. Parents can see that setting higher academic standards or hiring better teachers will not on average improve their child's rank in class or grade point average (GPA). The Scholastic Aptitude Test (SAT) does not assess knowledge and understanding of science, history, social science, trigonometry, statistics, and calculus or the ability to write an essay. Consequently, improving the teaching of these subjects at the local high school will have only minor effects on how a child does on the SAT, so why worry about standards? In any case, doing well on the SAT matters only for those who aspire to attend a selective college. Most students plan to attend open-entry public colleges, which admit all high school graduates from the state, with the requisite courses. Scholarships are awarded on the basis of financial need, not academic merit.

The parents of children not planning to go to college have an even weaker incentive to demand high standards at the local high school. They believe that what counts in the labor market is getting the diploma, not learning algebra. They can see that learning more will be of only modest benefit to their child's future, and that higher standards might put at risk what is really important—the diploma.

Only when educational outcomes are aggregated, at the state or national levels, do the real costs of mediocre schools become apparent. The whole community loses because the workforce is less efficient, and it becomes difficult to attract new industry. Competitiveness deteriorates and the nation's standard of living declines. This is precisely why employers, governors, and state legislatures have been the energizing force of school reform. State governments, however, are far removed from the classroom, and the instruments available to them for inducing improvements in quality and standards are limited. States do not have effective control of the standards and expectations that prevail in the classroom. State aid can be increased but econometric studies suggest that the primary effect of increases in state aid is reductions in local property tax collections (Carroll, 1982; Ehrenberg and Chaykowski, 1988).

A consensus appears to have emerged that the first wave of top-down reforms had only modest effects and that a new wave of bottom-up reform "empowering" teachers and principals is required. In our system all the really important decisions—budget allocations, hiring selections, salary levels, homework assignments, teaching strategies, grading standards, course offerings, pupil assignments to courses and programs, disciplinary policies, etc.—are made by classroom teachers and school administrators who are responding to local political pressures. If the parents voting in school board elections do not believe that a more rigorous math and science curriculum will help their children get a better job or into the college of their choice, state mandates designed to raise standards will have no lasting effect.

E. Incentives to Learn in Other Nations

The tendency not to reward effort and learning in high school appears to be a peculiarly American phenomenon. School grades are the major determinant of who gets the most preferred apprenticeships in West Germany. In Canada, Australia, Japan, and West Europe, educational systems administer achievement exams that are closely tied to the curriculum. While the Japanese use a multiple-choice exam, all other nations use extended-answer examinations in which students write essays and show their work for mathematics problems. Generally, regional or national boards set the exam and oversee the blind grading of the exams by committees of teachers. These are not minimum-competency exams. In many subjects the student may choose to take the exams at two different levels of difficulty. Excellence is recognized as well as competence.

Performance on these exams is the primary determinant of admission to a university and to particular fields of study such as medicine and law. Good grades on the toughest exams—physics, chemistry, advanced mathematics—carry particular weight. Exam grades are included in resumes and are asked for on job applications (see Figures 5 and 6).

In Japan, clerical, service, and blue-collar jobs at the best firms are available only to those who are recommended by their high school. The most prestigious firms have long-term arrangements with particular high schools to which they delegate the responsibility of selecting the new hire(s) for the firm. The criteria by which the high school is to make its selection is, by mutual agreement, grades and exam results. In addition, most employers administer their own battery of selection tests prior to hiring. The number of graduates that a high school is able to place in this way depends on its reputation and the company's past experience with graduates from the school. Schools know that they must be forthright in their recommendations because if they fail just once to make an honest recom-

Figure 5. Resume from Republic of Ireland, including Intermediate and Final National Examination Grades

```
┌─────────────────────────────────────────────────────────────┐
│              C U R R I C U L U M    V I T A E                │
│                                                               │
│ NAME:                                                         │
│ ADDRESS:                                                      │
│                                                               │
│ DATE OF BIRTH:                           AGE:                 │
│ NATIONALITY:                                                  │
│ TELEPHONE NO:                                                 │
│                                                               │
│ EDUCATIONAL DETAILS                                           │
│ Primary School                                                │
│ Post Primary                                                  │
│ Secretarial Course                                            │
│ Office Procedures                                             │
│ Course                                                        │
│                                                               │
│ EXAMINATIONS                                                  │
│                   Intermediate Certificate      1985          │
│ SUBJECTS          English             B - L.C.                │
│                   Irish               C - L.C.                │
│                   Maths               B - L.C.                │
│                   Science             C                       │
│                   Geography           C                       │
│                   History             C                       │
│                   Home Economics      D                       │
│                   Leaving Certificate           1987          │
│ SUBJECTS          English             D - L.C.                │
│                   Irish               C - L.C.                │
│                   Maths               C - L.C.                │
│                   Biology             C - H.C.                │
│                   Geography           C - L.C.                │
│                   French              D - L.C.                │
│                   Home Economics      B - L.C.                │
└─────────────────────────────────────────────────────────────┘
```

Figure 6. British Job Application Requiring Grades as well as Course Information

APPLICATION FOR AN APPOINTMENT HANDLED BY MVP
16, Highfield Road, Edgbaston, Birmingham, B15 3DU Tel: 021 455 9765/0559

[mvp logo] 3319

Appointment applied for __DISTRIBUTION PROJECTS MANAGER (B.X.Q.)__ Ref.No. ___

PERSONAL DETAILS: (block capitals)

Surname _____ Title _MR_ Forenames _____

Address ____ CAERNARVON GARDENS _____

_____ Postal Code _____ Tel.No.Home _____ Work _____

Marital Status ___M___ Children/Dependants (with ages) _1 x 4-YRS   1 x 1 YR_

Age _33_ Date of Birth _5.8.55_ Nationality _BRITISH_ Place of Birth _ILFRACOMBE, DEVON_

State of health ___OK___ Height _6'_ Weight _13st. 12lbs_

Any disabilities/recurrent medical problems? _____ Regd.disabled _____

Driving Licences ___CAR___ Car Owner _✓_ Company Car _____

Endorsements, convictions, accidents, etc ___NONE___

Leisure activities and offices held in clubs and societies ___CYCLING/WALKING___

EDUCATION:
Secondary Education

From	To	School	Exams Taken (inc. grades)	Other achievements
1966	1972	BARNSTAPLE GRAMMAR	'O' LEVEL :- ENG. LANG. (2), MATHS (2) FRENCH (2) GEOGRAPHY (3), STATISTICS (3), CHEMISTRY (3), ADDL. MATHS (6), HISTORY (6), PHYSICS (6) 'A' LEVEL :- CHEMISTRY (E) PHYSICS (E), MATHS (O)	MIDDLE SCHOOL GAMES CAPTAIN

Further Education

From	To	College/University	Course & results (inc.class/grades)	Other achievements
1972	1973	UNIVERSITY OF BRADFORD	APPLIED CHEMISTRY - LEFT AFTER 1 YEAR - DOMESTIC REASONS	

Other training and qualifications (inc. in-company and external courses, etc.)

From	To	Establishment	Training/Qualifications
1979		FARLEY COLLEGE, LEEDS	CERTIFICATE OF PROFESSIONAL COMPETENCE (TRANSPORT OPS)
1983	1984	EAVERS COLLEGE	INSTITUTE OF INDUSTRIAL MANAGEMENT CERT.
1984	1989	IN - COMPANY	NUMEROUS, MANAGEMENT COURSES.

Membership of professional bodies

Date	Association/Institute	Grade of membership	Offices held
1988	I.I.D.M.	A.M.	

33

mendation, the relationship will be lost and their students will no longer be able to get jobs at that firm (Rosenbaum and Kariya, 1989).

Parents in these countries know that a child's future depends critically on how much is learned in secondary school. In many countries the options for upper secondary schooling depend primarily on the child's performance in lower secondary school, not on where the parents can afford to live, as in the United States. Since the quality and reputation of the high school is so important, the competitive pressure often reaches down into lower secondary school. National exams are the yardstick, so achievement tends to be measured relative to everyone else's in the nation and not just relative to the child's classmates. As a result, parents in most other Western nations demand more and get more from their local schools than we do—nevertheless, they are more dissatisfied with their schools than American parents.

Japanese teenagers work extremely hard in high school, but once they enter college, many stop working. For students in nontechnical fields, a country club atmosphere prevails. The reason for the change in behavior is that when employers hire graduates with nontechnical majors, they base their selections on the reputation of the university and a long series of interviews and not on teacher recommendations or other measures of academic achievement at the university. Students in engineering and other technical programs work much harder than their liberal arts counterparts largely because job opportunities depend entirely on the recommendation of their major professor. Studying hard is *not* a national character trait, it is a response to the way Japanese society rewards academic achievement.

American students, in contrast, work much harder in college than in high school. This change is due, in part, to the fact that academic achievement in college has important effects on labor market success. When higher-level jobs requiring a bachelor or associate degree are being filled, employers pay more attention to grades and teacher recommendations than when they hire high school graduates. The NFIB survey found that when college graduates were hired, 26% of the employers had reviewed the college transcript before making the selection, 7.8% had obtained a recommendation from a major professor, and 6.3% had obtained a recommendation from a professor outside the graduate's major or from the college's placement office.

III. POLICY RECOMMENDATIONS

The analysis presented in the first part of the paper implies that student incentives to learn and parental incentives to demand a quality education are maximized when the following is true: (1) *significant* rewards depend directly and *visibly* on academic accomplishments, (2) the accomplishment is defined relative to an *externally imposed standard of achievement* and not relative to one's classmates,

(3) the reward is received quickly, (4) everyone, including those who begin high school with serious academic deficiencies, has an *achievable goal,* which will generate a significant reward, and (5) progress toward the goal can be monitored by the student, parents, and teachers.

These principles suggest that individual learning goals should be established that challenge the student to the maximum extent possible and achievement of these goals should be recognized at a school awards ceremony and communicated to the labor market. If employers know who has learned, they will provide the rewards. There must be significant rewards for learning and real consequences for failing to learn. Learning accomplishments need to be described on an absolute scale so that improvements in the quality and rigor of the teaching and greater effort by all students make everybody better off.

The policy recommendations have been grouped into four categories: school-sponsored signals of academic achievement made available to employers, reforming college admissions criteria, greater use of more valid broad-based achievement tests for selecting workers, and more powerful school-administered incentives for academic achievement. The discussion of the distributional consequences of making academic achievement a more important factor in hiring selections is postponed to the final section of the paper.

A.   Improving Measures of Academic Achievement So the Labor Market Will Reward Effort in High School

The first best solution to the incentive problem is for the educational system to take on the job of deciding what academic and vocational competencies are to be measured and how they are to be signaled to employers. Schools should provide graduates with certificates or diplomas that certify the students' knowledge and competencies, not just their attendance. Competencies should be defined relative to an absolute standard in the way Boy Scout merit badges are. Different types of competency need to be distinguished and different levels of competency signaled.

Instituting Statewide Achievement Examinations

States should adopt statewide tests of competency and knowledge that are specific to the curriculum being taught (e.g., New York State's Regents Examinations and California's Golden State Examinations) and then give students a competency profile certifying performance on each of these exams. State merit-based scholarships should be awarded on the basis of student performance on these achievement exams and employers should be encouraged to factor examination results into their hiring decisions. An exam system such as this maximizes incentives to study. All employers now have access to information on the academic achievements of job candidates, not just the employers who choose to give employment tests. It makes the connection between effort in school, performance on the exams, and job placement clearly visible to all. This approach to signaling academic achievement has a number of advantages. By retaining control of exam content, educators and the public influence the kinds of academic achievement that are rewarded by the labor market. Societal decisions regarding the curriculum (e.g., all students should read Shakespeare's plays and understand the Constitution) tend to be reinforced by employer hiring decisions. Tests developed solely for employee selection purposes would probably place less emphasis on Shakespeare and the Constitution. Because it is centralized and students take the exam only once or twice, job applicants do not have to take a different exam at each firm they apply to and the quality and comprehensiveness of the test can be much greater. There is no need for multiple versions of the same test and it is much easier to keep the test secure.

Shifting emphasis away from teacher assessment to external assessment also has important pedagogical benefits. It transforms the relationship between teachers and students into a more cooperative one in which they work jointly to prepare the students for the external assessment.

Promote the Development of New Assessment Mechanisms

Linking assessment to the curriculum requires a greater diversity of assessment mechanisms. States should not be prevented from having their own unique curriculum simply because examinations keyed to this curriculum are not available. However, the need for multiple versions and for fairness to minorities make test development very expensive. The federal government should underwrite state consortia and other organizations that seek to develop alternatives to currently available tests and assessment mechanisms. Priority needs to go to developing methods of assessing higher-order thinking skills and competencies that cannot be evaluated using a multiple-choice format. There should be a conscious effort to maximize philosophical and educational diversity in the selection of consortia for funding. The push for better measures of student learning should not be limited to the academic arena. A similar effort should be made in the vocational area. Consideration should be given to federal subsidies of the administration cost of more expensive assessment mechanisms such as essays, judged portfolios, hands-on performance tests, and simulations designed to measure higher-order thinking skills.

Local Competency Profiles

Another way to motivate students is to give them feedback on their accomplishments through the mechanism of a criterion-referenced competency profile. Competency profiles are checklists of competencies that are the goals of instruction. By evaluating students against an absolute standard, the competency profile avoids a negative feedback of one student's effort into another student's grade and encourages students to share their knowledge and teach each other.

A second advantage of the competency profile approach to evaluation is that students can see their progress as new skills are learned and checked off. The skills not yet checked off are the learning goals for the future. Seeing such a checklist get filled up is inherently reinforcing.

With a competency profile system, goals can be tailored to the student's interests and capabilities, and progress toward these goals can be monitored and rewarded. Students who have difficulty in their required academic subjects can nevertheless take pride in the occupational competencies that they are developing and that are now recognized just as prominently as course grades in academic subjects.

A great many vocational programs currently use competency profiles both to structure instruction and as a system for articulating with the labor market and further training. At present, the profiles assess occupational skills and employability skills but there is no reason why academic competencies could not be included in the profile.

Graduation Credentials ("Career Passport," "Competency Portfolio") that Signal the Student's Accomplishments in High School

The coverage and format of graduation credentials and competency portfolios should probably be worked out cooperatively by a committee that includes school administrators, employers, and other interested parties. Developing and using such a document might be part of a campaign to enlist commitments from major local employers to hire new graduates and summer interns. Some degree of compactness and standardization is desirable in order to make it easier for employers to use the information in their hiring decisions. Students might also be encouraged to develop a portfolio of completed projects (e.g., a research report, pictures of a cabinet made in shop class, artwork). Employers should be encouraged to ask to see the portfolio and make a copy of it to attach to the application.

Releasing Student Records

The school can help students get good jobs by developing an equitable and efficient policy for releasing student records. School officials have the dual responsibility of protecting the student's right to privacy and helping them find good, suitable jobs. The student and his or her parents should receive copies (encased in plastic) of transcripts and other records that might be released so that they may make them available to anyone they choose. Schools might also develop a sheet explaining to parents and students their rights, as well as the pros and cons of disclosing information.

According to the Federal Education Rights and Privacy Act, all that a student/graduate must do to have school records sent to a prospective employer is sign a form specifying the purpose of disclosure, which records are to be released, and who is to receive the records. The waiver and record request forms used by employers contain this information, so when such a request is received, the school is obliged to respond. Requiring that graduates fill out a school-devised form—as one high school I visited did—results in the employer not getting the transcript requested and the graduate not getting the job. There are probably millions of high school graduates who do not realize that they failed to get a job they were hoping for because their high school did not send the transcript that was requested. Schools can best serve students by handling all inquiries expeditiously and without charge.

Credential Data Bank and Employee Locator Service

It may, however, be unrealistic to expect 22,902 high schools to develop efficient systems of maintaining student records and responding quickly to requests for transcripts. An alternative approach would be to centralize the record keeping and dissemination function in a trusted third-party organization. This organization would be easy to regulate and thus everyone could be assured that privacy mandates are being observed. The student would determine which competencies to have assessed and what types of information to include in his/her competency portfolio. Competency assessments would be offered for a variety of academic subjects and occupational skills. Tests with many alternative forms (or administered by computer based on a large test item bank) would be used so that students could retake the test a month later if desired. Only the highest score would remain in the system. Students would be encouraged to include descriptions of their extracurricular activities, their jobs, and any other accomplishments they feel are relevant and to submit samples of their work such as a research paper, artwork, or pictures of a project made in metal shop. Files could be updated after leaving high school.

Students would have three different ways of transmitting their competency profile to potential employers. First, they would receive certified copies of their portfolio, which they could carry to job interviews or mail to employers. Second, they would be able to call an 800 number and request that their portfolio be sent to specific employers. Third, they could ask to put themselves in an employee locator data bank similar to the student locator services operated by the Educational Testing Service and American College Testing. A student seeking a summer or postgraduation job would specify the type of work sought and dates of availability. Employers seeking workers could ask for a printout of the portfolios of all the individuals living near a particular establishment who have expressed interest in that type of job and who pass the employer's competency screens. Student locator services have been heavily used by colleges seeking to recruit minority students, and an employee locator service would almost certainly be used in the same way. This will significantly increase the rewards for hard study because the employee locator service is likely to result in a bidding war for the qualified minority students whose portfolios are in the system.

B.   Reform College Admission Policies

Promote Advanced Placement Courses

The advanced placement (AP) program is a cooperative educational endeavor that offers course descriptions, examinations, and sets of curricular materials in 28 different academic subjects. Students who take these courses and pass the examinations receive college credit for high school work. Expanding and up-grading the AP program should be a centerpiece of any effort to promote excellence in American secondary education. It clearly meets a felt need, for it is growing rapidly. The numbers of students taking AP exams more than doubled between 1983 and 1988. Nevertheless, only 8022 of the 22,902 U.S. high schools participate in the AP program and only 52 AP exams are taken on average in each participating high school. In 1988 only 6.6% of the seniors and 3.3% of the juniors took one or more AP exams (College Board, 1988). The nation should set a goal of doubling these percentages by 1992 and quadrupling them by 1995.

A survey of college placement officials conducted by *USA Today* and interviews of officials at Cornell and SUNY Binghamton conducted for this report found that students were expected to take AP courses if they are offered and grade point averages were adjusted for the difficulty level of the courses taken. High school students and parents are generally unaware of this policy, however, and many have not factored it into their high school course selections. They need to be better informed about this policy. Acting in concert, the college presidents of the 200 most selective colleges in the nation should send a letter to every high school principal in the country (with copy to the school board and local newspaper) urging them to create an AP program or expand the one they have. They should announce that starting in 1994, students seeking admission to their school should have taken and passed at least one AP course in junior year and be taking more than one AP course their senior year.

The federal government can facilitate the growth of the AP program by financing summer institutes for the teachers of AP courses and by offering a $100 AP excellence award (larger if the student is eligible for Pell Grant aid) to every student who gets an "eligible for college credit" score on the exam and a $300 award for getting a top score. To insure that attending a summer institute is considered a plum, compensation should be generous. In 1988 approximately 42,000 teachers taught AP courses (College Board, 1988). Rapid expansion of the program will require a yearly increase of 8000 in the stock of teachers teaching AP courses and if half of the increment to the stock were to experience summer institute training for six weeks, the cost would be about $28 million. In 1988, 286,009 students would have been eligible for an AP excellence award so the program would have cost about $71 million. If a good deal of publicity were attached to these awards, they would have major symbolic effects.

Induce Either a Complete Transformation of SAT and ACT Tests or a Substitution of AP and State-Sponsored Achievement Exams for Purposes of Awarding State Scholarships and Selection for Competitive Colleges

While national tests are necessary, the SAT is not the kind of test that is helpful. The SAT suffers from two very serious limitations: the limited range of the achievements that are evaluated and its multiple-choice format. The test was designed to be curriculum free. To the extent that it evaluates the students' understanding of material taught in schools, the material it covers is vocabulary and elementary and junior high school mathematics. Most of the college pre-paratory subjects studied in high school—science, social studies, technology, art, music, computers, trigonometry, and statistics—are completely absent from the test. As a result, it fails to generate incentives to take the more demanding courses or to study hard. The new version of the American College Test (ACT) test is somewhat better for it tests science and social science knowledge and also assesses problem solving in science. Both tests suffer from the common prob-lems that arise from their multiple-choice format. National and provincial exams in Europe are predominantly essay and extended-answer examinations. The ab-sence of essays on the SAT and ACT tests contributes to the poor writing skills of American students. The tests are advertised as ability tests but are in fact achievement tests measuring a very limited range of achievements (Jencks and Crouse, 1982). Jencks and Crouse have recommended that either the SAT evalu-ate a much broader range of achievements or be dropped in favor of AP examina-tions. Knowledge and understanding of literature, history, technology and sci-ence, and higher-order thinking skills should all be assessed. These exams should not be limited to a multiple-choice format and essays should be required where appropriate. Foreign language exams, for example, should test conversational skills as well as reading and writing. Students taking science courses should be expected to conduct experiments and demonstrate the use of lab equipment.

C.   Greater Use of Improved Employment Tests

Add Subtests Measuring Technical, Scientific, and Advanced Mathematical Competency to the General Aptitude Test Battery

The employment service's program of validity research for the GATB has made this test one of the few employment tests whose validity (as a predictor of job performance) has been generalized for a great variety of jobs. The content of the GATB was set in the 1940s and there has been little change in the content of the academic subtests since then. The nature of jobs has changed substantially and it is time to rethink the content of the GATB. Research on the validity of the Armed Services Vocational Aptitude Battery (ASVAB) indicates that the GATB's validity would be substantially increased by adding subtests measuring technical, scientific, and advanced mathematical knowledge and skills. The Department of Labor should immediately add subtests similar to the technical, mathematical knowledge, and science subtests of the ASVAB to the GATB and include these subtests in the composites that are used for recommending clients to civilian jobs that are similar to the jobs studied in the military. The employment service should also undertake a major study of the validity of the new GATB in the full spectrum of civilian jobs.

Fear of litigation has significantly inhibited testing research outside government. Companies no longer share the results of their validity studies or allow them to be published (even when the company's name is withheld) for fear of revealing their defense strategy to a potential litigant. As a result, research on tests other than the GATB has been inhibited. The government needs to step into the vacuum it has created and sponsor a major increase in research into the development and validation of improved employment tests.

EEOC Regulations Should Encourage the Use of Broad Spectrum Achievement Test Batteries rather than IQ Tests and the Current GATB

EEOC regulations and case law have in the past required that a very expensive validation study be conducted before a firm can use any test to help select employees (Friedman and Williams, 1982). The result has been greatly to diminish the use of tests for employee selection and substantially to reduce the rewards for learning. The Supreme Court's decision in the Wards Cove Packing case has shifted the burden of proof in adverse impact cases onto the plaintiff and has therefore opened the door to increased use of employment tests assessing verbal and mathematical competencies. It appears that employers will be able to justify the use of employment tests without having to undertake costly validity studies in their own firm by citing validity research done for similar jobs in other firms. Since civilian research on test validity has used the GATB almost exclusively, there is a very real danger that most firms will choose to use the simple reading, vocabulary, and arithmetic reasoning tests that are demonstrably similar to their GATB counterparts. Unfortunately, however, we now know that GATB does a poor job of assessing the cognitive skills necessary to succeed on the job. Research conducted in the military using the ASVAB has established that test batteries that also include assessments of competence in algebra, geometry, science, mechanical reasoning, electronics, and shop and auto knowledge are considerably more valid than composites based solely on the simple verbal and arithmetic subtests of the GATB (Hunter et al., 1985).

Courts have in the past required that employers demonstrate that each question on an employment test has a specific application in each job for which it is a proposed selection device. To avoid having to redesign tests for each job, test developers are likely to "dumb" the test down and include only simple questions covering mathematical, scientific, and technical principles that are learned in grade school. Litigation costs and the potential liability are enormous, so companies have become extremely cautious about testing. When selecting a test, defensibility in court has become a much more important criterion than maximum validity. Given the uncertainty of whether ASVAB research will be accepted as evidence on the validity of similar tests for civilian jobs, broad spectrum achievement test batteries will probably be judged too risky. A well-designed validity study can protect a firm using an unconventional test battery, but in most cases the potential benefit of finding a more valid selection method will not outweigh the costs of the study and the greater risks of litigation. If things are left as they are, it will be at minimum a decade before tests measuring competence in algebra, science, and the technical arena can be used as general selection devices for craft and other blue-collar jobs. Firms need to be given a signal by the EEOC that broad-spectrum achievement tests are acceptable selection devices and in fact are preferred over the low-level basic skills test that serves as the g aptitude of the GATB.

For employment tests to generate incentives to learn, students, parents, and teachers must be aware that local employers are using tests for selection and what kind of material is included on these tests. Unfortunately, the fear of litigation has caused many employers to give only limited publicity to their use of tests. This is another reason why employers need to be told by people in authority that they are acting in the national interest when they seek out and reward those who have high-level academic skills.

The Federal Government Should give Greater Weight to Academic Achievement in its own Hiring

The federal government is the largest employer in the country. It should set an example for the private sector by announcing that henceforth it is giving greater weight to academic achievement in high school and college than it has in the past.

The military currently selects recruits on the basis of Armed Forces Qualification Test (AFQT) scores and the high school diploma. The current AFQT is an average of scores on the verbal, arithmetic reasoning, and mathematical knowledge subtests of the ASVAB. By adding the general science, electronics knowledge, mechanical comprehension, and auto/shop knowledge tests to the composite that defines the AFQT, the military would simultaneously increase the validity of their selection and improve incentives to study science and technical subjects in high school.

The Office of Personnel Management is designing a biodata form to be used for selecting professional and managerial personnel for the federal government. The current draft of the form asks applicants a number of questions about grades in high school and college and about class rank. It does not ask about the difficulty level of the courses taken. Current plans are to request that transcripts be sent only for a sample of the applicants and to use these data only for checking the accuracy of the information provided. If discrepancies are discovered for people who were hired, the cases will be referred to investigators. The questions are worded in such a way, however, that only the most outrageous of distortions can be proved to be a lie and could therefore be grounds for dismissal. The following changes in civil service hiring procedures are recommended:

- All candidates for civil service jobs (including clerical jobs) should be required to send their high school and college transcripts.
- After a preliminary screening on the basis of the biodata key, course grades and difficulty level indicators should be coded for the most recent school attended.
- Final rankings should be based on a combination of the transcript information, biodata, scores on job-relevant tests, and other relevant information.

This change will increase hiring costs, but the benefits of greater validity and improved incentives would outweigh these costs by a large margin.

D.   School-Based Rewards for Learning

Cooperative Learning

One effective way of inducing peers to value learning and to support effort in school is to reward the group for the individual learning of its members. This is the approach taken in cooperative learning. Research results (Slavin, 1983) suggest that the two key ingredients for successful cooperative learning are as follows:

- A cooperative incentive structure—awards based on group performance—seems to be essential for students working in groups to learn better;
- A system of individual accountability in which everyone's maximum effort must be essential to the group's success and the effort and performance of each group member must be clearly visible to the others in the group.

For example, students might be grouped into evenly matched teams of four or five members that are heterogeneous in ability. After the teacher presents new material, the team works together on worksheets to prepare each other for periodic quizzes. The team's score is an average of the scores of team members, and high team scores are recognized in a class newsletter or through group certificates of achievement.

What seems to happen in cooperative learning is that the team develops an identity of its own, and group norms arise that are different from the norms that hold sway in the student's other classes. The group's identity arises from the extensive personal interaction among group members in the context of working toward a shared goal. Since the group is small and the interaction intense, the effort and success of each team member is known to other teammates. Such knowledge allows the group to reward each team member for his or her contribution to the team goal—and this is what seems to happen.

Turn Schools into All-Day Learning Centers

Schools should remain open after the end of the regular school day and a full range of remedial and enrichment programs and extracurricular activities and interscholastic sports should be offered.

Keep the Schools Open During the Summer

Longitudinal studies of learning have found that the pace of learning slows considerably during the summer and that disadvantaged students especially lose ground during the summer months (Heyns, 1987). Experimental evaluations of STEP, a program for disadvantaged youth that combines a part-time summer job with about 90 hours of remediation, has found that adding the remediation to the summer job results in gains in academic achievement of 0.5 grade level equivalents relative to youth who received a job only (Sipe, Grossman, and Milliner, 1988). It would appear that summer programs targeted on educationally and economically disadvantaged children are likely to have high payoffs.

A Massive Dose of Mastery Learning

Students who are not learning at the desired rate should be required to commit additional time to the task after school and during the summer. At the beginning of the school year, school personnel should meet with the student and his or her parents to set goals. Students who are not performing at grade level in core subjects and who do not make normal progress during the school year should be kept after school for tutoring and remedial instruction and required to attend summer school. Assessment of progress should be made at appropriate points during the school year to inform students of their progress and to enable those who are participating in remedial programs after school to demonstrate they are now progressing satisfactorily. Course grades and teacher evaluations would be a central part of the assessment process, but there should be an external yardstick as well. The external yardstick might be a competency checklist, a mastery test keyed to the textbook, or an exam specified by the state or the school, or collectively by the teachers in that grade level or department. The reason for the external yardstick is that it helps ensure the students perceive the standard to be absolute rather than relative to others in the class, and it helps create a commonality of interest between teacher and student. Teachers need to be perceived as helping the student achieve the student's goals, not as judges meting out punishment. Since students will want to avoid being required to get remedial instruction after school and during the summer, this will be a powerful incentive for them to devote themselves to their studies.

Honoring Academic Achievement

Schools should strengthen their awards and honors system for academic and nonacademic accomplishments. The medals, trophies, and school letters awarded in interscholastic athletics are a powerful motivator of achievement on the playing field. Academic pursuits need a similar system of reinforcement. Awards and honors systems should be designed so that almost every student can receive at least one award or honor before graduation if he or she makes the effort. Outstanding academic performance (e.g., high grades or high test scores) would not have to be the only way of defining excellence. Award could be given for significant improvements in academic performance since the previous year or since the beginning of the school year, for public service in or out of school, for perfect attendance records, and for student of the week (criteria could vary weekly). The standard for making an award should be criterion referenced: if greater numbers achieve the standard of excellence, more awards should be given.

A prominent place in the school should be reserved for bulletin boards where pictures of the most recent winners and reasons for their receiving recognition could be posted. Another form of recognition could be displays of student work: art, science, social studies, vocational education projects, and so forth. Periodically, the parents of the most recent award winners and sponsoring teachers should be invited to an evening assembly at which the principal would award the students the certificate or plaque recognizing their accomplishments.

IV. EFFECTS OF PROPOSED REFORMS ON UNDERREPRESENTED MINORITIES

What impact would the reforms just described have upon the labor market chances of minority youth? Since minority students receive lower scores on achievement tests, it might appear at first glance that greater emphasis on academic achievement will inevitably reduce their access to good colleges and to good jobs. This is not the case, however, for four reasons.

If academic achievement becomes a more important basis for selecting students and workers, something else becomes less important. The consequences for minorities of greater emphasis on academic achievement depend on the nature of the criterion that becomes deemphasized. Substituting academic achievement tests for aptitude tests in college admissions *improves minority access* because minority–majority differentials tend to be smaller (in standard-deviation units) on achievement tests (e.g., the NAEP reading and math tests) than on aptitude tests (e.g., the SAT). Greater emphasis on academic achievement *improves the access of women* to high-level professional, technical, craft, and managerial jobs because it substitutes a criterion on which women do well for criteria—sex-stereotyped beliefs about which jobs are appropriate for women—that have excluded women in the past.

For the same reason, greater emphasis on academic achievement when selecting young workers will not reduce minority access to jobs if it substitutes for other criteria that also place minority youth at a serious disadvantage. The current system in which there is almost no use of employment tests and little signaling of high school achievements to the labor market clearly has not generated jobs for minority youth. In October 1985, 1986, 1987, and 1988, only 45% of previous spring's black high school graduates not attending college were employed (Bureau of Labor Statistics, 1989). One reason why minority youth do poorly in the labor market is that most of the criteria now used to make selections—previous work experience, recommendations from previous employers, having family friends or relatives at the firm, proximity of one's residence to stores that hire youth, performance in interviews, and prejudices and stereotypes—work against them. These criteria will diminish in importance as academic achievement becomes more important. There is no way of knowing whether the net result of these shifts will help or hinder minority youth seeking employment. In some models of the labor market the relative position of minority workers improves when academic achievement is better signaled (Aigner and Cain, 1977).

The second way in which minority youth may benefit from improved signaling of school achievements is that it will give recent high school graduates, both black and white, the first real chance to compete for high-wage, high-training jobs. At present all youth are frozen out of these jobs because primary labor market employers seldom consider job applicants who lack considerable work experience. Experience is considered essential partly because it contributes to productivity but also because it produces signals of competence and reliability that employers use to identify who is most qualified. Recent high school graduates have no such record and information on the student's high school performance is not available, so the entire graduating class appears to employers as one undifferentiated mass of unskilled and undisciplined workers. A supervisor at New York Life Insurance commented on television, "When kids come out of high school, they think the world owes them a living" (PBS, 1989). Surely this generalization does not apply to every graduate, but the students who are disciplined and academically well prepared currently have no way of signaling this fact to employers. State exams, competency portfolios, and informative graduation credentials would change this unfair situation and give students a way of demonstrating that the stereotype does not apply to them. Young people from minority backgrounds must overcome even more virulent stereotypes, and they often lack a network of adult contacts who can provide job leads and references. By helping them overcome these barriers to employment, competency portfolios are of particular help to minority youth.

The third way in which these proposals will assist minority students is by encouraging greater numbers of firms to undertake affirmative-action recruitment. The creation of a competency portfolio data bank that can be used by employers seeking qualified minority job candidates would greatly reduce the costs and increase the effectiveness of affirmative-action programs. Affirmative action has significantly improved minority representation in managerial and professional occupations and contributed to a substantial increase in the payoff to schooling for blacks (Freeman, 1981). One of the reasons it has been particularly effective in this labor market is that college reputations, transcripts, and placement offices provide brokering and prescreening services that significantly lower the costs of recruiting minority job candidates. The competency portfolio data bank would extend low-cost brokering and prescreening services to the labor market for high school graduates. The creation of such a data bank would almost certainly generate a great deal of competition for the more qualified minority youth in the portfolio bank.

The final and most important way in which these reforms will benefit minority youth is by bringing about improvements in academic achievement and productivity on the job. Student incentives to study hard, parental incentives to demand a better education, and teacher incentives both to give more and to expect more from students will all be strengthened. Because of the way affirmative action is likely to interact with a competency profile data bank, the rewards for learning will become particularly strong for minority students. Learning will improve and the gap between minority and majority achievement will diminish. Society has been making considerable progress in closing achievement gaps between minority and majority students. In the early NAEP assessments, black high school seniors born between 1952 and 1957 were 6.7 grade level equivalents behind their white counterparts in science proficiency, 4 grade level equivalents behind in mathematics, and 5.3 grade level equivalents behind in reading. The most recent NAEP data for 1986 reveals that for blacks born in 1969, the gap has been cut to 5.6 grade level equivalents in science, 2.9 grade level equivalents in math, and 2.6 grade level equivalents in reading (NAEP, 1988, 1989). Koretz et al.'s (1986, Appendix E), analysis of data from the state testing programs supports the NAEP findings. Hispanic students are also closing the achievement gap. These positive trends suggest that despite their limited funding, Head Start, Title I, and other compensatory interventions have had an impact. The schools attended by most minority students are still clearly inferior to those attended by white students, so further reductions in the school quality differentials can be expected to produce further reductions in academic achievement differentials.

The students of James A. Garfield's AP calculus classes have demonstrated to the nation what minority students from economically disadvantaged backgrounds can accomplish. The student body is predominantly disadvantaged minorities; yet in 1987 only three high schools in the nation, Alhambra High School in Los Angeles and Bronx Science and Stuyvesant High School in New York, had a large number of students taking the AP calculus exam. The two calculus teachers at this school, Jaime Escalante and Ben Jimenez, account for 17% of all Mexican Americans taking the AP calculus exam and 32% of all Mexican Americans who pass the more difficult (BC) form of the test (Matthews, 1988). There is no secret about how they did it: they worked extremely hard. Students signed a contract committing themselves to extra homework and extra time in school, and they lived up to the commitment. What this success establishes is that minority youngsters can be persuaded to study just as hard as the academic-track students in Europe and that if they do they will achieve at world class levels. The success at Garfield High is replicable.

POSTLUDE

Institutional arrangements of schools and the labor market have profound effects on the incentives faced by students, teachers, parents, and school administrators. The passivity and inattention of students, the low morale of teachers, the defeat of so many school levies, and low rankings on international measures of achievement are all logical outcomes of institutional arrangements that weaken student incentives to study and parental incentives to fund a high-quality education. Only with an effective system of rewards within schools and in the labor market can we hope to overcome the pervasive apathy and achieve excellence.

ACKNOWLEDGMENTS

This project was funded under Purchase Order No. 99-9-4757-75-009-04 from the U.S. Department of Labor, Commission on Workforce Quality and Labor Market Efficiency. Opinions stated in this document do not necessarily represent the official position or policy of the U.S. Department of Labor, Commission on Workforce Quality and Labor Market Efficiency. The paper has been prepared for the secretary of labor's Commission on Workforce Quality. The research that has culminated in this paper was sponsored by the Center for Advanced Human Resource Studies, the National Center for Research in Vocational Education, and the Commission on Testing and Public Policy. I would like to thank Peter Mueser, Richard Murnane, and James Rosenbaum for helpful comments on earlier versions of the paper.

NOTES

1. Results of a survey, designed by the author, of the National Federation of Independent Business. The survey (taken in 1987) was of a stratified random sample of the NFIB membership. Larger firms had a significantly higher probability of being selected for the study. The response rate to the mail survey was 20% and the number of usable responses was 2014.

2. Studies that measure output for different workers in the same job at the same firm, using physical output as a criterion, have found that the standard deviation of output varies with job complexity and averages about 0.164 in routine clerical jobs and 0.278 in clerical jobs with decision-making responsibilities (Hunter et al., 1988). Because there are fixed costs to employing an individual (facilities, equipment, light, heat, and overhead functions such as hiring and payrolling), the coefficient of variation of marginal products of individuals is assumed to be 1.5 times the coefficient of variation of productivity. Because about two-thirds of clerical jobs can be classified as routine, the coefficient of variation of marginal productivity for clerical jobs is 30% [$1.5 * (0.33 * 0.278 + 0.67 * 0.164)$]. A 0.5 validity for general mental ability then implies that an academic achievement differential between two individuals of one standard deviation (in a distribution of high school graduates) is associated with a productivity differential in the job of about 11% ($0.5 * 0.74 * 3$ 0%). The ratio of the high school graduate test score standard deviation to the population standard deviation is assumed to be 0.74. This issue is more thoroughly discussed in Bishop (1987b).

3. In game theory language, we have here a repeated game in which players may make side payments using the currency of friendship. Parents and college admissions officers (but not employers) offer prizes to those who do best in the academic game, but if everyone improves together the total amount of prize money does not rise. Some players are offered larger prizes than others. For most players the offered prizes are small by comparison to the costs of hard study and the side payments available from peers. The result is that only a few students (those facing the biggest prizes and the smallest costs of study) choose the noncooperative solution and the great majority of students choose the cooperative, "let's all take it easy," solution.

REFERENCES

Aigner, Dennis J. and Glen Cain (1977). "Statistical Theories of Discrimination in Labor Markets." *Industrial and Labor Relations Review*, January:175–187.

Berlin, Gordon and Andrew Sum (1988), *"Toward a More Perfect Union: Basic Skills, Poor Families, and Our Economic Future."* Occasional Paper # 3, Ford Foundation Project on Social Welfare and the American Future, New York.

Bishop, John (1985), *Preparing Youth for Employment*. Columbus: The National Center for Research in Vocational Education, The Ohio State University.

———— (1987a), "The Recognition and Reward of Employee Performance." *Journal of Labor Economics* 5(4):S36–S56.

———— (1987b), "Information Externalities and the Social Payoff to Academic Achievement." Center for Advanced Human Resource Studies, Working Paper # 87-06, Cornell University, Ithaca, New York.

———— (1988a), "The Economics of Employment Testing." Center for Advanced Human Resource Studies, Working Paper #88-14, Cornell University, Ithaca, New York.

———— (1988b), "The Productivity Consequences of What Is Learned in High School." Center for Advanced Human Resource Studies, Working Paper #88-18, Cornell University, Ithaca, New York.

———— (1989a), "Is the Test Score Decline Responsible for the Productivity Growth Decline?" *American Economic Review* 79(1).

———— (1989b), "Achievement, Test Scores and Relative Wages." Conference on Wages in the 1980s, American Enterprise Institute, Washington, DC., November 3, 1989.

Bureau of the Census (1990), *Current Population Reports*, Series P60.

Bureau of Labor Statistics (1989), "Nearly Three-Fifths of the High School Graduates of 1988 Enrolled in College." USDL 89-308, June.

Cain, Glen and Arthur Goldberger (1983), "Public and Private Schools Revisited." *Sociology of Education* 56:208–218.

Carroll, Stephen (1982), "The Search for Equity in School Finance." In Walter McMahon and Terry Geske (eds.), *Financing Education: Overcoming Inefficiency and Inequity*. Urbana: University of Illinois Press, pp. 237–66.

College Board (1988), *AP Yearbook 1988*. Princeton, NJ: College Entrance Examination Board.

Covington, M. V. and R. G. Beery (1976). *Self Worth and School Learning*. New York: Holt, Reinhart & Winston.

Ehrenberg, Ronald and Richard Chaykowski (1988), "On Estimating the Effects of Increased Aid to Education." In Richard Freeman and Casey Ichniowski (eds.), *When Public Sector Workers Unionize*. Chicago: University of Chicago Press, pp. 245–269.

Fischer, C. W., N. N. Filby, R. S. Marliave, L. S. Cahen, N. N. Dishaw, J. E. Moore, and D. C. Berliner (1978), "Teaching Behaviors, Academic Learning Time and Student Achievement: Final Report of Phase III-B." Technical Report V-I, Far West Laboratories, San Francisco.

Frederick, W. C. (1977), "The Use of Classroom Time in High Schools above or below the Median Reading Score." *Urban Education* 11(4):459–464.

Frederick, W., H. Walberg, and S. Rasher (1979), "Time, Teacher Comments, and Achievement in Urban High Schools." *Journal of Educational Research* 73(2):63–65.

Freeman, Richard (1976), *The Overeducated American*. New York: Academic Press.

——— (1981), "Black Economic Progress after 1964: Who Has Gained and Why." In Sherwin Rosen (ed.), *Studies in Labor Markets*. Chicago: University of Chicago Press.

Friedman, Toby and E. Belvin Williams (1982), "Current Use of Tests for Employment." In Alexandra K. Wigdor and Wendell R. Gardner (eds.), *Ability Testing: Uses, Consequences, and Controversies, Part II: Documentation Section*. Washington, DC: National Academy Press, pp. 999–1069.

Gardner, John A. (1982), *Influence of High School Curriculum on Determinants of Labor Market Experience*. Columbus: The National Center for Research in Vocational Education, The Ohio State University.

Ghiselli, Edwin E. (1973), "The Validity of Aptitude Tests in Personnel Selection." *Personnel Psychology* 26:461–477.

Goodlad, J. (1983), *A Place Called School*. New York: McGraw-Hill.

Griggs v. Duke Power Company, 3 FEP 175 (1971).

Hashimoto, M. and B. Yu (1980), "Specific Capital, Employment and Wage Rigidity." *Bell Journal of Economics* 11(2):536–549.

Heyns, Barbara (1987), "Schooling and Cognitive Development: Is There a Season for Learning?" *Child Development* 58(5):1151–1160.

High School and Beyond (HSB) (1982), *Data File Users Manual*. Chicago: National Opinion Research Corporation.

Hollenbeck, K. and B. Smith (1984), *The Influence of Applicants' Education and Skills on Employability Assessments by Employers*. Columbus: The National Center for Research in Vocational Education, The Ohio State University.

Hotchkiss, Lawrence, John H. Bishop, and John Gardner (1982), *Effects of Individual and School Characteristics on Part-Time Work of High School Seniors*. Columbus: The National Center for Research in Vocational Education, The Ohio State University.

Hunter, John (1983), *Test Validation for 12,000 Jobs: An Application of Job Classification and Validity Generalization Analysis to the General Aptitude Test Battery*. Washington, D.C.: U.S. Employment Service, Department of Labor.

Hunter, John E., J. James Crosson, and David H. Friedman (1985), "The Validity of the Armed

Services Vocational Aptitude Battery (ASVAB) for Civilian and Military Job Performance." Department of Defense Report, Washington, DC., August.

Hunter, John E., Frank L. Schmidt, and Michael K. Judiesch (1988), "Individual Differences in Output as a Function of Job Complexity." Department of Industrial Relations and Human Resources, University of Iowa, Iowa City.

International Association for the Evaluation of Educational Achievement (IAEEA) (1987), *The Underachieving Curriculum, Assessing U.S. School Mathematics from an International Perspective*. Champaign, IL: Stipes Publishing Co.

———— (1988), *Science Achievement in Seventeen Nations*. New York: Pergammon Press.

Jencks, Christopher and James Crouse (1982), "Aptitude vs. Achievement: Should We Replace the SAT?" *The Public Interest*, pp. 21–35.

Kang, S. and J. Bishop (1984), "The Impact of Curriculum on the Non–College Bound Youth's Labor Market Outcomes." In Larry Hotchkiss, John Bishop, and Suk Kang (eds.), *High School Preparation for Employment*. Columbus: The National Center for Research in Vocational Education, Ohio State University, pp. 95–135.

Klein, M. F., K. A. Tyle, and J. E. Wright (1979), "A Study of Schooling Curriculum." *Phi Delta Kappan* 61(4):244–248.

Koretz, Daniel et al. (1986), *Trends in Educational Achievement*. Washington, DC: Congressional Budget Office.

Lazear, Edward P. (1986), "Pay Equality and Industrial Politics." Research paper, The Hoover Institution, Stanford University, Stanford, CA.

Leestma, Robert et al. (1987), "Japanese Education Today." Report from the U.S. Study of Education in Japan, prepared by a special task force of the OERI Japan Study Team, Washington, DC.

Longitudinal Survey of American Youth (LSAY) (1988), *Data File User's Manual*. Dekalb, IL: Public Opinion Laboratory.

Maier, Milton H. and Frances C. Grafton (1981), *Aptitude Composites for ASVAB 8, 9, and 10*. Research Report 1308, U.S. Army Research Institute for Behavioral and Social Sciences, Alexandria, VA.

Matthews, Jay (1988). *Escalante: The Best Teacher in America*. New York: Henry Holt.

Meyer, R. (1982), "Job Training in the Schools." In R. Taylor, H. Rosen, and F. Pratzner (eds.), *Job Training for Youth*. Columbus: The National Center for Research in Vocational Education, The Ohio State University.

———— (1989), "The Curricular Production Function: An Analysis of the Sources of Mathematics Proficiency." National Assessment of Vocational Education Technical Report, LaFollette Institute of Public Affairs, University of Wisconsin, Madison.

National Assessment of Educational Progress (NAEP) (1988), *The Mathematics Report Card*. Princeton, NJ: Educational Testing Service.

————(1989), *Crossroads in American Education*. Princeton, NJ: Educational Testing Service.

Organization of Economic Cooperation and Development (1986), "Living Conditions in OECD Countries: A Compendium of Social Indicators." Social Policy Studies No. 3, OECD, Paris.

Public Broadcasting System (PBS) (1989), "Learning in America." March 27.

Rosenbaum, James and Tobe Kariya (1989), "From High School to Work: Market and Institutional Mechanisms in Japan." *American Journal of Sociology* 94(6):1334–1365.

Sipe, Cynthia, Jean Grossman, and Julita Milliner (1988). *Summer Training and Education Program: Report on the 1987 Experience*. Philadelphia, PA: Public/Private Ventures, April.

Sizer, Theodore, R. (1984), *Horace's Compromise: The Dilemma of the American High School*. Boston: Houghton Mifflin.

Slavin, Robert (1983), "When Does Cooperative Learning Increase Student Achievement?" *Psychological Bulletin* 99:429–445.

Stevenson, Harold, Shin-Ying Lee, and James W. Stigler (1986), "Mathematics Achievement of Chinese, Japanese, and American Children." *Science* 231:693–699.

Stiglitz, Joseph E. (1974), "Risk Sharing and Incentives in Sharecropping." *Review of Economic Studies* 61(2):219–256.

Taubman, P. and T. Wales (1975), "Education as an Investment and a Screening Device." In F. T. Juster (ed.), *Education, Income, and Human Behavior*. New York: McGraw-Hill.

Thomas, John W. (1988). Agency and Achievement: Self-Management and Self-regard." *Review of Educational Research* 50(2):213–240.

THE FIRM'S DECISION TO TRAIN

Donald O. Parsons

I. INTRODUCTION

Job training is a fundamental part of the total educational system in any industrialized economy, and the efficient provision of such training an important
element in any comprehensive industrial strategy. In his classic study of on-the-
job training, Jacob Mincer concluded a careful assessment of the aggregate
importance of on-the-job training with the remark, "It is probably correct to say
that, in the male half of the world, on-the-job training—measured in dollar
costs—is as important as formal schooling" (Mincer, 1962, p.63). This paper
provides a critical review of economic models of the firm's decision to train
workers: what training is undertaken, where it is undertaken, and who finances
it. In the final section, I consider ways in which the government can encourage
the more efficient provision of on-the-job training.

Many critical job skills, for example, reading and mathematical skills, are not
typically learned on the job, but are developed in a formal schooling environment. Presumably these attributes are almost universally demanded, so that
economies of scale argue for collective provision. Many of these skills also have
returns beyond any direct labor market returns, for example, an informed electo-
rate, and are collectively provided (subsidized) for that reason as well. The

Research in Labor Economics, Volume 11, pages 53–75.
ISBN: 1-555938-080-2

efficiency of the schooling system in providing these skills is often questioned, but only modest variations or reform have been proposed, suggesting that the basic structure (publicly financed, specialized training centers) is perceived as reasonable.

Skills more directly linked to the job are more eclectically supplied, reflecting perhaps the diversity of the skills required. Some job skills are learned in formal job-training programs, either on-site or in specialized centers not unlike public schools, while others are the informal outcome of work activity (learning by doing). Imposing some sort of logical structure on these disparate activities has been an important contribution of economic analysis.

In the final analysis, training is an investment decision. The training process absorbs the worker's time as well as the time of coworkers and supervisors, various materials, and the indirect costs of mistakes made by the inexperienced worker. If the training is to be economically rational, these costs must be offset by the highest future productivity of the trained worker. Because these returns (and costs) are distributed over time, the financial aspects of the transactions are important as well. The financing of intensive on-the-job training activities is a serious obstacle to the efficient provision of a highly trained work force.

The distinction between the *training activity* itself and the *financing* of the training activity is an important one. The form of the training activity is in the first instance technological. What is the nature of the on-the-job learning mechanism? In what environment is the learning of job skills most cheaply provided: in the firm or in some specialized training program, for example, schools? The financing issue is fundamentally one of access to capital and is intimately related to the structure of the property rights system. The financing decision depends in an important way on the legal environment in which firm and worker exchange goods and services as well as promises of future exchanges. As in many economic decisions, the action decision (training) and the financing decision (who pays for the training) are intimately related.

The focus of this review is on the provision of job training to workers with no unusual training problems. The provision of job-training programs to seriously disadvantaged individuals is itself a major policy issue, possibly justifying extensive direct government intervention, but the direct government supply of trained (disadvantaged) workers is not a significant portion of the total supply of job skills in the economy. Job training in the United States has been overwhelmingly private, forged in a variety of ways among workers, firms, and unions. It is this market that is examined below.

The review proceeds in the following way. I first consider the nature of on-the-job training more precisely, emphasizing the role of the firm in the supply of on-the-job training opportunities. Two alternative models of on-the-job training are considered and a few implications for the efficient supply of training services are derived. In Section III, I develop the basic investment model of on-the-job training, the analytical structure that will be used to frame the discussions to follow. The economic logic of this human-capital paradigm is discussed at length because of its central role in forming the economist's conception of this market. In Section IV, conditions under which the free market will generate the efficient amount of on-the-job training are outlined. The discussion then proceeds to the important issue of why this market may fail to yield efficient results, most prominently the financing problem. The relationship of human capital finance to the deeper issue of property rights structures is explored: the right of contract has been socially abridged for a variety of reasons, both by design (bankruptcy laws) and by the inadvertent decisions of judges and juries. Analyses of variations on this fundamental problem comprise much of the remainder of this review, including the policy discussion of the final section. The potential for an alternative supply mechanism—employer training cooperatives—is critically examined.

II. THE FIRM AS SUPPLIER OF TRAINING OPPORTUNITIES

The distinction between schooling and on-the-job training is not always a clear one. The issue is more than one of academic vs. vocational skills. Vocational skills that are obvious candidates for on-the-job training, for example, carpentry, are often taught in public schools or in specialized training centers. In that sense, on-the-job training must be considered as part of a broader educational structure, with the observed mix of formal schooling and on-the-job training an equilibrium outcome. Neither is the issue simply one of the geographic locus of training. During the English industrial revolution, firms often provided traditional schooling activities to young workers, much as Hollywood provides tutors to young actors today and for the same reason: the convenient integration of work schedules and legal requirements for schooling. This is not what is normally implied by on-the-job training, which includes the notion of a paid or "on-the-clock" activity. In this review, on-the-job training refers to any activity undertaken on the job (during work hours) that increases the worker's subsequent productivity.

Given the diffuse nature of this definition, the physical training activity is difficult to conceptualize neatly. The standard investment model of on-the-job training, discussed at greater length in the next section, is simply an extension of a schooling model into a period of incomplete specialization in education (Mincer, 1962, 1974; Ben-Porath, 1967; Heckman, 1976; Rosen, 1976; Haley, 1976). Individuals who wish to undertake a human-capital investment program that involves less than complete time specialization in schooling are presumed to choose on-the-job training. Why such activities should be undertaken during paid hours is not obvious.

The implications of this view for the optimal geographic locus of training activities are few: the part-time schooling could be carried on in schools or in the firm. The usual balance between economies of scale (in training) and commuting costs would presumably affect the outcome. For example, one could imagine that, if a large number of individuals in the same workplace wanted to undertake the same course of study at the same time, transportation economies would lead to the activity being undertaken at the workplace. If the labor market is competitive, one could also imagine that the training activity would be provided efficiently, with the individual's own time and assorted other inputs combined in a rational fashion. The incomplete specialization model is in many ways like the Hollywood tutoring model; the training may occur at the workplace, but does not capture much of the interaction of work activity and learning that is commonly associated with the notion of on-the-job training.

An intuitively plausible alternative model of the learning process is the learning-by-doing or learning-as-a-by-product model. Evidence from the National Longitudinal Survey of Youth reveals that on-the-job learning is intimately related to what the individual does on the job, that is, in his or her occupation (Parsons, 1985). Among male youth in 1982 who had jobs and were not enrolled in school, approximately two-thirds of all professionals, managers, and craftsmen reported that their jobs had high learning content. In contrast, only one-third of laborers and service workers and only one-fourth of farm laborers reported that their jobs had high learning content. This suggests that much on-the-job learning is the by-product of work activities and not simply incomplete specialization in schooling.

The learning-by-doing model emphasizes the importance of the underlying work activity and also the notion of learning rather than training. In this vein, Rosen (1972) has stressed the unique supply characteristics of training in the workplace. Specifically, Rosen proposes that individuals be viewed as choosing among jobs based on a compensation bundle that includes both current wages and on-the-job training, which itself is determined by the technological characteristics of the job and on the firm's efficiency at providing such training. The interaction of these individual and employer choices yields the equilibrium level of on-the-job learning in the economy as well as the rate of return to the activity.

In many circumstances the distinction between these two training activity models is not an important one. In other circumstances, however, the differences may be pronounced. A key difference in the models is the implied degree of flexibility in the provision of learning opportunities. If firms are simply schools within the plant, the opportunities for on-the-job training should respond flexibly to shifts in worker demand. Conversely if such learning is primarily a by-product of work activities, then the firm may have much less flexibility in varying learning activities.

For example, as a by-product of work activity, the aggregate supply of on-the-job learning opportunities will be positively linked to the business cycle through new hires, etc. On-the-job learning will increase or decrease more or less in proportion to the expansion and contraction of employment opportunities. Conversely, formal schooling tends to be mildly countercyclical; when current business conditions are difficult, individuals are more likely to remain in school. If on-the-job training is, in fact, well characterized by an incomplete-specialization-in-schooling model, then one might expect to see a similar expansion of the training component of work when product demand contracts; the learning content of jobs should increase.

The focus on the supply characteristics of the training activity raises other issues as well. Specialization in the training function may occur across firms and industrial sectors; on-the-job training need not be conducted in the firm at which the worker is trained (Cho, 1983). If the process involves explicit, controllable training programs, specialization will only occur if the training function is characterized by increasing returns. If on-the-job training is largely learning by doing, however, the learning accumulated by a firm's employees at one point in time may bear no systematic relationship to the amount demanded subsequently. Individuals may find that they cannot use their newly acquired skills profitably in the current firm. In this case, learning may induce mobility.

Evidence for such specialization is reported by several investigators. Schiller (1986), for example, provides evidence that learning among new entrants to the labor force occurs disproportionately in small firms. These firms, on net, lose experienced workers to larger firms. Weiss (1985) attempts to resolve theory and evidence that (1) union workers are better trained than nonunion workers, but that (2) union workers are less likely to receive training (Mincer, 1983), by arguing that experienced, nonunion workers disproportionately migrate to unionized firms. I argue below (although this is no more than a conjecture) that the training provided in small firms is disproportionately in rudimentary job skills, especially work discipline and cooperation, and that intensive on-the-job training is primarily carried on in large firms, principally because of the ease of internal financing.

On the production side, on-the-job training can be viewed as simply another product of the firm. To the extent the final product market activities are efficiently organized, one could assume that the time of worker, supervisor, and coworkers and the related direct costs devoted to the training will in general be in efficient proportions and combined rationally into a final trained product. One unique problem that arises in the provision of training is obtaining the cooperation of coworkers (Reagan, 1988). The heart of the cooperative problem is that workers are being asked to train their own potential replacements. This is not a serious problem if the market is large and the trainers are specialists, but may be serious in internal labor markets in which the trainers are coworkers. The problem is an ancient one. Noncompetitive provisions were an important part of early apprenticeship contracts; the apprentice's right to compete with the master was often limited. For example, he could not establish a shop within a fixed range of the master's own shop. If the employees doing the training are closely monitored, this type of malfeasance may be limited. If the training personnel have a great deal of discretion, however, as would be the case in less-formal training programs, the problem may be an important one.

Reagan (1988) has argued that seniority rules on layoffs and promotions are in part an institutional way of reducing this obvious conflict of interest. I assume below that these institutional rules are in fact sufficient to enable the firm to produce the training activity efficiently, *given* the amount of training that is to be undertaken. In the next several sections, I develop more carefully the issue of the efficient *amount* of on-the-job training. The training specialization issue is considered again in Section VII, when the implications for training of the recent restructuring of the industrial base in the United States are derived.

III. ON-THE-JOB TRAINING: AN INVESTMENT PERSPECTIVE

The on-the-job training decision is one of a broad class of human capital investment decisions (Jacob Mincer, 1962, 1974). The heart of the decision calculus is as simple as it is powerful. The training activity typically involves a period in which the worker is not as productive as he or she might otherwise be. The training activity may involve other costs as well, including the diversion of supervisor and coworker time and energies to the training process, purchased training materials, and unusually high scrappage rates (or lost business opportunities at the management trainee level) due to a high incidence of mistakes. Set against these costs is the increase in worker productivity after the training period.

It will be useful to formalize the investment decision. Denote the workers' productivity flow in the absence of training as v_t, which when discounted at the interest rate r, promises lifetime wealth (W) of

$$W \text{ (no training)} = \int_0^\infty v_t \, e^{-rt} \, dt. \tag{1}$$

If productivity is fixed forever at a level v, that is $v_t = v$ for all t, the wealth formula takes on the simple form

$$W \text{ (no training)} = v/r. \tag{2}$$

Productivity is likely to decline at some point and indeed fall to zero at death or retirement, but the constant-productivity assumption underlying Eq. (2) may still be a useful approximation, especially if retirement is many years in the future or if the interest rate is high.

The training alternative also involves a time flow of productivity, say v_t^* and may include some direct costs of training at each instant, say d_t. The lifetime wealth implied by the training alternative is

$$W \text{ (Training)} = = \int_0^\infty (v_t^* - d_t) \, e^{-rt} \, dt. \tag{3}$$

If, for example, the training period is of duration T, during which the worker's productivity is v_0^* and direct training costs are d, and after which the worker's productivity is v_1^*, the worker's lifetime wealth in the training regime is

$$W \text{ (training)} = (1/r)[(v_0^* - d)(1 - e^{-rT}) + v_1^* e^{-rT}]. \tag{4}$$

The *efficiency criterion* is a simple one: the training activity should be undertaken if and only if the worker's productive wealth in the training regime equals or exceeds his or her productive wealth if untrained, where all wealth computations are undertaken at the social discount rate, say ρ. Formally this means that training is economically efficient if and only if

$$W \text{ (training} \mid r = \rho) \geq W \text{ (no training} \mid r = \rho), \tag{5}$$

or in the special case represented by Eqs. (2) and (4):

$$(1/\rho)[(v_0^* - d - v)(1 - e^{-\rho T}) + (v_1^* - v)e^{-\rho T}] \geq 0. \tag{6}$$

In the typical case in which $v_0^* < v$, and $d > 0$, the posttraining productivity v_1^* must exceed the untrained productivity by an amount sufficient to cover the foregone earnings $(v - v_0^*)$ and the direct training costs incurred during the training period T:

$$v_1^* \geq v + (v - v_0^* + d)(e^{\rho T} - 1). \tag{7}$$

As with any investment that yields returns over an extended period, the present value of the investment (and its economic efficiency) is sensitive to the interest rate that must be paid to finance the investment. The set of efficient training opportunities is likely to be seriously reduced in the high-interest-rate regime.

IV. TRAINING EFFICIENCY AND THE FREE MARKET

The question naturally arises, What institutional structure, if any, will generate the efficient job-training outcome? A free labor market composed of wealth-maximizing individuals will be efficient if:

1. the worker has access to capital at the social discount rate;
2. a large number of firms demand the skills developed; and
3. job changing is costless.

In such a world, the worker would receive at each instant a wage equal to his or her net productivity; assuming that the firm provides all training materials, the competitive wage at each instant t should be

$$w_t = \begin{cases} v_t & \text{if no training,} \\[2ex] v_t^* - d_t & \text{if training.} \end{cases} \tag{8}$$

This market outcome has strong efficiency implications. The wealth-maximizing worker facing this wage structure would train when training is efficient, and would not train when training is inefficient. If the direct training costs are paid directly by the worker, the wage in the training alternative would not include an implicit charge for this material; the conclusion that the individual would choose efficiently among the alternatives is unchanged.

A model of this sort has provided the basis for a highly successful model of life cycle wages in the postschooling period. The pioneering work in this area, especially that of Mincer (1962, 1974), is based on this theoretical linkage between training and wage growth in a competitive spot market for labor services: in such a market, on-the-job learning leaves predictable patterns in the wage/experience profiles of young workers. The optimal time path of life cycle learning and earnings was first formally derived within a simple structural environment by Ben-Porath, and was extended and empirically implemented by Haley (1976), Heckman (1976), Rosen (1976), and others [see Weiss (1986) for a review of this literature]. Empirical implementation of these models requires strong assumptions on a variety of environmental and technological conditions. As a consequence, the simple log earnings function approximation to this process remains a standard estimating tool. For an excellent critical review of the standard model, see Hanushek and Quigley (1985).

Becker (1975) used a simple investment model to assess the efficiency of the provision of a college education in the United States. In particular, he found that the after-tax rate of return on a college education was comparable to that on physical capital, a strong indication of efficiency in the college market. Unfortunately the same analysis cannot be used to assess the aggregate efficiency of the market for on-the-job training. To understand why, it is necessary to sketch out briefly the standard wage model. In the standard log wage function, t years following school departure, the log wage can be represented by the approximation (ignoring individual subscripts)

$$\text{Log}(w_t) = \text{Log}(w_0) + rH_t - \Delta H_t + \epsilon_t, \tag{9}$$

where w is the observed wage rate, H the stock of accumulated on-the-job learning capital, ΔH the current-period addition to that stock (current learning activity), and ϵ a random element. The initial postschooling wage $\text{Log}(w_0)$ is assumed to be a linear function of a variety of attributes:

$$\text{Log}(w_0) = X\beta, \tag{10}$$

where X is a vector of personal productivity attributes, such as schooling and intelligence. With all variables directly observable, the coefficients as well as their standard errors can be estimated efficiently using ordinary least-squares techniques under common assumptions on the error term ϵ (iid normal). The coefficient r on the stock of human capital variable H can be interpreted as a rate of return on on-the-job training.

Unfortunately, the stock of on-the-job training is not directly observable. Instead, the model is normally implemented by assuming a simple investment pattern. In particular, assume that

$$H_t \equiv \sum_{i=0}^{t-1} \Delta H_i = \sum_{i=0}^{t-1} \lambda_i k_i, \tag{11}$$

where λ_i represents the individual's work intensity in period i, and k_i is the share of total human capital in period i devoted to learning activities. The standard treatment for male earnings is to impose the assumption that $\lambda_i = 1$ for all i and that on-the-job investment shares decrease at a linear rate with job market experience:

$$k_i = \kappa_0 + \kappa_1 E_i, \quad 0 < \kappa_0 < 1, \quad \kappa_1 \leq 0, \tag{12}$$

where $E_i = i$ in this model. This investment structure induces a log wage model with experience and experience-squared terms, at least over the range of value for which k_i is feasible (positive):

$$H_i = \kappa_0 E_i + (\kappa_1/2)(E_i)^2. \tag{13}$$

In almost all empirical applications of this model in which the sample age intervals are sufficiently broad to permit precise estimation, log wage is estimated to be a positive, concave function of experience. Unfortunately, the rate of return on on-the-job training is not identified in this structure; it can only be jointly estimated with the share of training time parameters κ_j, unless individuals differ in work intensity λ (Hanushek and Quigley, 1985).

Direct measures of on-the-job learning permit a more persuasive test of the on-the-job-training hypothesis, but also fail to identify the critical rate of return on training parameter. In Parsons (1989), for example, an on-the-job learning variable is constructed from a question designed to elicit the respondent's self-perception of learning activities. The instrument had four categories of response, indexed by L_j, $j = 1,2,3,4$, with 4 denoting the highest learning condition. This instrument provides an alternative, *direct* measure of human capital investment and stock under competitive assumptions:

$$\Delta H_i = \sum_{j=1}^{4} \alpha_j L_{ji}, \tag{14}$$

and

$$H_t = \sum_{i=0}^{t-1} \sum_{j=1}^{4} \alpha_j L_{ji}. \tag{15}$$

Presumably $0 < \alpha_1 < \alpha_2 < \alpha_3 < \alpha_4$ if the self-assessment measures are valid. Since the no-job status is the base category, the empirical equivalence of the learning content of no job and of a no-learning job can be tested as the hypothesis that $\alpha_1 = 0$. Estimates of such a model are consistent with the basic on-the-job hypothesis (Parsons, 1989), but the rate of return measure is again not identified, being jointly estimated with α_i. The fact that the on-the-job-training hypothesis is broadly consistent with the observed pattern of postschooling wages does *not* imply that this training is efficiently provided, but rather that the market for on-the-job training is not fundamentally perverse.

Institutional features of the U.S. labor market raise the possibility that the market mechanism set out in Eq. (8) may not be feasible. The competitive-labor-market model suggests that equalizing or compensating differentials should exist, so that individuals in high-learning jobs (with the prospect of higher future wages) will receive lower current wages, much as individuals in formal schooling must forego current income. A variety of plausible institutional forces, however, may support wage rates above competitive levels, most obviously a legal wage minimum. A number of studies report evidence that on-the-job training is restricted by effective minimum wages (Fleisher, 1981); Leighton and Mincer, 1981; Hashimoto, 1982). Social forces may also limit the ability of workers to pay for job training through wage deductions during the training period. Lazear (1979), for example, has recently argued that affirmative-action pressures have had perverse effects on the provision of on-the-job training activities to black youth. In particular, he argues that average current wages are the most visible indicator of discrimination, so that employers have an incentive to shift black workers systematically into low-learning/high-current-wage jobs (under the standard equalizing differential argument). The logic of the argument depends on the specific observability assumption—that affirmative-action enforcers observe wages and not learning activities. This empirical assumption is not plausible for formal training programs. It seems unlikely that an employer under affirmative-action pressures would restrict entry by blacks into training programs. The insight may be valid, however, for more informal learning-by-doing activities for which no statistics or measurements are available.

Works by Barron et al. (1989), based on employer reports of training activity, and by Parsons (1989), based on self-reporting of on-the-job learning activity by workers, suggest that compensating differentials are not significant. The Barron et al. data contained only modest individual quality controls, and they attribute the absence of an observed compensating differential to unmeasured quality characteristics of trainees. The phenomenon is also observed in the Parsons study, however, which includes much richer individual controls, including the extensive aptitude and achievement information in the Armed Services Vocational Aptitude Battery.

In any case it is *theoretically* possible for the firm to work around the minimum-wage constraint by having the worker enter explicitly into a financial transaction (an explicit loan) that breaks the link between current wages and current training. Full payment of wages and a corresponding bill for the training, appropriately financed, should provide an equivalent solution to the investment problem. In the next section we shall see why this is not done.

V. THE FINANCING PROBLEM

Prominent among the sufficient conditions for the free market in on-the-job training to be efficient is the requirement that workers have access to capital at the social rate of discount. One would suspect that this condition does not hold empirically, even approximately. Workers undertaking substantial job-training investments are often young, with only insignificant capital holdings. Even among older workers, a substantial fraction of those considering substantial human-capital investments are displaced workers, many of whom have similar financial difficulties. If the training investment is a significant one, the financing problem may substantially increase the costs of undertaking the activity.

The incentive for the employer to supply its workers with some form of funds for training is evident. In this section, I first explore the nature of the borrowing problem that limits the worker's access to funds in general and then explain why the firm has a unique role as provider of the resources required to finance the training.

A. The Worker's Ability to Borrow: The Property Rights Issue

Obviously, limitations on worker credit are a serious problem if the worker is expected to finance a major investment activity. The amount of training activity will be less than the efficient level and the more-limited supply of trained workers will translate into higher costs to the firm. To consider solutions to the problem, it is necessary to understand more completely the nature of the borrowing difficulty; a property rights perspective is useful.

Consider a world of certainty with completely enforceable contracts, so that an individual who commits to a specified payment scheme is not able to avoid these payments. The financing of the training program in this environment is unlikely to be a problem; the least-cost provider would supply the funds, whether that provider is the worker, the firm, or a financial intermediary, and, ceteris paribus, the training would be supported at least cost.

Two important processes arise that make financial contracts of this type incompletely enforced: default and bankruptcy. Individuals who die with debts exceeding assets do, in a sense, take it with them; their creditors are out of luck. Less-drastic means of avoiding repayment also exist. If the debt is sufficiently small or the costs of collection sufficiently high, then the creditor may write off a specific debt. Bankruptcy introduces social values into the debt collection mechanism. If the individual's debts exceed his or her assets, he or she may from time to time declare bankruptcy, distribute the assets proportionately among the creditors, and return to a zero net asset position. A special problem with human-capital investments is that the resulting capital is not viewed as an asset in this computation; such investments do not create their own collateral, they are an invitation to bankruptcy.

To illustrate the importance of the financing aspect, consider an historical example that illustrates the basic principles of the problem in an extreme way, the practice of indentured servants. In the colonial period, land and natural resources were abundant in the United States, but labor shortages were severe. A basic problem was the high cost of transportation from areas of relative labor surplus, the Old World, to areas of labor shortage, the New. The cost of passage in the early seventeenth century was almost one-and-one-half times the annual income per person in a laboring family (Galenson, 1981, p.230). Equally important was the financing. The individuals most likely to find migration to the New World economically attractive were those in the most unfavorable economic conditions, a group unlikely to have significant capital holdings to finance the cost of passage.

An institutional response to this problem was the development of the practice of indenturing servants. Individuals could purchase passage to the colonies by promising to work for a master for a fixed period of time, typically for four years or more, depending on skill and other personal characteristics. Indentured servants were a major source of labor in the colonial period; Galenson (1981, pp. 3–4) cites two accounts that claim that one-half to three-quarters of the immigrants to the colonies in the seventeenth century were indentured servants. Over time, slave labor came to dominate this market, but for an extended period of time this alternative, the long-term commitment of labor services, was the dominant institution for handling the problem of financing migration.

More than a simple labor contract was involved: "indentured servitude . . . involve[d] a stricter obligation than most forms of labor contract because the system provided for the enforcement of the agreement by requirement of specific performance of the work described in the contract" (Galenson, 1981, p.3). Commercial law developed around indentured-servants' contracts; they could be, and were, freely bought and sold for the duration of their indenture periods. The control problem with indentured servants was a serious one. Such contracts could not permit bankruptcy; few of these individuals had significant physical assets upon arrival to set against their transportation debt. The problem was deeper; the new arrivals had to be secured to their place of employment and motivated to work for another without the usual free-market incentives. In this natural-resource–abundant society, runaways were a problem. To assist in the enforcement of this type of contract, colonists were required to carry internal passports.

A modern and somewhat less exotic example is the government's funding of training of military officers, most prominently in military academies. These institutions provide an expensive college education at no cost to those selected to participate. Indeed, the various armed services pay attendees a substantial wage during the training period. At the end of the training period, attendees are very much in debt to the government. Payment again is by specific performance: the individual is required to serve a minimum length of time with the "firm," in this case one of the military services. The individual can also be funded to attend professional school, with an additional number of years added to his or her service requirement. The commitment is not subject to personal bankruptcy.

Both examples, the historical and the modern, illustrate (1) the basic problem of financing an expensive training activity, (2) the institutional responses to the problem—contracts with specific performance requirements, and (3) the difficulties that the response themselves generate—any long-term contract involves some limitation on the individual's freedom. Private employers today do not have the specific-performance option. Nonetheless, they have a unique role in providing personal financing to workers with modest capital. The nature of the lending mechanism and its limitations are developed next.

B.   The Unique Role of the Firm

The problem of funding human-capital investments with third-party loans is a serious one. Of particular importance here, the employer has an alternative debt repayment mechanism, one that provides for repayment despite the bankruptcy constraint, namely, job mobility costs. If mobility costs are high, the employer can invest in the worker, knowing that the worker cannot strategically respond by leaving the firm. The bankruptcy problem is preempted: the individual cannot go to court and have the debt erased. Mobility costs are an essential element in a variety of long-term implicit contracts, for example, if the firm supplies productivity insurance, either across the business cycle or across the life cycle (Bailey, 1974; Gordon, 1974; Azariadis, 1975; Freeman, 1977; Harris and Holmstrom, 1982). The firm cannot pay above-average wages when conditions are adverse without paying below-average wages when times are good, an arrangement that is only possible if mobility costs are significant. The limitations on this mechanism are clear. No individual is completely immobile; if the firm becomes a sufficiently large (implicit) creditor to the worker, the worker has an incentive to leave the firm and seek work elsewhere.

One interesting model combines on-the-job investment and the mobility process within a life cycle framework (Jovanovic, 1979). Jovanovic argues that the time profile of on-the-job learning will interact with expected mobility in a systematic way in an optimal investment program. Given the high turnover rates among new hires, perhaps due to job shopping over nonpecuniary aspects of the job, employers may not offer valuable training opportunities to new entrants until they have shown that they are stable and unlikely to leave the firm for an alternative employer [see also Lester (1954), Bishop (1985), and Parsons (1989)]. As a consequence, the life cycle profile of job learning intensity may *increase* early in the individual's career, not decline as assumed in the standard on-the-job-training model, Eq. (12). The Jovanovic hypothesis assumes that on-the-job learning activities include important worker/firm match–specific elements; the returns to on-the-job learning are partly (or wholly) dependent on the worker having a continuing relationship with the firm in which the investment takes place. By definition, interfirm mobility will completely depreciate the specific human capital. Similar results hold for general capital with positive mobility costs.

VI. WORKER IMMOBILITY AND THE EMPLOYER HOLDUP PROBLEM

The employer has mechanisms for providing the worker with a loan that is not vulnerable to bankruptcy or to default in the usual sense. To the extent the worker's job mobility is limited by effective long-term employment contracts or by high transaction costs, the firm can finance the worker's training costs by paying the worker more than his or her productivity during the training period and then recovering the expenditures by paying the worker less than his or her productivity in the posttraining period. Both explicit long-term contracts and intrinsically high worker mobility costs introduce their own difficulties, however. A few of these are considered here, as are the market forces that ameliorate their effects.

Long-Term Employment Contracts

If it were possible to bind the worker to the firm, it would not be difficult in a static world to design a long-term employment contract that permits the employer to absorb some or all the training costs, if that is efficient. If the labor market in which the basic employment contract is negotiated is competitive, posttraining wages will be set at a level that just compensates the firm for its training outlays. The least-cost provider of capital in this relationship will absorb the majority, perhaps all, of the training costs as efficiency dictates.

Unfortunately, the world is dynamic, not static; conditions are constantly changing and in unpredictable ways. Complete worker immobility is almost surely inefficient in such a dynamic environment; an unexpected increase in the worker's productivity outside the firm or a sudden decline in the worker's productivity inside the firm calls for the reallocation of the worker to a more-productive work setting. Explicit mobility bonding schemes can in principle handle this problem [Mortensen, 1978; Hashimoto, 1981; see also the review in Parsons (1986)]. The party that wants to break the contract can be required to pay a penalty to the other party for the breach; properly designed in an ideal environment, such a bonding mechanism can induce efficient behavior.

The use of explicit bonding schemes in this case is limited by information problems, most obviously the identification of the party that precipitated the job change. This critical information may not be observable to an outside (enforcement) party. The worker may voluntarily leave the firm (quit), but only under (unobservable) pressure from the firm; conversely, the firm could lay off or fire the worker, but only after the worker became slack or malfeasant on the job. Hashimoto and Yu (1980) consider more efficient contracts with imperfect observability. The mobility bond is indexed to observable proxies correlated with separation culpability; the efficiency of the bond then is a function of the quality of the proxies.

Casual empiricism suggests that such elaborate mobility-bonding schemes are not often observed in practice, and that the difficulties in implementing explicit long-term contracts are serious ones. Whether this is the result of intrinsic problems in the approach or to legal problems of enforcement of long-term employment contracts is unclear. The legal enforcement of long-term contracts is at best fitful (Green, 1989). Enforcement depends in the main on interpretations by the various state court systems, which vary in their commitment to contractual agreements of this sort over time and across states. In general, courts seem reluctant to restrict the worker's freedom to seek alternative jobs.

High Mobility Costs

High interfirm mobility costs provide an alternative to enforceable long-term contracts. If it is expensive for the worker to relocate, then the firm can hope to pay the worker a wage less than productivity in the posttraining period without losing him or her to another firm. A concern naturally arises, however: What keeps the firm from extracting more than its share of training costs? Once the worker is in place, the potential for exploitation of immobile workers would seem a real one. What keeps the employer from squeezing all quasi-rents out of the worker? Of course, there exists a symmetry here: If the firm invests in the worker, the worker may attempt to extract a disproportionate share of the returns by threatening to leave the firm; such a threat becomes less credible the higher mobility costs, but it is never totally absent.

If the labor market in which the original job commitment is made is a competitive one, the firm could not expect to extract more than its share of training costs out of the worker, at least if the worker correctly anticipates the firm's posttraining wage behavior. If the worker anticipates that the employer is going to act exploitively in the posttraining period, then the worker will require a higher current wage from the firm. In a sense, the unreliable firm will be forced to accept a larger share of the investment. Conversely, if the firm anticipates that the worker is going to capture a disproportionate share of the rents, it will insist that the worker bear a greater share of the investment costs.

The efficiency problem is that the investment cost–sharing decision may be made, not on the basis of differential access to capital, but on the basis of expectations of future quasi-rent sharing. This problem has been considered at length in the employment-contracting literature. Specifically, a literature has developed considering the most extreme possibility of an employer–employee lockin, "firm-specific human capital," in which a skill *only* has value in one firm, presumably the firm in which the training occurs (Becker, 1975; Oi, 1962). More widely valued human capital with positive mobility costs can be considered a generalization of the specific human-capital model (mobility costs induce economic specificity).

Two approaches to implicit contracting and specific human-capital investment sharing have been proposed, both of which stress the anticipation of subsequent quasi-rent sharing in the determination of investment cost shares. The early literature—Becker, Oi, and also Parsons (1972)—focused explicitly on the interplay between the specific human-capital financing decision and job mobility. The worker is never completely immobile. Individual heterogeneity ensures that worker mobility is only a probability statement; some workers will stay, others leave, with only the proportion of stayers and movers in the workplace changing as compensation changes.

This literature explores a weak form of employment contract; wages are fixed (with mobility processes in mind) and firms and workers respond through layoffs and quits, respectively. In these models, the worker quits whenever outside productivity exceeds the (fixed) wage, and the firm lays off the worker whenever the wage exceeds inside productivity. Job separation is not fully efficient under this simple contract if outside and inside productivity are subject to random shocks due to product market demand fluctuations or technological shifts (Hashimoto, 1981; Parsons, 1986). The incentives of the two parties do not adjust optimally in this stochastic environment. Becker (1975) first proposed that there may be some optimal investment sharing between firm and worker that will minimize this inefficient separation. The financing of and returns to the investment will be shared between firm and worker because some investment by each reduces the incentives for unilateral withdrawal from the relationship by the other; investment sharing is a form of mobility bond. The investment sharing is not fully optimal, depending as it does on the bonding device, namely, the shapes of the quit and layoff functions as well as on more fundamental factors.

A second approach to investment cost sharing also places much emphasis on the forces that determine posttraining rent sharing (Grout, 1984). As in the turnover model, Grout argues that the worker and firm are forward looking, that they can anticipate the outcome of subsequent bilateral bargaining, and that they accept financial shares based on this perspective. He employs a bargaining model rather than a relative turnover model as the structure that underlies rent sharing in the posttraining period. Specifically, he assumes that a Nash bargaining model can be used to formalize the "solution" of the bargaining process. Bargaining models of this sort *assume* that the bargaining outcome has features consistent with some set of stylized facts. The Nash model, for example, assumes that the bargaining outcome meets an intuitively plausible fairness criterion. The efficiency problem is the same as in the turnover model—the sharing is driven by a process other than access to capital.

Reputational Enforcement of Implicit Contracts

The market itself may generate (partial) solutions to the "holdup" problem, especially through reputational forces. Employers, especially large employers, may find it profitable to behave as if they are legally bound to a contract, even when they are not. In the current case, the firm may behave *as if* it has a commitment not to exploit the worker once the worker is locked in to the firm. Despite the potential importance of these reputational forces, empirical evidence on the situations in which they are operative remains limited. The evidence indicates that reputational enforcement of implicit employment contracts is a large-firm phenomenon (e.g., Clark et al., 1986; Parsons, 1988).

VII. SECULAR TRENDS IN WORK PLACE STRUCTURE: CONSEQUENCES FOR THE SUPPLY OF TRAINING

Recent industrial trends have favored smaller, nonunion workplaces (Blau, 1987; Farber, 1987; Parsons, 1988). The decline in the large-firm sector is largely attributable to the well-noted (relative) decline in manufacturing employment and the growth of the service sector. The economies of scale that induced the rapid growth of large industrial enterprises in earlier periods are apparently more limited in the service economy that has blossomed in the last two decades. This industrial restructuring is a long-term one; between 1970 and 1986, employment in the manufacturing sector declined as a share of total employment from 26.4 to 19.1% (U.S. Bureau of the Census, 1987, p. 379). Over the same time interval, employment in the service sector expanded from 25.9 to 31.3%. Even within industrial sectors, trends appear unfavorable to the growth of large enterprises. Although consistent time series data on recent trends in firm size *within* industries is unavailable, casual evidence suggests that firm size has declined within sectors as well as in aggregate, for example, the rise of minimills in the steel industry.

Reflecting in part this structural shift, the unionized sector of the labor market has shrunk dramatically. The decline in union representation in the workforce has been precipitous, with union membership dropping from 25.6% of non-agricultural employment in 1973 to 14.1% in 1985 (Farber, 1987). This decline again is only partly explained by sectoral shifts (Farber, 1987).

Less clear are the implications of this industrial restructuring for the provision of on-the-job training. As noted in Section II, it has been argued that training is disproportionately carried on in the nonunionized, small-firm sector. Schiller

(1986) reports that learning among new entrants to the labor force occurs dispro-portionately in small firms. These firms, on net, lose experienced workers to larger firms. Mincer (1983) finds that union workers are less likely to receive training than are nonunion workers.

Does this mean that the aggregate supply of trained workers is improved by these recent sectoral shifts? I think not. I suspect that the preponderance of training activities in small, nonunionized firms is limited to the provision of relatively rudimentary job skills. Employment in a fast-food outlet, a common entry level job, no doubt teaches the young person a number of useful job skills, including the value of punctuality and cooperation. What is more difficult to undertake efficiently in the small-firm setting is the training of highly skilled craftspeople and operatives. The individual worker's problem in financing a training program is likely to increase with the size of the investment. A highly skilled machinist, under current limitations on contracting, may have serious difficulty financing his or her investment. At the same time, the low mobility costs implied by a large number of similar firms make the investment an unat-tractive one for the small employer to finance; the likelihood that the employer will be able to capture a significant share of the training returns is small. If true, the training of highly skilled workers may become a matter of increasing concern in coming years.

VIII. PUBLIC POLICY ISSUES: SUPPORT FOR PRIVATE JOB TRAINING

The policy issue is an important one: how best to foster the efficient provision of job training. I have argued above that the main problem is one of financing. The firm typically has access to credit at rates substantially below those available to most trainees. The firm cannot simply lend the worker the resources, however, because of the possibility of bankruptcy and default. If the worker is relatively immobile (has high job-changing costs), it may be possible for the firm to lend resources implicitly to the worker through its wage policy, in a sense absorbing the investment costs (and returns) itself. This avenue of finance is partly depen-dent on high job mobility costs, however, and especially in this period of sectoral shifts toward smaller firms (and perhaps lower intrinsic mobility costs), consid-eration of alternative financing mechanisms is important.

Direct provision of training programs by the government is not likely to be productive (beyond the provision of basic skills to seriously disadvantaged indi-viduals). The main argument against direct government involvement is informa-tional; the market is a complex one, with thousands of firms demanding thou-sands of skills and, in turn, supplying a corresponding number of job-training opportunities. Knowing which services to offer and which to eliminate is an immense coordinating task. Clearly this is a market in which decentralized decision making is essential.

The issue is how to encourage and support job training at arms length, that is, with limited direct governmental micromanagement. An obvious solution is the public provision of job training loans to workers, comparable to educational-loan programs. To state the solution is to state the problem; the government student loan program has faced the same sort of problems that have beset the private capital market. Particularly among the young, access to a large amount of capital is an invitation to default and bankruptcy. More importantly, it is an invitation to fraud, of which this group, especially the least educated, are themselves likely to be victims. To the extent that job training is less well defined than is formal schooling, the invitation to deception and fraud by suppliers of training is increased. Without a fundamental change in the rules of the game, the problem is likely to be severe.

One recent public policy initiative, the compromise legislation to increase the minimum wage, is likely to have reduced the efficient functioning of the private on-the-job-training market. The minimum-wage increase is likely to be most damaging to the least skilled, those whose training wage would drop them below minimum-wage levels. The policy is likely to have had little impact on highly skilled workers, such as machinists, whose training wages are likely to be well above the minimum wage (although this fact may be changing with increased competition in this sector). In that sense, eliminating the minimum wage is only a partial step toward a more complete solution of the training problem, although perhaps an important one, given the social interest in the well-being of the least skilled.

Tax policy is another potential mechanism for governmental encouragement of job training in the private sector (Smolensky and Quigley, this volume). Current tax laws permit (require) training costs to be "expensed" rather than amortized over the life of the investment as with physical capital investments. If (1) the tax structure is not progressive and (2) the interest rate is positive, this tax system favors human-capital investments, whether undertaken by the firm or by the worker. The rate-of-return measurement problem (discussed in Section IV) makes a quantitative assessment of the impact of the tax structure on training activity difficult. While the use of tax policy to foster governmental nonrevenue objectives indirectly is currently out of fashion, this condition may eventually change.

Given that the financing problem is, at its core, a property rights issue, reformation of the contract system would seem to offer an alternative approach. The issue is a delicate one, however, since the limitations on the ability to contract—(1) the right to declare bankruptcy when debts exceed assets, and (2) the right to (relatively) unrestricted job mobility—are based on important social values. It is possible, however, that modest adjustments could be made in each that would facilitate the supply of credit to trainees. It may be enough to strengthen the worker's right to contract with the firm over a specific employment period, or at least a period in which the individual could not work for a competitor, thereby encouraging worker–firm training relationships that are now partly, and imperfectly, cemented by positive mobility costs. Elimination of bankruptcy possibilities for a certain class of loans is another alternative, although the potential for creditor abuse of financial structure is a real one. In a sense, what is required is a refashioning of apprenticeship contracts.

The encouragement of employer training collectives for the development of skills specific to an industry or type of technology may also be useful. If a highly specialized skill is demanded by a relatively small number of employers, a training cooperative may be designed so that the employers (with their access to capital at lower cost) may have an incentive to finance the investment activity themselves. As argued at length above, employers will agree to finance investments in worker skills only if they are able to capture the returns on the investment through subsequent wage payments that are less than the worker's productivity (by an amount sufficient to compensate them for the training costs they incur). An agreement to share the costs of training in proportion to the employer's share of new-trainee hires would achieve the desired object *if* combined with a "no-raiding" agreement on previously hired workers. In the absence of such an agreement a charging mechanism based on the new hires of trainees would break down, with rational employers bidding up the wages of experienced workers to the value of marginal product, thereby eliminating the necessary payback period. A no-raiding agreement is unattractive for a variety of reasons: workers may want to change jobs, not because of wages, but because of changes in geographic preferences or personality conflicts with supervisors and coworkers.

An alternative charging mechanism that would permit workers to change jobs freely and at the same time protect the employer's investment in the worker would be an agreement by the employer to share training costs according to the *total* number of cooperatively trained workers currently on the employer's payroll. If aggregate training levels are stable over time, this charging scheme is efficient; employers could hire trained workers from other firms, but they would be responsible for the workers' training costs as well as for the workers' current wages. The employer's wage offer would therefore reflect the value of the worker's product less the appropriately amortized charge for the costs of training incurred by the cooperative. The worker would not be able to "capture" the gains in his or her productivity that resulted from the employers' joint investment in the worker.

The collective provision of training reduces the free-rider problem that makes the employer financing of training unprofitable. The level of interfirm cooperation required in the training cooperative, however, raises serious antitrust concerns. It may be necessary to give an explicit antitrust exemption to the activity if it is to be attractive to employers, perhaps along the lines of existing legislation designed to foster joint research and development activities among firms, the National Cooperative Research Act of 1984. Such a relaxation would not be likely to increase significantly the probability of a successful product market cartel, which is the primary focus of the antitrust laws.

The problem of an efficient training mechanism is an important one, especially in this period of intense international competition. Japanese employers, a major focus of competitive concern, are felt to have significant advantages in the provision of training opportunities, because of cultural biases against job mobility and toward greater industrial harmony (Hashimoto, 1989; Mincer and Higuchi, 1988). Whether these cultural factors are a cause or a consequence of the rapid, sustained growth of the Japanese economy is not clear. Nonetheless the concern is a significant one, given the importance of job training. Deeper consideration of the property rights system that both supports and retards the training process is warranted.

ACKNOWLEDGMENTS

This paper was funded under Purchase Order No. 99-9-4757-75-009-04 from the U.S. Department of Labor, Commission on Workforce Quality and Labor Market Efficiency. Opinions stated in this document do not necessarily represent the official position or policy of the U.S. Department of Labor, Commission on Workforce Quality and Labor Market Efficiency.

REFERENCES

Azariadis, Costas (1975), "Implicit Unemployment and Underemployment Equilibrium." *Journal of Political Economy* 83:1183–1202.

Bailey, Martin M. (1974), "Wages and Employment under Uncertain Demand." *Review of Economic Studies* xx:37–50.

Barron, John M., Dan A. Black, and Mark A. Loewenstein (1989), "Job Matching and On-the-Job Training." *Journal of Labor Economics* 7 (January):1–19.

Becker, Gary S. (1975), *Human Capital*. New York: Columbia University Press.

Ben-Porath, Yoram (1967), "The Production of Human Capital and the Life Cycle of Earnings." *Journal of Political Economy* 75 (August):352–365.

Bishop, John (1985), "Preparing Youth for Employment." Mimeo, The National Center for Research in Vocational Education, The Ohio State University, Columbus.

Blau, David M. (1987), "A Time-Series Analysis of Self-Employment in the United States." *Journal of Political Economy* 95 (June):445–467.

Cho, Woo (1983), "Promotion Prospects, Job Search, and the Quit Behavior of Employed Youth." Mimeo, The Ohio State University, Columbus.

Clark, Robert L., Steven C. Allen, and Daniel Sumner (1986). "Inflation and Pension Benefits." In Richard A. Ippolito and Walter W. Kolodrubetz (eds.), *Handbook of Pension Statistics 1985*. Chicago: Commerce Clearing House, Inc., pp. 177–250.

Farber, Henry S. (1987), "The Decline of Unionization in the United States: What Can Be Learned from Recent Experience?" NBER Working Paper No. 2267, Washington, D.C.

Fleisher, Belton, M. (1981), *Minimum Wage Regulation in Retail Trade*. Washington, DC: American Enterprise Institute.

Freeman, Smith (1977), "Wage Trends as Performance Displays Productivity Potential: A Model and Application to Academic Early Retirement." *Bell Journal of Economics* 8:419–443.

Galenson, David W. (1981), *White Servitude in Colonial America*. Cambridge: Cambridge University Press.

Gordon, Donald F. (1974), "A Neo-Classical Theory of Keynesian Unemployment," *Economic Inquiry* 12:431–459.

Green, Wayne E. (1989), "Courts Skeptical of 'Non-Compete' Pacts." *Wall Street Journal*, Wednesday, January 11:B1.

Grout, P. (1984), "Investment and Wages in the Absence of Binding Contracts: A Nash Bargaining Approach." *Econometrica* 52:449–461.

Haley, William J. (1976), "Estimation of the Earnings Profile from Human Capital Accumulation." *Econometrica* 44:1223–1238.

Hanushek, Eric A. and John M. Quigley (1985), "Life-Cycle Earning Capacity and the OTJ Investment Model." *International Economic Review* 26(June):365–385.

Harris, Milton and Bengt Holmstrom (1982), "A Theory of Wage Dynamics." *Review of Economic Studies* 49:315–333.

Hashimoto, Masanori (1981), "Specific Human Capital as a Shared Investment." *American Economic Review* 71:475–482.

——— (1982), "Minimum Wage Effects on Training on the Job." *American Economic Review* 72 (December):1070–1087.

——— (1989), "Employment and Wage Systems in Japan and Their Implications on Productivity: A Transaction-Cost Perspective." Paper presented at Brookings Institution Conference on Alternative Compensation Schemes,

Hashimoto, Masanori and Benjamin T. Yu (1980), "Specific Human Capital, Employment Contracts and Wage Rigidity." *Bell Journal of Economics* 11:536–549.

Heckman, James (1976), "A Life Cycle Model Of Earnings, Learning, and Consumption." *Journal of Political Economy* 84 (August, Supplement):S11–S44.

Jovanovic, Boyan (1979), "Firm-Specific Capital and Turnover." *Journal of Political Economy* 87 (December):1246–1260.

Lazear, Edward (1979), "The Narrowing of the Black–White Wage Differential Is Illusory." *American Economic Review* 69 (September):553–563.

Leighton, Linda and Jacob Mincer (1981), "Effects of Minimum Wages on Human Capital Formation." In Simon Rottenberg (ed.), *The Economics of Legal Minimum Wages*. Washington, DC: American Enterprise Institute, pp. 155–173.

Lester, Richard A. (1954), "Hiring Practices and Labor Competition." Industrial Relations Section Report, Princeton University, Princeton, NJ.

Mincer, Jacob (1962), "On-the-Job Training: Costs, Returns and Some Implications." *Journal of Political Economy* Suppl. 70 (October): 50–79.

——— (1974), *Schooling, Experience, and Earnings*. New York: Columbia Univ. Press, for NBER.

——— (1983), "Union Effects: Wages, Turnover, and Job Training." *Research in Labor Economics* Suppl. 2:217–252.

Mincer, Jacob and Yoshio Higuchi (1988), "Wage Structure and Labor Turnover in the United States and Japan." *Journal of the Japanese and International Economies* 2:97–133.

Mortensen, Dale (1978), "Specific Human Capital and Turnover." *Bell Journal of Economics* 9:572–586.

Oi, Walter Y. (1962), "Labor as a Quasi-Fixed Factor." *Journal of Political Economy* 70:538–555.

Parsons, Donald O. (1972), "Specific Human Capitol: Layoffs and Quits." *Journal of Political Economy* 80:1120–1143.

——— (1985), "Wage Determination in the Post-Schooling Period: The Market for On-the-Job Training." In R. D'Amico et al. (eds.), *Pathways to the Future*, Volume VI. Columbus: Center for Human Resource Research, Ohio State University, Chapter 7.

——— (1986), "The Employment Relationship: Job Attachment, Work Effect, and the Nature of

Contracts." In Orley Ashenfelter and Richard Layard (eds.), *Handbook of Labor Economics.* Amsterdam: North-Holland, pp. 789–848.

———— (1988), "The Provision of Private Pensions: An Equilibrium Approach." Mimeo, Ohio State University, Columbus.

———— (1989), "On-the-Job Learning and Wage Growth." Mimeo, Ohio State University, Columbus.

Reagan, Patricia (1988), "On-the-Job Training, Layoff by Inverse Seniority, and the Incidence of Unemployment." Mimeo, Ohio State University, Columbus.

Rosen, Sherwin (1972), "Learning and Experience in the Labor Market." *Journal of Human Resources* 7 (Summer):326–342.

———— (1976), "A Theory of Life Earnings." *Journal of Political Economy* 84 (August, Suppl.):S45–S68.

Schiller, Bradley R. (1986), "Early Jobs and Training: The Role of Small Business." Final Report on Contract SBA-9281-AER, Capital Research, Inc., Washington, DC.

Weiss, Yoram (1985), "The Effect of Labor Unions on Investment in Training." *Journal of Political Economy* 93 (October):994–1007.

———— (1986), "The Determination of Life Cycle Earnings: A Survey." In Orley Ashenfelter and Richard Layard (eds.), *Handbook of Labor Economics.* Amsterdam: North-Holland, pp. 603–640.

U.S. Bureau of the Census (1987), *Statistical Abstract of the United States: 1988,* 108th edition. Washington, DC: U.S. Government Printing Office.

IMPROVING EFFICIENCY IN THE TAX TREATMENT OF TRAINING AND EDUCATIONAL EXPENDITURES

John M. Quigley and Eugene Smolensky

I. INTRODUCTION

This paper evaluates the tax treatment of investments in the education and training (E&T) of workers under both the personal and corporate tax codes. It focuses on the ways in which the current tax laws affect the attractiveness of investments in human capital relative to other investments. Section II summarizes past research on the effects of taxation on human-capital investment in contrast to physical-capital investment. The current treatment of E&T costs under the personal income tax is detailed in Section III. Distortions created under the Tax Reform Act of 1986 and subsequent legislation are examined. Two effects of personal income taxation are of particular concern: nonneutrality in the choice between investment in human and in physical capital; and nonneutrality in the choice among different categories of E&T investment. The current personal tax law distinguishes between educational investments related to a taxpayer's current "trade or business" and those investments that qualify the taxpayer for an alter-

Research in Labor Economics, Volume 11, pages 77–95.
Copyright © 1990 by JAI Press Inc.
All rights of reproduction in any form reserved.
ISBN: 1-555938-080-2

native occupation. The distinction in tax treatment discourages training that would facilitate economically efficient occupational changes.

Section IV describes the current treatment of worker E&T expenditures under the corporate tax laws. It compares the tax treatment of spending on human capital, physical capital, and research and development (R&D). Section V outlines proposals to improve the allocation of resources through changes in the personal and corporate tax codes. Conclusions are summarized in Section VI.

II. TAX OBJECTIVES

A. Criteria

Tax laws are traditionally evaluated according to the criteria of equity and efficiency. The equity objective is judged by how well the tax base conforms to the concept of Haig–Simons income. The efficiency objective of taxation is met when revenues are generated without distorting the choices that would have been made in the absence of taxation, that is, by tax neutrality.[1] While equity and efficiency are reasonable goals, implementing them consistently in the tax code is difficult for many reasons, including ambiguities in the definition of taxable income. The problem is familiar: The Haig–Simons concept of net income attempts to measure net *well-being*. Whereas *income* needs to be measured in tangible monetary quantities if it is to be equitably taxed, well-being is often derived from intangibles not explicitly priced in the market. Examples include the value of leisure time, time used in productive nonmarket activities, and good health. For convenience, we shall refer to all nonmarket uses of time as "leisure."

Because the value of leisure is not assessed as income, people who choose different consumption or production mixes yielding equivalent levels of personal satisfaction can be liable for different amounts of federal income tax. If the goal is to minimize the distortion of individual choices, then the tax base should include items like the monetary value of leisure. Clearly, however, the inclusion of these income components can violate other conceptions of fairness (Warren, 1980; Stephan, 1984).

By the same argument, intangible costs undertaken to create income should be as fully deductible from taxable income as are out-of-pocket costs. Time invested in education and training is thus as much a cost as the training materials purchased (i.e., books, tuition), and both should be deductible expenses against additional well-being generated. The full cost of acquiring education or training thus includes both direct outlays and foregone opportunities. For most students beyond the high school level, at least some portion of expenses for tuition, books, and other related fees are incurred directly. Occupational training can involve direct spending by the trainee, for example, through formal training schools, or by the firm, for example, through on-the-job training given by senior employees. When employers pay wages to trainers and trainees for time spent in training rather than production, they are incurring direct costs for workforce training. Employers also incur direct costs in purchasing and developing training materials.

Students also forego currently attainable earnings to invest in themselves, and workers receiving on-the-job training in generally productive activities forego the higher wages attainable in jobs that do not involve training. Current production sacrificed by firms in favor of training in firm-specific skills is also costly. Together, foregone personal earnings (or foregone leisure) and foregone production, together with direct expenses for E&T, comprise the full investment cost of the activity.

These concepts—Haig–Simons income, neutrality, foregone earnings, and leisure—play important roles in principle in the evaluation of tax systems, but they can be incorporated into the tax system only imperfectly. Nevertheless, paying due attention to them has consequences of great practical importance for the appropriate tax treatment of E&T expenditures, as we shall now indicate.

B.   The Literature

Many theoretical models have been developed indicating how tax incentives affect the choice between investment in physical and human capital (Boskin, 1975; Stephan, 1975; Heckman, 1976; Eaton and Rosen, 1980; Sgontz, 1982).[2] Boskin (1975) has shown that when foregone earnings are the only cost of investment in education, a proportional personal income tax does not distort investment in human capital. Boskin's result applies more generally to those circumstances in which the full cost of E&T is immediately deductible and in which proportional taxes are imposed on earned income only. No tax is paid in the initial period (because the trainee sacrifices all income in order to invest), but the resulting income is fully taxed. Since taxes are proportional to earned income, the taxpayer is indifferent between the alternatives: expensing capital acquisition costs immediately but paying a tax on all income in the future; or else paying tax in the future on earned income less a proportionate share of capital acquisition costs.

Heckman (1976) analyzed a more realistic circumstance, a proportional tax on both earned and unearned income (wages and interest). Taxation now favors investment in human capital since the costs of education are immediately and fully deductible. By taxing interest earnings, the after-tax interest rate is lowered relative to the return on human capital. While the amount invested or saved is taxed as soon as it is first obtained, the tax on human capital is applied to future earnings. Because future taxes are valued less than the same current tax payment, the taxpayer prefers to invest in human capital.[3] This model resembles the current corporate tax treatment of human and physical-capital investment since most training costs are immediately deductible but physical-investment costs must be amortized.

Eaton and Rosen (1980) added uncertainty to the analysis. Taxation of earnings buffers expected wage gains and losses, but also reduces expected income. These two aspects of taxation have opposing effects on the incentive to invest in human capital. The first reduces risk and thus encourages more human capital investment, while the second curtails investment in human capital as long as risky investing is less desirable at lower income levels. Thus the net effect of taxation on human-capital investment is ambiguous—even under a proportional earnings tax and even when foregone earnings are the only cost of human-capital investment.

Sgontz (1982) analyzed a fairly general model in which the tax base includes both wages and interest earnings and in which educational costs include both foregone earnings and direct expenditures. In this analysis only foregone earnings are excluded from taxable income; the model thus resembles current personal income tax treatment when educational fringe benefits and direct costs of educational investment are not excludable from income. Under these circumstances, with proportional taxation, the effect of taxation on human-capital investment varies with the ratio of direct educational costs to foregone earnings. The proportional tax rate and the rate of return on physical-capital investment determine a critical ratio between direct educational costs and foregone earnings. If the critical ratio is exceeded, increases in tax rates reduce investment in human capital. As long as actual direct expenditures for education or training are less than the critical ratio, increasing taxes favors investment in human capital. Since different students face different direct-cost shares, they may react differently to increases in tax rates. As noted below, the variations in the incentive structure in this model may correspond to real-world differences in educational investment according to whether or not it is job related.

Progressive taxation greatly complicates these models. With reduced tax progressivity under the Tax Reform Act of 1986, however, the less-complicated results arising from models with proportional tax rates are quite credible. The results based on foregone earnings alone are also reasonable if foregone earnings dominate total education costs or if all educational costs are immediately deductible from earnings for tax purposes. The Sgontz model illustrates the extent of dominance required when direct costs are not fully deductible. Based on simple calculations from this model, even a small ratio of direct E&T costs to foregone earnings is sufficient to make human-capital investment less attractive than physical capital investment at higher tax rates.

In summary, when a proportional tax is levied on earned income and interest income and when foregone earnings are the only cost of investment in human capital, then human-capital investment is favored relative to physical-capital investment (Heckman, 1976; Sgontz, 1982). For those students incurring direct educational expenditures that are high enough, the current income tax will discourage investment in human capital (since tax rates are essentially proportional over the relevant range). In all probability, however, any distortion between investment in human and physical capital is quantitatively small, suggesting that distortions among different types of E&T under the personal tax code may be more important. Under the corporate tax code, investment in human capital and R&D might be favored over investment in physical capital within the firm. However, because firms have little incentive to train their workers for new jobs outside the firm, the distinction between current and other jobs is also relevant in the corporate tax analysis.[4]

III. EDUCATION AND TRAINING UNDER THE PERSONAL INCOME TAX

A. Current Tax Treatment

Foregone Earnings

Earnings foregone in order to undertake investments in E&T are fully excluded from taxable income. No one suggests they be treated otherwise, but the consequences are significant—foregone earnings typically comprise a large share of total educational costs. For those participating in employee training programs provided by firms, foregone earnings might well comprise all of the individual's cost of training. For individuals, this exclusion is tantamount to the expensing for tax purposes of the major cost of acquiring human capital. Since immediate expensing of most long-lived physical capital is not permitted, human-capital investment is favored by the exclusion of foregone earnings. This advantage is inherent in tax systems, and any suggestions for policy change must begin from the advantaged position conferred on E&T.

Out-of-Pocket Costs

Direct expenses on E&T are treated differently under the personal tax code, depending on the nature of the education undertaken and the method of financing utilized. Only those personal expenditures directly related to an employee's *current* occupation reduce taxable personal income. Two constraints limit deductibility. First, courses taken cannot be educational prerequisites for the employee's current occupation. Second, the job-related courses cannot enable the worker to choose a new occupation upon their completion.

Employee-Financed Training

Current, job-related, employee out-of-pocket expenditures on education can be reported as itemized deductions from personal income (Federal Income Tax

Schedule A). Unreimbursed educational expenses related to the employee's current occupation are deductible, but are subject to a floor. The tax code treats educational expenses related to employment as a component of "job expenses and most other miscellaneous deductions"; only the excess over 2% of adjusted gross income qualifies as an itemized deduction on Federal Income Tax Schedule A (Internal Revenue Service, 1988a).

These complications cloud the impact of tax deductibility on the decision to undertake education. For those who itemize and who have current job-related expenses equaling at least 2% of adjusted gross income, educational expenditures related to the employee's current job are immediately and fully deductible from income even though the returns from the investment in education are likely to be earned over several tax years.

For those able to take advantage of this deduction, both direct costs and foregone earnings associated with current job-related investment in E&T reduce taxable income immediately by the full cost of the investment. An equal amount invested in physical capital would have to be amortized. Those unable to take full advantage of this deduction do not face the same clear incentive. For them, one component of education cost is fully deductible (foregone earnings) but the other does not reduce taxable income (education expenditures). Depending on the relative shares of these components, the educational investment may or may not be favored by the tax code (Sgontz, 1982). If lower-income taxpayers are less likely to have the supplemental deductions, they are also less likely to benefit from the advantages of job-related out-of-pocket human-capital investment. Sgontz's results suggest that nondeductibility of large direct education costs more than eliminates the inherent advantage conferred on human-capital investments by the exclusion of foregone income from the income tax base.

Employer-Financed Training

Tuition financed by employers was treated differently from those educational expenses fully paid by an employee until quite recently. Until December 1988, educational costs paid by an employer were subject to a maximum tax-free annual income exclusion of $5250, with some restrictions, if distributed through an employer's "educational assistance program" (Internal Revenue Code, Section 127, Internal Revenue Service (1988a). For 1988, the law restricted this exclusion to undergraduate level education.) Employer payment for educational expenditures beyond the tax-free limit was reportable as taxable income by the employee.[5] Congress extended the life of this provision for one year retroactive to January 1, 1989. Treatment changed beginning with tax year 1990.

Under Section 127 as recently extended, education is treated as a fringe benefit. The exclusion for education in this guise removes the distinction between the individual's current job and other jobs as long as the firm is willing to finance both types of education. Human-capital investment is tax favored once again, since comparable physical-investment costs would be amortized. The tax incentive is provided to an employee at the employer's discretion. If a firm chooses to offer full educational assistance under Section 127, its employees gain the tax advantage. A firm may choose, however, to provide educational assistance only for current-job–related courses. For those working in firms not offering this assistance at all, the tax incentive is once again dependent upon the ratio of direct costs to foregone earnings.

Without a further legislative extension of Section 127, when an employer provides full financing for educational expenses that would be deductible if the employee financed the expenses alone, then these amounts need not be included in taxable income at all. If employers finance broader training expenditures, the total education benefit could be considered to be taxable income. The employee, however, could deduct any eligible job-related proportion from taxable income (Ernst & Whinney, 1988; Internal Revenue Service, 1988a,b; White, 1989).

Special Circumstances

Several additional features of the personal income tax code address specific types of educational costs. Scholarships and fellowships receive preferential treatment under the tax code. Some universities grant tuition waivers to employees and their dependents. This, too, is treated preferentially by the tax code. In contrast, interest payments paid on educational debt are *not* deductible from current or subsequent income and hence do not receive preferential treatment.

The Tax Reform Act of 1986 taxes some previously tax-free components of scholarship and fellowship income. Amounts covering tuition and other direct costs of education are still excludable from taxable income. Under the current law, scholarships are taxable, as are all scholarship and fellowship amounts requiring the recipient to work. For example, compensation paid to research or teaching assistants is taxable under current law (Internal Revenue Service, 1988d; Madoff, 1987). For students receiving allowable scholarship and fellowship income, the tax treatment is certainly not neutral.

Some universities offer their employees tuition waivers or reductions for courses taken by their employees or their employees' dependents. As long as this benefit is available to a broadly defined group of employees rather than a relatively exclusive group (tenured faculty, for example), this tuition waiver or reduction, when used for undergraduate courses, escapes federal income taxation (Internal Revenue Service, 1988d; Madoff, 1987).

The Tax Reform Act of 1986 reduced the incentive to finance personal consumption through debt by ending all consumer interest deductions except for those associated with mortgage finance. However, when educational spending is financed by home equity, the interest payments can be included as an itemized deduction. Gross (1988) has written at length on the deductibility of interest payments for educational investment since the Tax Reform Act of 1986. He argues that this nondeductibility favors homeowners unjustly.

There may be two justifications for making interest payments for training deductible. First, if education spending is more of an investment than is the purchase of consumer durables, then treating educational interest payments differently from consumer debt is appropriate. Second, since the corporate tax code allows interest payments associated with physical-capital investment to be deducted from corporate income, the same treatment should be given to interest payments associated with human-capital investment. If not, interest payments on human capital are a nondeductible cost of earning income adding to other nondeductible costs, thereby reducing the advantage of human- relative to physical-capital investments.

Union Wage Concessions

When unions negotiate wage concessions in return for retraining benefits, the tax treatment of those benefits is unclear. In the absence of explicit new legislation, most such retraining arrangements could be treated as compensation to employees.[6] However, if the external retraining benefits can be packaged so as to fall within a qualified educational assistance program as defined by Section 127, and if the retraining benefits cost less than $5250 per employee per year, the benefit might be excluded from employee income just like any other employer-financed educational fringe benefit that is broadly available to employees.[7] Without an extension of Section 127 of the tax code, all retraining benefits paid to finance training outside the firm will be taxable income to the recipient.

Large and taxable retraining benefits (when combined with small foregone earnings costs) may actually discourage retraining by the individual. From the firm side, as we shall describe in more detail in Section IV, the full deductibility of employee compensation favors retraining over physical-capital investment as long as the retrained workers remain with the firm. (Or, to put it another way, full deductibility of employee training offsets, at least to some degree, the chance that a trained worker will leave the firm that paid for the training.)

B.   Tax Incentives

Education and Training Compared to Physical Capital

Currently the advantages of human- relative to physical-capital investment differ for an individual by type of E&T undertaken. As long as Section 127 remains, the relative advantage also depends on the source of finance—the taxpayer or the employer.

When the full costs of E&T are excluded or deducted from income (Section

127–type education benefits, current-job–related education for some taxpayers, scholarships, fellowships, and tuition waivers), human-capital investment is favored. When E&T costs are nonexcludable or nondeductible (non–current-job–related education financed by student loans, work–study, savings, research assistantships, teaching assistantships, and all other arrangements where students work to pay their way through school), the tax incentive is less clear-cut. If the non–deductible-cost portion is large enough, amortization will favor physical-over human-capital investment.

Current Job Compared to Another Job

As a general rule, only those expenses related to skills or learning used in a taxpayer's current occupation qualify as deductions from income by the earner. An incentive is given to further current skills, but retraining or education that might lead to an occupational change is discouraged. This tax treatment is inconsistent with a human-capital representation of educational expenses.

That the tax code biases human-capital investments against interoccupational mobility is infrequently criticized or defended. Three reasons can be advanced for tolerating this bias. First, it is difficult to distinguish learning not required for a current job from consumption. Second, the rationale for exclusion would have to differ from that of an expense necessary for acquiring contemporaneous income—the current rationale for the deduction. Third, treating human capital symmetrically with physical capital raises other conceptual and administrative difficulties (see McNulty, 1973; Stephan, 1984; Gross, 1988).

Education and Training Compared to Research and Development

Like physical- and human-capital investment, investment in R&D is undertaken to achieve higher future earnings. R&D is more relevant to the corporate tax code since few self-employed are likely to incur substantial R&D costs. Consequently, the issue is afforded more detailed treatment in Section IV. Nevertheless, for consistency, the personal choice between human-capital investment and investment in R&D by the self-employed is noted briefly.

The federal tax code allows some R&D costs to be expensed immediately. Investors have the option of an immediate deduction or amortization over time. As is the case with physical capital, amortized treatment of R&D costs may or may not favor investment in human capital, depending on the ratio of nondeductible to deductible or excludable costs. Immediately deductible R&D is favored. (Incentives are further complicated by a federal R&D tax credit. These complications are discussed below in the context of corporate taxation.)

The current- vs. non–current-job bias carries over into this analysis. Unless an employer is specifically allowed to finance employee education subject to Internal Revenue Code specifications and limitations, initial training and retraining expenditures are not deductible from personal taxable income. If an individual wants to self-invest in education to generate a higher stream of future income, tuition and other out-of-pocket costs are not deductible unless clearly linked to the taxpayer's current occupation. No such limitations are applied to R&D expenditures. R&D that allows someone self-employed to develop a brand new product is as deductible as research allowing improvement to current lines of business. Neutrality suggests that out-of-pocket expenditures for E&T be deductible from gross income by an investor in education even if the training can lead to a new occupation.

IV. EDUCATION AND TRAINING UNDER THE CORPORATE INCOME TAX CODE

A.   Current Tax Treatment

Foregone Production

When firms invest in capital equipment there need be no sacrifice in current production. Prior capital remains in place; the workforce operates on the existing capital as usual. Investment in E&T may take place differently. A firm choosing to retrain its workforce might sacrifice current production by devoting current labor resources to training rather than production. These indirect firm costs are fully excludable from taxable income for the firm. In this respect, it is as if these indirect costs of investment in human capital were deductible from taxable corporate income.

Direct Training Costs

Training expenditures made by firms are generally tax deductible.[8] Deductible training costs generally fall into one of two expenditure categories for corporations: compensation or direct business expenses. Firms make direct expenditures for training in a variety of ways. On the one hand, firms may purchase materials and develop in-house programs. Expenses for short-lived training materials are deducted from firm revenues as business operating expenses. Compensation paid to any of these training personnel is immediately deductible from firm revenues as is any other reasonable employee compensation.[9] Thus, for most in-house training, much of the direct cost of human-capital investment is currently deductible by the firm.[10]

Another way to finance employee training is through tuition or training program reimbursement (for example, Section 127 education plans). In most cases, educational-benefits payments and reimbursements are considered to be employee fringe benefits. Fringe benefits are a component of employee compensation and can be deducted from corporate revenue as costs of doing business for corporate tax purposes (Internal Revenue Service, 1988c).

B. Tax Incentives

Education and Training Compared to Physical Capital

The immediate deductibility of most E&T costs combined with full excludability of foregone production biases corporate investment in favor of human-capital investment, or at least investment of special importance to the specific firm relative to other firms. The tax code requires amortization of physical-capital investment. By spreading the total cost of physical-capital investment over several tax periods, the tax code matches a share of the total cost of physical-capital investment against resultant income. Most investment expenditures for human capital are immediately expensed rather than amortized.

Education and Training Compared to R&D

Nondistortionary tax treatments of R&D, education, and training expenditures would follow the physical-capital treatment of investment costs. However, R&D, education, and on-going training are not treated in quite the same way as physical-capital investment.

Neutrality requires that, like physical-capital costs, R&D costs be allocated across those production periods where resultant income is generated. Instead, R&D expenditures are subsidized by allowing immediate expensing. For certain types of development expenses, the taxpayer can elect to deduct the spending immediately or to amortize (Internal Revenue Service, 1988c). Immediately expensed R&D costs are favored relative to physical- and to those human-capital investments not immediately and fully deductible. Amortized R&D costs might be favored relative to physical-capital investment depending on the relationship between income-generating years and amortization years. Except for capital equipment purchased for training purposes and start-up training, costs of training are immediately deductible under the corporate tax code. These expensed costs are treated much like deductible R&D costs.

The tax code also allows a tax credit for increasing R&D expenditures. If more R&D is undertaken in the current tax year relative to an average of previous years, one-fifth of the increase can be deducted directly from the taxpayer's tax liability.[11] No such explicit tax credit exists for education or physical-capital investment. Implicitly, training may also benefit from the Targeted Jobs Tax Credit if eligible workers are hired and trained as a result.

V. TAX CODE CHANGES TO RESTORE NEUTRALITY

Generally speaking, the tax code should not favor certain types of investment (unless a conscious decision is made to subsidize one type of investment relative to another). Neutrality with respect to human-capital investment would require several changes in the tax codes.

A.   Personal Income Tax Code

A variety of reforms could reduce disparities in the current personal tax treatment of investment in human capital. Each of three proposals—extension of the employer fringe benefit exclusion, complete deductibility of all investment costs for E&T, and amortization of these investments—is outlined and discussed in turn. However, before discussing the proposals, we return to an important problem in the measurement of investment in education. The problem involves separating education for investment from education for consumption.

In general, learning includes components of both consumption and investment. Courses taken purely for enjoyment but that never generate a stream of taxable income should not, in principle, be treated as an investment. Hence investment and consumption components of educational expenditures should be distinguished.[12] A potential approach is found in Section 127, where certain educational expenditures financed by employers and widely available within the firm are excluded from taxable income even though they might be for consumption purposes. This treatment is appropriate if employers are less likely to finance education for consumption purposes than are the individuals themselves (Stephan, 1984). As explained below, we propose the expensing or amortization of all educational expenses, in part, because the consumption component is not a great concern. Consumption is already favored by the tax code. The tax code allows subsidized meals provided by employers to escape taxation. Recreational facilities provided by employers are enjoyed by employees yet the value of this enjoyment is not included in taxable income. If consumption of education is a relatively small percentage of investment in education, then the consumption component can be treated rather innocuously like existing forms of subsidized consumption.

Extending the Educational Fringe Benefit Exclusion

Continuing the income exclusion for employer-paid education for employees would reduce the disparity in treatment between investment in skills useful in the current job and in another job. Current proposals exclude from income all education benefits paid by the employer up to some dollar limit, as long as the benefit program is available rather freely to different income levels of employees. The extension does not distinguish between job-related and non–job-related benefits; if firms permit non–job-related educational pursuits, so do the tax authorities.

Deductibility of All Education Costs

Another remedy would be to allow immediate deductibility of all educational investment.[13] The bias against investment in skills required for new jobs would thereby be removed. However, human-capital investment would then be favored over physical-capital investment in both personal and corporate taxation. Furthermore, education for pleasure could be deducted together with education for investment. An immediate tax savings, largely for middle- and upper-income families, would also result, since these families are more likely to incur higher out-of-pocket costs for education. This inequity could be reduced by phasing out the deduction at higher income levels and by limiting the deduction to the earned income of the trainee.[14] Another possibility would be to allow deductions for only selected types of E&T. For example, E&T undertaken by those served with plant-closing notifications could be declared tax deductible.

If human-capital investment and R&D are to be treated comparably by the tax code, immediate expensing of R&D investment favors it over investment in physical capital. If such an outcome is desired, then an option to expense education costs, parallel to the treatment of R&D costs, should be adopted in the personal tax code as well. If the objective of tax policy is to subsidize certain R&D costs relative to other investments even beyond the subsidy afforded by the research tax credit, then neutrality can be established between human- and physical-capital investment while maintaining the potential R&D tax advantage. This could be accomplished in the personal tax code by allowing out-of-pocket educational expenses to be amortized, as are long-lived physical capital investments, on schedule C. Corporate tax treatment would also require amortization of training costs.

Amortization

Amortization would make the treatment of educational-capital spending more comparable to that of physical capital. In theory, this would involve taxing (imputed) foregone earnings as income, but then amortizing the capital acquired over the working life of the trainee. Foregone earnings would have to be estimated. McNulty (1973) suggested that foregone earnings, based on the earnings of individuals of comparable age and education, could be included in the gross income of the student or trainee. However, individuals would then be inequitably treated to the extent that true foregone earnings differ from the cohort average (McNulty, 1973). It also raises the same issues of personal choice mentioned earlier (Warren, 1980; Stephan, 1984). Comparable treatment of human- and physical-capital investment are more easily achieved when the tax rates are proportional rather than progressive.

The current system, permitting no deduction of direct expenditures, is one extreme position. The other extreme would be to treat all human capital investments identically and in a manner similar to physical capital investments.[15] Since foregone earnings are already excluded, that cost component would not be amortized under this proposal. The amortization period could be determined by the tax authorities according to the same principles that govern amortization of physical capital. Human-capital investors unable to work for the full length of the amortization period could be allowed to take a large deduction in the final work period (Goode, 1976).[16]

Revisions to the current tax forms would be minor. Taxpayers could report their total income to the Internal Revenue Service on form 1040 as usual. If the taxpayer had undertaken formal training contributing to the income, these expenses could be amortized according to a common schedule. The amortized deduction could be taken on schedule A. It will be administratively difficult to devise a neutral amortization treatment for educational investment. While investment in physical capital involves only direct spending, investment in human capital also includes forgone earnings. Neutrality between investment in physical and human capital would require a more accelerated deduction schedule for the direct costs of physical-capital investments. The problem is not insurmountable, but further attention must be given to this issue before amortization can be made operational.

The treatment of self-employment income on Schedule C provides a model to remedy the distortion between investments in human capital that generate new skills and those which improve current skills. Schedule C allows self-employment gains (and losses) to be added to (or subtracted from) other income. If the self-employment activity were actively pursued during the current tax year, losses could be used fully to offset other income. If the self-employment did not meet particular participation rules for the tax year, deductions for losses could be limited or disallowed. A similar treatment could be applied to investments in human capital that involve the acquisition of new skills. The deductibility rules could be based on taxpayer earned income, which can be linked to earlier investment in human capital. If a link can be established, some portion of the human capital direct expenditures could be deducted against the resultant earnings. The amortization schedules for investments in human capital can be approximated in a manner comparable to the treatment of physical capital used to generate self-employment income, while taking into account the immediate deductibility of foregone earnings inherent in the investment in human capital.

A difficulty involves establishing criteria for deductibility to ensure that human-capital investments be amortized but that educational consumption be excluded from the deductible portion of total education expenses. The taxpayer would have to demonstrate that the educational expenses were incurred. For graduate or professional training, this criterion could be applied in a rather straightforward manner, at least as long as the student pursued a standard course of study. Complications arise in considering broader education costs such as the cost of undergraduate courses unrelated to the student's eventual major or job requirements. Provided that undergraduates take most courses broadly contributing to general human capital, the occasional course taken exclusively for pleasure might not be a cause for concern.[17]

B.   Corporate Tax Code

The corporate tax code treats costs incurred for investment in human capital differently from those costs incurred for investment in both physical capital and R&D. Complete tax neutrality would require that all three be treated in the same manner. According to the Haig–Simons definition, the costs of all three investments would be amortized against their corresponding streams of income. Human-capital costs and R&D costs would be amortized according to comparable predetermined schedules. The current treatment of physical capital could serve as a benchmark. While we prefer amortization of those costs which result in future streams of income, restructuring the corporate tax code to amortize the cost of human-capital investment and R&D may prove administratively difficult. Short of this, we propose that human-capital investment costs be treated comparably with R&D costs.

Nearly all costs of human-capital investment are immediately deductible by the firm, for example, wages of trainees and trainers, educational fringe benefits, and short-lived training materials. Firms can choose, however, how to expense R&D costs. At the firm's discretion, these costs can be expensed immediately or amortized against future income. The amortization choice will be preferred, for example, if the firm faces a loss. Currently, the firm must expense E&T investment costs but can defer deducting R&D costs in anticipation of profits in subsequent years. We propose that investment in human capital be treated the same way as R&D is treated. Firms should have the option of carrying the costs of investment in human capital forward to offset gains in subsequent periods.[18] The R&D tax credit complicates a neutral treatment of the costs of investment in human capital compared to R&D. Due to the complicated incentives introduced by the tax credit, further analysis of the tax credit incentives may be warranted. The more general treatment of the costs of investing in human capital and R&D can be made more comparable without explicit consideration of the tax credit.

VI.   CONCLUSIONS

Any analysis of tax incentives for E&T should proceed in two steps. First, the analysis should describe those changes necessary to achieve neutrality between E&T and other forms of investment. If some deviations from this neutral ideal are socially desirable, they should be recognized as such. We have concentrated on the first step—identifying the neutral tax treatment of human capital.

For consistent treatment between human- and physical-capital investment throughout the tax code, all investment spending should be amortized against earnings when those earnings occur. Amortization should apply to both employee expenditures on the personal income tax and employer expenditures on the corporate income tax. Such a tax system design would be highly complex. Therefore, we do not propose it, though it is conceptually preferable to any other.

Instead, for employee expenditures, we propose that all investment in E&T be immediately and fully deductible against current wages and salaries of the trainee. We propose that these expenditures be immediately deductible on Schedule A of the personal income tax rather than subjected to a 2% expenditure floor. To avoid adverse distributive impacts, the deduction should be phased out as reported income rises. For the same reason, we propose that the deduction be allowable against earned income only.

For employer expenditures on E&T, we recommend combining training and R&D into one category of expenditure to be treated identically under the corporate tax code. Since immediate expensing of R&D and human-capital investment would be allowable under this proposal, neutrality between investments in human and physical capital would not be achieved.

ACKNOWLEDGMENTS

This research was originally financed by the U.S. Department of Labor, commission on Workforce Quality and Labor Market Efficiency, which is not responsible for the opinions expressed. We acknowledge the assistance of Denis Jarvinen and the comments of Laurie J. Bassi and David L. Crawford.

NOTES

1. Purposeful nonneutrality is sometimes a warranted feature of the tax code. Some socially desirable activities may be underproduced in the absence of taxation and can therefore be encouraged through the tax code.

2. Also see results summarized in Rosen (1980) and Sgontz (1982).

3. Sgontz (1982) and Stephan (1984) offer good intuitive explanations of this result.

4. Little existing research recognizes capital market imperfections. Even without tax distortion, one type of investment might be favored over another because of the institutional structure of current capital markets. For example, 18-year-olds might have reasonable access to educational loans but might find it difficult to find funding for a self-initiated research or capital project. Even if all three possibilities generated equal expected returns, we might expect a bias in favor of educational investment because our society has selected to remedy only the education-related capital market constraint. The distorting consequences of capital market imperfections have not been explicitly considered in this paper either. These models also assume perfectly mobile labor markets. Finally, McNulty (1973) discusses various other reasons why human-capital investment might be advantaged under the tax code. Examples include the tax-exempt status of interest earned on state and municipal bonds, and the difference between the cost of providing education and the tuition paid by the student.

5. If the education benefits exceeding the limit were current-job related, the employee could deduct the surplus benefits from income using Schedule A.

6. See the 1982 decision regarding the FAA's "Second Career Training Program."

7. In each case, the retraining expenditures would be deductible from corporate revenue as employee compensation for tax purposes.

8. In defining training expenditures, we are excluding capital equipment purchased for training

purposes. Capital equipment used for training is amortized. A special case exists in which other training costs can be amortized. If the training can be considered as a component of firm start-up costs, the training can be amortized (Internal Revenue Service, 1988c).

9. On-the-job training could be integrated into the production process. If so, training components of wages would be inseparable from production components (Stephan, 1984; Doeringer and Piore, 1971). See Doeringer and Piore (1971) for descriptions of on-the-job and other forms of training.

10. Besides the immediate deductibility of employee wages and salaries paid for employee training time, the Targeted Jobs Tax Credit might be interpreted as a tax subsidy for human-capital investment in specific circumstances. The tax credit currently allows employers to credit 40% of the first $6000 in first-year wages paid to members of designated groups against the employer's total tax liability (Internal Revenue Service, 1988c). The requirement that the credit only apply to first-year wages is meant as an incentive to hiring. Employers who would hire workers from these designated groups as regular trainees would also receive a substantial federal subsidy on training wages paid under the tax credit. Rather than the ordinary tax advantage of training costs (in this case, wages) being fully and immediately deductible, the tax credit allows even more of an incentive to training. A percentage of training wages, rather than being deductible, is credited directly against the employer's federal corporate tax liability. This training subsidy only occurs when the subsidized wages represent training wages. In cases where an employer may hire "disadvantaged" workers for jobs requiring no simultaneous training, the tax credit subsidizes production wages and not training wages. In most cases, the tax credit will subsidize some combination of production and training.

11. Because all R&D is measured in nominal dollars, the tax credit may be allowed when no real increase in R&D has occurred (Eisner et al., 1984). Three-year averaging may also introduce a perverse incentive since increasing R&D currently increases the base in future years, thus possibly limiting future tax credits.

12. See McNulty (1973) for an explanation of this problem and some proposed remedies.

13. McNulty (1973) discusses the advantages and disadvantages of this approach.

14. See McNulty (1973) for further discussion of the impacts of these proposals.

15. Richard Goode (1976) suggested that investments in human capital be treated comparably with investments in physical capital. McNulty (1973) also agreed with the amortization proposal if the tax objective is to change the tax code toward more accurate measurement of Haig–Simons income.

16. This proposal raises the minor problem that temporary absences from the labor force may sometimes be indistinguishable from permanent withdrawals.

17. Gross (1988) argues that the current tax code favors education financed by home mortgage debt relative to other forms of educational debt. He further argues that human-capital investment components should be deducted from earned income in theory. However, Gross believes that to be administratively infeasible and therefore advocates that educational debt be exempted from the phase-out of consumer interest deductibility.

18. A complication may arise when an employee's wage includes components of both production and training. Conceptually, we would want to separate the production wage from the training wage, a difficult distinction to incorporate.

REFERENCES

Anonymous (1988a), "A Complete Guide to the Technical and Miscellaneous Revenue Act of 1988." In *Federal Taxes,* Bulletin 49 Extra. Englewood Cliffs, NJ: Prentice-Hall.

———— (1988b), *1989 U.S. Master Tax Guide,* 72nd edition. In *Standard Tax Reports.* Chicago: Commerce Clearing House.

———— (1988c), *Technical and Miscellaneous Revenue Act of 1988: Law and Explanation.* Chicago: Commerce Clearing House.

_____ (1989), "Study Says Targeted Jobs Tax Credit Is Necessary, But Needs Improvement."
    Daily Tax Report, February 17.

Becker, Gary S. (1975), *Human Capital: A Theoretical and Empirical Analysis with Special Refer-
    ence to Education,* 2nd edition. New York: Columbia University Press, for National Bureau of
    Economic Research.

Bernstein, Allen (1988), *1989 Tax Guide for College Teachers and Other College Personnel.*
    College Park, MD: Academic Information Service.

Boskin, Michael J. (1975), "Notes on the Tax Treatment of Human Capital." In *Conference on Tax
    Research 1975.* Washington, DC: U.S. Department of the Treasury.

Doeringer, Peter B. and Michael J. Piore (1971), *Internal Labor Markets and Manpower Analysis.*
    Lexington, MA: D.C. Heath.

Eaton, Jonathan and Harvey S. Rosen (1980), "Taxation, Human Capital, and Uncertainty." *Ameri-
    can Economic Review* 70(September 1980):705–715.

Eisner, Robert, Steven H. Albert, and Martin A. Sullivan (1984), "The New Incremental Tax Credit
    for R&D: Incentive or Disincentive?" *National Tax Journal* 37(June):171–183.

Ernst & Whinney (1988), *Tax Notes* (July).

Goode, Richard (1976), *The Individual Income Tax.* Washington, DC: The Brookings Institution.

Gould, Carole (1989), "Paying for Employee Education Benefits." *The New York Times,* March 12.

Gross, Clifford (1988), "Tax Treatment of Education Expenses: Perspectives from Normative Theo-
    ry." *University of Chicago Law Review* 55(Summer):916–942.

Heckman, James J. (1976), "A Life-Cycle Model of Earnings, Learning, and Consumption." *Journal
    of Political Economy* 84(August):S11–S44.

Internal Revenue Service (1987), *Statistics of Income: 1984 Corporation Income Tax Returns,*
    Publication 16. Washington DC: U.S. Department of the Treasury, 1987.

_____ (1988a), *Educational Expenses,* Publication 508. Washington, DC: U.S. Department of the
    Treasury.

_____. *Miscellaneous Deductions,* Publication 529. Washington, DC: U.S. Department of the
    Treasury.

_____ (1988c), *Tax Guide for Small Business,* Publication 334. Washington, DC: U.S. Department
    of the Treasury.

_____ (1988d), *Your Federal Income Tax,* Publication 17. Washington, DC: U.S. Department of
    the Treasury.

Kelman, Mark G. (1979), "Personal Deductions Revisited: Why They Fit Poorly in an 'Ideal'
    Income Tax and Why They Fit Worse in a Far from Ideal World." *Stanford Law Review*
    31(May):831–883.

Kramer, John R. (1987), "Will Legal Education Remain Affordable, by Whom, and How?" *Duke
    Law Journal* 1987(April):240–275.

Levitan, Sar A. and Frank Gallo (1986), "Individual Accounts for Training: A New But Not
    Improved Idea." *Labor Law Journal* 37(December):841–848.

Madoff, Ray D. (1987), "Back to School after the Tax Reform Act of 1986: Effect of the New Law
    on Educational Funding." *Taxes* 65(September):570–574.

McNulty, John K. (1973), "Tax Policy and Tuition Credit Legislation: Federal Income Tax Allow-
    ances for Personal Costs of Higher Education." *California Law Review* 61(January):1–80.

Office of Tax Analysis (1988), *Report to the Congress on Certain Employee Benefits Not Subject to
    Federal Income Tax.* Washington, DC: U.S. Department of the Treasury.

Rosen, Harvey S. (1980), "What Is Labor Supply and Do Taxes Affect It?" *American Economic
    Review* 70(May):171–176.

Schultz, Theodore W. (1961), "Investment in Human Capital." *American Economic Review*
    51(March):1–17.

Sgontz, L. G. (1982), "Does the Income Tax Favor Human Capital?" *National Tax Journal* 35:99–
    104.

Simons, Henry C. (1938), *Personal Income Taxation: The Definition of Income as a Problem of Fiscal Policy*. Chicago: University of Chicago Press.

Stephan, Paul B. III. (1984), "Federal Income Taxation and Human Capital." *Virginia Law Review* 70(October):1357–1427.

Stephan, Paula E. (1975), "The Impact of Income Taxes on Labor's Productivity: A Human Capital Approach." *Public Finance Quarterly* 3 (October):361–379.

U.S. Congress (1988), *Employment in the Year 2000: A Candid Look at Our Future*. Hearings before the Subcommittee on Investment, Jobs, and Prices of the Joint Economic Committee, Senate Hearing 100–728, 100th Congress, 2nd session, April 11, 12, 18, and 19, 1988.

Warren, Alvin (1980), "Would a Consumption Tax Be Fairer Than an Income Tax?" *Yale Law Journal* 89(May):1081–1124.

White, Patrick E. (1989), "When Must an Employer Withhold on Educational Assistance Payments?" *Journal of Taxation* 70(March):162–165.

EMPIRICAL EVIDENCE
ON PRIVATE TRAINING

Charles Brown

I. INTRODUCTION

A number of recent developments—concern about the ability of American firms to compete in international markets, the perception (as yet unreflected in official productivity figures) that we are in the midst of unusually rapid technological change, and the belief that taking advantage of technological opportunities will require a better-trained workforce—have combined to increase interest in improving the education and training of the labor force. While this interest has not yet led either to major increases in resources devoted to upgrading the workforce or to a decision to welcome many highly educated would-be entrants from abroad—indeed, perhaps *because* major changes have not yet occurred—this is a good time to take stock of what we know about the training of the U.S. labor force.

This paper focuses on training provided by private employers, with some comparisons with training received by government workers. After a discussion of the difficulties of measuring training, the paper summarizes recent evidence on the extent of training in recent data, and available evidence on trends over time.

Research in Labor Economics, Volume 11, pages 97–113.
Copyright © 1990 by JAI Press Inc.
All rights of reproduction in any form reserved.
ISBN: 1-555938-080-2

Differences in access to training among different population groups are discussed next. Finally, attention is turned to two narrower questions of more direct policy interest: training offered by different-sized employers and training in minimum-wage jobs. Implications of these findings for policy are discussed in the concluding section.

II. MEASURING TRAINING

Obtaining information on the extent of training of the workforce is complicated both by conceptual problems and by difficulty in actually measuring those aspects of training which seem relatively well-defined.

While there are difficulties in measuring formal training, what we would like to measure is relatively well defined: an individual is either in a training program or not, formal training has a identifiable start and end, and one should *in principle* be able to determine either how many hours the worker spent or how many dollars the employer spent on any particular training program.

In contrast, informal training is produced jointly with the primary output of the worker, and is therefore more elusive. Workers learn from watching other workers, may share easier ways to do the work either while working or during breaks, and are indirectly instructed whenever a supervisor constructively criticizes their work. Knowing whether informal training is happening in any given week may be difficult to determine; one hopes that for most workers it never ends. The dollar cost is elusive not only because the time spent by supervisors and other workers is not logged, but also because the worker's productivity is likely to be reduced while in training. Thus, it is difficult to measure informal training in hours (from the worker's side) or in dollars (from the firm's side). This poses problems for understanding what is happening to employer-provided training, overall.

In addition to conceptual problems, there are narrower problems of measurement as well. While in principle the costs of formal training programs should be known to firms, in fact reliable figures seem to be hard to come by. Moreover, surveys that are directed toward firms typically elicit little information about workers (detailed information about their education is thought too burdensome, while other characteristics such as race are thought too sensitive); questions directed to workers may lead to inaccurate data about things one might think the worker knew (the size or industry of the firm, and even the worker's own wage rate).

In addition to these conceptual and measurement problems, which are reasonably well known, there is another (unanticipated) recurrent shortcoming in many of the studies discussed below: They are known to be based on stratified samples of workers or firms, but no weighting to a population total of interest is undertaken.

Faced with these difficulties in directly sighting training, economists often look instead for its tracks: If training makes people more productive, wages of workers receiving training should rise faster than wages of those who do not. If one assumes wages rise only because of training, one can indirectly infer how much training is occurring from wage data alone (Mincer, 1962).

Unfortunately, wages may also change for reasons unrelated to training. Medoff and Abraham (1981) present evidence that wages rise with seniority, independent of productivity. Others have noted that wages rising with tenure provide incentives for workers to work hard, in order to collect the implied bonus; Lazear and Moore (1984) claim that such incentives may be more important than rising productivity in explaining wage increases. Freeman (1979) notes that demographically-induced shifts in age–earnings profiles argue against assuming that age–earnings profiles are driven solely by individual human-capital investments. Topel and Ward (1988) argue that job changing is an important source of earnings growth. While one can treat such job changing as the result of individual investments in job search, and hence as human capital, it clearly is not investment in training as generally understood. Consequently, direct measurement of private training is emphasized in this paper.

All of this is an extended apology for the fact that much of what we would like to know about training is not known. Data on informal on-the-job training is sparse compared to formal training programs, and hard data on the extent or cost of training is much less common than information on participation. Thin as our knowledge base is at a point in time, it is even harder to know whether things are getting better or worse. For all their shortcomings, data on educational attainment are far more extensive than comparable data on postschool training.

III. EXTENT OF TRAINING

Table 1 provides both an introduction to the major sources of information about employer-provided training and an overview of the extent of training as measured in these surveys.

All of the surveys in Table 1 that ask whether an individual has received training are population surveys, which when weighted should be representative of the U.S. labor force. The three studies that present estimates of the proportion of those employed who received formal training from their current employer (Haber, 1988; Lillard and Tan, 1986; and Hollenbeck and Willke, 1985) all find that roughly 10% of those employed have ever received such training. Tierney's (1983b) estimate of 5% is lower because it refers only to the year preceding the survey; indeed, given the difference in reference periods, it is surprising that it is as high as it is. Lillard and Tan (1986) is the only study in this group with explicit data on informal on-the-job training; they show it to be somewhat more common than formal training (15% of those employed having learned needed skills this

Table 1. Summary of Extent of Employer-Provided Training[a]

Type of measure	Study	Data set[b]	Time interval	Specific measure	Proportion or average value
Received training	Haber (1988)	1984 SIPP	Time with current employer	Employer-provided training program	8%
	Lillard and Tan (1986)	1983 CPS	Time with current employer	Company (formal) training program	12%
				Informal OJT	15%
				Other training	5%
	Hollenbeck and Willke (1985)	1983 CPS	Time with current employer	Company (formal) training program	11%
	Tierney (1983b)	1981 CPS	Last year	Informal OJT	14%
				Employer-provided training programs	5%
	Duncan and Hoffman (1978)	1975 PSID	Currently receiving	Formal training or OJT	20%

100

Weeks of training	Haber (1988)	1984 SIPP	Time since 1980 with current employer	Weeks of employer-paid training at work	6 weeks
	Tierney (1983a)	1978 CPS	Last year	Weeks of employer-provided training	9 weeks
	Bishop and Kang (1984)	1982 EOPP	NA	Weeks to become fully trained	7 weeks
	Duncan and Hoffman (1978)	1975 PSID	NA	Weeks to become fully trained	86 weeks
Hours of training	Tierney (1983a)	1978 CPS	NA	Hours of employer-provided training	120 hours
	Bishop and Kang (1984)	1982 EOPP	First three months on job	Hours of formal training	11 hours
				Hours of informal training by supervisors	51 hours
				Hours of informal training by coworkers	24 hours

Note: aNA, not applicable; OJT, on-the-job training.
bSIPP, Survey of Income and Program Participation;
CPS, Current Population Survey
PSID, Panel Study of Income Dynamics
EOPP, Employment Opportunity Pilot Project

way). Even allowing for the fact that this figure does not count skills learned informally on previous jobs, it is lower than one would expect if such training is the major force behind the tendency of earnings to rise with earnings on the job.

Duncan and Hoffman's (1978) estimate that 20% of those employed are currently receiving training is based on a different way of approaching the question. Rather than asking whether one had received training and if so what sort of training [as the Current Population Survey (CPS) analyzed by Lillard and Tan did), the PSID sequence used by Duncan and Hoffman asked workers how long it takes a new worker to become fully trained and qualified. Duncan and Hoffman then count as receiving training anyone who has been on their current job for that length of time or less. That their estimate of those currently receiving is close to Lillard and Tan's estimate of those who have received training on their job suggests to me that rather subtle semantic distinctions ("receiving training" vs. "becoming fully trained and qualified") may have a rather large impact on our estimate of the extent of training—particularly for the more elusive informal on-the-job training.

This difference in approaches to measuring training leads to even more striking differences in estimates of weeks of training for those who have received it. For those studies based on direct questions about formal training, the estimates for length of training range from six to nine weeks. Of course, some individuals will not have completed their program, so completed training should be somewhat longer in average duration. Duncan and Hoffman's estimate of how long it takes to become fully trained and qualified runs *much* higher—over 1.5 *years*.

Also shown in the table is an estimate of how long it takes to become fully trained and qualified from Bishop and Kang's (1984) analysis of the Employment Opportunities Pilot Project (EOPP) data. While the difference between this estimate and Duncan and Hoffman's is striking, the unusual sampling frame of EOPP explains at least a significant share of the difference. EOPP oversampled low-wage employers, and the question refers to the most recent hire, so that even within the firm, low-wage, high-turnover jobs are overrepresented. Unfortunately, none of the published analyses of EOPP data appear to have reweighted the data to be representative of jobs at all points on the wage scale. Whether one focuses on workers or new hires depends on one's question: focusing on workers is more appropriate for characterizing the stock of training in the workforce, while focusing on new hires may be more appropriate for assessing the costs to employers.[1]

Data on hours of training are sparser still. Tierney's (1983a) tabulation of CPS data on formal training produces an estimate of about 120 hours. In contrast, Bishop and Kang's estimate for the EOPP population is only 11 hours. What is striking in Bishop and Kang's data is the relative importance of formal and informal training. Depending on whether or not one counts time spent watching others do the job, informal training (for those who receive it) lasts considerably longer than does formal training. While I strongly suspect that the disparity is enhanced by the sample being studied (one typically imagines formal training to be more concentrated on higher-wage workers (see Bishop's (1982a, p. 2) data on white- and blue-collar workers), I also suspect the message that formal training is the tip of the iceberg is not completely an artifact.[2]

While one might be inclined to dismiss the EOPP data as referring to a special and unrepresentative population, it is certainly a population of considerable policy interest. It also contains one of the few estimates of the costs to firms of training workers. By combining data on time spent by new employees, their supervisors, and coworkers on training with productivity indices for newly hired and more senior workers, Bishop (1982a) estimates that training costs in the first three months amount to 30–64% of a more experienced worker's productivity or wage over the same three-month period. The range in the above estimate is due partly to assumptions used in combining training and productivity indices, but the largest difference is between different occupational groups, with estimates for professional, technical, and managerial workers roughly twice as high as those for service workers, with other white- and blue-collar workers falling in between.

Hill (1987) collected specific estimates of components of training costs (formal training programs, informal training, wages in excess of productivity, materials, and outside training) in occupations in which employers typically prefer, but do not require, education beyond high school.[3] She concluded that firms spend an average of $8500 and from six months to two years to train high school graduates for these occupations. Postsecondary education reduced these costs by more than a quarter on average, but they remain substantial. Informal training costs were roughly twice those of formal training, with wages in excess of productivity the largest component of all.

Finally, information from a study by the Bureau of National Affairs's Personnel Policy Forum (1985) illustrates just how difficult it is to get reliable information on training costs from employers. Roughly half of the sample (which over-represents large firms) has a separate training budget (so, presumably the relevant fraction is considerably less than half among all firms). Only 7% of the 140 panel firms reported (formal) training costs per employee; for these 10 or 11 firms (depending on year), median costs per trainee were $122–250. The study correctly flags the low response rate.

IV. TRENDS OVER TIME

Data on trends in employer-provided training over time appear to be limited to tabulations of CPS Surveys of Adult Education in 1969, 1972, 1975, 1978, and 1981. Medoff's (1982) analysis of the first four of these surveys finds no trend in the probability of private sector workers participating in employer-provided training programs at their place of work. He does find an increase between 1978 and 1981 in the probability of participating in any employer-sponsored programs, suggesting an increase in off-worksite but employer-sponsored training in this period.

He finds a sharp *drop* in hours of training programs provided by employers at the workplace between 1972 and 1978,[4] and no increase in total hours of employer-sponsored training programs (regardless of location) over the 1969–1978 period. Given evidence (from help-wanted advertising data) that employers were finding it harder to recruit suitable workers over much of this period, Medoff finds the lack of evidence of increased training surprising. From a more recent perspective—claims that increased interest in short-term payoffs has led to reductions in training—the participation numbers are encouraging and the hours numbers perhaps less surprising.

Tierney (1983b) presents trends in participation in employer-provided (i.e., employer-sponsored, at-the-workplace programs) between 1968 and 1981, presenting both private-sector and government worker participation rates. He finds no trend for private workers, but an upward trend of 2% per year in the proportion of workers participating in training for government workers.

V. DIFFERENCES AMONG WORKERS

Several studies have compared the training (typically, the probability of having received any) between different groups of workers. Here I summarize findings for several such comparisons.

The most surprising result is the lack of consensus on whether men or women acquire more training. Duncan and Hoffman (1978) and Haber (1988) report, as one might expect given the literature on labor force interruptions and postschool training, that women receive less training than men. Tierney (1983b) also finds this to be the case, though the differences are small and have declined significantly in recent years. Hollenbeck and Willke (1985) find that males and female household heads receive more training. Lilland and Tan (1986) report that women are more likely to have received formal training, and have the same likelihood of receiving informal on-the-job training (OJT) in their CPS data. The National Longitudinal Surveys [(NLS), which followed four birth/sex cohorts starting in 1966–1967], however, seem to support the traditional view—mature women receiving less training than either young men or older men—though any conclusion is complicated by lack of a direct comparison between men and women the same age. The "new NLS," which followed a cohort of males and females, ages 14–21 in 1978, also finds young men are more likely to receive OJT than are young women (Lynch, 1989).[5]

Whites receive more training than blacks (Lillard and Tan, 1986; Tierney, 1983b; Duncan and Hoffman, 1978; Lynch, 1989). The only surprise here is that Lillard and Tan find the difference is in access to formal programs rather than informal OJT.

More-educated workers get more training (Bishop, 1985; Lillard and Tan, 1986; Haber, 1988; Hollenbeck and Willke, 1985; Duncan and Hoffman, 1978).[6] The only debate here seems to be whether the relationship persists among those when those with a Ph.D. or professional degree are compared to those with master's degrees.

Results for differences in previous experience are somewhat richer, though not completely consistent between studies. Mincer (1988) finds that more-experienced workers are more likely to have received training, but less likely to be receiving it. Duncan and Hoffman (1978) find that both general experience and years of experience with current employer prior to current position increase the training in one's current position. Lynch (1989) finds positive effects of general experience but not years with employer. Bishop (1985) reports that greater relevant experience is associated with jobs that require more time for an untrained worker to learn, but less training investment for the *typical* new hire—firms place those with more-relevant experience in jobs in which they have more to learn, but such experience helps them learn more cheaply.

Studies of differences in training between union and nonunion workers appear not to have reached a consensus. Mincer (1988) finds unionization significantly negatively related to both training required by the job and the probability of being in training. Barron et al. (1989) report that union workers are less likely to receive the types of training covered by EOPP, though the differences are typically not statistically significant. Bishop (1985) finds no appreciable relationship between unionization and either weeks to become fully trained or an index of hours of training. Lynch (1989) finds union workers more likely to receive training. Unfortunately, none of these studies explains why its results differ from others.

A number of other differences have been less frequently studied. Part-time workers receive less (formal) training (Haber, 1988; Hollenbeck and Willke, 1985). Lillard and Tan (1986) find some positive relationship between the rate of technical change in an industry and the probability of its workers receiving formal training, though evidence for this hypothesis is consistent only for those with education beyond a B.A. Bishop (1982b) finds no statistically significant differences in training for workers hired under hiring subsidies (WIN for welfare recipients, or the Targeted Jobs Tax Credit for various disadvantaged groups), but significantly more training by both management and coworkers in jobs that received CETA OJT subsidies.

VI. TRAINING AND EMPLOYER SIZE

There is considerable interest in the relationship between employer size and training, both because small employers are disproportionate hirers of young workers and because the role of small firms in generating new jobs has received so much attention. (In fact, existing small firms do not grow faster than large ones; small firms' role in job creation just reflects the fact that new firms create jobs and that new firms tend to be small. It would be important to distinguish between small firms and new ones, but available data do not permit this.)

Haber (1988) reports that SIPP respondents who worked for larger firms (at least 100 workers) were about twice as likely to participate in formal training programs. Given economies of scale in providing such training, this is the expected result. Barron et al. (1987a) report that larger establishments and firms with multiple locations are more likely to provide the types of training detailed in the EOPP data, and these differences are typically significant statistically. Bishop (1982a) finds that more training is provided by the largest and smallest firms; this U-shaped pattern persists when one controls for industry and occupation (Bishop, 1985). Consequently, there is no significant linear relationship between employer size and training in these data (Barron et al., 1987b). Hill (1987, 1988) also reports mixed results.

Overall, the evidence suggests that larger employers provide more training, but the very smallest ones do, too. However, much of the evidence so far is based on the EOPP survey, in which low-wage, high-turnover jobs are overrepresented. If training, wages, and employer size are positively related, the EOPP sampling scheme should attenuate the size–training relationship.

VII. MINIMUM WAGES AND TRAINING

Employers do not provide training on the job unless it is worthwhile for them to do so. Because training is costly, it is generally assumed that those receiving training earn lower wages while in training than they would if the firm were making no such costly outlays. However, for an individual whose value to employers is at or slightly above the minimum wage, "buying" training by accepting a lower wage is illegal! Consequently, it is sometimes proposed that young workers—those most in need of training—be subject to a lower minimum wage in order to not interfere with the training process. The recent amendments to the Fair Labor Standards Act were at least in part motivated by a desire to minimize the impact of the minimum wage on training.

It is tempting to dismiss this line of argument with the assertion that minimum-wage jobs have so little training content that—whatever the desirability of minimum-wage laws on other grounds—concern about effects on training is misplaced. If employers' reports about training of minimum-wage workers are correct, however, more training than one might have guessed is going on in minimum-wage jobs. Converse et al. (1981) report that about half of minimum-wage workers are in jobs that require formal training, and that this training lasts (on average) 12 days. Moreover, it takes a new worker four to five weeks to reach company standards of performance. Bishop and Kang's (1984) results for EOPP workers (who are disproportionately but not exclusively low wage) are broadly consistent with Converse et al.'s results. While these are not overwhelming levels of training, they are high enough that it is worth asking whether they are changed by the minimum wages.

Evidence on this question is quite mixed. Perhaps the most direct evidence on the issue comes from Bishop's (1982b, pp. 182–183) analysis of EOPP data. He finds that, after controlling for wage rates, generally those who receive the minimum wage receive less training, both by management and peers. In fact, however, his dummy variables for minimum-wage workers include both those paid the legally required minimum and those whose jobs are not subject to the Fair Labor Standard Act (some of which pay less than the minimum). If the minimum wage is constraining training received by those who receive the minimum, we would not expect those paid less than the minimum to obtain even less training than those at the maximum wage. But this is what Bishop's estimates show. (Bishop attributed this discrepancy to confusion about whether respondents gave the starting wage for the job at the time of the survey, as they were supposed to, or at the time of the most recent hire. *If* respondents did the latter, the dummary variables for wage rates below the minimum may really refer to minimum-wage jobs.)

Leighton and Mincer (1981) find that earnings growth and participation in training programs is lower in states where the impact of the minimum wage (measured by the ratio of the minimum wage to average wage adjusted for differences in coverage across industries) is higher. However, it is not clear whether this means that there is more training and wage growth in high-wage states generally, or whether the minimum wage is directly implicated by the evidence.[7]

Lazear and Miller (1981) compared earnings growth in industries newly covered by the 1967 amendments to the Fair Labor Standards Act, to see whether the payoff to work experience was lower there than in uncovered industries (which should not reduce their training in response to the minimum wage). They find no evidence for this hypothesis, though they emphasize the weakness of the data rather than claiming the training hypothesis has been disproved.

Hashimoto (1982) asked whether each period of work experience does less to increase earnings for those workers most likely to be constrained by the minimum wage (by virtue of low wages or employment in covered industries). He obtains sensible results for young white males, but not for young black males. Once again, however, it is not clear whether this is evidence that low-wage workers profit less from experience or whether the minimum wage is an important constraint on their training.

My reading is that the evidence is inconclusive, and that trying to measure the effects of minimum-wage laws on training by observing their effects on earnings growth is unlikely to succeed. Consider this back-of-the-envelope calculation: Suppose that investments in training earn a return on costs of 10% per year. If the production forgone in formal training equals the wage, while time in informal training costs half of the wage (as would be true if productivity rose linearly from zero to the wage during the period of training), the typical individual in Converse et al.'s (1981) sample of minimum wage jobs would invest about 15 days' earnings in his/her training, or about $500 for a full-time worker. A 10% return on that investment would be $50 per year, or about 2.5 cents per hour for a full-time worker. So if this level of investment were precluded altogether by the minimum wage, its tracks in wage gain equations would be awfully hard to detect. Obviously, this calculation is only a crude guesstimate, but I think it is dramatic enough that refinements are unlikely to alter the basic conclusion.

It is possible, however, that using the level of training from a period of relatively high minimum-wage laws seriously distorts the calculation. One might argue that the Converse et al. (1981) data just show how much the minimum wage had, by then, reduced training. Retabulating the Bishop (1982a) and Converse et al. (1981) data in a way that highlighted coverage status would also be helpful.

VIII. POLICY IMPLICATIONS

Often, learning that what we know about a particular policy is less than we had hoped "merely" undercuts the rationale for a policy we think is needed. In the case of training, the lack of information signals a serious limitation in what a direct policy attack might hope to achieve. The limited data available suggests that informal OJT is at least as important as—and probably considerably more important than—formal training. But the major reason our knowledge about OJT is limited is that it is so difficult to measure with any precision. Researchers face some unique problems trying to measure training—neither firms nor workers have much incentive to respond thoughtfully to the questions we ask—but at least those answering our questions have no obvious incentive to mislead us. If one were to try to subsidize informal training, on the other hand, the incentives to exaggerate are obvious. Consequently, attempts to use subsidies have either focused on formal training or provided hiring subsidies that are not directly linked to any training commitment. The elusiveness of informal training makes it more difficult to subsidize than to measure.[8]

The current method of collecting information about training does not give any reason to hope that we will know much more about the subject in ten years than we do today. Occasional, uncoordinated efforts have their advantages, but they leave us with very little information about representative national samples of individuals, apart from counts of those participating in formal training programs. If policymakers believe that concern about employer-provided training is likely to persist, the time to start a systematic data collection program is yesterday. The current volume of concerns about training voiced by firms may even be enough to drown out complaints about the costs of complying with an employer-based survey. But whether the data should be collected from employers or workers—or from a matched sample of workers and employers—depends on what it is about training that we most want to know.[9]

Because most of the training data summarized in this paper has asked about training on current job, and the sample is restricted to the civilian labor force, little has been said about training provided by the military. According to Hollenbeck and Willke (1985), about 2% of the labor force participated in armed forces training, which provided skills or training for their present (civilian) job. While this training may not loom large in the overall total of job-related training, the fact that the armed forces provides training to many thousands of individuals each year, that it has a serious interest of its own in evaluating the performance of those it trains, and that most of its trainees pursue civilian careers after completing their military service means that there is probably a great deal about training in civilian occupations to be learned from the military.[10] Much of the training provided by the armed forces is for blue-collar and service specialties, and is directed toward the middle rather than the top of the ability distribution. And, unlike many of the projects one might design, the major barriers to a serious study of military training and civilian labor markets are organizational (interagency cooperation) rather than conceptual.

IX. SUMMARY

A.   Research Findings

Measuring employer-provided training is complicated by the fact that informal OJT is much more difficult to measure than time (or dollars) spent on formal training, and by the fact that employers find it difficult to determine how much they spend on training. Consequently, more is known about participation in training and especially formal programs, than about the extent of training (particularly informal OJT).

Roughly 10% of those who are employed have participated in formal training programs on their current job. Participation in informal OJT is probably more widespread, though hard numbers are scarce. Studies that have provided estimates of informal OJT indicate that about 15% of those employed have learned skills this way on their current job, though this estimate is sensitive to how the question is phrased.

There is little evidence to suggest that private-sector workers are receiving increased levels of formal employer-provided training over time. There is some evidence of a decline in length of such training. In contrast, public-sector workers have received more formal training over time.

In general, workers with characteristics associated with higher earnings receive more training. Thus, more-educated workers get more training than less-educated workers, and whites (still) receive more than blacks with the difference being in access to formal training rather than informal OJT. Male–female differences appear to have been reduced, though not eliminated.

Other findings include: part-time workers receive less formal training; there may a positive relationship between the rate of technological change in an industry and the probability of workers with education beyond a bachelor's degree receiving formal training; and workers hired under hiring subsidies (WIN, TJTC) receive about the same training as similar unsubsidized workers.

On balance, large firms seem to provide more training, though very small ones seem to provide more than medium-sized ones as well. Minimum-wage employers report modest training levels, and there is little evidence that the minimum wage itself limits the amount of training provided.

B.   Policy Recommendations

- Avoid direct subsidization of informal training since monitoring such training is too difficult.
- Consider a systematic data collection program on employer-provided training at the national level by the Department of Labor.
- Consider a study of military training for insights into training middle-skill workers, and disseminate the findings to the private sector.

ACKNOWLEDGMENTS

This project was funded under Purchase Order No. 99-9-4757-75-009-4 from the U.S. Department of Labor, Commission on Workforce Quality and Labor Market Efficiency. Opinions stated in this document do not necessarily represent the official position or policy of the U.S. Department of Labor, Commission on Workforce Quality and Labor Market Efficiency.

NOTES

1.   If one worker quits, and is replaced and trained by the employer, one might argue the stock of relevant training was unchanged (depending on what the first worker's new job involves). But it is clear from the employer's viewpoint that the cost of training has increased.

2.   The EOPP numbers are no doubt biased downward by limiting the question to the first three months on the job. However, since the mean estimate of time to become fully qualified is roughly half of three months (seven weeks), I would not want to put too much stress on this quirk of the data. Converse et al. (1981) report considerably more formal training (an average, for those receiving formal training, of 52 hours or 12 days) among minimum-wage workers, but that on average it takes about twice that long for workers to "reach company standards"—a lower level of performance, one would suspect, than "fully trained and qualified."

3. Specifically, the occupations were computer programmer, EDP equipment operator, electric/electronic engineering technician, mechanical engineering technician, drafter, surveying technician, and secretary.

4. Medoff offsets the potential distortion caused by a change in the maximum number of weeks of training allowed by census coding procedures, by recoding all years' data with the tighter top-coding convention.

5. Lynch notes that the NLS training measure may miss informal OJT.

6. Lynch's (1989) education effects are positive but not statistically significant.

7. Moreover, their results on earnings growth do not test directly whether the effect of experience on earnings growth is reduced by the minimum wage; yet this is the real question. Minimum-wage laws could reduce earnings by reducing the probability of getting any experience, even if they do not change the training content of a given amount of experience.

8. It is possible to tie a hiring subsidy to indicators of subsequent performance that one believes are related to training, for example, wage growth or employment stability. Apart from the obvious incentive this creates for employers to shun those without a stable record of past employment, it is also unsuited to markets where promotions come from changes in employer rather than progress through an internal labor market. It is often alleged (though I am skeptical) that small employers provide entry level training only to find their workers "kidnapped" by larger firms.

9. For example, data on costs must come from employers. Surveying employers is not without disadvantages; for example, sampling designs that adequately represent small, new firms are difficult, whereas worker surveys contact the employees of such firms automatically.

10. An anonymous reviewer suggested an in-process review of the army apprenticeship program could usefully be studied from this perspective.

REFERENCES

Barron, John M., Dan A. Black, and Mark A. Loewenstein (1987a), "Employer Size: The Implications for Search, Training, Capital Investment, Starting Wages, and Wage Growth." *Journal of Labor Economics* 5(January):76–89.

———— (1987b), "Gender Differences in On-the-Job Training." Center for Business and Economic Research Working Paper No. E111-87, University of Kentucky, Lexington.

———— (1989), "Job Matching and On-the-Job Training." *Journal of Labor Economics* 7(January):1–19.

Bishop, John (1982a), *The Social Payoff from Occupationally Specific Training: The Employer's Point of View.* Columbus: National Center for Research in Vocational Education, Ohio State University.

———— (ed.) (1982b), *Subsidizing On-the-Job Training: An Analysis of a National Survey of Employers.* Columbus: National Center for Research in Vocational Education, Ohio State University.

———— (1985), "The Magnitude and Determinants of On-the-Job Training." In John H. Bishop et al. (eds.), *Training and Human Capital Formation.* Columbus: National Center for Research in Vocational Education, Ohio State University, pp. 2-1–2-19.

Bishop, John H. and Suk Kang (1984), "Why Do Employers Underinvest in On-the-Job Training?" In John H. Bishop (ed.), *Hiring and Training Workers.* Columbus: National Center for Research in Vocational Education, Ohio State University.

Blakemore, Arthur E. and Stuart A. Low (1988), "Human Capital Formation of Youth: The Impact of Minimum Wages." Mimeo, Arizona State University, Tempe, AZ.

Bureau of National Affairs (1985), *Training and Development Programs.* Report No. 140, Bureau of National Affairs, Rockville, MD.

Converse, Muriel, Richard Coe, Mary Corcoran, Maureen Kallick, and James N. Morgan (1981), "The Minimum Wage: An Employer Survey." In *Report of the Minimum Wage Study Commission*, Volume 6. Washington, DC: US Government Printing Office.

Duncan, Greg J., and Saul D. Hoffman (1978), "Training and Earnings." In Greg Duncan and James Morgan (eds.), *Five Thousand American Families—Patterns of Economic Progress*, Volume 6. Ann Arbor, MI: Institute for Social Research.

Freeman, Richard B. (1979), "The Effect of Demographic Factors on Age–Earnings Profiles." *Journal of Human Resources* 14 (Summer):289–318.

Haber, Sheldon, E. (1988), "Participation in Industrial Training Programs." SIPP Working Paper No. 8813, Bureau of the Census, U.S. Department of Commerce, Washington, DC.

Hashimoto, Masanori (1982), "Minimum Wage Effects on Training on the Job." *American Economic Review* 72 (December):1070–1087.

Hill, Elizabeth T. (1987), "Postsecondary Vocational Training in Pennsylvania—In School and on the Job." Mimeo, Pennsylvania State University, Mont Alto, PA.

——— (1988), "Effects of Postsecondary Technical Education on the Job." Mimeo, Pennsylvania State University, Mont Alto, PA.

Hollenbeck, Kevin and Richard Willke (1985), "The Nature and Impact of Training: Evidence from the Current Population Survey." In John H. Bishop et al. (eds.), *Training and Human Capital Formation*. Columbus: National Center for Research in Vocational Education, Ohio State University.

Lazear, Edward and Frederick Miller (1981), "Minimum Wage versus Minimum Compensation." In *Report of the Minimum Wage Study Commission*, Volume 5. Washington, DC: US Government Printing Office.

Lazear, Edward P. and Robert L. Moore (1984), "Incentives, Productivity, and Labor Contracts." *Quarterly Journal of Economics* 99 (May):275–296.

Leighton, Linda and Jacob Mincer (1981), "The Effects of the Minimum Wage on Human Capital Formation." In Simon Rottenberg (ed.), *The Effects of Legal Minimum Wages*. Washington, DC: American Enterprise Institute.

Lillard, Lee A. and Hong W. Tan (1988), *Private Sector Training: Who Gets It and What Are Its Effects*. Santa Monica, CA: The Rand Corporation.

Lynch, Lisa M. (1989), "Private Sector Training and Its Impact on the Earnings of Young Workers." NBER Working Paper 2872, NBER, Cambridge, MA.

Medoff, James L. (1982), "The Importance of Employer-Sponsored Job-Related Training." Mimeo, Harvard University, Cambridge, MA.

Medoff, James L. and Katharine G. Abraham (1981), "Are Those Paid More Really More Productive? The Case of Experience." *Journal of Human Resources* 16 (Spring):186–216.

Mincer, Jacob (1962), "On-the-Job Training: Costs, Returns, and Some Implications." *Journal of Political Economy* 70 (October):50–79.

——— (1988), "Job Training, Wage Growth, and Labor Turnover." NBER Working Paper No. 2690, NBER, Cambridge, MA.

Tierney, Michael (1983a), "Employer-Provided Education and Training in 1981." In Robert Zemsky (ed.), *Training's Benchmarks: A Statistical Sketch of Employer-Provided Training and Education: 1969–1981*, Task I Report: "The Impact of Public Policy on Education and Training in the Private Sector." Philadelphia: Higher Education Finance Research Institute, University of Pennsylvania,

——— (1983b), "Trends in Employer-Sponsored Education and Training: 1969–78." In Robert Zemsky (ed.), *Training's Benchmarks: A Statistical Sketch of Employer-Provided Training and Education: 1969–1981*. Task I Report: "The Impact of Public Policy on Education and Training in the Private Sector." Philadelphia: Higher Education Finance Research Institute, University of Pennsylvania,

Topel, Robert H. and Michael P. Ward (1988), "Job Mobility and the Careers of Young Men." NBER Working Paper No. 2649, NBER, Cambridge, MA.

Zemsky, Robert (ed.) (1983), *Training Benchmarks: A Statistical Sketch of Employer-Provided Training and Education: 1969–1981*. Task I Report: "The Impact of Public Policy on Education and Training in the Private Sector." Philadelphia: Higher Education Finance Research Institute, University of Pennsylvania.

LABOR FORCE PARTICIPATION AND EMPLOYMENT AMONG YOUNG MEN: TRENDS, CAUSES, AND POLICY IMPLICATIONS

Harry J. Holzer

I. INTRODUCTION

In this paper I will review recent secular trends in labor force participation and employment among young men.[1] Special attention will be paid to specific demographic groups, such as high school dropouts and minorities, whose participation and employment rates have particularly declined.

I will then review several potential causes of these developments, as well as the empirical literature and evidence on these causes. With regard to labor force participation, I will consider factors on both the demand side and supply side of the labor market. The former will include evidence on changes in relative and absolute real wages, caused by demographic changes (i.e., baby boom/baby bust) and changing returns to education. The latter will include the attractiveness on nonmarket, alternative income sources (e.g., transfer payments, illegal activities), which affect reservation (i.e., minimum acceptable) wages, as well as the interaction between participation and family/household structure. We will

Research in Labor Economics, Volume 11, pages 115–136.
Copyright © 1990 by JAI Press Inc.
All rights of reproduction in any form reserved.
ISBN: 1-555938-080-2

also discuss factors that might affect participation and/or employment rates specifically for minorities.

The rest of the paper will be laid out as follows: Section II presents evidence on recent trends in participation and employment for different groups of young people. Section III reviews the empirical literature and demand side and supply side shifts as causes of participation changes, as well as additional evidence on employment changes for minorities. In Section IV, I conclude and discuss policy implications.

II. TRENDS IN EMPLOYMENT AND PARTICIPATION

In Table 1 we find population levels as well as labor force participation rates, employment-to-population ratios, and unemployment rates (for those in the labor force) of young people for selected years between 1955 and 1987. The particular years are chosen to reflect comparable points in the business cycle (so as to consider only secular trends) and to include at least one observation prior to the baby boom/baby bust years.[2] Separate data are presented for the four race-by-sex groups among young people, as well as for those aged 16–19 and 20–24.

Several important trends emerge from Table 1. The rapid growth in the population levels of young people shows the effects of the baby boom between 1964 and 1978, while those for 1987 begin to show effects of the baby bust. Labor force participation trends are quite divergent between males and females in this age group. Young white females show significant increases in participation, while young black females show a slower rise and growing gap relative to their white counterparts. Among young white males, participation rates increased quite sharply for teens through the late 1960s and 1970s, but they have declined significantly since 1978. Among white males aged 20–24, participation has been relatively constant over time. In contrast, participation for young black males has consistently declined in both age categories since the early 1970s. Finally, we note unemployment rate increases for all groups through the 1970s. The increases were largest for blacks and females, and these groups have begun to show some limited improvement (both absolutely and relative to white males) by 1987. Still, unemployment rates of young blacks remain 2½ to 3 times larger than those of young whites, while their participation and employment rates are considerably lower.

In Table 2 we focus more specifically on the labor force participation rates of young people and their relationships to rates of school enrollment. We provide participation and enrollment rates for teens and for those aged 20–24, as well as for males and females in each of the years considered in Table 1.

The results show that since 1964, school enrollment has declined for all groups except females aged 20–24. As the nonenrolled have higher participation rates than do the enrolled, these trends alone should tend to raise overall participation

Table 1. Population, Labor Force, and Employment/Unemployment Rates, Youth and Others, 1955–1987[a]

Year	White males				White females				Black males				Black females			
	Pop.	LFPR	EP	UR	Pop.	LFPR	EP	UR	Pop.	LFPR	EP	UR	Pop.	LFPR	EP	UR
								Ages 16–19								
1955	3507	0.586	0.520	0.113	3785	0.407	0.370	0.091	—	—	—	—	—	—	—	—
1964	5184	0.527	0.450	0.147	5468	0.378	0.322	0.149	—	—	—	—	—	—	—	—
1972	6627	0.601	0.515	0.142	6673	0.481	0.413	0.142	978	0.463	0.316	0.317	1040	0.322	0.192	0.405
1978	7022	0.650	0.563	0.135	7038	0.567	0.485	0.144	1093	0.448	0.285	0.367	1195	0.373	0.221	0.408
1987	6015	0.590	0.499	0.155	5924	0.565	0.490	0.134	1065	0.436	0.285	0.344	1098	0.396	0.258	0.349
								Ages 20–24								
1955	3074	0.856	0.804	0.070	4720	0.458	0.435	0.051	—	—	—	—	—	—	—	—
1964	4862	0.857	0.793	0.074	5706	0.488	0.454	0.071	—	—	—	—	—	—	—	—
1972	7042	0.843	0.771	0.085	7855	0.594	0.546	0.082	921	0.826	0.704	0.149	1106	0.571	0.469	0.179
1978	8335	0.872	0.806	0.076	8704	0.693	0.636	0.083	1120	0.788	0.622	0.210	1363	0.628	0.486	0.227
1987	7729	0.850	0.796	0.084	8079	0.748	0.693	0.074	1173	0.778	0.621	0.203	1405	0.644	0.493	2.233

Note: [a] Pop., LFPR, EP, and UR refer to population (in thousands), labor force participation rate, employment-to-population ratio, and unemployment rate, respectively. Sources are the relevant tables of the *Handbook of Labor Statistics* and *Employment and Earnings*.

117

Table 2.   School Enrollment and Labor Force Participation Rates of Youth,
1955–1987[a]

	Males			Females		
Year	Fraction enrolled	LFPR, enrolled	LFPR, nonenrolled	Fraction enrolled	LFPR, enrolled	LFPR, nonenrolled
			Ages 16–19			
1955	0.640	0.392	0.929	0.487	0.230	0.581
1964	0.739	0.335	0.874	0.688	0.233	0.565
1972	0.718	0.401	0.872	0.652	0.346	0.621
1978	0.693	0.471	0.886	0.658	0.440	0.693
1987	0.621	0.433	0.770	0.600	0.442	0.670
			Ages 20–24			
1955	0.181	0.417	0.967	0.061	0.420	0.486
1964	0.238	0.480	0.966	0.109	0.378	0.518
1972	0.277	0.533	0.949	0.161	0.500	0.627
1978	0.243	0.554	0.946	0.193	0.583	0.721
1987	0.217	0.568	0.931	0.200	0.608	0.761

Note: [a]Sources are the same as those of Table 1.

rates of young people. Among the enrolled, participation rates of both males and females have generally risen since 1964 (though a small decline has occurred for male teens in the 1980s). As for the nonenrolled, participation has generally risen among females and declined among males. The decline among males has been gradual but consistent for those in their twenties, while for nonenrolled male teens the decline has been very sharp since 1978.

Furthermore, the sharp decline among nonenrolled male teens suggests that much of the change involves high school dropouts, who would constitute most of the nonenrolled below the age of 18. More evidence of this issue appears in Table 3, where we find participation rates for young nonenrolled males in 1978 and 1987. The results show that participation rates of high school dropouts declined from 86.5 to 76.8% between 1978 and 1987 for males aged 16–24. Among nonenrolled high school graduates and those with college degrees we find much smaller declines in participation.

It is also particularly disturbing to find nonparticipation growing among those who are not engaged in another productive activity, such as schooling. Both their lack of current employment and their lack of schooling may further inhibit their employment opportunities in future years.

In sum, we find that participation rates among females are generally rising while those among nonenrolled and/or minority males are declining. The declines appear to be most serious for the least educated in these groups.

Table 3. Participation Rates of
Nonenrolled Males, Ages 16–24, by
Educational Attainment, 1978 and 1987

	1978	1987
<4 years high school	0.865	0.768
High school graduates	0.954	0.931
1–3 years college	0.952	0.940
College graduates	0.968	0.967

III. PARTICIPATION AND EMPLOYMENT OF YOUNG MALES: THE EVIDENCE

In this section we review the empirical literature on the labor force participation of young males (generally defined as those aged 16–24), for whom secular declines appear to be occurring. We will review the direct evidence on the determinants of participation, and then consider some possible causes of the trends over time and differences across groups (e.g., blacks and whites) that were noted in Section II. Because of the potentially close link between employment/unemployment and participation effects noted above, we will include some evidence on the former set of issues as well. We consider labor demand and then labor supply effects separately below.

A. Labor Demand Shifts: Wage and Employment Effects on Participation

A number of empirical studies have been done that show the effects of labor demand shifts on labor force participation of youth. The classic work of Bowen and Finegan (1969), using data on individuals from the 1960 census (U.S. Bureau of the Census, 1961), showed that participation of young males rose with average earnings. Of course, earnings are not observed for those out of the labor force; in this case, they must either be taken from a previous period when the individual did work, be statistically imputed, or be proxied by other factors. Among proxies, the individual's education attainment is often used. Bowen and Finegan, and others since then (e.g., Welch, 1989), have found positive effects of such attainment (though not of enrollment) on participation as well.

More recent evidence on the effects of wages on participation of youth confirm these findings. Gustman and Steinmeier (1981), focusing on those aged 17–22, find positive effects of local youth wages (relative to those of adults) on the participation rates of those not enrolled in school, though their estimated effects are not large.[3] Williams (1987) focuses on male teens and also finds positive (and somewhat larger) effects of wages for both whites and blacks on transitions into the labor force, while Cain (1987) finds that youth participation rises with family income. Since family income could be a source of nonwage income for young people that would reduce the participation of those from high-income families, the observed positive effects of family income are instead attributed to the higher wages attained by youth from these families. In fact, moving from families with incomes under $15,000 (1980 dollars) to those at or above $30,000 we generally see wages rising by about 10% and participation rates rising 5–10%.

The effects of overall (i.e., including adult) local or national unemployment on youth labor force participation also appear to be negative in virtually all studies, thereby suggesting an additional role for labor demand through "discouraged worker" effects. In particular, Freeman (1982) finds participation rates of young workers falling 1–2% for every percentage point rise in the national prime-age male unemployment rate in time-series data.

Bowen and Finegan also found negative effects of local unemployment in cross-sectional data, as do Gustman and Steinmeier, (1981), Freeman (1982), and Cain and Finnie (1987). Bowen and Finegan as well as Freeman also considered the effects of various indices of demand for young labor based on local industrial structure. In Freeman's case, the fraction of each industry's nationwide employment that is accounted for by youth is weighed by the fraction of area employment accounted for by that industry, thus creating an index measuring overall local demand for youth. For Bowen and Finegan as well as Freeman, these indices showed positive and significant effects on participation of young males.

Furthermore, several authors find ever larger effects of local demand on the participation of young blacks. In particular, Williams finds larger effects on blacks in both time-series data (using lagged unemployment rates and controlling for trend) and cross-sectional data, which seem to account for substantial fractions of the observed black–white differences in participation of young workers. Cain and Finnie find significant positive effects of the employment of young whites and negative effects of adult black unemployment on the participation of young black males. Gustman and Steinmeier also find effects of local unemployment to be substantially larger for young blacks than young whites, though wage effects are fairly comparable.

A further effect of labor demand on participation of young males might occur through its effect on school enrollment, which we have seen to be negatively correlated with participation. In fact, Gustman and Steinmeier find enrollment to be negatively related to wages and positively related to local unemployment, thus moving in the opposite directions from participation. A few authors have also considered the effects of minimum wages on both enrollment and participation. This effect is somewhat ambiguous a priori, since higher minimum wages may also mean higher unemployment for young workers (an issue considered in greater detail below). In fact, Mattila (1978) finds higher enrollments in years of high minimum wages, while Ehrenberg and Marcus (1982) find negative effects on enrollments for young people from low-income families and positive effects on those from higher-income families. The higher minimum wages thus seem to induce low-income workers to leave school for the labor market while higher-wage workers show an opposite effect.

Declining Wages of Young Men

Since the evidence clearly indicates that labor demand factors play an important role in determining participation rates for both young blacks and whites, we must next consider how changes in demand may have contributed to the observed declines in participation of the nonenrolled and black males in recent years. The labor market for young males has been buffeted by several major demographic and secular economic shifts during this period which should have caused large changes in the demand for particular groups of young males. These changes include:

1. the entrance of the baby boom cohort into the labor market in the mid-to-late 1960s and 1970s;
2. the subsequent aging of this cohort and the entrance of the baby bust cohort in the 1980s;
3. the huge growth of the female labor force in the 1960s and 1970s;
4. shifts in demand away from the manufacturing/heavily unionized sectors toward service/unionized sectors;
5. dramatic slowdowns in productivity growth; and
6. changes in enrollment patterns.

There has been convincing evidence for quite some time now that the baby boom lowered wages and raised unemployment among young workers in the 1970s (Welch, 1979; Freeman, 1979; Wachter and Kim, 1982). Given the rise in college enrollment rates of the 1960s, the fall in earnings was largest for college graduates (Freeman, 1977; Berger, 1983).[4] The baby boom effect appears to have been compounded by the growth of the female labor force, since women seem to be most "substitutable" (or competitive) with young men in the labor market (Grant and Hamermesh, 1981). The substitution seems particularly strong for young black men (Borjas, 1986).

As the baby boom cohort has aged in the 1980s and has been replaced among youth by the baby bust group, some of this has changed. In particular, employment prospects and wage levels should improve for that latter group. However, the wage gains appear to be concentrated primarily among college graduates. This has been predicted by some models as a consequence of the boom–bust phenomenon and the limited scope for substitution between younger and older college graduates, as the skills of the latter became more obsolete (Dooley and Gottschalk, 1984; Stapleton and Young, 1988). The falling rate of college enrollments in the 1970s and 1980s (see Table 2) has made the current group of young college graduates even scarcer and high school graduates more plentiful, thus further increasing the gap in earnings between them.

On top of these demographic and enrollment changes have been some larger changes in the economy that reinforce the developments described here. In particular, the relative shifts in demand away from manufacturing and related industries toward the service and financial sectors seem to be further raising the demand for college graduates and lowering it for non–college graduates, though there remains some doubt about the magnitude of this effect (Murphy and Welch, 1988; Bound and Johnson, 1989). Slow productivity growth, industrial relocation toward the South, and the rise of involuntary part-time work among men all appear to have further reduced the relative and real earnings of young, less-educated males (Beach, 1988; Levy, 1988).[5] Finally, declines in unionization rates and the real value of the minimum wage (since it was last increased in 1981) presumably hurt the wages of the young and least educated as well, though their effects on both employment and participation for young workers may be somewhat more positive [Brown et al. (1982) for minimum wages; Holzer (1982) and Montgomery (1989) for unionism].[8]

The net effects of all of these changes on employment and unemployment were seen in Table 1, where improvements for the youngest group by 1987 begin to appear. Some evidence on earnings appears in Tables 4 and 5. The tables show median income of males for various age groups and education groups in 1972 and 1986. In Table 4, we find median income by age group for all those with income during the year and only for those who worked year-round and full-time. The latter measure is in many ways preferable, since it reflects only wage effects rather than employment effects. In Table 5, we find median income by education for year-round, full-time workers only. These are presented for all aged 25 and over as well as for the group aged 25–34 in each year (data by education are not available for those below age 25). All amounts reported are in 1986 dollars.

Table 4. Males' Median Income by Age, 1972 and 1986[a]

	Age			
	All males	16–19[b]	20–24	25–34
1972				
All with income	17,768	2,402	11,004	21,985
Year-round, full-time workers	25,133	10,153	16,740	24,635
1986				
All with income	17,114	1,928	8,961	19,162
Year-round, full-time workers	25,894	9,730	14,152	22,692

[a] Data are obtained from US Bureau of the Census (1961). All figures are in 1986 dollars, with 1972 adjusted by the fixed-weight personal consumption expenditures deflator.
[b] Ages 15–19 in 1986.

Table 5.   Males' Median Income by Education, 1972 and 1986,
Year-Round, Full-Time Workers[a]

	8 years	1–3 years high school	High school grads	1–3 years college	College grads
1972					
Ages 25+	18,753	22,567	26,409	29,641	37,559
Ages 25–34	16,266	19,982	23,628	26,292	30,857
1986					
Ages 25+	16,389	20,003	24,701	28,025	36,665
Ages 25–34	12,056	16,165	20,438	23,594	30,162

[a]See notes to Table 4.

The data of Tables 4 and 5 show clearly declining real incomes for virtually all groups of male workers between 1972 and 1986. For all age groups combined, the median income reported in 1986 is about 96% of that in 1972 for all with income, though it is about 3% higher for year-round, full-time workers of all ages. Younger workers show the largest declines between 1972 and 1986. Teens in 1986 earned about 90% of their incomes in 1972 and about 96% for year-round, full-time workers. At least the latter group thus appears to be benefiting from the baby bust effects. Those aged 20–24 in 1986 are making only about 81% of their earlier incomes, and about 85% for year-round, full-time workers. For those aged 25–34, the comparable numbers are 87 and 92%, respectively.

The median incomes by education groups (for year-round, full-time workers only) in Table 5 tell a similar story. Among college graduates, real incomes in 1986 are 98% of those in 1972, both for those above age 25 and for those aged 25–34. Comparable numbers for high school graduates are 94 and 87%, while for those without high school diplomas the numbers are about 88 and 74–81%, respectively (i.e., 74% for those with eight years or less schooling, 81% for those with some high school). Clearly, young workers without college degrees and especially those without high school degrees are facing dramatic declines in their real earnings. The results of Table 4 suggest that these trends are even stronger for those in their early twenties. Furthermore, the decline in earnings of young blacks relative to young whites that has occurred in the late 1970s and 1980s (Bound and Freeman, 1987) implies that these results could be even more severe if calculated separately for young black males.[7]

All of these results strongly suggest that the observed decline in labor force participation among nonenrolled young males and especially young black males should be at least partly explained by their fall in real earnings (though it is difficult to say with any degree of confidence how much of the observed effect is so explained). The fact that participation, employment, and real market wages are all falling also points to the predominance of labor demand over labor supply shifts in explaining these developments. But the full explanation must also examine alternative uses of time and sources of income for these young people, which we will consider in the section on labor supply below.

Black–White Demand Differences

Before moving to the next section, it may be useful to review more evidence on differences in relative demand facing young blacks and whites. As noted above, the declines in demand caused by growing female labor force participation and other factors appear to have been larger for young blacks than for whites (Borjas, 1986), and in general the demand for young blacks seems to be more sensitive to overall demand conditions. It is at least possible that the decline of manufacturing and unionized employment, on which young blacks have traditionally been more dependent, has hurt them relatively more as well; however, the evidence to date on this issue is very incomplete.[8] Shifting demand from agriculture toward manufacturing appears to have hurt the employment of young, southern blacks between 1950 and 1970 (Cogan, 1982); changes since then are more ambiguous in their relative effects.

At any point in time, the relatively lower demand faced by young blacks is usually thought to be caused by some combination of lower skills and discrimination. It is clear, for instance, that educational performance as measured by grades has important effects on employment for both young blacks and whites, and that young blacks do less well in such performance measures (Meyer and Wise, 1982b). But it is not clear why either skill or discrimination problems of young blacks should have grown worse in the last two decades. If anything, government equal opportunity and affirmative-action activities appear to have raised the relative demand for black males (Freeman, 1981; Leonard, 1984).[9] Relative skills as measured by years of education as well as test scores have also converged over time (Smith and Welch, 1987).

It is, however, possible that employer *perceptions* of less-educated, low-income blacks have grown more negative over time because of growing concerns about absenteeism, turnover, crime, vandalism, etc. (Jencks, 1987). High rates of discharge for black youth when they are employed can be at least partly traced to absenteeism and other problems of performance on the job (Jackson and Montgomery, 1986); Ferguson and Filer, 1986). It is also possible that the information and "connections" of young blacks in the labor market have diminished because of their growing tendency to live in female-headed, welfare households in which no other adults are employed. We have no direct evidence on changes over time in information or connections. But there is clear evidence that the employment status of their siblings has significant effects on the employment of young people in general (Rees and Gray, 1982), which therefore reflects some direct family effects. Also, most of the employment problems faced by young blacks occur when searching informally for jobs, that is, when using friends and relatives for information or applying directly to employers without referrals (Holzer, 1987).

Furthermore, any early difficulties that young blacks face in obtaining employment seem to reproduce themselves in later years. Both Meyer and Wise

(1982a,b) and Ellwood (1982) find that the lost labor market experience caused by early unemployment has longer-term negative effects on wages. For younger blacks (and, to a lesser extent, young whites) this seems to mean lower participation and employment rates in future years. Indeed, Ballen and Freeman (1986) find that the employment rates of inner-city young blacks do not increase with age to the same extent as do those of young whites and blacks more generally. They trace this effect (through employer interviews) at least partly to the poor work histories that many young blacks clearly have as they apply for new jobs. Also, the successive spells of nonemployment that these young blacks experience do not seem to diminish in duration, which implies that many inner-city young blacks are gaining little in the way of useful work experience and/or talents from the jobs they do obtain.

One final source of demand problems often hypothesized to exist for young blacks is the movement of firms to suburban areas while blacks remain concentrated in inner-city areas. While such movement has clearly occurred over time, there has been conflicting evidence recently on this question. Some papers suggest that the overall employment effects for young blacks may not be large (Ellwood, 1986; Leonard, 1985), while others (Ihlanfeldt and Sjoquist, 1990) find them to be substantial. This issue thus remains a topic of much continuing research and controversy.

B. Effects of Labor Supply Shifts on Participation and Employment

As noted in Section IIIA, labor supply effects on participation will usually reflect an individual's nonwage income sources and alternative uses of time outside the labor market, such as in school or in caring for a family. These factors, as well as the general value of income relative to time, will determine the reservation wage of an individual, which is compared to the expected value of the market wage. Our direct evidence on these issues is somewhat mixed and incomplete, especially with regard to changes over time. However, some inferences about their effects are still possible.

With regard to school enrollments, the data are quite clear. As noted above, enrollments for most groups of young workers have declined since the mid-1960s. This decline would be expected on the basis of the falling rates of return to higher education that were experienced during the 1960s and 1970s (Freeman, 1971, 1977). As the rate of return has risen again in the 1980s, this trend should be reversed. But even as enrollments were declining for most youth, they rose for young blacks between the 1960s and 1980s. This rise (along with rising participation in the military) helps to explain a third or more of the decline in overall civilian participation and employment rates of young blacks relative to young whites during that time (Mare and Winship, 1983; Ellwood and Wise, 1983).

While marriage is generally negatively correlated with labor force participation among women, it is positively correlated for young males (Cain, 1989). Marriage for men seems to imply responsibilities that translate into a higher value of income relative to time (although marriage also seems to have positive effects on wages). Thus, the falling marriage rates of young males in recent years may have contributed to their lower participation. Furthermore, black young men have significantly lower rates of marriage than do young whites [11 and 18% of those aged 16–24, respectively, according to Cain (1987)]. Of course, distinguishing cause from effect is difficult here, since labor market difficulties might also explain low marriage rates (Wilson, 1987).[10]

A related issue involves household structure, since for young people living with parents is negatively related to labor market activity (McElroy, 1985). With no obvious downward trend in the fraction of young males who live on their own, it is unlikely that this factor contributes to the downward trend in participation for young males. Young blacks do live with their families more frequently than do young whites, but once again the direction of causation is unclear here.

With regard to nonwage income sources, we note that unemployed young males are generally not eligible to receive transfer payments such as AFDC directly unless they are heads of households with children, which the vast majority are not. Lerman (1986) finds that young males living in AFDC households are less likely to be employed than are comparable youth from non-AFDC homes; but he considers it unlikely that this is due to a high marginal tax rate on their income (i.e., tendency to lose benefits as earned income rises), since most states do not put great emphasis on the earnings of nonheads when calculating benefits. A more general negative effect of such income on participation is also unlikely, since families on AFDC generally are low-income and since family income seems to be positively correlated with participation (as noted above). Freeman (1986) also finds negative effects on employment for black youth in female-headed households or whenever there is no employed adult in the household. Possible interpretations of these results include low (unobserved) skills, lack of connections in the labor market, or lack of work ethic. The potential role of attitudes and work ethic on employment of black youth is also stressed by Datcher-Loury and Loury (1986), though again the potential correlation of expressed attitudes with other individual characteristics makes it difficult to interpret these results exactly.

Another source of nonage income for young males involves illegal activity, whether it be unreported work in the "underground economy" or more serious criminal activity, especially that involving drug trafficking. These factors are likely to be particularly important for young men who are neither enrolled in school nor participating in the regular labor force.

Of course, the very nature of this income (i.e., its illegality) makes it very difficult to analyze in survey data on employment and participation. The literature on this issue generally shows negative but weak relationships between crime and employment (Freeman, 1983), and once again the direction of causation remains in doubt (i.e., does weak employment lead to participation in crime or vice versa?).

For inner-city black youth, Viscusi (1986) finds that an expected gap between income from illegal activity and from market work raises the probability of participating in such activity, while higher expected probabilities of arrest and conviction lower such activity. Given that the expected gap between these income sources is likely to be higher for black youth than for whites, it is likely that substitution of illegal activity for market work occurs to a greater extent for them. For young men of both races, prison time is clearly negatively correlated with employment, education, and labor force activity in the 1980 census (Welch, 1989). The rise in criminal activity over time by the young as reported in official government records also suggest a possible link between crime and declining participation of young males overall.

Another approach to these issues involves the analysis of reservation wages of young males. High reservation wages can potentially cause lengthy durations of unemployment as well as nonparticipation in the labor force; and a great deal more attention has been placed on studying the former in empirical work to date.[11] Also, the subjective and hypothetical nature of responses to survey questions on reservation wages has led some economists to prefer drawing inferences from (presumably) more reliable data on wages and employment.

With regard to youth, Welch (1990) has recently argued that the observed declines in employment and participation rates of black youths during times when their wages have been rising suggests that their relative reservation wages must have risen substantially during this period. Analyzing self-reported reservation wages from survey data, Holzer (1986a,b) finds some evidence of comparable reservation wage *levels* between young blacks and whites. This implies that, *relative* to market wages, reservation wages are about 10–15% higher for young blacks. These higher relative reservation wages then appear to explain significant fractions (i.e., up to about 20%) of the higher unemployment rates of young black males. In interviews conducted among inner-city youth in Philadelphia Anderson (1980) also finds evidence of young blacks refusing to accept low-wage employment.[12]

As for changes in reservation wages among young males over time, there has been little explicit analysis to date on this issue. Only Kim (1981) has compared self-reported reservation wages for both blacks and whites between the late 1960s and late 1970s/early 1980s, and he finds some evidence of rising reservation wages relative to market wages for both (and especially for young blacks). However, small sample sizes and other statistical problems in this work leave us with some questions on this issue.

To sum up, the evidence reviewed here suggests a significant role for illegal income and high reservation wages relative to market wages in explaining the low employment and participation rates of black youth. The evidence on changes over time in these factors for both young blacks and whites is sketchier but still suggests the possibility of a role here as well in explaining falling participation rates over time.

IV.   CONCLUSIONS AND POLICY IMPLICATIONS

The evidence presented in the preceding sections of this paper shows a decline in labor force participation of nonenrolled young men that has been independent of the business cycle and has been heavily concentrated among blacks and those less educated. Among the potential causes of these developments, a decline in the demand for the labor of these young men (and the resulting fall in the wages they face in the market) seems to have the greatest potential explanatory power. Other factors, such as the greater willingness of young men to remain unmarried and to participate in illegal activities, may be important as well in keeping reservation wages high relative to falling market wages. Potentially positive developments for these youth, such as the small size of the baby bust cohort that is now entering the labor force, appear to have lowered unemployment rates among young people but have not yet had a large effect on the wage of the less educated.

It therefore seems as though large-scale economic and demographic forces, as well as the responses of youth to those factors, are driving the observed changes in the labor force. At least to some extent, these forces should generate self-correcting mechanisms over time that will help to alleviate the problems discussed here. For instance, there is some evidence that the wages of less-educated young workers have risen quite substantially recently in various tight local labor markets, such as that of Boston (Freeman, 1988). If economic growth and/or the baby bust continue to generate tight labor markets in other parts of the country, the implications for the young and less educated will be quite positive. Furthermore, the currently high rates of return to education and low returns to high school dropouts should themselves encourage higher post secondary school enrollments and lower dropout rates. By changing the relative supplies of young workers with different levels of education, such changes in enrollments will help to equalize wages somewhat across these groups.

But it is also quite unlikely that economic and demographic forces alone will totally resolve these problems. For one thing, a cyclical downturn in the coming years would dampen these developments by reducing the positive effects of demand for the young and less educated. Furthermore, employment problems of groups such as young black men have steadily worsened (or remained very serious) over time despite major cyclical shifts and other economic changes. Thus new policy responses to combat these developments may be appropriate. Given the apparent causes of the declines in participation, the goals of such policies should be to (1) discourage dropping out from high school, and (2) raise the demand for labor among the less educated, either by enhancing their skills or by lowering their costs to employers.

A. Education/Training Programs

Of course, these are not particularly new policy goals, and some evidence exists on the efficacy of previous attempts to achieve them. For instance, several experimental employment and training programs for young men have had the goals of enhancing their skills and work experience as well as discouraging their dropping out from school. The Youth Incentive Entitlement Pilot Project (YIEPP) from 1978 through 1981 provided part-time employment during the school year and full-time employment during the summer on the condition that the participants remain enrolled. Post program evaluations (Gueron, 1984) indicated that YIEPP succeeded in raising employment of youth as much as a year afterwards but did not raise wages. Furthermore, high school graduation rates were not significantly higher for program participants. In the more recent Summer Training and Education Program (STEP), developed by Public/Private Ventures in 1984, disadvantaged youth receive part-time work and part-time skills remediation over a few summers and a school year. Evaluations (Sipe et al., 1988) show positive effects on participants' performance on standardized tests but only small and statistically insignificant effects on dropout rates.

Thus, these programs seem to show positive effects on various aspects of participant behavior but little success in preventing dropping out. Other approaches to providing dropouts (as well as other low-skilled, nonenrolled people) with basic or employment-related skills may show more promise. These include government-funded "human-capital" grants, where low-skill people would receive training vouchers and could choose between a variety of public and private modes of skill acquisition. But there is little in the literature to date that carefully evaluates such ideas.[13]

A great deal more evidence exists on what is and is not cost-effective in the realm of more traditional government training programs for disadvantaged workers (e.g., Bassi and Ashenfelter, 1986). These approaches, as well as more recent attempts to improve the effectiveness of informal job search behavior among these workers, should be considered here as well.[14]

B. Wage Subsidies

A different approach to the problem of low-wage workers involves wage subsidies, paid to either employers or employees. If paid to employers, the subsidy would effectively lower the cost of hiring workers and thereby raise employment. If paid to employees, it would raise the income they receive per wage dollar. At least in theory, payment to employers or to employees should produce comparable outcomes in the labor market. In the latter case, workers would be more willing to accept low-wage jobs than before, thus enabling employers to reduce their costs. But in reality, legal minimum wages and other constraints on the firm's ability to lower wages for specific groups of workers make the two kinds of payments less comparable. The employer subsidy is therefore regarded as a way of generating higher labor demand and the employee subsidy is often thought of as an income supplement. Either by lowering employer costs or by raising the worker's effective wage, both should tend to raise the demand facing workers and therefore their labor force participation.

The relevant question for government policy is whether the amount of net job creation of subsidy justifies the budgetary cost of the program. The amount of net job creation depends on the elasticity of labor demand. The lower this elasticity, the greater the extent to which an employer wage subsidy would simply represent a windfall to employers whose hiring practices do not change and who merely substitute government finances for their own.

An important related question involves the degree to which a subsidy should be "categorical," or targeted on specific groups such as disadvantaged workers (however defined). Targeting reduces the overall costs and lessens the windfall to employers, but it raises the degree to which subsidized workers may displace nonsubsidized workers, especially if their skills are comparable. Targeting also has the disadvantage of creating a stigma for eligible workers, since it signals to the employer that these workers have labor market problems in the absence of the subsidy. The stigma may more than fully counteract the benefits in terms of lower employer costs for hiring these workers.

An intermediate strategy involves subsidies only for "marginal" workers, or for any who are hired above some base level of employment. Such a strategy eliminates some of the windfall problem, since only those hired above the base level are subsidized; and it also limits substitution against unsubsidized workers for the same reason. By focusing on the last group of employees to be hired, this policy should also disproportionately benefit less-skilled employees without the stigma of targeting. This last attribute is reinforced if the subsidy is designed to cover a fixed fraction of wage costs up to some total dollar limit, since this will cover a larger fraction of total wage costs for low-wage than for high-wage workers.

The federal government has had experience with both marginal and targeted subsidies. The New Jobs Tax Credit (NJTC), begun in 1977 but discontinued after 1978, paid 50% of the first $6000 of wages for up to 50 new workers after the firm had reached 102% of the previous year's employment. Budgetary costs of the program were under $2 billion (1977 dollars), and several studies suggest that employment growth in eligible firms (as well as among those who knew about the program at all) was 2–3% higher than in comparable firms (Bishop and Haveman, 1979; Perloff and Wachter, 1979; Bishop, 1981).

On the other hand, targeted employer subsidy programs for disadvantaged workers had longer lives but smaller effects. The Work Incentive (WIN) program for heads of welfare households and the Targeted Jobs Tax Credit (TJTC) are two programs that have provided employer subsidies for different groups of disadvantaged workers. Response rates from firms on both have been low (Hamermesh,

1978). Experimental programs on smaller scales have shown similar results (Burtless, 1985), again suggesting a large stigma effect from targeted subsidies.

What does all of this imply for labor force participation of young people? In local labor markets that are now tight and where upward pressure on wages of youth already exists, there is little point in an employer subsidy program. But in states or metropolitan areas where local demand is slack, a marginal worker subsidy focusing only on less-educated youth might be quite cost-effective in raising employment and participation. Complementing this with an *employee* subsidy for particularly disadvantaged groups would further enhance the labor force effects but would avoid the stigma problem discussed above. In the event of a cyclical downturn over the next few years, the employer subsidy would be especially timely as a means of combating labor demand problems, which always fall disproportionately on the young and/or less educated (Clark and Summers, 1981).

It is also important to consider federal minimum wage policy in any discussion of subsidies. Since the federal minimum will again rise in the next few years, employer subsidies might tend to offset any negative effects on labor demand that might result. The two policies might therefore be seen as being complementary. On the other hand, the additional employee subsidy for disadvantaged workers may be viewed as a more efficient way of raising their earnings than are large minimum-wage increases (though it is also more costly for the federal treasury).

Finally, we note the important link that may exist between illegally obtained income and the participation of low-wage workers in inner-city areas. To the extent that more effective law enforcement can make such activity costlier (in terms of expected arrest) and/or less profitable, positive effects on participation might result. But more specific recommendations in this area are clearly beyond the scope of this paper.[15]

ACKNOWLEDGMENTS

This project was funded under Purchase Order No. 99-9-4764-75-026-04 from the U.S. Department of Labor, Commission on Workforce Quality and Labor Market Efficiency. Opinions stated in this document do not necessarily represent the official position or policy of the U.S. Department of Labor, Commission on Workforce Quality and Labor Market Efficiency.

NOTES

1. This paper will not cover the general issue of youth unemployment and why its levels are always higher than those of adults. For discussions of these issues, see Osterman (1980) or Ellwood and Feldstein (1982). Important cyclical effects on the youth market, such as those discussed in Clark and Summers (1981), are also ignored in this discussion of *secular trends*. Finally, the analysis below assumes that labor force participation is a meaningful and measurable category, thus abstracting from the unemployment/nonemployment issue stressed by Clark and Summers in their other work (1979).

2. Unemployment rates for adult males (ages 20 and above) in the five years listed are 3.8, 3.9, 4.0, and 4.2%, respectively for 1955, 1964, 1972, and 1978. For married males, they are 2.6, 2.8, 2.8, and 2.8%, respectively.

3. Separate rates for blacks by age in the pre-1972 years are not available in the published annual data.

4. Some disagreement remains over whether wage *growth* (as opposed to levels) for the baby-boomers will allow their wages to converge over time to more normal levels, relative to other cohorts. Welch (1979) and Bloom and Freeman (1986) argue that they will, while Berger (1985) argues against this view.

5. The rather lengthy literature on deindustrialization began with Bluestone and Harrison (1983) and was disputed by Lawrence (1984). On the related issue of growing inequality in earnings and family income, see Bell and Freeman (1986), Blackburn and Bloom (1985), and Montgomery and Stockton (1987).

6. According to Brown et al. (1982), the elasticity of labor demand for teens with respect to the minimum wage is 0.1 to 0.2, implying only a small trade-off between higher minimum wages and employment levels of youth. Montgomery also shows that the negative effects of unions on employment are not large in magnitude.

7. Median income by race for year-round, full-time workers is not available for all years. Looking at all workers' income would exaggerate the decline in wages for black males, given the dramatic decline in their employment levels over this period.

8. The argument that recent declines in black youth employment reflect a mismatch of jobs and worker skills caused by declining manufacturing employment is stated in Kasarda (1986) and Wilson (1987).

9. While government antidiscrimination activity should have shifted out the labor demand curve for blacks, thereby raising both wages and employment, it is possible that this activity has raised wages of blacks at the expense of employment. A more plausible argument is that labor demand has risen for some blacks (i.e., those with education and skills) and declined for others (for reasons discussed in the text).

10. The view that black male unemployment is responsible for lower marital rates and high female headship among black households is disputed by Bassi (1987), among others.

11. The literature on employee job search focuses on unemployment rather than participation. See Mortensen (1986) for a review of this literature.

12. The argument that relative reservation wages are higher for blacks is disputed by Borus (1982), though he presents no data on market wages. Various Manpower Development Research Corporation (MDRC) publications (e.g., Gueron, 1984) also dispute this viewpoint, on the basis of the ease with which minimum-wage jobs in government programs are filled. This, however, does not contradict the notion that large segments of the black and white youth populations are unwilling to accept these jobs.

13. Proposals for a voucher system in which young people would be able to purchase the remedial education or training of their choice appear, for example, in Haveman (1988). A few states, such as Michigan, are initiating comprehensive programs designed to evaluate and identify particular skill deficiencies of individual adults in the population and to direct them to appropriate remedial services. Apprenticeship programs, in which youth are trained for specific skills at low wages, have never been widely used outside unionized construction, though government subsidies for such programs more generally might be considered.

14. Programs that aid disadvantaged workers in the job search process have recently been included in many statewide programs for AFDC recipients (Gueron, 1986), though their specific effects have not been frequently evaluated.

15. Even the general direction of policies to achieve such a goal are unclear. For instance, the apparently growing importance of the high-priced, illegal drug traffic has led some public officials to argue for legalization rather than stricter law enforcement. I defer to others with greater expertise in these matters.

REFERENCES

Anderson, Elijah (1980), "Some Observations on Black Youth Unemployment." In J. Palmer and I. Sawhill (eds.), *Youth Employment and Public Policy.* Englewood Cliffs, NJ: Prentice-Hall.

Ballen, John and Richard Freeman (1985), "Transitions between Employment and Unemployment." In R. Freeman and H. Holzer (eds.), *The Black Youth Employment Crisis.* Chicago: University of Chicago Press.

Bassi, Laurie (1987), "Changing Family Structure: Economic Choice or Economic Constraint?" Mimeo, Georgetown University.

Bassi, Laurie and Orley Ashenfelter (1986), "The Effect of Direct Job Creation and Training Programs on Low-Skilled Workers." In S. Danziger and D. Weinberg (eds.), *Fighting Poverty.* Cambridge, MA: Harvard University Press.

Beach, Charles (1988), "The Vanishing Middle Class? Evidence and Explanations." Discussion Paper, Institute for Research on Poverty, University of Wisconsin.

Bell, Linda and Richard Freeman (1986), "The Facts About Rising Industrial Wage Dispersion in the U.S." *IRRA Proceedings*, pp. 331–337.

Berger, Mark (1983), "Changes in Labor Force Composition and Male Earnings: A Production Approach." *Journal of Human Resources,* Spring.

—————— (1985), "The Effect of Cohort Size on Earnings Growth: A Reexamination of the Evidence." *Journal of Political Economy,* June.

Bishop, John (1981), "Employment in Construction and Distribution Industries: The Impact of the New Jobs Tax Credit." In S. Rosen (ed.), *Studies in Labor Markets.* Chicago: University of Chicago Press.

Bishop, John and Robert Haveman (1979), "Selective Employment Subsidies: Can Okun's Law Be Repealed?" *American Economic Review,* May.

Blackburn, McKinley and David Bloom (1986), "Family Income Inequality in the United States: 1967–1984." *IRRA Proceedings*, pp. 349–357.

Bloom, David and Richard Freeman (1986), "The Youth Problem: Age of Generational Crowding?" NBER Working Paper, NBER, New York.

Bluestone, Barry and Bennett Harrison (1983), *The De-Industrialization of America.* New York: Basic Books.

Borjas, George (1988), "The Demographic Determinants of the Demand for Black Labor." In R. Freeman and H. Holzer (eds.), *The Black Youth Employment Crisis.* Chicago: University of Chicago Press.

Borus, Michael (1982), "Willingness of Youth to Work." *Journal of Human Resources* , pp. 581–593.

Bound, John and Richard Freeman (1987), "Black Economic Progress: Erosion of the Post-1964 Gains in the 1980's?" Mimeo, Harvard University.

Bound, John and George Johnson (1989), "Changes in the Structure of Wages During the 1980's: An Evaluation of Alternative Explanations." Unpublished. Mimeo, University of Michigan.

Bowen, William and T. Aldrich Finegan (1989), *The Economics of Labor Force Participation.* Princeton, NJ: Princeton University Press.

Brown, Charles et al. (1982), "The Effects of the Minimum Wage on Employment and Unemployment." *Journal of Economic Literature,* June.

Burtless, Gary (1985), "Are Targeted Wage Subsidies Harmful? Evidence from a Wage Coucher Experiment." *Industrial and Labor Relations Review,* October.

Cain, Glen (1987), "Black–White Differences in Employment of Young People: An Analysis of 1980 Census Data." Discussion Paper, Institute for Research on Poverty, University of Wisconsin.

Cain, Glen and Ross Finnie (1987), "The Black–White Difference in Youth Employment: Evidence for Demand-Side Factors." Discussion Paper, Institute for Research on Poverty. University of Wisconsin.

Clark, Kim and Lawrence Summers (1979), "The Dynamics of Unemployment Reconsidered."
    Brookings Papers on Economic Activity , pp. 13–60.
_____ (1981), "Demographic Differences in Cyclical Employment Variation." *Journal of Human
    Resources,* Winter.
Cogan, John (1982), "The Decline in Black Teenage Employment: 1950–70," *American Economic
    Review,* September.
Datcher-Loury, Linda and Glen Loury (1988), "The Effects of Attitudes and Aspirations on the Labor
    Supply of Young Men." In R. Freeman and H. Holzer (eds.), *The Black Youth Employment
    Crisis.* Chicago: University of Chicago Press.
Dooley, Martin and Peter Gottschalk (1984), "Earnings Inequality Among Males in the United
    States: Trends and the Effects of Labor Force Growth." *Journal of Political Economy,* February.
Ehrenberg, Ronald and Alan Marcus (1982), "Minimum Wages and Teenagers' Enrollment and
    Employment." *Journal of Human Resources,* Winter.
Ellwood, David (1982), "Teenage Unemployment: Permanent Scars on Temporary Blemishes?" In
    R. Freeman and D. Wise (eds.), *The Youth Labor Market Problem.* Chicago: University of
    Chicago Press.
_____ (1986), "The Spatial Mismatch Hypothesis: Are There Jobs Missing in the Ghetto?" In R.
    Freeman and H. Holzer (eds.), *The Black Youth Employment Crisis.* Chicago: University of
    Chicago Press.
Ellwood, David and Martin Feldstein (1982). "Teenage Unemployment: What Is the Problem?" In R.
    Freeman and D. Wise (eds), *The Youth Labor Market Problem,* Chicago: University of Chicago
    Press.
Ellwood, David and David Wise (1983), "Youth Employment in the Seventies: The Changing
    Circumstances of Young Adults." Working Paper, NBER, New York.
Ferguson, Ronald and Randall Filer (1986), "Do Better Jobs Make Better Workers? Absenteeism for
    Work Among Inner-City Black Youths." In R. Freeman and H. Holzer (eds.), *The Black Youth
    Employment Crisis.* Chicago: University of Chicago Press.
Freeman, Richard (1971), *The Market for College-Trained Manpower.* Cambridge, MA: Harvard
    University Press.
_____ (1977), "The Decline in Economic Rewards to College Education." *Review of Economics
    and Statistics,* February.
_____ (1979), "The Effects of Demographic Factors on Age–Earnings Profiles." *Journal of
    Human Resources,* Summer.
_____ (1981), "Black Economic Progress Since 1964: Who Has Gained and Why." In S. Rosen
    (ed.), *Studies in Labor Markets.* Chicago: University of Chicago Press.
_____ (1982), "Economic Determinants of Individual and Geographic Variation in the Labor
    Market Positions of Young Persons." In R. Freeman and D. Wise (eds.), *The Youth Labor
    Market Problem.* Chicago: University of Chicago Press.
_____ (1983), "Crime and the Labor Market," In J. Q. Wilson (ed.), *Crime and Public Policy.* San
    Francisco: Institute for Contemporary Studies.
_____ (1986), "Who Escapes? The Relation of Church-Going and Other Background Factors to the
    Performance of Black Male Youths." In R. Freeman and H. Holzer (eds.), *The Black Youth
    Employment Crisis.* Chicago: University of Chicago Press.
_____ (1988), "How Do Young, Less-Educated Workers Fare in a Labor Shortage Economy?"
    Mimeo, Harvard University.
Grant, James and Daniel Hamermesh (1981), "Labor Market Competition Among Youths, Women
    and Others." *Review of Economics and Statistics* 63:354–360.
Gueron, Judith, (1984), "Lessons From a Job Guarantee: The Youth Incentive Entitlement Pilot
    Projects." New York: Manpower Development Research Corporation.
_____ (1986), "Work Initiatives for Welfare Recipients." Manpower Development Research
    Corporation.

Gustman, Alan and Thomas Steinmeier (1981), "Wages, Unemployment, and the Enrollments of Youth." *Review of Economics and Statistics,* November.

Hamermesh, Daniel (1978), "Subsidies for Jobs in the Private Sector." In J. Palmer (ed.), *Creating Jobs.* Washington, DC: The Brookings Institution.

Handbook of Labor Statistics (1983), Washington, DC: Bureau of Labor Statistics, US Department of Labor.

Haveman, Robert (1985), *Starting Even.* New York: Twentieth Century Fund.

Holzer, Harry (1982), "Unions and the Labor Market Status of White and Minority Youth." *Industrial and Labor Relations Review,* April.

———— (1986a), "Black Youth Unemployment: Duration and Job Search." In R. Freeman and H. Holzer (eds.), *The Black Youth Employment Crisis.* Chicago: University of Chicago Press.

———— (1986b), "Reservation Wages and Their Labor Market Effects for Black and White Male Youth." *Journal of Human Resources,* June.

———— (1987), "Informal Job Search and Black Youth Unemployment." *American Economic Review,* June.

Ihlanfeldt, Keith and David Sjoquist (1990), "Job Accessibility and Racial Differences in Youth Employment Rates." *American Economic Review* 80:267–276.

Jackson, Peter and Edward Montgomery (1986), "Layoffs, Discharges, and Youth Unemployment." In R. Freeman and H. Holzer (eds.), *The Black Youth Employment Crisis.* Chicago: University of Chicago Press.

Jencks, Christopher (1987), "Deadly Neighborhoods." *The New Republic,* June 13.

Kasarda, John (1986), "The Regional and Urban Redistribution of People and Jobs, in the U.S." Mimeo, University of North Carolina, Chapel Hill.

Kim, Choongsoo (1981), "On the Determinants of Reservation Wages: An Empirical Specification." Paper, Center for Human Resource Research, Ohio State University, Columbus.

Lawrence, Robert (1984), *Can America Compete?* Washington, DC: The Brookings Institution.

Leonard, Jonathan (1984), "The Impact of Affirmative Action on Employment." *Journal of Labor Economics,* October.

———— (1985), "Space, Time, and Unemployment: Los Angeles, 1980." Mimeo, University of California, Berkeley.

Lerman, Robert (1986), "Do Welfare Programs Affect Schooling and Work Patterns of Young Black Men?" In R. Freeman and H. Holzer (eds.), *The Black Youth Employment Crisis.* Chicago: University of Chicago Press.

Levy, Frank (1988), *Dollars and Dreams.* New York: Russell Sage Foundation.

Mare, Robert and Christopher Winship (1983), "Racial Socioeconomic Convergence and the Paradox of Black Youth Joblessness." Chicago: National Opinion Research Center (NORC).

Mattila, J. Peter (1978), "Youth Labor Markets, Enrollment, and Minimum Wages." *IRRA Proceedings,* pp. 134–140.

McElroy, Marjorie (1985), "The Joint Deterioration of Household Membership, and Market Work: The Case of Young Men." *Journal of Labor Economics,* July.

Meyer, Robert and David Wise (1982a), "High School Preparation and Early Labor Market Experience." In R. Freeman and D. Wise (eds.), *The Youth Labor Market Problem.* Chicago: University of Chicago Press.

———— (1982b), "The Transition for School to Work: The Experiences of Blacks and Whites." Working Paper, NBER, New York.

Montgomery, Edward (1989), "Employment and Unemployment Effects of Unions." *Journal of Labor Economics,* April.

Montgomery, Edward and David Stockton (1987), "Evidence on the Causes of Rising Dispersion of Relative Wages." Mimeo, Board of Governors, Federal Reserve Bank.

Mortensen, Dale (1986), "Job Search and Labor Market Analysis." In O. Ashenfelter and R. Layard (eds.), *Handbook of Labor Economics.* Amsterdam: North-Holland.

Murphy, Kevin and Finis Welch (1988), "The Structure of Wages." UNICON Discussion Paper, UNICON, Los Angeles.

Osterman, Paul (1980), *Getting Started: The Youth Market*. Cambridge, MA: MIT Press.

Perloff, Jeffrey and Michael Wachter (1979), "The New Jobs Tax Credit: An Evaluation of the 1977–78 Wage Subsidy Program." *American Economic Review*, May.

Rees, Albert and Wayne Gray (1982), "Family Effects in Youth Employment." In R. Freeman and D. Wise (eds.), *The Youth Labor Market Problem*. Chicago: University of Chicago Press.

Sipe, Cynthia et al. (1988), "Summer Training and Education Program: Report on the 1987 Experience." Philadelphia: Public/Private Ventures.

Smith, James and Finis Welch (1987), *Closing the Gap*. Santa Monica, CA: Rand.

Stapleton, David and Douglas Young (1988), "Educational Attainment and Cohort Size." *Journal of Labor Economics*, July.

U.S. Bureau of the Census (1961), *Current Population Reports*, Series P-60. Washington, DC: US Government Printing Office.

Viscusi, W. Kip (1986), "Market Incentives for Criminal Behavior Among Inner-City Black Youth." In R. Freeman and H. Holzer (eds.), *The Black Youth Employment Crisis*. Chicago: University of Chicago Press.

Wachter, Michael and Choongsoo Kim (1982), "Time-Series Changes in Unemployment of Teenagers." In R. Freeman and D. Wise (eds.), *The Youth Labor Market Problem*. Chicago: University of Chicago Press.

Welch, Finis (1989), "The Employment of Black Men." *Journal of Labor Economics* 8:526–574.

——— (1979), "Effects of Cohort Size on Earnings: The Baby-Boom Babies' Financial Bust." *Journal of Political Economy* 87:565–598.

Williams, Donald (1987), *Labor Force Participation of White and Black Male Youth*. Ann Arbor, MI: UMI Press.

Wilson, William (1987), *The Truly Disadvantaged*. Englewood Cliffs, NJ: Prentice-Hall.

UNDERSTANDING PART-TIME WORK

Rebecca M. Blank

In 1988, 18.4% of all workers worked part-time, including 26.8% of all female workers and 11.4% of all male workers. Furthermore, the percentage of part-time workers has been increasing over time, growing from 10.5% of the labor force in 1955. Of course, given the overall growth in employment in this country, increases in the percentage working part-time imply very large increases in the number of part-time workers—from 5.6 million in 1955 to 19.5 million in 1988.[1] These changes indicate the importance of understanding the role of part-time work in the U.S. labor market, both for employers as well as for workers.

This paper is designed to analyze what we do and do not know about part-time work. Section I reviews the trends in part-time work, and discusses who works part-time and in which jobs. Section II discusses the decision to use part-time workers from the employer's perspective. Section III discusses differences in compensation between full-time and part-time workers. Section IV discusses the well-being and income levels of households with part-time workers. Section V focuses on three major policy issues relating to the current nature of part-time work in the U.S. labor market. Finally, Section VI summarizes and highlights four research areas where our knowledge regarding part-time work and its impact is inadequate.

Research in Labor Economics, Volume 11, pages 137–158.
Copyright © 1990 by JAI Press Inc.
All rights of reproduction in any form reserved.
ISBN: 1-555938-080-2

I.   DESCRIBING THE PART-TIME LABOR MARKET

A.   Defining Part-Time Work

Part-time work is officially defined by the department of labor as regular employment involving less than 35 hours of work per week. Individuals who indicate they work part-time are asked to identify their reasons for part-time work. Some, categorized as "voluntary part-time workers," indicate they are only looking for part-time work. Others indicate that they are working part-time for economic reasons, because they could only find a part-time job, or because of slack work or material shortages. These workers are considered "involuntary part-time workers."[2] At times it is also useful to distinguish between part-time workers, those currently employed on a part-time job, and the part-time labor force, which includes the unemployed who seek part-time work (Nardone, 1986).

The cutoff at 35 hours for part-time workers has been used since the mid-1940s and there is at present little indication that this cutoff is inappropriate. The number of individuals who consider themselves working full-time, but whose hours are less than 35, is small. Analysis of the jobs held by workers who work 30–34 hours indicates that they are more similar to the jobs held by 25–29-hour workers than to the jobs held by 35–39-hour workers (Hedges and Gallogly, 1977). There has also been little change in the average hours per week worked by full-time workers, which has remained at around 43 for the past two decades.[3]

An additional question often arises as to how part-time work relates to part-year work, usually defined as working less than 50 weeks per year. Research has indicated that there are significant differences between the part-time and the part-year workforces (Blank, 1988). In addition, it has been noted that while part-time work has increased, part-year work has decreased in recent years. However, it is true that part-time workers are more likely than full-time workers to work only part-year (Mellor and Parks, 1988).

B.   Trends in Part-Time Work

The number of part-time workers has grown steadily for the past four decades. As Figure 1 shows, the share of part-time workers expanded in the 1950s and 1960s, but remained relatively stable at around 17–18% through the 1970s.[4] The deep recession of the early 1980s drove the share to its historical high of over 20% in 1982, but it has since declined to 18.4% It is clear that the underlying trend has been an increasing percentage of workers in part-time work.

Part of this trend has been due to expansions in the supply of part-time workers, as a growing number of teenagers and married women entered the labor market, both groups that were more likely to seek part-time jobs. There has also been a growing propensity for workers over 65 to work part-time, if they work at

Figure 1. Percentage of Part-time Workers (persons age 16+, at work, nonagricultural industries), 1955–1988

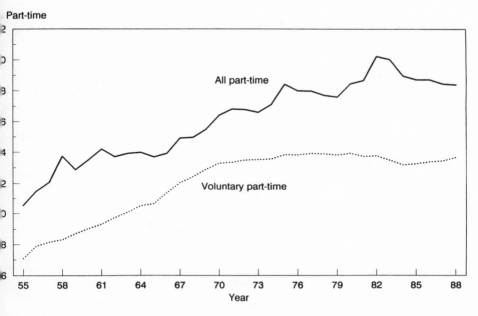

all. At the same time, the demand for part-time workers has also expanded as the retail and service sectors have grown, both of which rely more heavily on part-time jobs (Stein and Meredith, 1960; Holland, 1966; Deutermann and Brown, 1978). It is virtually impossible to separate the impact of increased supply vs. increased demand in the growth of part-time work. Both have occurred simultaneously and each has almost surely stimulated further change in the other.

The percentage of teenagers in the labor market has declined since the mid-1970s; concurrently, the percentage of jobs filled by part-time teenage workers has also declined. But this decline has been somewhat offset by the fact that teenagers who work are increasingly likely to work part-time (U.S. Department of Labor, 1989, Table 23).

Figures 2 and 3 plot the percentage of part-time workers among all female and male nonagricultural workers between 1968 and 1988. The percentage of female workers in part-time jobs is virtually constant over this time period, varying around 27%. The percentage of male workers in part-time jobs is rising.[5]

Figures 1–3 also plot the percentage of all nonagricultural workers who are voluntary part-time workers. The distance between this line and the total percentage part-time is the percentage of involuntary part-time workers. As the figures make clear, the percentage of involuntary part-time workers has been rising among both men and women and is far more cyclical than the percentage of

Figure 2. Percentage of Part-time Workers among Women (age 16+, at work, nonagricultural industries), 1968–1988

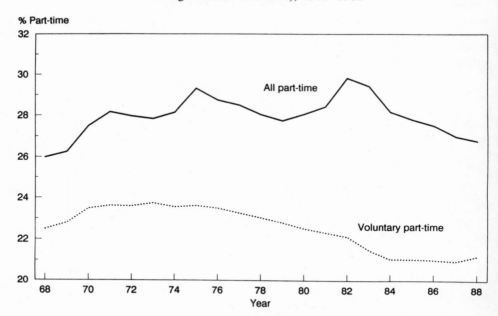

Figure 3. Percentage of Part-time Workers among Men, (age 16+, at work, nonagricultural industries), 1968–1988

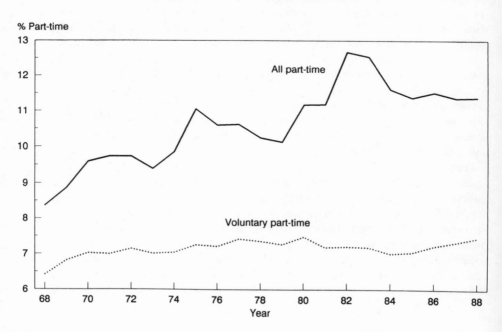

voluntary part-timers. Increases in involuntary part-time work tend to lead movements in the unemployment rate, as firms cut back on hours before they lay off workers (Bednarzik, 1975).

The percentage of workers in voluntary part-time employment can be regressed against the aggregate unemployment rate, a time trend, and a constant; a similar regression can be estimated using involuntary part-time employment as the dependent variable. The results for these two regressions indicate that both the percentage of voluntary and involuntary part-time work increases with the unemployment rate, although the impact of unemployment on involuntary part-time work is much larger. In addition, even after changes in unemployment are controlled for, there remains an underlying positive time trend in the percentage of workers in involuntary part-time work over the past two decades (Bednarzik, 1975; Ichniowski and Preston, 1986; Blank, 1990). Essentially, the share of involuntary part-time workers has increased in each recession and then declined, but each time it does not quite return to its prerecession level. While this trend has been much discussed, the reasons behind it have not been seriously investigated and are not understood. Among men, voluntary part-time work also shows a positive time trend. Among women, once the unemployment rate is controlled for, voluntary part-time work shows a declining trend (Blank, 1990).

In summary, the percentage of workers in part-time jobs varies over the business cycle, but has an underlying upward trend. This is due to two primary factors: the increase in part-time work among men, and the increase in the percentage of the labor force composed of women, who have a higher propensity to work part-time. Much of the increase in men's part-time work is the result of an increase in involuntary part-time employment. In recent years, however, the percentage of workers in part-time jobs has actually declined somewhat as the nation has recovered from the deep recession of the early 1980s.

C. Who Are the Current Part-Time Workers?

Part-time workers are disproportionately likely to be teenagers, women with young children, and workers over the age of 65. In fact, among teens and elderly workers, over half are employed part-time (Nardone, 1986). The result is a very heterogeneous group of part-time workers; the labor market issues of concern to teenagers are likely to be quite different from those of concern to elderly part-timers, and also different from those facing women with children. Part-time workers are disproportionately in retail and service occupations. They are less likely to be in professional and managerial positions, and they are also less likely to be in blue-collar positions (Leon and Bednarzik, 1978; Blank, 1990). Part-time workers are also more likely to be in sex-segregated jobs (Holden and Hansen, 1987).

Compared to voluntary part-time workers, involuntary part-time workers are more likely to be male, teens, black, and lower skilled (Bednarzik, 1975, 1983; Shank, 1986). There are also demographic differences among involuntary part-time workers, depending on the reason for such work (Terry, 1981; Bednarzik, 1983).

Part-time workers are much more likely to work nonstandard (nondaytime and/or nonweekday) shifts than are full-time workers. While only 16% of full-time workers regularly work nonstandard shifts, fully 49% of part-timers do so (Mellor, 1986). Teens are more likely than other part-time workers to work nonstandard shifts (Smith, 1986). Women who work part-time and have children are more likely to be off work in the late afternoons than are other part-timers (Owen, 1978).

Part-time workers also have generally shorter job tenure. The propensity to leave part-time work is high, either to move out of the labor market or to move into full-time work (Long and Jones, 1981; Moen, 1985). There is very little research on the dynamics of part-time work over a worker's lifetime. Preliminary current work indicates that part-time work among adult women is only rarely used as a stepping stone between nonemployment and full-time employment, but is instead used as an alternative either to full-time employment or to nonemployment (Blank, 1989).

A growing literature is concerned with estimating labor supply choices that include part-time work option. These papers estimate the effect of a range of variables on the probability of choosing part-time vs. full-time jobs (Morgenstern and Hamovitch, 1976; Nakamura and Nakamura, 1983; Simpson, 1986). These estimates have also been extended to include a third labor market choice, namely, nonemployment. An ordered probit can estimate the probability of having desired hours that go from 0 (nonemployed), greater than 0 to 34 (part-time), and greater than 34 (full-time) (Long and Jones, 1980). More recent work has estimated even less restrictive maximum-likelihood models of labor market choices, allowing the determinants of labor force participation to differ from the determinants of part-time vs. full-time work. The results indicate that these two equations are different and should be separately estimated (Blank, 1988).

Most of this work produces similar results regarding the determinants of part-time work, although the data, the time periods, and the estimating techniques differ. Among workers, women with younger children and more children are more likely to work part-time, while nonwhites are more likely to work full-time. Women in households with higher levels of other income, either higher spousial earnings or larger amounts of nonearned household income, are more likely to work part-time.

Only one study has separated voluntary from involuntary part-time workers. Sundt (1988) estimates a joint model of desired and actual hours of work, allowing the actual hours of unemployed and involuntary part-timers to differ from their desired hours. She finds, consistent with raw data tabulations, that younger, less-educated, and nonwhite part-time workers are more likely to be involuntarily working part-time. The determinants of involuntary part-time work are very similar to the determinants of unemployment.

Overall, these estimated labor supply equations reinforce the conclusions from less statistically sophisticated studies. Part-time workers are a clearly distinguishable group of workers, whose personal and household characteristics provide explicit reasons for working fewer hours. In addition, the potential importance of differentiating involuntary from voluntary part-timers is underscored.

II. EMPLOYERS' USE OF PART-TIME WORKERS

A. How Do Firms Decide Whether to Use Part-Time Workers?

Firms can hire a given number of person-hours in a variety of ways, using combinations of part-time and full-time workers. The choice of employment patterns must depend upon the technological demands of firm production, the availability of workers willing to work certain hours, and the relative costs of employing workers on different hourly schedules.

Very little research is available that investigates part-time work from an establishment perspective. The most comprehensive survey was conducted by Nollen et al. (1978) in 1976 and interviewed 68 firms about their use (or nonuse) of part-time workers. The Bureau of National Affairs (BNA) has recently conducted a survey of 223 of its members on this issue (BNA, 1988). There are also other firm surveys with at least some information on part-time workers (Daski, 1974; Montgomery, 1988b; Tilly, 1988). Both Nollen et al. and the BNA conclude that the primary reason firms hire part-time workers is to resolve scheduling problems. Firms with high weekly and daily variance in workload were most likely to employ part-time workers. With far less frequency, firms also indicated they occasionally hired part-time workers because of an inability to recruit full-time, to avoid fringe benefit payments, to avoid layoffs, or to retain valued employees. Both studies conclude that firms appear to do little analysis of the overall economic benefits and costs of part-time vs. full-time workers; their strategy is to hire full-time, unless there are scheduling problems that part-time workers appear to solve. These surveys also indicate that it is larger, less unionized firms, in retail trade, finance, and service industries, with high percentages of clerical and service workers, who are most likely to employ part-time workers.

In recent years, part-time work has often been discussed as one aspect of firms' growing use of contingent workers. *Contingent work* has no formal definition, but is typically used as an inclusive term for all part-time, temporary, contracted, and leased workers (U.S. Department of Labor, 1988b). It is not clear, however, that all part-time workers should be included in this category. There is a clear implication in the term *contingent* that the employer does not consider either the worker or the job permanent. However, many part-time workers may stay in their jobs for as long as they desire and as long as their work performance is acceptable to the firm. Even when these workers leave, the firm will seek to hire new workers for these same jobs. In contrast, temporary work, defined as an employment situation in which both employer and employee share an ex ante understanding that the job is of limited duration, appears far more closely related to the idea of contingent work. Survey data indicate that the majority of temporary workers work full-time, although they are more likely to be part-time than are nontemporary workers (Hartmann and Lapidus, 1989). Thus, although some part-time workers are clearly contingent workers, considering part-time work per se as a manifestation of contingent work is probably neither accurate nor useful.

In contrast to research that focuses on direct survey questions asking firms to identify why they hire part-time workers, there are a variety of studies that attempt to estimate the determinants of part-time employment within a firm. Theories of employment demand emphasize the role of quasi-fixed labor costs (such as hiring and training costs) in determining the number of workers hired (Oi, 1962). Several papers have extended these models to encompass part-time and full-time employment choices (Owen, 1979; Montgomery, 1988b). Both the quasi-fixed costs associated with hiring a worker as well as the hourly compensation differential between part-time and full-time workers will affect the part-time/full-time mix in the firm. Regression analysis estimating the determinants of the share of part-time employment within firms finds that it is sensitive to the part-time/full-time wage differential (Owen, 1979; Ehrenberg et al., 1988), as well as to measures of training and hiring costs (Montgomery, 1988b). These estimates also confirm the survey results indicating that firms that use more part-timers are more likely to be in service industries and to be less capital intensive.

More recent work has also recognized that when the relative price of labor changes there may be both employment and hours effects; that is, firms can employ a different mix of part-time and full-time workers and they can also employ existing part-time and full-time workers for longer or shorter hours. Increases in fixed costs per worker, for instance, should decrease the number of part-time workers as well as increase the hours worked by existing part-timers (Fitzroy and Hart, 1986). Montgomery (1988a) finds that hours among part-timers are responsive to training costs, size of firm, and relative wage differentials.

Fringe benefit differences between part-time and full-time workers may also significantly affect their relative costs. This may be an increasingly important issue as the share of fringe benefits in total compensation has grown, although there has been a slight decline since the mid-1980s (Woodbury, 1983, 1989). Statutory fringe benefits, such as social security, unemployment compensation, disability insurance, and workers' compensation payments typically require a firm to make contributions based on a share of each worker's salary up to a maximum salary level. This increases the relative cost of part-time workers since their entire salary is usually subject to such taxes (Nollen et al., 1978). Other forms of fringe benefits, such as vacation pay, pensions, and health insurance, may or may not affect relative part-time/full-time costs. If part-timers are excluded from major fringe benefits, then they may have lower fringe costs than full-time workers. If fringes are prorated to hours and wages, there may be no part-time/full-time differential. If part-time workers are provided with the same fringes as full-time workers, they will have higher relative costs.

We have virtually no information on the extent to which fringe benefit costs affect the use of part-time workers. The only available estimates indicate that greater fringe benefit coverage for part-time workers is positively correlated with greater use of part-time workers, a seemingly perverse effect (Ehrenberg et al., 1988). However, the information available on fringe benefits is extremely limited in this study. It is true that fringe benefits have increased as a share of compensation at the same time as the use of part-time work has expanded; if expanded fringe benefits make part-time workers more costly, this at least has not been a dominant factor in determining part-time employment over the past few decades.

B. What Are the Advantages and Disadvantages of Using Part-Time Workers?

Given that a firm has decided to hire part-time workers (probably because of scheduling needs), how is the performance of those workers evaluated? While the standard image of a part-time worker may be that he or she is less stable and less reliable, this does not appear to be the experience of firms who employ these workers. Firms that use part-time workers tend to indicate that there is less absenteeism and less turnover among them than among full-time workers (Nollen et al., 1978; Ronen, 1984; Barnett, 1984). The suggestion is often made that part-time workers take fewer breaks and less personal time while on the job, and there is some evidence to support this (Mintz, 1978). Firms using part-time workers provide much more positive evaluations of their job performance than firms not using them, although this may merely reflect underlying differences in these firms' technology (Nolan et al., 1978).

Firms that use part-time workers list their disadvantages as additional administrative record keeping, training and supervision problems (especially when part-timers do not work standard hours), and lack of promotability. Part-timers are also considered particularly unsuitable for jobs involving coordinational or managerial tasks. Overall, employers generally indicate part-time workers are best suited for jobs involving discrete tasks that are necessary to meet peak demand problems (Nollen et al., 1978; Owen, 1979; BNA, 1988).

This perspective on part-time work is in conflict with the efforts of groups like the Association of Part-Time Professionals to expand the image of part-time work. "Permanent, professional part-timer" is still a contradiction in terms for many employers. Efforts to promote a more expanded role for part-time employees include Kahne's work on "new concept" part-time jobs (Kahne, 1985) and Applebaum's call for a restructuring of part-time work (Applebaum, 1986).

A recent survey of 31 firms by Tilly (1988) identified a few employers who used selected part-timers in an expanded role. Tilly distinguishes between "secondary" part-timers, members of the secondary labor force in low-wage jobs with few career opportunities, and "retention" part-timers, typically highly skilled and committed workers, once employed full-time, who are switched into part-time work in order to prevent them from leaving the firm (often women with young children). However, while some firms may treat certain part-time workers as skilled and permanent employees, the vast majority of employers do not appear to view their part-time workers in this way.

III. COMPENSATION FOR PART-TIME WORK

While the evidence indicates that it is scheduling and not compensation issues that determine whether employers hire part-time workers, nonetheless economists have paid a great deal of attention to part-time and full-time compensation differentials. The standard wisdom is that part-time jobs pay lower wages than full-time jobs, and virtually all of the evidence supports this conclusion. Every comparison of average part-time and full-time wages shows negative part-time differentials. It is clear that part-time jobs are disproportionately lower-wage jobs; among all individuals working at the minimum wage, 65% of them were part-time workers in 1986 (Mellor, 1987; Levitan and Conway, 1988).

Because economists generally expect that similar workers on similar jobs should earn similar wages, regardless of their hours of work, most research has explored whether part-time workers and part-time jobs are really similar to full-time workers and full-time jobs. Two primary differences are immediately apparent. First, on average, part-time workers are typically younger, less skilled, and less experienced than full-time workers. This implies that some of the part-time/full-time differential has nothing to do with part-time work per se, but relates to the human-capital characteristics of the workers. For instance, because teenagers compose such a large percentage of the part-time labor force, the average part-time/full-time wage differential for all workers is much larger than it is among adult workers only. Second, part-time jobs are often concentrated in low-wage industries and occupations. Full-time workers in these areas typically receive lower wages as well. While these lower wages may be a concern, they are again not the result of part-time work, per se.

Studies have attempted to estimate the effect of part-time work on wages using multivariate regressions that control for individual skills and (in some cases) job characteristics. Some researchers assume the effect of part-time work is simply to shift the average level of wages downward, equivalent to including a dummy variable in a wage regression (Ehrenberg et al., 1988); others estimate entirely separate wage regressions for part-time and full-time workers, allowing all the coefficients on the determinants of wages to vary (Owen, 1979; Long and Jones,

1981). Ehrenberg et al. estimate wage equations for workers in 44 separate industries and find significant negative part-time effects in 40 of them. Owen finds that almost half of the raw part-time/full-time differential is due to individual human-capital differences among workers; Long and Jones estimate that 30% of the raw differential is due to individual differences among workers and another 55% is due to the industry and occupational location of the workers. All of these studies find significant negative part-time differentials even after accounting for individual and job characteristics.

More recent work has included an adjustment for individual selection into part-time or full-time work as part of the wage estimates. If there are particular characteristics of workers that make them more likely to work part-time and also lower their wage rate, then estimating wages without taking account of the fact that certain workers have explicitly chosen part-time work will overestimate the part-time/full-time wage differential. Most of these studies estimate a probit equation on part-time/full-time work among workers and use these results to calculate the so-called Heckman selectivity term, which is then included in separate part-time and full-time wage regressions (Nakamura and Nakamura, 1983; Simpson, 1986; Gordon, 1987; Main, 1987). The effect of this correction differs across the samples. Nakamura and Nakamura (1983) and Gordon (1987) both find that this correction is important, while Simpson (using Canadian data) and Main (using British data) find that it is not. Results as to the importance of individual characteristics are similar to those cited above. For instance, Main finds that half of the part-time/full-time difference in his British data is due to human-capital differences among the workers. Simpson finds that as much as two-thirds of the differential in his 1981 Canadian data is due to individual differences between workers.

Blank (1990) has attempted to account even more fully for the self-selection of workers into particular labor market slots. She estimates a full maximum-likelihood model using an intercorrelated set of equations for part-time wages, full-time wages, choice into the labor market, and choice into part-time work. With this fuller selectivity adjustment (accounting for both selection into the labor market as well as selection into part-time work), her results are notably different from earlier studies: the impact of part-time work on wages becomes positive for women, with particularly strong effects in professional and managerial jobs. These estimates, based on 1987 *Current Population Survey* (CPS) data on women, have been duplicated on similar data for 1983. In this earlier year, part-time work negatively affects wages in a few occupations (primarily service and sales), but again has a positive effect on professional and managerial workers' wages. In contrast to the results for women, male part-time workers continue to receive lower wages than equivalent full-time workers, even with full selectivity adjustments. These results indicate the important role that selection into part-time work (heavily determined by household demographics, particularly children) has on the wages women receive. In addition, Blank's study of wages explicitly includes information on involuntary part-time workers in the wage regressions. She finds that involuntary part-timers receive lower wages than either voluntary part-timers or full-time workers, even after personal and job-related characteristics are accounted for.

Separate estimation of part-time/full-time wage equations allows the wage effects of such characteristics as education and experience to differ between the two groups of workers. It is often assumed that part-time work offers lower returns to human-capital investments. Interestingly, most of the research cited above shows no difference in the returns to education between part-time and full-time workers.[6] However, virtually all of the studies find that worker age (a proxy for experience in much of this research) or actual worker experience (when available) has a lower return for part-time workers. Several researchers have gone beyond investigating the effect of total past experience on current wages and have utilized data sources that allow them to include information on past involvement in part-time vs. full-time work (Jones and Long, 1979; Corcoran et al., 1983; Sundt, 1987). All of these studies uniformly conclude that past spells of part-time work have no positive effect on current wages (for part-time or full-time workers), while past spells of full-time work clearly increase current wages. In a similar manner, part-time workers receive little "rebound" effect on their wages when reentering the workforce after a period of absence, while full-time workers' wages will recover quite rapidly from the effects of a period of nonemployment (Sundt, 1987).

Total compensation includes fringe benefits as well as wages. As noted above, fringes were an increasing share of the compensation package until the mid-1980s. It is possible that lower part-time cash wages for some workers could offset higher fringe compensation, however, the evidence does not support this idea. All evidence indicates that part-time workers unambiguously receive lower fringes. This evidence ranges from employer survey data (BNA, 1988), to tabulations of worker-reported data (Conway, 1988; Blank, 1990), to multivariate regressions estimating the likelihood of receiving particular fringe benefits (Ichniowski and Preston, 1986; Ehrenberg et al., 1988), to full selectivity-corrected models (Blank, 1990).[7] It should be noted that much of this research focuses on very limited and poorly defined fringe benefit measures (the CPS only asks if workers are covered by a pension plan and if they are covered by a health plan on their primary job). However, it appears that employers are far more likely to exclude part-time workers completely from fringe benefit plans than to include them in some prorated fashion. In general, most fringe benefits are received by only about half as many part-time as full-time workers.[8]

While the evidence seems overwhelming that part-time workers are paid less than full-time workers when total wage and fringe compensation is calculated, none of these studies have adequate data to explore the effects of nonwage, nonfringe differentials between part-time and full-time jobs. There is virtually no information on the extent to which part-time workers value the shorter hours, more flexible hours, or simpler set of work tasks that part-time work often involves. Among those who work part-time voluntarily, their household constraints and/or personal tastes must lead them to value the time flexibility that part-time work allows for non–labor market activities more highly than the compensation. The heavy use of part-time work among individuals who have major non–labor market commitments (teenagers in school, women with children) indicates the importance of these nonwage issues.

IV. HOUSEHOLD WELL-BEING AMONG PART-TIME WORKERS

There is an ongoing concern among observers of the labor market that part-time work is a policy problem, and that part-time jobs create hardship for those in them (Nine to Five, 1986; Conway, 1988). The lower average compensation received by part-time workers and their lack of protection through fringe benefits is cited as consistent with this perspective. However, whether part-time work represents a problem or a positive labor market choice depends largely on the household situation of part-time workers. Many teenage and married female part-time workers are in households in which there are other household members working full-time. This does not imply that the labor market situation of these part-time workers is unimportant, since some of these workers may provide an important supplement to household income with their earnings. However, many part-time workers may focus more on the nonwage advantages of part-time jobs rather than on their financial implications.

In contrast, the evidence indicating particularly low compensation among involuntary part-time employees, whose hours of work are clearly constrained, may be a serious concern indeed. And even among those workers who indicate that they were only seeking part-time work, there may be some individuals who face difficult hours constraints. For instance, lack of adequate child care, transportation difficulties, or health problems on the part of the household head can lead to "voluntary" part-time work that results in inadequate household income levels. Particularly among women heading households with young children, the lack of health insurance, life insurance, or pension coverage in part-time work may create long-term problems. Unfortunately, there is no research that explicitly addresses the question, When does part-time work cause household distress? But there are bits of evidence that can be brought to bear upon this issue.

In the mid-1980s 20% of all part-time workers were household heads. These were primarily single women with young children, young single individuals, and elderly workers. Part-time workers were disproportionately likely to be poor, especially involuntary part-timers. More than one-third of all households containing an involuntary part-time worker also received some type of government transfer assistance (Nine to Five, 1986; Levitan and Conway, 1988).

One of the main determinants of part-time work for women with children is the availability of child care arrangements. Evidence indicates that this is a serious constraint for many. In a survey from the late 1970s, fully 23.5% of all part-time working women with children indicated that they would work more if they could find child care (Presser and Baldwin, 1980). In part, this is a statement about low part-time wages (at a high enough price, child care can almost always be purchased).

Another indicator of problem part-time work is the extent of multiple job holding among part-time workers. People holding multiple part-time jobs are typically women. (Men who hold multiple jobs tend to have one full-time and one part-time job.) Multiple part-time job holders are likely to include at least one job that is involuntarily part-time (Applebaum, 1986; Levitan and Conway, 1988).

All of these facts do not fit together neatly. But there is evidence here that at least some subgroup of part-time workers is experiencing serious household income shortfalls, although the exact size and significance of this problem is not known. A disproportionate number of these workers are surely working part-time because of inadequate labor market demand. But even among the voluntary part-timers, there may be exogenous constraints that prevent greater work effort and that result in family hardship. Our understanding of the advantages and disadvantages of part-time work would benefit by closer research attention to the correlations between part-time work and household income adequacy.

V.   POLICY ISSUES FOR PART-TIME WORKERS

Much of the public discussion of part-time jobs focuses on the differences in average compensation between part-time and full-time work. Lower part-time wages and fringes are generally decried by many observers of part-time work (Nine to Five, 1986; Applebaum, 1986). This is perhaps because wages are the most visible measure of a job's return to the worker. However, the preceding discussion indicates that average compensation differences between part-time and full-time work should probably not be a primary policy concern, for at least four reasons.

First, some large amount of the part-time/full-time wage differential is clearly due to the different skills and experience levels of part-time workers and to the occupational distribution of part-time jobs.

Second, it appears that certain part-time workers are not seriously disadvantaged in terms of wages. Among professional and managerial employees who select part-time work, there is evidence they may earn even more than their equivalent full-time coworkers. Many of these workers are likely to be previous full-time employees who have switched to a part-time job during a period when other family or personal involvements limit their labor market commitment. Yet, instead of leaving the labor market entirely, they choose to remain as part-timers, indicating their strong career orientation as well as the desire of firms to retain their skills and experience.

Third, even for those workers who are earning less than equally trained full-time colleagues, there are few good measures of the value of the nonwage advantages they may be receiving from their jobs; these may provide a compensating differential for lower hourly wages or fringes. Given the commitment many part-time workers have to nonmarket activities such as family and school, and given that many part-timers are in households with full-time earners, part-time work—even at lower wages—will often represent an optimal choice.

Fourth, appropriate wage payments require not only an understanding of the skills of the worker, but also the demands of the job. As long as employers primarily use part-timers in narrowly defined jobs that require little training and have few promotion opportunities, the productivity of part-time workers may well remain below that of full-time workers. In this case, the policy concern is not with the wages of the available jobs, but with the set of jobs that are offered to potential part-time workers.

For these reasons, observed differences in compensation between part-time and full-time workers may or may not signal real policy concerns. However, there are at least three policy issues, strongly correlated with certain aspects of part-time/full-time compensation differences, which relate more clearly to well-defined problems.

A. Encouraging Employers to Explore a Broader Set of Part-Time Options

The heterogeneity of the part-time labor force implies that current part-time work options are surely very appropriate for some group of part-time workers. A teenager seeking to earn extra income may find a part-time job at a local fast-food chain completely acceptable. However, certain groups of part-time workers are more limited by low-wage, noncareer-oriented part-time jobs.

Women's education levels and labor market experience have increased steadily during this century. Women have labor market talents that firms want, and many women have strong work commitments. Yet, at the same time, many married women experience periods when their commitments to family and children make full-time employment difficult. Employers will face a growing challenge to provide job options for these women during years when they seek to be committed and loyal—but part-time—workers. This may require reconceptualizing the organizational structure and task assignments within jobs, to allow for easier coordination between workers on different hours schedules. It may lead to a variety of alternative job arrangements such as job sharing and flexible schedules for full-time workers as well.

Some initial steps in this direction have been taken. The Federal Employees Part-Time Career Employment Act of 1978 lays out guidelines for part-time compensation and encourages federal employers to offer part-time jobs to interested workers (Ronen, 1984). A number of states have similar legislation (Olmsted, 1983). Further work in this area should include research into the ways in which current employers are successfully dealing with the coordination and use of permanent part-time employees.

B.   Encouraging Part-Time Employers to Design Flexible Fringe Benefit Plans

One of the biggest stumbling blocks to providing career-oriented part-time jobs is the demand that such jobs include fringe benefits, which many firms fear will create unacceptably large fixed costs for part-time workers. However, from the worker's perspective, the lack of fringe benefits in part-time jobs may cause serious hardship, and clearly decreases the compensation associated with such jobs.

However, there are ways to make fringe benefits available to part-time workers without raising their cost relative to full-time workers. Some fringes can easily be prorated to the hours of the part-time worker. But other fringes may be more "lumpy" and not easily divisible. One option is to provide "cafeteria" benefit plans, in which workers can choose the mix of fringe benefits they want to receive, with the total value prorated to their work hours (Chollett, 1984).

The changes in tax provisions governing pensions have increased the popularity of defined-contribution plans relative to defined-benefit plans. The former are easier to prorate, as they base pension payments on the amount paid into the fund, while the latter establish a guaranteed future pension payment, and then adjust payments accordingly.

With regard to health insurance, often a very difficult fringe benefit to prorate, firms may experiment with higher copayments for part-time workers. In addition, the concern about lack of health insurance coverage for many households has prompted increasing government interest in incentive schemes (tax incentives are suggested most frequently) that encourage employers to provide health coverage for more employees. There is also increasing discussion of the potential for small employers (who often face extremely high health insurance premiums) to form multiple-employer trusts to engage in risk pooling. The Tax Reform Act of 1986 included a clause (to have been implemented in 1989) requiring employers to be nondiscriminatory in health benefits for all employees working more than 17.5 hours/week (Conway, 1988; BNA, 1988). Although this clause was repealed before its implementation, serious interest in similar legislation continues.

C.   Assisting Involuntary Part-Time Workers

The one group of part-time workers who appear to face the greatest problems are involuntary part-timers. The growing share of involuntary part-time work in the labor force over the past two decades makes this a very current concern. The relatively large number of involuntary part-time workers is particularly surprising in the late 1980s, a period of sustained growth and falling unemployment.

The many similarities between involuntary part-time workers and the unemployed implies that the solutions for unemployment are also the solutions for involuntary part-time employment. Strong macroeconomic growth that results in rising labor demand is clearly the best way to shrink the size of the involuntary part-time work force.

However, given the regular occurrence of economic cycles, involuntary part-time employment is unlikely to disappear in the near future. One concern is that unemployment insurance (UI), which partially replaces the wages of those who lose their jobs entirely, is not available to cushion the wage losses of involuntary part-timers who have been put on shortened hours.[9] In some circumstances, being placed on shortened hours involuntarily may leave a worker in a worse situation than he or she would face if completely unemployed and eligible for UI. One policy alternative is an expansion of the UI system to include short-time compensation, which would partially replace the earnings of those constrained to low levels of employment due to slack labor market demand. In fact, a few states do have some provision for this in their UI system. Research indicates that short-time compensation results in greater work sharing, rather than layoffs, thereby spreading the costs of unemployment more broadly across the labor market (Hamermesh, 1989).

VI. CONCLUSIONS AND RESEARCH SUGGESTIONS

The primary conclusion in this paper is that part-time work is a significant aspect of the U.S. labor market, encompassing almost 20 million workers in 1988. The share of part-time workers has increased gradually over time, with recent increases in the incidence of involuntary part-time employment. Part-time work is used by a very diverse range of workers, particularly teens, older workers, and women with children. As a result, thinking about the part-time labor market as a single group of workers is probably not useful; different part-time workers may have very different concerns and needs.

The evidence available indicates that most employers think of part-time workers in a single context: as nonpromotable workers who solve particular scheduling and peak-demand problems within the firm. However, there is evidence of a growing awareness among employers that there may be other types of part-time workers and other types of part-time jobs. Part-time workers in professional and managerial occupations appear to be at least as well-paid as their full-time fellow workers. The demands of skilled women who seek to work during their child-rearing years may lead to a growing number of "professional part-time" jobs, and some reconceptualization of part-time work and part-time workers.

Economywide growth is forecast in the service, retail, and financial industries, which hire a substantial fraction of part-time workers. This will surely continue to open up part-time jobs to workers interested in taking them. Continued increases are expected in the percentage of women who remain in the labor market while their children are young, providing an ongoing stream of part-time workers (although an increasing number of these women may be interested in more challenging jobs than part-time work has typically provided). While teenagers are currently a shrinking percentage of the labor force, the coming decade will begin to see the maturing of the baby boom children's children, increasing the number of teenagers. In addition, shortages of teen workers in some areas have led firms to offer incentives to older workers to work part-time following retirement from their primary job. The current macroeconomic conditions, with steady growth and a low unemployment rate, suggest that involuntary part-time employment will continue to fall over the next few years. However, any future economic slowdown may turn this around quickly.

There are several issues relating to part-time work about which we currently know too little. To understand the part-time labor market better and to make intelligent public policy choices, useful future research and data projects might include the following:

(1) The lack of fringe benefits in part-time jobs is an ongoing point of concern among part-time workers—voluntary and involuntary alike. For some households this clearly causes severe problems. Yet we know very little about the relationship between part-time jobs and fringe benefit provisions. A significant number of part-time workers are covered by a wide range of fringes, while other part-time workers receive almost none. It would be useful to conduct an employer survey that inquires into fringe benefit policies among employers with part-time employees, identifying which employers offer fringes to part-time workers, why they offer them, and the type of fringe benefits programs they operate. Other useful research might involve pilot studies of potential schemes designed to encourage prorated fringe benefit coverage among employers of part-time workers, such as "cafeteria plans" or health plans with prorated cost sharing.

(2) We have tended to treat all part-time workers who say they were only looking for part-time work as identical, without inquiring into their reasons for seeking part-time work. This leaves a great deal of uncertainty about the nature of the labor market and household constraints faced by those who choose part-time work. It would be an extremely useful project to fund research (perhaps a supplement to the CPS) that inquires more closely into the child care, transportation, health, and work options of those who are classified as voluntary part-time workers. This would provide information on the extent to which the part-time employment of these workers is a positive labor market choice, or a second-best alternative chosen because of other serious household constraints. Understanding the nature of the constraints on voluntary part-time workers will also help in the

planning of other government programs designed to enhance women's labor market opportunities, such as child care assistance or welfare reform.

(3) There is a need to understand better the impact of part-time work on the well-being of households that contain part-time workers. There is no serious research that cohesively studies the relationship between part-time work and household financial responsibilities, or the causality between part-time work and household poverty, government transfer usage, or other measures of household economic security. An important aspect of such research should be to investigate the impact of the increase in involuntary part-time employment and in part-time employment among men on household well-being.

(4) We need to understand better how the labor market meets the demand by women for part-time jobs at certain points in their life, particularly when these women are predominantly skilled, full-time, and long-term employees. First, we need to understand how women workers manage this transition. What part-time jobs do they find? Do they change jobs or make arrangements with current employers? What is the career cost of spending time as a part-time worker? How does their part-time labor market work affect the structure of their household work? How do these workers reenter full-time work? Second, we need to understand the effect of these labor market choices on employers. How many employers retain former full-time employees as current part-time employees? Under what circumstances do they make these arrangements? What are the effects on the operation, organization, and productivity of the workplace? The phenomenon of women who marry, raise children, and also pursue lifelong labor market involvements is an increasingly important one in our society, and one that is only poorly understood. Similar questions can also be asked regarding elderly workers who may seek to move from full-time into part-time work rather than retiring completely.

ACKNOWLEDGMENTS

This project was funded under Purchase Order No. 99-9-4757-75-009-04 from the U.S. Department of Labor, Commission on Workforce Quality and Labor Market Efficiency. Opinions stated in this document do not necessarily represent the official position or policy of the U.S. Department of Labor, Commission on Workforce Quality and Labor Market Efficiency.

NOTES

1. All 1955–1967 data used in this paper are from the U.S. Department of Labor (1988a, Table A-22). All 1968–1988 data are from the U.S. Department of Labor (1989, Table 23). These numbers are based on all persons at work, age 16 and over, in nonagricultural industries, tabulated from the *Current Population Survey*.

2. There is also a category for individuals who typically work full-time, but are working part-

time for noneconomic reasons (sickness, vacation, holiday, etc.). In official data, these persons are counted as full-time workers.

3. In contrast to the United States, Canada in 1976 redefined part-time work as less than 30 hours per week. A number of European countries also use lower definitions (Hedges and Gallogly, 1977).

4. See note 1 for data sources for Figures 1, 2, and 3.

5. In comparison to European economies, the United States has generated far fewer part-time jobs in recent decades. Between 1973 and 1981 half of all new jobs in Europe were part-time, while in the United States the number was one-fifth (Plewes, 1984). Cross-country comparisons of part-time work are often difficult, however, because of widely varying definitions.

6. The Long and Jones (1981) study is an exception.

7. In a similar manner to wages, Blank finds that involuntary part-timers receive even fewer fringes than other part-timers.

8. Provision of some fringe benefits is regulated by law. For instance, if a firm offers a pension plan, ERISA requires that all workers who are employed for more than 1000 hours over the year must be included in it.

9. Even voluntary part-time employees may be losers with regard to UI, since many states set minimum-earnings and/or minimum-hours requirements. Unemployed workers with prior annual earning or hours below these levels are ineligible for UI.

REFERENCES

Applebaum, Eileen (1986), "Restructuring Work: Temporary, Part-Time and At-Home Employment." In Heide I. Hartmann, Robert E. Kraut, and Louise A. Tilly (eds.), *Computer Chips and Paper Clips: Technology and Women's Employment*, Volume 2. Washington, DC: National Academy Press.

Barnett, Nancy (1984), "Part-Time: Workers' Mandate?" In *Part-Time Employment in America*. First National Conference on Part-Time Employment, 1983, National Association of Part-Time Professionals.

Bednarzik, Robert W. (1975), "Involuntary Part-Time Work: A Cyclical Analysis." *Monthly Labor Review* 98 (September):12–18.

——— (1983), "Short Workweeks During Economic Downturns." *Monthly Labor Review* 106 (June):3–11.

Blank, Rebecca M. (1988), "Simultaneously Modelling the Supply of Weeks and Hours of Work Among Female Household Heads." *Journal of Labor Economics* 6 (April):177-204.

——— (1989), "The Role of Part-Time Work in Women's Labor Market Choices over Time." *American Economic Review* 79 (May):295–299.

——— (1990), "Are Part-Time Jobs Bad Jobs?" In Gary Burtless (ed.), *A Future of Lousy Jobs?* Washington DC: Brookings Institution.

Bureau of National Affairs (BNA)(1988), "Special PPF Report: Part-Time and Other Alternative Staffing Practices." *Bulletin to Management* 39 (June 23).

Chollett, Deborah (1984), "Setting Up Employee Benefit Packages: Issues and Trends." In *Part-Time Employment in America*. First National Conference on Part-Time Employment, 1983, National Association of Part-Time Professionals.

Conway, Elizabeth (1988), "Working Along the Edge." *Business and Health* 6 (October):12–15.

Corcoran, Mary, Greg J. Duncan, and Michael Ponza (1983), "A Longitudinal Analysis of White Women's Wages." *Journal of Human Resources* 18 (Fall):497–519.

Daski, Robert S. (1974), "Area Wage Survey Test Focuses on Part-Timers." *Monthly Labor Review* 97 (April):60–62.

Deutermann, William V., Jr., and Scott Campbell Brown (1978), "Voluntary Part-Time Workers: A Growing Part of the Labor Force." *Monthly Labor Review* 101 (June):3–10.

Ehrenberg, Ronald G., Pamela Rosenberg, and Jeanne Li (1988), "Part-Time Employment in the United States." In Robert A. Hart (ed.), *Employment, Unemployment, and Labor Utilization.* London: George Allen and Unwin.

Fitzroy, Felix R. and Robert A. Hart (1986), "Part-time and Full-Time Employment: The Demand for Workers and Hours." Unpublished paper, University of Stirling, Stirling, Scotland.

Gordon, Anne R. (1987), "The Full-Time/Part-Time Wage Differential and the Choice to Work Part-Time for Young Married Women." Unpublished paper, University of Wisconsin, Madison.

Hamermesh, Daniel S. (1989), "Unemployment Insurance Financing, Short-Time Compensation, and Labor Demand." In *Investing in People, Background Papers,* Volume I. Commission on Workforce Quality and Labor Market Efficiency, U.S. Department of Labor. Washington, DC: U.S. Government Printing Office.

Hartmann, Heidi and June Lapidus (1989), "Temporary Work." In *Investing in People, Background Papers,* Volume II. Commission on Workforce Quality and Labor Market Efficiency, U.S. Department of Labor. Washington DC: U.S. Government Printing Office.

Hedges, Janice N. and Stephen J. Gallogly (1977), "Full and Part-Time: A Review of Definitions." *Monthly Labor Review* 100 (March):21–28.

Holden, Karen C. and W. Lee Hansen (1987), "Occupational Segregation among Part-Timers and Full-Timers." In Claire Brown and Joseph A. Peckman (eds.), *Gender in the Workplace.* Washington DC: The Brookings Institution.

Holland, Susan S. (1966), "Trends in Full- and Part-Time Employment." *Employment and Earnings* 12 (June):6–22.

Ichniowski, Bernard E. and Anne E. Preston (1986), "New Trends in Part-Time Employment." *Industrial Relations Research Association, 38th Annual Proceedings, December 28–30, 1985,* pp. 60–71.

Jones, Ethel B. and James E. Long (1979), "Part-Week Work and Human Capital Investment by Married Women." *Journal of Human Resources* 14 (Fall):563–578.

Kahne, Hilde (1985), *Reconceiving Part-Time Work.* Totawa, NJ: Rowman and Allenheld.

Leon, Carol and Robert W. Bednarzik (1978), "A Profile of Women on Part-Time Schedules." *Monthly Labor Review* 101 (October):3–12.

Levitan, Sar A. and Elizabeth A. Conway (1988), "Part-Timers: Living on Half Rations." *Challenge* 31 (May–June):9–16.

Long, James E. and Ethel B. Jones (1980), "Part-Week Work by Married Women." *Southern Economic Journal* 46 (January):716–725.

———— (1981), "Married Women in Part-Time Employment." *Industrial and Labor Relations Review* 34 (April):413–425.

Main, Brian G. (1987), "Hourly Earnings of Female Part-Time Versus Full-Time Employees." Unpublished paper, University of St. Andrews, St. Andrews, Scotland.

Mellor, Earl F. (1986), "Shift Work and Flexitime: How Prevalent Are They?" *Monthly Labor Review* 109 (November):14–21.

———— (1987), "Workers at the Minimum Wage or Less: Who They Are and the Jobs They Hold." *Monthly Labor Review* 110 (July):34–38.

Mellor, Earl F. and William Parks II (1988), "A Year's Work: Labor Force Activity from a Different Perspective." *Monthly Labor Review* 111 (September):13–18.

Mintz, Judith (1978), "Part-Time Work: The Effect of Fragmentation on Employees." Report to the Manpower Administration, U.S. Department of Labor, Washington, DC.

Moen, Phillis (1985), "Continuities and Discontinuities in Women's Labor Force Activity." In Glen H. Elder, Jr. (ed.), *Life Course Dynamics: Trajectories and Transitions, 1968–1980.* Ithaca, NY: Cornell University Press.

Montgomery, Mark (1988a), "Hours of Part-Time and Full-Time Workers at the Same Firm." *Industrial Relations* 27 (Fall):394–406.

———— (1988b), "On the Determinants of Employer Demand for Part-Time Workers." *Review of Economics and Statistics* 70 (February):112–117.

Morgenstern, Richard D. and Hamovitch, William (1976), "Labor Supply of Married Women in Part-Time and Full-Time Occupations." *Industrial and Labor Relations Review* 30 (October):59–67.

Nakamura, Alice and Masao Nakamura (1983), "Part-Time and Full-Time Work Behavior of Married Women." *Canadian Journal of Economics* 16 (May):229–257.

Nardone, Thomas J. (1986), "Part-Time Workers: Who Are They?" *Monthly Labor Review* 109 (February):13–19.

Nine to Five (1986), *Working at the Margins: Part-Time and Temporary Workers in the United States.* Clevland, OH:National Association of Working Women.

Nollen, Stanley D., Brenda B. Eddy, and Virginia H. Martin (1978), *Permanent Part-Time Employment.* New York: Praeger.

Oi, Walter (1962), "Labor as a Quasi-Fixed Factor." *Journal of Political Economy* 70 (December):538–555.

Olmsted, Barney (1983), "Changing Times: The Use of Reduced Work Time Options in the United States." *International Labour Review* 122 (July–August):479–492.

Owen, John (1978), "Why Part-Time Workers Tend to Be in Low-Wage Jobs." *Monthly Labor Review* 101 (June):11–14.

——— (1979), *Working Hours.* Lexington, MA: D.C. Heath.

Plewes, Thomas (1984), "Profile of the Part-Time Worker." In *Part-Time Employment in America.* First National Conference on Part-Time Employment, 1983, Association of Part-Time Professionals.

Presser, Harriet B. and Wendy Baldwin (1980), "Child Care As a Constraint on Employment." *American Journal of Sociology* 85 (March):1202–1213.

Ronen, Simcha (1984), *Alternative Work Schedules.* Homewood, IL: Dow Jones–Irwin.

Shank, Susan E. (1986), "Preferred Hours of Work and Corresponding Earnings." *Monthly Labor Review* 109 (November):40–44.

Simpson, Wayne (1986), "Analysis of Part-Time Pay in Canada." *Canadian Journal of Economics* 19 (November):798–807.

Smith, Shirley J. (1986), "The Growing Diversity of Work Schedules." *Monthly Labor Review* 109 (November):7–13.

Stein, Robert L. and Jane L. Meredith (1960), "Growth and Characteristics of the Part-Time Work Force." *Monthly Labor Review* 83 (November):1166–1175.

Sundt, Leslie A. (1987), "The Effect of Work Interruption on Subsequent Earnings." Unpublished paper, University of Arizona, Tucson.

——— (1988), " 'Involuntary' Employment and Labor Market Constraints upon Women." Unpublished paper, University of Arizona, Tucson.

Terry, Sylvia L. (1981), "Involuntary Part-Time Work: New Information from the CPS." *Monthly Labor Review* 104 (February):70–74.

Tilly, Chris. (1988), "Highs and Lows of Part-Time Employment." Unpublished paper, University of Lowell, Lowell, MA.

U.S. Department of Labor (Bureau of Labor Statistics) (1988a), *Labor Force Statistics Derived from the Current Population Survey, 1948–1987.* Washington, DC: U.S. Government Printing Office.

——— (1988b), *Flexible Workstyles: A Look at Contingent Labor.* Washington DC: U.S. Government Printing Office.

——— (1989), (Bureau of Labor Statistics) *Handbook of Labor Statistics,* Bulletin 2340. Washington, DC: U.S. Government Printing Office.

Woodbury, Stephen A. (1983), "Substitution Between Wage and Nonwage Benefits." *American Economic Review* 73 (March):166–182.

——— (1989), "Current Economic Issues in Employee Benefits." In *Investing in People, Background Papers,* Volume II. Commission on Workforce Quality and Labor Market Efficiency, U.S. Department of Labor. Washington, DC: U.S. Government Printing Office.

ECONOMIC INCENTIVES AND THE LABOR FORCE PARTICIPATION OF OLDER WORKERS

Richard V. Burkhauser and Joseph F. Quinn

No demographic phenomenon has provided a greater ongoing challenge to the policymaker's art than the aging of the post–World War II baby-boomers. In the 1950s they created a shortage of maternity beds and four-bedroom housing in the suburbs. In the 1960s they forced a massive increase in public-school facilities. In the 1970s and 1980s, boomers sorely tested the economy's ability to create jobs for young adults.

This continuing shift in the age structure has been a leading cause of economic and social changes in American society over the past four decades. It is notable that these changes have led to expansions as well as contractions of services. The trek to the suburban ranch homes of the 1950s is now matched by a return to the two- and three-bedroom condos in the central cities. Despite the echo effect of the baby-boomers' own babies, maternity facilities are well below their peak years. School enrollment is down and belt tightening is seen throughout the education industry.

Such ebbs and flows in the product market have their counterpart in the labor market. Many policies that developed in an era when job creation was the major

Research in Labor Economics, Volume 11, pages 159–179.
Copyright © 1990 by JAI Press Inc.
All rights of reproduction in any form reserved.
ISBN: 1-555938-080-2

labor market issue must be reconsidered as the possibility of future labor shortages arise.

In this chapter, we describe the changes in labor force participation of older workers over the last two decades and summarize the available evidence regarding the importance of economic and other factors in those decisions. We argue that our current retirement system is far from neutral with respect to work effort across one's lifetime. Rather it systematically encourages individuals to work full-time with a single firm until retirement age and then to go into full-time retirement. Reforms initiated in the 1970s and early 1980s are not likely to change these incentives dramatically unless employers also change the benefit calculation rules of their retirement plans.

I. LABOR SUPPLY AT OLDER AGES

The recent decline in the labor force participation rates of older Americans is well known and well documented. Since some of the retirement incentives discussed below go into effect at particular ages, it is useful to look at trends for one-year age categories.

Table 1 shows that participation trends during the last half-century have varied over time and across ages. The first great reduction in the work efforts of older men occurred during the 1950s, as the coverage of the Social Security system expanded dramatically. The participation rates of men aged 65 and over fell by about a quarter, while those of men aged 55, 60, and 63, ineligible for benefits, remained about the same. Between 1960 and 1970 there were only modest declines for these older men. Labor force participation of those aged 55 and 60 continued to increase slightly during this decade of strong economic growth. Men aged 62 to 64 were first eligible for Social Security retirement benefits in 1961, and their labor force participation fell by nearly 10% between then and 1970. Between 1970 and 1980 substantial reductions in labor force participation occurred at each age between 55 and 70. In the early 1980s, the declines were more modest. And over the last few years, the labor force participation rates of men aged 65, 68, and 70 have actually increased.

Figure 1 shows the dramatic changes in male participation rates by individual ages (55 to 70) between 1968 and 1989. Over these two decades, participation fell for every single age. In absolute terms, the declines are the largest between ages 62 and 65, the ages of eligibility for reduced and full Social Security retirement benefits. But the declines are substantial as early as age 55 and as late as 70. In proportional terms (as a percentage of the 1968 rate), the decreases stay large past age 65. For men 62 and older, participation rates have dropped by 33 to 45% over the past 20 years.

The trends for older women are much less dramatic. The five-year cohort pictures over the past two decades are basically flat—the combined effects of

Table 1.   Male Labor Force Participation Rates
by Age, 1940–1989[a]

Year	Age					
	55	60	63	65	68	70
1940	90.9	82.9	78.2	66.1	54.9	43.4
1950	87.8	82.1	77.6	67.7	54.2	44.5
1960	89.9	83.2	75.7	53.6	39.4	33.2
1970	91.8	83.9	69.4	49.9	39.4	30.1
1972	90.7	82.1	66.5	45.2	33.8	27.1
1974	88.0	79.0	59.2	39.8	27.7	23.5
1976	87.1	75.5	55.7	36.6	26.7	22.4
1978	85.8	74.4	52.2	36.3	28.7	21.7
1980	84.9	74.0	52.3	35.2	24.1	21.3
1982	86.4	72.1	45.2	30.6	24.8	21.1
1984	84.3	70.2	48.2	30.4	21.3	18.8
1985	83.7	71.0	44.7	30.5	20.5	15.9
1986	84.1	69.2	44.3	30.7	20.7	17.1
1987	83.9	69.8	45.6	31.7	22.9	17.1
1988	82.5	68.8	45.0	31.1	22.5	18.1
1989	83.7	70.7	44.5	31.4	22.2	17.9

[a]*Source:* Labor force participation rates for 1940, 1950, and 1960 are
based on decennial U.S. census data. Thereafter, they are
from unpublished department of labor statistics, based on annual *Consumer Population Survey* (CPS) labor force participation questions.

increased participation by women and decreased participation by the elderly. For
elderly women, they approximately cancel. Slight declines are observed for
women 60 and older, and a small increase for those 55 to 59.

Further investigation reveals that the retreat from work at older ages is even
greater than these participation statistics reveal. Fewer older Americans are
working and, of the ones who are, fewer are working full-time. In 1989, nearly
half of the employed men and more than half of the employed women aged 65
and over were working part-time (and the vast majority voluntarily), compared to
about 6% of the men and 23% of the women less than 65. The proportion of older
Americans employed part-time has been growing over time—from one-third to
nearly one-half for men, and from 50 to 60% for women between 1968 and the
present.

Finally, older workers are more likely to be self-employed than are members
of any other age group. In 1988, one-quarter of all working men over 64 were
self-employed, compared to less than 10% overall. The self-employed are less
likely to retire than are wage and salary workers, and many of the latter have
turned to self-employment late in life (Quinn, 1980; Fuchs, 1982). Both Becker
(1984) and Blau (1987) suggest that the number of self-employed is currently on
the rise.

Figure 1.   Decrease in Labor Force Participation Rates between 1968 and 1989,
Men Aged 55 to 70

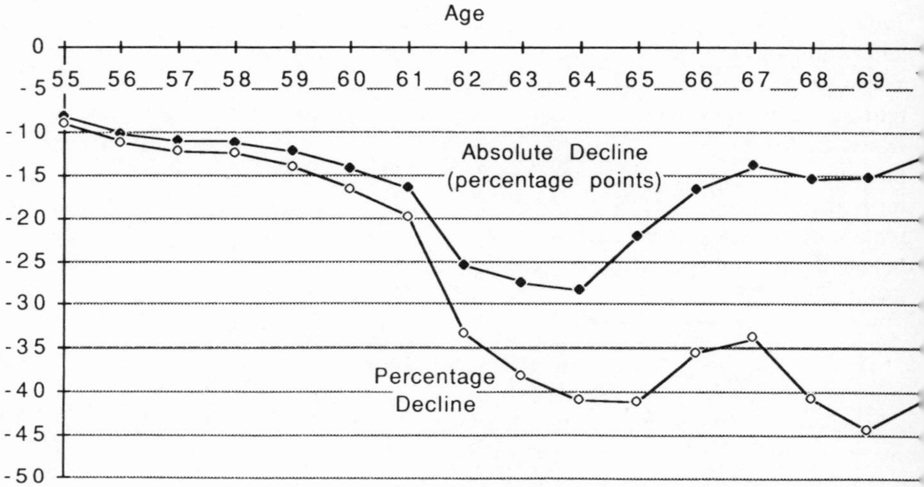

II.   DETERMINANTS OF THE RETIREMENT DECISION

The labor supply of older Americans has declined dramatically over the past four decades. Work beyond age 65 was once common but is now rare. Circumstantial and econometric evidence suggests that our retirement income programs have played an important role in this drama. Social Security and employer pensions grew significantly over this same period and the financial incentives imbedded in these plans discourage work late in life.

Since its inception in 1935, the Social Security program has expanded coverage (which is now nearly universal), relaxed eligibility rules, and provided large increases in real benefits. Ycas and Grad (1987) estimate that by 1984 over 90% of all aged couples and single persons received Social Security benefits, and that this one source provided almost 40% of their aggregate income. Since 1950, real Social Security expenditures in 1987 dollars (excluding Medicare) have grown from $5 billion to well over $200 billion per year, from 2 to 20% of all federal spending, and from negligible to almost 5% of GNP (Quinn et al., 1990).

Over the postwar period, employer pensions have grown as well. Kotlikoff and Smith (1983, Table 4.1.1) report that the number of private pension plans in America rose from 14,000 to over 600,000 between 1950 and 1980. Turner and Beller (1989, Table 1.3) estimate that there were 870,000 plans in 1987, covering 42 million workers, 16 million of whom were covered by two or more plans.

Pension coverage increased from a quarter to a half of all private-sector wage and salary workers, and from 60 to 90% among state and local government workers (Kotlikoff and Smith, 1983, Tables 3.1.2 and 3.1.3; Turner and Beller, 1989, Table 13.2). The growth of Social Security and pension plans and the declining labor supply of the aged could be related for at least two reasons. Burkhauser and Warlick (1981), Moffitt (1984), and Boskin et al. (1987) have shown that cohorts retiring up to now have received aggregate Social Security benefits that far exceeded the present value of the contributions made by them and their employers. These intergenerational transfers of wealth may have financed earlier retirement. In addition, Social Security and pension plans alter the lifetime pattern of compensation for many workers, subsidizing work at some ages and penalizing it at others. We argue that these wage changes may have induced early retirement for many workers.

A.   Economic Incentives

There is growing evidence that the financial incentives inherent in our Social Security and employer pension plans are important determinants of work across an individual's life. Social Security and employer pensions not only affect work decisions at older ages but may also influence behavior at younger ages as well.

A one-period framework is inadequate for understanding retirement incentives. Social Security and employer pensions are multi-period in nature. Contributions are made during the work life and a stream of benefits is repaid later. The two are usually connected, although the association can be very loose. Current work decisions alter future benefits. Social Security benefits depend on one's average monthly earnings, which change with continued work. Employer pension plans are many and varied. Defined-benefit pensions, which provide primary coverage for most covered workers, are usually based on some combination of years of service and average salary, often over just the last few years.

Since retirement income rights are entitlements to future income, they are best described by the present discounted value of the expected stream—their asset or wealth equivalent. This depends on the size of the future benefits, when they are claimed, the life expectancy of the individual (and spouse, in some cases), and the discount rate. When viewed this way, these rights have positive value even before one is eligible to receive them.

Prior to eligibility, an additional year of work usually increases future benefits and therefore the asset value of pension rights. This *increase* in pension wealth (called pension accrual) is really part of compensation—the reward for working another year.

Kotlikoff and Wise (1985) and Ippolito (1987) have shown that the method by which defined-benefit accrual is usually calculated leads to substantial losses in pension wealth if a worker leaves full-time employment with a firm before the first age of pension eligibility. Allen et al. (1987) provided empirical evidence supporting this view. After eligibility, however, if one stays on the job, accrual is likely to fall and may become negative.

An employee already eligible for benefits who is considering working another year is really choosing between two retirement income streams, one starting today and another beginning in a year but with higher annual benefits. If the asset value of the second stream is larger, the employee receives a paycheck *plus* the wealth accrual for working that year. Total compensation exceeds traditionally defined earnings. But if the second (delayed) stream is smaller in present value, true compensation is less than the paycheck by the amount of the wealth loss. Research suggests that the latter is the case for many older workers. They suffer pay cuts if they stay on the job too long, not directly via the paycheck, but more subtly, through the details of their retirement income plans.

Burkhauser (1979) found that the value of the pension stream for a sample of United Auto Worker (UAW) workers fell by more than half between the ages of early and normal retirement. We used a large sample of older men from the Retirement History Study (RHS; Irelan, 1973) to estimate the size and the effect of the incentives imbedded in Social Security and in employer pension schemes (Burkhauser and Quinn, 1983a,b; Quinn and Burkhauser, 1983). Social Security benefits grow with additional years of work for two reasons. Average indexed monthly earnings (AIME) rise, which in turn increase the annual retirement benefit. In addition, those who claim benefits before age 65 suffer a permanent actuarial reduction of 6⅔% for each year of early receipt—a maximum reduction of 20% for those who start benefits at age 62. Viewed from the other end—age 62—there is an actuarial *reward* of 8.33% (6.67/0.8) for each year receipt is delayed, in addition to the benefit recalculation via the AIME. At age 65, this delayed retirement credit drops to 3% per year of delay. The price paid for higher benefits in the future is a year without benefits in the present. Social Security wealth may rise or fall, depending on the asset value of the two streams.

We found that for the median full-time worker in 1973, Social Security wealth rose slightly with continued work at ages 63 and 64. But at age 65, because of the drop in the delayed retirement credit, Social Security wealth decreased sharply for those who worked to age 66. The median wealth loss was about a third of annual pay—a significant pay cut indeed. The pension story was similar, although the estimates were less reliable because the pension data were much more limited.

Fields and Mitchell (1984a,b,c) examined the details of 14 specific pension plans and estimated the incentives facing workers at each age between 60 and 68. They found that the asset value of pension rights tended to rise and then fall with delayed retirement, peaking between ages 60 and 65. With samples of men from one of their pension plans and from the RHS, they calculated total lifetime income (from age 60 on) for each retirement age between 60 and 68. This is the sum of the present values of earnings, Social Security, and employer pension benefits. The total always rises with additional work, since earnings exceed retirement benefits. But the *increase* in the total (the true compensation for the additional year of work) falls monotonically, and at age 68 was less than 40% of what it was at age 60. This is the declining compensation profile facing older Americans.

Rhine (1984) surveyed executives of 363 companies and found that nearly two-thirds of the firms had attractive early-retirement provisions—either unreduced pension benefits, usually at age 62, for employers who met age and service requirements, or less than actuarial reductions, usually at age 55. These all encourage early retirement. One-third had also made "open-window" offers—additional financial incentives for older workers to leave available to them over short periods of time.

Finally, Kotlikoff and Wise (1989) studied the accrual patterns of nearly 1200 plans and found a wide variety of incentives. Their accrual rate is the annual change in pension wealth divided by wage earnings for that year. Positive accrual rates describe a wage supplement, and negative ones a wage cut. They find considerable evidence of the latter.

It is now generally agreed that retirement income rights are best viewed as assets whose values depend on when they are claimed. Changes in these asset values with continued work are part of compensation and wealth losses are equivalent to pay cuts. At some age—certainly by 65 but often much earlier—these retirement plans provide strong incentives to retire. Do workers respond to these inducements by leaving the job and perhaps the labor force as well?

Considerable research suggests that people behave as though they understand and respond to these incentives. Burkhauser (1979) showed that auto workers were more likely to accept pension benefits and leave the firm the larger the pension wealth loss associated with continued work. Rhine (1984) found that "employees in companies that provide attractive early-retirement benefits tend to retire earlier than those in companies without such incentives." With a much larger and more representative sample from the RHS, we found the same for both Social Security and pension wealth changes. In fact, we concluded that much of what looked like a mandatory retirement effect at age 65 was really due to the financial incentives that occurred at the same time (Burkhauser and Quinn, 1983b).

Burtless and Moffitt (1984, 1985) confirmed that the Social Security system influences retirement behavior. They defined retirement as a discontinuous drop in hours of work and found dramatic clustering of retirement around ages 62 (the earliest age of eligibility) and 65 (when the delayed-retirement credit drops). They also showed that retirees who continued to work reported earnings clustered around the amount that Social Security permitted without loss of benefits. More than a third earned between 80 and 110% of the exempt amount, and many more were below than above (Burtless and Moffitt, 1985).

Sickles and Taubman (1986), also using the RHS, combined earnings and the change in Social Security wealth into one variable and found that "the gain from postponing retirement [was] the most significant of the income variables." With a different methodology and data set, Mitchell and Fields (1984) concluded that "individuals who have more to gain by postponing retirement do in fact retire later." Kotlikoff and Wise (1989) studied the employees of one particular firm and showed that "inducements in the [pension] plan provisions to retire early have had a very substantial effect on the departure rates from the firm." In summary, it has even established that financial incentives do influence retirement behavior, although debate continues on the size of the effect.

B. Health

Financial incentives are important retirement determinants but they are certainly not the only ones. Individual decisions are extremely complex and depend on a vast number of factors, only some of which researchers can observe and measure. Physical and mental health, social networks, attitudes toward work and leisure, living arrangements, job characteristics, local labor market conditions, and expectations about the future are all undoubtedly important. They interact with the financial incentives on which economists have focused to bring about the final result.

In empirical work, poor health is almost always associated with earlier retirement [see Sammartino (1987) for a review of the recent literature on health and retirement]. The effects are large and significant, and generally more so for early (prior to age 65) and very early (prior to 62) retirees (Parnes, 1988). Exact comparisons between studies are impossible because of the variety of definitions of retirement and health. Many researchers are skeptical about the usefulness of subjective health evaluations, especially when given as a reason for retirement or as part of an application for health-related benefits (Johnson, 1977; Myers, 1982; Parsons, 1982; Bazzoli, 1985; Parnes and Less, 1985; Baily, 1987). One fear is that health may be viewed as a socially legitimate reason for stopping work and be mentioned even when it is not the primary reason. Quinn (1977) found that among RHS respondents who claimed that they had no health limitations and health better than that of their peers, 10% still claimed health as the primary motivation for retirement. On the other hand, Sammartino (1987) and Burtless (1987) argue that self-evaluated health may be a superior measure because it implicitly incorporates information about the quality of health required on the individual's actual job. No one denies that health is, was, and always will be an important factor. The debate concerns its measurement and the precise nature of its effect.

Some recent studies have focused on health measures other than self-defined status at retirement. Parsons (1982), Kingson (1982), and Anderson and Burkhauser (1985) utilized subsequent mortality. Bazzoli (1985) and Parnes and Less (1985) used self-reported health, but from a survey wave prior to retirement, and

Chirikos and Nestel (1981) and Bazzoli (1985) created indices of impairment. Butler et al., (1987) compared self-reports on a specific condition—arthritis—with a clinical measure. Burtless (1987) compared three subjective measures with subsequent mortality and found them highly correlated.

These studies suggest that the use of self-defined health status at retirement exaggerates the importance of health in the retirement decision (although it remains important under any definition), and may muffle the measured effect of economic factors such as Social Security (Parsons, 1982), wages (Anderson and Burkhauser, 1985), and pension entitlement (Burtless, 1987). There is no general consensus on what the best measure is. What is known is that health is a key determinant, despite recent emphasis on financial incentives, and that the magnitude of the estimated effect depends on the measure chosen.

Sickles and Taubman (1986) and Butler et al. (1989) have proposed models in which health is endogenous. Since medical care depends on income, the financial variables in these models have two effects on the retirement decision—a direct one and an indirect one via the impact on health status.

One reason for the interest in health and retirement is the recent improvement in the life expectancy of the elderly. This suggests to some that workers may be able to work more years in the future than they do now and has been used as one justification for the legislated increase in the age of eligibility for full Social Security benefits to 67. But recent reviews by Chapman et al. (1986) and by Ycas (1987) have cast some doubt on the presumption that life expectancy and health status go hand in hand. The trends on longevity are clear—older Americans are living longer now than they did two decades ago. The increases in life expectancy at ages 60 or 65 are well documented (see Chapman et al. 1986, pp. 27–28) and are significant for males and females and for whites and nonwhites. What is surprising is that they do not seem to be accompanied by increases in average health status. Chapman et al., reporting on a variety of studies and data sources, concluded that morbidity and the prevalence of disability have actually increased. Ycas used a number of measures of health status and found that they produced very similar patterns over time, suggesting increasing health problems at least through the late 1970s and perhaps a leveling off or reversal during the 1980s. One explanation of the declining health is the "failure of success"—that medical advances keep people alive today who would have died in the past (Berkowitz, 1988). The additional years may be ones of chronic illness, not good health. Regardless of the explanation, poor health remains a serious problem among the elderly and the impact of health on the retirement decision will be as important in the future as it is now.

C. Labor Market Obstacles

According to Jondrow et al. (1987), many workers would like to retire gradually. In one survey, 80% of respondents over age 55 preferred part-time work to complete retirement. In another, 60% of a sample of managers preferred phased retirement. Two-thirds of another group said they would consider a transitional step of part-time employment. Most of these would have liked part-time work with their full-time employer. Despite these preferences, the modal (but by no means the only, as we will see below) pattern of retirement still involves an abrupt transition from full-time work to complete labor force withdrawal. Most wage and salary workers who are able to reduce hours must switch jobs to do so. Why do desires and opportunities not match?

One reason is that part-time wage rates are much lower than full-time compensation. According to Gustman and Steinmeier (1985a), older workers in the RHS who reported themselves partially retired suffered an hourly wage loss of 10% if they remained with their previous full-time employer and 30% if they did not. Quinn et al. (1990), using the same data set but a retirement definition based on hours of work, report similar findings—severe wage losses associated with movement to part-time work, especially if accompanied by a change in employer.

Why do workers not reduce hours on their career jobs? According to Gustman and Steinmeier (1983, 1985a), they do not because they cannot. Only 15% of firms responding to a 1979 survey permitted some employees to reduce hours as they approached retirement. Only 7% offered this option to all employees. A survey of individuals suggested that two-thirds to three-quarters of older wage and salary workers were unable to work fewer hours. Rhine (1984) reported that only 3% of a sample of over 350 large firms permitted phased retirement. The reasons for this inflexibility are not clear. Some have mentioned the fixed costs of employment (which would make two half-time employees more expensive than one full-time) or a fear that the productivity of older workers does not justify their wages. The self-employed, on the other hand, with more control over their hours, are much more likely to utilize a transitional period of partial retirement.

But even if workers were permitted to work part-time on their career jobs, they would have to do so for reduced compensation. Social Security and most defined-benefit plans offer declining and often negative wealth accruals to workers who stay on the job. Many older workers, then, face unattractive alternatives as they age. Continued full-time employment on a career job eventually results in significant losses of retirement income wealth; in essence, a pay cut. Part-time work on this job is rarely available for the wage and salary population, and even if it is, it also may result in reduced retirement income wealth. New part-time (and to a lesser extent, new full-time) employment means a significantly lower wage rate. Faced with these alternatives, many older Americans stop working. Is the decision voluntary? Yes, in the sense that they choose to do it under the circumstances. But no, in that the circumstances may have changed dramatically as they aged.

III. PATTERNS OF WITHDRAWAL FROM THE LABOR FORCE

Most recent research has focused on the theoretical formulation of the retirement decision and on the specification of the explanatory variables, particularly the financial incentives. Much less attention has been paid to the left-hand side of the equation—the behavior being explained. Retirement has generally been modeled as dichotomous and irreversible. Recent work suggests that for many Americans, actual withdrawal patterns are far more varied than the simple views that have dominated the literature.

A. The Extent of Partial Retirement

Partial retirement is actually a common phenomenon in the United States. With the initial wave of the RHS, Quinn (1980, 1981) found that 5% of wage and salary workers (aged 58 to 63) and 12% of the self-employed described themselves as partially retired in 1969. Fuchs (1982) showed that many of the self-employed turned to self-employment late in their careers (after age 58) and that they are more likely to work reduced weekly hours than are salaried employees. Data on annual labor supply confirm that the self-employed have a much wider distribution of hours. The distribution of wage and salary workers is dominated by the mode around 2000 hours, while the self-employed are more evenly spread around it (Quinn, 1981).

Honig (1985) and Honig and Hanoch (1985) classified as partly retired anyone earning less than 50% of their maximum annual earnings. With this definition, they found that from 14 to 27% of white married wage-earning men aged 58 to 67 became partly retired between 1969 and 1973. Honig and Reimers (1987) analyzed monthly earnings, raised the definition of partial retirement to less than 80% of maximum *monthly* earnings, and of course found even more of it. Although this definition may be overly broad, they are correct to conclude that retirement in the United States is a much more complex phenomenon than the either–or framework implies.

Gustman and Steinmeier (1984a,b, 1985a), using four waves of the RHS, found that the proportion of wage and salary workers (aged 58 to 69) who call themselves partially retired rises with age and that about a third of the sample was partially retired at some time during that period. They also showed that partial retirement usually involves a job change and a pay cut, which led them to conclude that most career jobs have minimum-hours constraints. All this work illustrates that dichotomizing older workers as either retired or not retired obscures partial retirement as an important avenue of labor force withdrawal.

B.   Exit Patterns from Career Jobs

Quinn et al. (1990) have used the full ten years of the RHS to analyze patterns of disengagement from career jobs, defined as full-time jobs held at least ten years. We show, as did Hall (1982) and Addison and Castro (1987), that most Americans spend considerable time on a single job. This pattern of long tenure on a career job is consistent with the view that defined pension plans substantially penalize those who leave a career job "too early." The transition from this job is an important event. Many leave this career job and the labor force simultaneously, but many do not.

Over a quarter of the wage and salary employees in our sample did not stop work when they left full-time career employment. Of those who remained employed, most took on a new position quickly and stayed at it for at least two years. The new positions often represented a new line of work, lower down the socio-economic scale, often at considerably lower pay. Many workers, of course, were augmenting these earnings with Social Security and/or employer pension checks.

Although people of all types utilized these intermediate steps toward retirement, those at the extreme ends of the economic scale were most likely to do so. We suspect that the poor continue to work because they have to and because they do not face dramatic age-specific pay cuts since they are not likely to be eligible for pension benefits. The wealthy work because their employment provides more than a paycheck and also because they also are probably less affected by Social Security and defined-benefit employer pensions than are middle-class workers.

Iams (1987) reported similar findings with a recent sample of new Social Security retired-worker beneficiaries. Between a fifth and a quarter were still working 18 to 30 months after initial receipt of benefits. Most were working part-time, usually by reducing hours per week. The median wage of those who switched employers was about half of that on their longest job or latest job, and many earned under the Social Security earnings test threshold.

Ruhm (1990) has argued that the "job-stopping" process with which older workers leave the labor force is similar to the "job-shopping" process with which they enter. Between these periods, which are often characterized by multiple job holdings and part-time work, the typical worker has a career job for a significant number of years.

Ruhm defines the career job as the longest job held, regardless of when that was or how long it lasted. He finds that fewer than half of the RHS sample retired directly from a career employment. Most held at least one "bridge" job before labor market exit. Given his definition of career, Ruhm finds a wide distribution of years on postcareer jobs; many in fact are really second careers. He finds that three-quarters of his sample changes industry or occupation between career and bridge jobs, and almost half changed both.

What this research suggests is that work after retirement is not a rare event. But substantial changes are required in both current Social Security and employer pension legislation before the majority of middle-class workers are likely to stay at work past their early sixties.

IV. RECENT CHANGES IN THE INSTITUTIONAL ENVIRONMENT

The institutional environment surrounding retirement is itself changing. Important legislation concerning mandatory retirement and Social Security has passed in recent years and the nature of employer pension plans continues to evolve. These changes and others prompted by the aging of the population may combine to reverse the recent trend toward earlier retirement.

A. Mandatory-Retirement Rules

In 1978, an amendment to the Age Discrimination in Employment Act outlawed mandatory retirement before age 70 for most American workers. Many states went further, and outlawed mandatory retirement at age 70 as well (Rhine, 1984). In 1986 the federal government followed suit, and mandatory retirement, with a few exceptions, has been eliminated.

Casual empiricism suggests that these changes might drastically alter retirement patterns, since many workers used to retire at mandatory-retirement age (Barker and Clark, 1980). But econometric evidence indicates otherwise. Burkhauser and Quinn (1983b) found that mandatory retirement was closely intertwined with both Social Security and employer pension incentives. As described above, the Social Security delayed-retirement credit drops significantly at age 65, from about 8% per year of delay to 3% (and was only 1% before 1982), which is less than actuarially fair. This implies a pay cut at age 65, which was also the most common age of mandatory retirement before 1978. In addition, mandatory retirement was often accompanied by an employer pension plan that added work disincentives of its own. We argued that at least half of the difference in behavior between those with and without mandatory retirement was due to other factors, primarily financial incentives, and that even the unexplained residual was an overestimate of the mandatory-retirement effect (Burkhauser and Quinn, 1983b). Therefore, we expect that mandatory-retirement legislation will have only a modest effect on elderly labor supply [see Morrison (1988) for more detail]. The stick is gone, but the carrots remain.

B. Social Security

Because of fears about the future financial solvency of the Social Security system and the labor market implications of earlier retirement in an aging society, the Greenspan Commission was appointed to investigate policy options. Their recommendations formed the base for the 1983 Amendments to the Social Security Act, several of which were designed to prolong the working life of older Americans [see Svahn and Ross (1983) for details of the amendments]. Two amendments are now affecting older workers. The delayed-retirement credit after age 65 was increased to 3.5% for those reaching age 65 in 1990 and will increase by 0.5% every other year until it reaches 8% in 2009. In addition, in 1990 the benefit loss associated with an additional dollar of earnings above the exempt amount dropped from 50 to 33 cents for full-benefit retirees. A third amendment will begin after the turn of the century. The age of eligibility for full Social Security benefits is scheduled to rise from 65 to 66 by the year 2009 and to 67 by 2027. Benefits will still be available as early as age 62, but the reduced benefits will only be 70% of the full amount rather than the current 80%. All of these changes reward additional work and should help reverse the trend toward earlier retirement. Analysts agree on the direction but not the size of the effect.

Burtless and Moffitt (1984), Fields and Mitchell (1984b), and Gustman and Steinmeier (1985b) have simulated the effects of reforms like those of 1983. They all find that the aggregate impact on retirement age is modest—average delays on the order of months, not years. Burtless and Moffitt (1984) and Sickles and Taubman (1986) have hinted that delaying or eliminating Social Security eligibility at age 62 (which has not been legislated) would have much a larger effect on behavior. But all of these estimates are only preliminary, because they assume that the rest of the environment, in particular, employer pensions, remains unchanged. As we argue below, this is the great unknown.

C. Employer Pensions

The growth in employer pension coverage has ceased. According to Turner and Beller (1989, Table 13.2), the proportion of private-sector workers covered has hardly changed since 1970. Recent news has not been in overall coverage, but rather in the changing distribution of types of plans.

Most workers with pensions still have primary coverage in a *defined-benefit* plan, in which the worker is promised an annuity upon retirement from the firm. The benefit is usually based on some combination of earnings and years of service (Schulz, 1988). There are also *defined-contribution* plans, in which the firm periodically deposits funds into an account that belongs to the worker upon retirement. These are basically just savings accounts with tax advantages.

According to Turner and Beller (1989, Table 4.12), fewer than 13% of the private sector workers with pension plans had their primary coverage in a defined-contribution plan in 1975. Ten years later, this had risen to nearly 30%. Defined-contribution plans are even more popular as supplementary coverage, where they are nearly universal. There are at least two implications of this. First, the investment risk is shifting from the firm to the employee. But more important from our perspective, the retirement incentives are very different. The complex and powerful accrual patterns discussed above all come from the benefit calculation formulas of *defined-benefit plans,* which discourage work after the age of normal retirement if not sooner. There is no such work disincentives with defined-contribution plans, because the employer's contribution is merely a constant wage supplement. Nearly half of all private pension coverage is still in defined-benefit plans (Turner and Beller, 1989, Table 4.11) [and Ippolito (1986, Chapter 6) argues that this will remain so], so the discussion above is still relevant to understanding the current environment. But if the trend toward defined-contribution plans continues and if the Social Security delayed-retirement credit after age 65 becomes close to actuarially fair as scheduled, then the importance of these work disincentives at older ages will diminish.

V.   WHAT CAN PUBLIC POLICY DO TO INCREASE WORK EFFORT AT OLDER AGES?

Economic research suggests that retirement trends are not exogenous. On the contrary, they are influenced by public policy. The institutional environment continues to evolve. Some changes are already underway or legislated for the future, others may occur as the composition of the work force shifts, and others may require additional legislation.

What changes are currently underway? Mandatory retirement has virtually been eliminated. The proportion of workers covered by age-neutral defined-contribution pension plans is on the rise. Social Security amendments already on the books will delay the age of eligibility for full retirement benefits to 67, increase the penalty for retiring at age 62 from 20 to 30% of full benefits, decrease the earnings test tax rate from a half to a third, and augment the delayed-retirement credit for work beyond normal retirement age from 3 to 8% per year of delay. All of these changes should work to increase the labor force participation of older workers. But recent research suggests that the impact of the removal of mandatory retirement and the legislated changes in the Social Security rules on retirement patterns will be small.

These results must be viewed with caution, however, since they are estimates of first-round effects only. In the simulations mentioned above, Burtless and Moffitt (1984), Fields and Mitchell (1984b), and Gustman and Steinmeier (1985b) changed Social Security rules but assumed that employer pension plans remain as they are. But we believe pension plans will change. As we have shown, recent evidence suggests that pension incentives are very important in determining individual and aggregate behavior. The fact that work effort has fallen dramatically between ages 55 and 61, ages below the minimum for early Social Security retirement benefits, suggests that Social Security incentives are not the only reason for reduced work at older ages.

A key factor, about which very little is known, is how employer pension plans will change in response to Social Security rule changes. Some of the interaction, in "integrated plans," is automatic. Pension benefits in these plans depend directly on the amount of Social Security benefits, and an implicit tax rate is built into the benefit calculation rules. If Social Security benefits decrease, the pension automatically rises, though not always dollar for dollar. This tends to offset the effect of Social Security changes. Since about two-thirds of full-time participants in defined-benefit pension plans are in plans integrated in some way, this factor could be important (Herz and Rones, 1989). But beyond this, the rules of the pension plans are subject to change, and it is this response that is unknown, yet important for predicting the future. Will pensions augment or offset the changes in Social Security incentives? Would congressional initiatives concerning pensions be nullified by other alterations in the compensation package? In general, how would the long-run general-equilibrium impacts compare to the short-run effects that have been estimated?

We simply do not know the answers to these questions. But we do know that the pension rules set and negotiated in the future will significantly affect the decisions workers make with respect to retirement. Most people do not retire because they can no longer find or perform work, as we once thought. Many now retire voluntarily, when they are still able to work and there is demand for their services. They do so because of the trade-offs they face in the marketplace. There are always people at the margin, and these people will change their behavior in response to changes in the choices before them.

As the first-round simulations show, changes in Social Security legislation will have some effect in delaying retirement. But the currently slated changes will not in themselves dramatically affect lengths of stay in career jobs. And it is this labor market decision—the departure from the career job—that is most important in determining work effort at older ages. Defined-benefit pension plans continue to encourage job exit from a career job, often at the earliest possible retirement age. It is more likely that changes in pension rules, rather than Social Security rule changes, will have the greatest effect on full-time work on such jobs.

Bureau of labor statistics projections (U.S. Department of Labor, 1989) show that over the next 15 years the population 55 and older will increase, while the population aged 16 to 34 will decline. Some foresee labor market shortages emerging from these demographic shifts and the trend toward earlier retirement. If employers share this concern, then we may see substantial changes in current pension policy. If not, employers may tilt lifetime benefits even more toward those who leave at early retirement age in order to offset the Social Security changes now underway.

There is already some evidence that employers changed pension plans to offset the effects of delaying (and later eliminating) mandatory-retirement age. Mitchell and Luzadis (1988) studied changing incentives over time in a small number of specific pension plans. Between 1960 and 1970, when "social security reforms encouraged employees to opt for earlier retirement," they found that "in many cases private pension offerings adapted to accommodate these new retirement patterns." But during the 1970s, when the mandatory-retirement age was increased fro 65 to 70 and the movement to eliminate it altogether was gathering momentum, "pensions requiring mandatory retirement . . . altered their benefit incentives by 1980 so as to encourage earlier retirement."

If employers want to buck the Social Security trend, it is not easy to prevent them. For instance, the 1986 Amendments to the Age Discrimination Act require firms with pension plans to continue to provide service credit to those who continue with the firm past normal retirement age. But this will not prevent the firm from making early-retirement benefits even more generous, in order to offset this rule.

But the ability to offset government policy does not necessarily translate into counteraction. One might argue that the opposite will occur. One reason that most pension plans in the United States chose age 65 as the normal retirement age was that Social Security used that age. One of the original purposes of Social Security policy was to encourage older workers to leave the labor force and, until 1972, earnings above an exempt amount were taxed at 100% and benefits postponed beyond age 65 earned no actuarial credit. Given these strong disincentives to full-time work, it is not surprising that firms developed institutions that conformed. To do otherwise would have required firms to pay workers higher wages past age 65 to offset the Social Security penalties. Although the following is more debatable, the establishment of early Social Security benefits at age 62 may have encouraged firms to follow suit, to the degree that workers believed Social Security pension accrual fell past this age. The scheduled changes in benefit rules will reduce the fall in Social Security accrual after age 62, and change the foundation on which private pensions were built.

A final speculation concerns the influence of these rule changes on the type of work that will be done by older Americans. If pension rules do not change, we expect more work after departure from the career job and more second careers. This is because the easing of Social Security work disincentives will make work more attractive relative to complete retirement, but pension rules will continue to discourage continued employment on career jobs. The result? Keep working but switch jobs to do so.

If firms actually counter Social Security rule changes with even stronger incentives to leave full-time work at early-retirement age, then we predict even more part- and full-time work on postcareer jobs. If, however, firms match the changes in the Social Security system with similar attempts to flatten pension accrual across the life cycle, then workers should delay departure from their career jobs.

A final and very important variation on this theme is the possibility of part-time work on a career job. This has the advantage of eliminating the loss of specific human capital that accompanies a job change and reducing the wage loss associated with part-time employment. Research has established that the self-employed, who rarely have pension-related work disincentives, are much more likely than wage and salary workers to move from full- to part-time work on the same job. Currently, defined-benefit pension rules, especially when benefits are based on earnings in the last few years of employment, make this a costly choice for wage and salary workers who desire part-time work. What may be needed is the introduction of partial-pension schemes in which workers can combine partial-pension benefits, as they can now with Social Security, with part-time employment on the career job. Such a program for workers aged 60 to 64 exists in Sweden. The labor force participation rate of older workers there is higher than in the United States, and response to this program has been very positive (Ginsberg, 1985). As the age of eligibility for full Social Security benefits rises to 67, the importance of such flexible pension schemes will grow. The key question again is whether labor market demands will induce firms to offer such flexibility on their own.

It is important for policymakers to recognize the difference between policies that encourage continued work *on any job* and those that induce people to stay *on the career job*. The former include many of the Social Security changes already enacted and others that have been proposed, such as the total elimination of the earnings test, an earlier phase-in of the 8% delayed retirement credit for work past age 65, or the exemption of Social Security recipients from Social Security taxes on part-time earnings. The latter relate to employer pension plans, and include policies favoring defined-contribution plans, age-neutral defined-benefit plans, or flexible partial-pension schemes.

Surveys of older workers suggest that many workers would like to retire gradually, to incorporate a period of partial retirement into the transition from full-time work to complete labor force withdrawal. Currently, only a minority do. Policies that facilitate this desire by making it less costly for firms to hire part-time workers and less costly for older workers to accept part-time employment should be considered and encouraged.

ACKNOWLEDGMENTS

This project was funded by the U.S. Department of Labor, Commission on Workforce Quality and Labor Market Efficiency. Opinions stated in this document do not necessarily represent the official position or policy of the U.S. Department of Labor, Commission on Workforce Quality and Labor Market Efficiency. We thank T. Aldrich Finegan for supplying us with the unpublished labor force participation numbers from the 1940 census and John Stinson of the Bureau of Labor Statistics for supplying us with the unpublished labor force participation numbers from the *Current Population Surveys*.

REFERENCES

Addison, John T. and Alberto C. Castro (1987), "The Importance of Lifetime Jobs: Differences Between Union and Nonunion Workers." *Industrial and Labor Relations Review* 40:393–405.

Allen, Steven, Robert Clark, and Ann McDermed (1987), "Pensions and Lifetime Jobs: The New Industrial Feudalism Revisited." Unpublished paper.

Anderson, Kathryn H. and Richard V. Burkhauser (1985), "The Retirement–Health Nexus: A New Measure of an Old Puzzle." *Journal of Human Resources* 20:315–330.

Baily, Martin N. (1987), "Aging and the Ability to Work." In Gary Burtless (ed.), *Work, Health, and Income Among the Elderly*. Washington, DC: The Brookings Institution, pp. 59–97.

Barker, David T. and Robert L. Clark (1980). "Mandatory Retirement and Labor-Force Participation of Respondents in the Retirement History Study." *Social Security Bulletin* 43(11):20–29, 55.

Bazzoli, Gloria J. (1985), "The Early Retirement Decision: New Empirical Evidence on the Influence of Health." *Journal of Human Resources* 20:214–234.

Becker, Eugene H. (1984), "Self-Employed Workers: An Update to 1983." *Monthly Labor Review* 107(7):14–18.

Berkowitz, Monroe (1988), "Functioning Ability and Job Performance as Workers Age." In Michael E. Borus et al. (eds.), *The Older Worker*. Madison, WI: Industrial Relations Research Association, pp. 87–114.

Blau, David M. (1987), "A Time Series Analysis of Self-Employment in the United States." *Journal of Political Economy* 95:445–466.

Boskin, Michael J., Laurence J. Kotlikoff, Douglas J. Puffert, and John B. Shoven (1987), "Social Security: A Financial Appraisal Across and Within Generations." *National Tax Journal* 40:19–34.

Burkhauser, Richard V. (1979), "The Pension Acceptance Decisions of Older Workers." *Journal of Human Resources* 14:63–75.

Burkhauser, Richard V. and Joseph F. Quinn (1983a), "The Effect of Pension Plans on the Pattern of Life-Cycle Compensation." In Jack E. Triplett (ed.), *The Measurement of Labor Cost*. Chicago: The University of Chicago Press, pp. 395–415.

————— (1983b)., "Is Mandatory Retirement Overrated? Evidence from the 1970s." *Journal of Human Resources* 18:337–358.

Burkhauser, Richard V. and Jennifer L. Warlick (1981). "Disentangling the Annuity from the Redistributive Aspects of Social Security in the United States." *Review of Income and Wealth* 27:401–421.

Burtless, Gary (1987), "Occupational Effects of the Health and Work Capacity of Older Men." In Gary Burtless (ed.), *Work, Health and Income Among the Elderly*. Washington, DC: The Brookings Institution, pp. 103–142.

Burtless, Gary and Robert A. Moffitt (1984), "The Effect of Social Security Benefits on the Labor Supply of the Aged." In Henry J. Aaron and Gary Burtless (eds.), *Retirement and Economic Behavior*. Washington, DC: The Brookings Institution, pp. 135–171.

————— (1985), "The Joint Choice of Retirement Age and Postretirement Hours of Work." *Journal of Labor Economics* 3:209–236.

Butler, J. S., Richard V. Burkhauser, Jean M. Mitchell, and Theodore P. Pincus (1987). "Measurement Error in Self-Reported Health Variables. *Review of Economics and Statistics* 69:644–650.

Butler, J. S., Kathryn H. Anderson, and Richard V. Burkhauser (1989). "Work and Health after Retirement: A Competing Risks Model with Semiparametric Unobserved Heterogeneity." *Review of Economics and Statistics*. 71:46–53.

Chapman, Steven H., Mitchell P. LaPlante, and Gail Wilensky (1986), "Life Expectancy and Health Status of the Aged." *Social Security Bulletin* 49(10):24–48.

Chirikos, Thomas N. and Gilbert Nestel (1981), "Impairment and Labor Market Outcomes." In

Herbert S. Parnes (ed.), *Work and Retirement: A Longitudinal Study of Men*. Cambridge, MA: MIT Press, pp. 93–131.

Fields, Gary S. and Olivia S. Mitchell (1984a), "Economic Determinants of the Optimal Retirement Age: An Empirical Investigation." *Journal of Human Resources* 19:245–262.

———— (1984b), "The Effects of Social Security Reforms on Retirement Ages and Retirement Incomes." *Journal of Public Economics* 25:143–159.

———— (1984c), *Retirement, Pensions, and Social Security*. Cambridge, MA: MIT Press.

Fuchs, Victor (1982), "Self-Employment and Labor Force Participation of Older Males." *Journal of Human Resources* 17:339–357.

Ginsburg, Helen (1985), "Flexible and Partial Retirement for Norwegian and Swedish Workers." *Monthly Labor Review* 108(10):33–43.

Gustman, Alan L. and Thomas L. Steinmeier (1983), "Minimum Hours Constraints and Retirement Behavior." *Contemporary Policy Issues* 3:77–91.

———— (1984a). "Partial Retirement and the Analysis of Retirement Behavior." *Industrial and Labor Relations Review* 37:403–415.

———— (1984b), "Modeling the Retirement Process for Policy Evaluation and Research." *Monthly Labor Review* 107(7):26–33.

———— (1985a), "The Effects of Partial Retirement on Wage Profiles for Older Workers." *Industrial Relations* 24: 257–265.

———— (1985b), "The 1983 Social Security Reforms and Labor Supply Adjustments of Older Individuals in the Long Run." *Journal of Labor Economics* 3:237–253.

Hall, Robert E. (1982), "The Importance of Lifetime Jobs in the U.S. Economy." *American Economic Review* 72:716–724.

Herz, Diane E. and Philip L. Rones (1989), "Institutional Barriers to Employment of Older Workers." *Monthly Labor Review* 112(4):14–21.

Honig, Marjorie (1985), "Partial Retirement Among Women." *Journal of Human Resources* 20:613–621.

Honig, Marjorie and Giora Hanoch (1985), "Partial Retirement As a Separate Mode of Retirement Behavior." *Journal of Human Resources* 20:21–46.

Honig, Marjorie and Cordelia Reimers (1987). "The Labor Market Mobility of Older Workers." Mimeo, Department of Economics, Hunter College.

Iams, Howard M. (1987), "Jobs of Persons Working After Receiving Retired-Worker Benefits." *Social Security Bulletin* 50(11):4–17.

Ippolito, Richard A. (1986), *Pensions, Economics and Public Policy*. Homewood, IL: Dow Jones–Irwin.

———— (1987), "The Implicit Pension Contract: Developments and New Directions." *Journal of Human Resources* 22:441–467.

Ireland, Lola M. (1973), "Retirement History Study: Introduction." *Social Security Bulletin* 35(11):3–8.

Johnson, William G. (1977), "The Effect of Disability on Labor Supply: Comment." *Industrial and Labor Relations Review* 30:380–381.

Jondrow, Jim, Frank Brechling, and Alan Marcus (1987), "Older Workers in the Market for Part-Time Employment." In Steven H. Sandell (ed.), *The Problem Isn't Age: Work and Older Americans*. New York: Praeger, pp. 84–99.

Kingson, Eric R. (1982), "The Health of Very Early Retirees." *Social Security Bulletin* 45(9):3–9.

Kotlikoff, Laurence J. and Daniel E. Smith (1983), *Pensions in the American Economy*. Chicago: The University of Chicago Press.

Kotlikoff, Laurence J. and David A. Wise (1985), "Labor Compensation and the Structure of Private Pension Plans: Evidence for Contractual versus Spot Labor Markets." In David Wise (ed.), *Pensions, Labor and Individual Choice*. Chicago: The University of Chicago Press, pp. 55–85.

———— (1989), *The Wage Carrot and the Pension Stick.* Kalamazoo, MI: The W. E. UpJohn Institute for Employment Research.

Mitchell, Olivia S. and Gary S. Fields (1984), "The Effects of Pensions and Earnings on Retirement: A Review Essay." In Ronald G. Ehrenberg (ed.), *Research in Labor Economics,* Volume 5. Greenwich, CT: JAI Press, pp. 115–155.

Mitchell, Olivia S. and Rebecca Luzadis (1988). "Changes in Pension Incentives Through Time." *Industrial and Labor Relations Review* 42:100–108.

Moffitt, Robert A. (1984), "Trends in Social Security Wealth by Cohort." In Marilyn Moon (ed.), *Economic Transfers in the United States.* Chicago: The University of Chicago Press, pp. 327–347.

Morrison, Malcolm (1988), "Changes in the Legal Mandatory Retirement Age: Labor Force Participation Implications." In Rita Ricardo Campbell and Edward Lazear (eds.), *Issues in Contemporary Retirement.* Stanford, CA: Hoover Institution Press, pp. 378–405.

Myers, Robert J. (1982), "Why Do People Retire From Work Early?" *Social Security Bulletin* 45(9):10–14.

Parnes, Herbert S. (1988), "The Retirement Decision." In Michael E. Borus et al. (ed.), *The Older Worker.* Madison: Industrial Relations Research Association, pp. 115–150.

Parnes, Herbert S. and Lawrence J. Less (1985), "The Volume and Pattern of Retirements, 1966–1981." In Herbert S. Parnes et al. (eds.) *Retirement Among American Men.* Lexington, MA: Lexington Books, pp. 57–77.

Parsons, Donald O. (1982), "The Male Labor Force Participation Decision: Health, Reported Health and Economic Incentives." *Economica* 49:81–91.

Quinn, Joseph F. (1977), "Microeconomic Determinants of Early Retirement: A Cross-Sectional View of White Married Men." *Journal of Human Resources* 12:329–347.

———— (1980), "Labor Force Participation Patterns of Older Self-Employed Workers." *Social Security Bulletin* 43(4):17–28.

———— (1981), "The Extent and Correlates of Partial Retirement." *The Gerontologist* 21:634–643.

Quinn, Joseph F. and Richard V. Burkhauser (1983). "Influencing Retirement Behavior: A Key Issue for Social Security." *Journal of Policy Analysis and Management* 3:1–13.

Quinn, Joseph F., Richard V. Burkhauser, and Daniel C. Myers (1990), *Passing the Torch: The Influence of Economic Incentives on Work and Retirement.* Kalamazoo, MI: The W. E. Upjohn Institute for Employment Research.

Rhine, Shirley H. (1984), *Managing Older Workers: Company Policies and Attitudes.* New York: The Conference Board.

Ruhm, Christopher J. (1990), "Career Jobs, Bridge Employment, and Retirement." In Peter B. Doeringer (ed.), *Bridges to Retirement: The Changing Labor Market for Older Workers.* Ithaca, NY: Institute for Labor Relations Press, Cornell University.

Sammartino, Frank J. (1987), "The Effect of Health on Retirement." *Social Security Bulletin* 50(2):31–47.

Schulz, James H. (1988), *The Economics of Aging.* New York: Van Nostrand Reinhold.

Sickles, Robin C. and Paul Taubman (1986), "An Analysis of the Health and Retirement Status of the Elderly." *Econometrica* 54:1339–1356.

Svahn, John A. and Mary Ross (1983), "Social Security Amendments of 1983: Legislative History and Summary of Provisions." *Social Security Bulletin* 46(7):3–48.

Turner, John A. and Daniel J. Beller (1989), *Trends in Pensions: 1988.* Washington, DC: U.S. Government Printing Office.

U.S. Department of Labor (1989), *Older Worker Task Force: Key Policy Issues for the Future.* Washington, DC: U.S. Government Printing Office.

Ycas, Martynas A. (1987), "Recent Trends in Health Near the Age of Retirement: New Findings from the Health Interview Survey." *Social Security Bulletin* 50(2):5–30.

Ycas, Martynas A. and Susan Grad (1987), "Income of Retirement-Aged Persons in the United States." *Social Security Bulletin* 50(7):5–14.

LABOR FORCE PARTICIPATION AMONG DISABLED PERSONS

Monroe Berkowitz and Edward Berkowitz

I. INTRODUCTION

This paper explores the factors that influence the labor force participation of disabled persons. It considers the problems involved in defining and counting the disabled population, the nature of the relationship between aging and disability, the institutions through which we conduct disability policy, the effects of income transfers on the labor force participation of disabled persons, the usefulness of rehabilitation programs, and the value of civil-rights programs on behalf of the disabled population. The paper concludes with some practical policy suggestions aimed at increasing the labor force participation of disabled persons.

Although the paper covers many topics, our aims are quite simple: We want to show how institutions encourage or discourage labor force participation and to suggest ways of improving the performance of our public policies.

II. DEFINING DISABILITY

Unlike other groups whose rates of labor force participation are the subject of scholarly inquiry, disabled persons cannot be identified with precision. The very

Research in Labor Economics, Volume 11, pages 181–200.
Copyright © 1990 by JAI Press Inc.
All rights of reproduction in any form reserved.
ISBN: 1-555938-080-2

concept of disability resists definition. The scholarly convention is to think of disability in terms of a continuum that begins with illness or impairment. Most people recover from such incidents; in some cases, however, the transient illness or other medically defined condition leaves the person with a functional limitation—some lasting inability to perform "normal" physical or mental functions, such as the inability to climb stairs or to maintain amiable relations with coworkers. Some people may adapt themselves to the functional limitation with no loss of productivity and thus maintain their attachment to the labor force. Others may perceive themselves as unable to carry on their normal, usual, and accustomed tasks because of their mental or physical conditions. Social scientists define such persons as disabled.

In the real world, the definition of disability seldom conforms to this typology. Social-insurance programs, for example, equate disability with actual or potential wage loss, and the administrators of those programs often use physical impairment as a proxy for wage loss. Hence, the distinctions between impairment or functional limitation and disability are not honored. To be impaired is to be disabled. Furthermore, some of the programs equate disability with the inability to perform one's customary occupation; other programs have a more stringent definition and insist on the inability of performing any job—however that concept might be measured—as a condition of receiving benefits. Finally, some definitions of disability do not depend on the condition of real or potential wage loss so much as on the existence of an impairment or physical and mental condition that triggers prejudice on the part of employers. In this definition, policymakers are encouraged to think of disabled persons as a minority group who face physical and attitudinal barriers. As a woman quoted in a popular health guide puts it, "We are not disabled; it is society which disables us by being so unsupportive" (Boston's Women's Health Book Collective, 1984).

III.   THE NUMBER OF DISABLED PEOPLE

Because no consensus has emerged on how to define disability, there can be no single unambiguous count of disabled persons. Even if we focus on a single standard such as a functional limitation that leads to wage loss, the fact remains that in a group of people with identical functional limitations, some will be disabled and some not. Factors such as age, education, personal motivation, alternative sources of income, physical barriers in the working environment, the attitude of employers toward the basic abilities of the handicapped, and the condition of the labor market all will play a part in the outcome. For that reason, it makes as much sense to think of disability as a socioeconomic phenomenon as a medically defined concept.

The results of surveys conducted by the Social Security Administration in 1966, 1972, and 1978 show that about 17% of the population considered themselves as having some degree of work disability in both 1966 and 1978. Despite this agreement, the surveys report a substantial increase in the degree of severe work disability, defined as a person unable to work altogether or unable to work regularly, from 6% of the population in 1966 to 8.6% in 1978. This outcome has important implications for labor force participation rates. In 1966, 19.2% of those in the severely disabled category reported themselves as being in the labor force; in 1978, this proportion had decreased to 13.6% (McNeil, 1983).

From a policy standpoint, it might be preferable to substitute verified measures of impairment and functional limitations for a person's own perceptions of his or her ability to work. With such measures, we could begin to understand better why some people join the labor force and others choose to accept a disabled status or, alternatively, whether people with certain impairments and functional limitation face discrimination in the labor market.

IV. AGING AND DISABILITY

In thinking about the definition and prevalence of disability, the relationship between aging and disability requires special consideration. It is no accident that in most discussions of disability, the population under consideration is restricted to those persons normally in the labor force age group. When it comes to children and older persons beyond normal retirement age, difficulties arise. What, for example, is the appropriate activity to test for in the case of a retired person: recreation, activities of daily living, or something else? And all persons become disabled before they die—some for long periods of time and others for only a microsecond—but presumably the disability rate and the mortality rate are not the same things.

The fact remains, however, that age and disability move together. The older a person, the more likely he or she is to be disabled. Older people are less healthy, more impaired and functionally limited, and more disabled than younger people (Berkowitz, 1988).

Demography and disability combine to pose some intriguing policy questions, particularly when one considers the almost certain rise in the median age of the population between 1990 and 2040 from 33 to 42 years. The best estimates also posit that the percentage of the population 65 years or over should grow from 12.7 in 1990 to 21.7 in 2040 (U.S. Senate, 1988, pp. 11, 13). We know that people are living longer as mortality rates in the older age groups decline, but we know less about comparable trends in morbidity and disability rates. Will the increasing number of older persons be healthier and able to participate in the labor force? Or will the same disability patterns prevail so that the increasing number of older persons will make for an increasingly dependent population?

The commonsense interpretation is that health should improve with falling death rates, but the elimination of infectious disease may have fundamentally changed the meaning of mortality as a health measure (Ycas, 1987). Gruenberg (1977) maintains that we may be suffering from "failures of success." Mortality has been postponed, not by curing the underlying causes of death, but by curbing the lethality of their side effects. Those alive today who would have died in an earlier era are not healthy; they are sick persons whose problems can be kept under control at a level of severity short of death.

As for empirical studies that attempt to measure the effects of age and disability on labor force and other forms of participation, Newquist (1984) uses National Health Interview Survey data to show that the number of older persons who report that they are unable to carry on their major activity has increased over time. Newquist hypothesizes that the older population may be restricting its activities in the face of chronic conditions in order to avoid serious illness consequences. Several other studies note this phenomenon of an increased willingness of persons diagnosed as having certain conditions or diseases to restrict their activities (Haynes et al., 1978), although Ycas (1987) casts some doubt on these inferences. He argues that in the first half of the 1970s, the trend was toward worsening health in age groups near retirement age; in the late 1970s, the trend was toward stable or improving health.

What does this confusing evidence mean? The literature lacks good explanatory models (Berkowitz, 1988; Robinson, 1986). Our best guess, after examining the literature (Fries, 1980; Fries and Crapo, 1981; Manton, 1982; Manton and Stallard, 1982; Wing and Manton, 1981), is that the trend toward declining health among the older age groups seems to be reversing. If we are correct in this guess, that is encouraging: The problems of increasing labor force participation may lie in the social arrangements we devise and not in the medical area.

V. THE AMERICAN DISABILITY SYSTEM—AN INSTITUTIONAL AND HISTORICAL OVERVIEW

Beyond these definitional, demographic, and epidemiological concerns, a discussion of labor force participation requires an overview of the many programs and policies that mark government and employer responses to disability (Berkowitz, 1987). In general, these programs reflect two approaches to the situation. Either they make the person better off by raising his or her level of income, whether through insurance payments or through public assistance, or they attempt to correct the situation that limits the worker's labor force participation, whether through individual training (rehabilitation) or environmental restructuring (ramps in buildings). Many people have access to formal systems that combine the two approaches.

A.   The Social Security Disability System

The most widely available public system includes the Social Security Disability Insurance (SSDI) program, the Medicare program, and the Vocational

Rehabilitation (VR) program. In 1986 these programs cost about $20.1 billion for disability benefits paid to approximately 2.8 million disabled workers, $8.8 billion for Parts A and B of Medicare (expenditures for disability beneficiaries), and about $4.2 million for the rehabilitation of Social Security disability beneficiaries [all program data from Virginia Department of Rehabilitative Services (1988)].

Designed to fit into the Social Security program, this system places a heavy emphasis on retirement, rather than labor force participation. To receive benefits, a worker needs to prove that he or she is "unable to engage in substantial gainful employment" as a result of medically demonstrable condition that is expected to last a year. In other words, the successful applicant proves the inability to work. Once a worker passes the test, he or she receives a pension that paid an average of $471 a month in 1984, with an additional $131 if the worker had an eligible spouse and $139 for the worker's children (Social Security Administration, 1985, p. 1). Since the program tests the ability to work, benefits are either payable in full (the formula reflects a worker's earnings and family structure) or not payable at all.

Just as disability insurance reflects the general design of the Social Security program, so does Medicare for disability beneficiaries. The program makes no distinction between the elderly and the disabled persons receiving Medicare, except that the disabled person needs to wait longer than an elderly person before becoming eligible. A disabled person must be entitled to benefits for 24 consecutive months before he or she can receive Medicare. For both the disabled and the elderly person, the program reimburses expenses incurred during hospital stays for acute conditions, as well as doctors' treatments related to those acute conditions. The program makes no provisions for long-term care or for what might be called permanent continuing care, such as an attendant who might assist a paraplegic in transferring from a bed to a wheelchair or in toileting.

In a similar sense, the disability insurance program has never made effective arrangements for the rehabilitation of disability beneficiaries. Although the program began with a rehabilitation referral system, that system never amounted to much. In 1965, Congress authorized the creation of the Beneficiary Rehabilitation Program (BRP). This program, run jointly by the Social Security Administration (SSA) and the Rehabilitation Services Administration (RSA), reimbursed 100% of the costs for rehabilitating disability insurance beneficiaries. In 1976, a gradual disenchantment with the BRP began that culminated in the drastic alteration of the program in 1981.

Part of the disenchantment stemmed from the evaluations made by SSA to assess the efficiency of the BRP. Although initial evaluations were ambiguous, the SSA estimated the benefit–cost ratio as 1.60 in 1970 and 1.93 in 1972. Independent evaluations soon began to cast further doubts on the program. The GAO examined a small sample of beneficiaries who had been terminated from the program after rehabilitation and found that 62% of the persons who left the benefit rolls would have left anyway without rehabilitation services. Other independent examinations found benefit–cost ratios slightly over one (Berkowitz et al., 1982).

Because of the disillusionment with the program, possibly because of overblown expectations, it was discontinued. In its stead, Congress instituted a program under which the VR agency would get reimbursed for its services plus a bonus only if the person left the benefit rolls and stayed off for a period of six months. Only modest use has been made of this program.

Despite the disappointment with the BRP, the SSDI program also includes a number of incentive provisions designed to encourage the rehabilitation of persons on the rolls. Most of these date from the 1980 amendments, in which Congress turned its attention to the difficulties that program beneficiaries had in leaving the rolls. The amendments included provisions for a trial work period, the disregard of impairment-related expenses, and an extension of Medicare coverage after a person returned to work and left the rolls.

B.   The Public Assistance Disability System

The Social Security–Medicare–Vocational Rehabilitation system applies only to people with a record of labor force participation. A parallel public system consisting of Supplemental Security Income (SSI), Medicaid, and VR assists those with a less-permanent record of labor force attachment. This system, which requires a means test of its recipients, permits more state discretion than does the Social Security system, since all states (Arizona has no Medicaid program) administer Medicaid and VR and some states supplement federal SSI payments. Hence, aggregate expenditure figures need to be considered with regard to the considerable variance that exists from state to state. In 1986, SSI cost $5.4 billion in disability-related expenditures (the program covers the blind, the elderly, and the permanently and totally disabled). Medicaid for the disabled cost $15.6 billion in that year, and expenditures for the rehabilitation of SSI beneficiaries amounted to $600,000.

C.   The Work Injury System

One of the most important features of the American disability system lies in the separation of work-related disability from other sources of disability. Work-related disability falls into the realm of workers' compensation (WC), which is restricted to the payment of benefits in the event of injuries incurred at work and arising out of the employment situation. The states run individual programs with no participation by the federal government. (The federal government does administer a significant program for its own employees as well as a program covering longshoremen and harbor workers.)

Unlike the Social Security program, which has welfare and insurance objectives and which is financed on a pay-as-you-go basis, the WC program is financed mainly through private insurance carriers. Since two million persons may receive an indemnity benefit in a single year, at an annual cost of $25 billion, WC insurance has emerged as a big business (Worrall and Butler, 1986). As with any private insurance program, WC is subject to the problems of adverse selection and moral hazard.

D. The Veterans System

Although most work injuries fall into the realm of WC, war injuries fall into a different category, since the Department of Veterans' Affairs maintains a large bureaucracy that provides injured veterans with income, medical care, and rehabilitation. In 1986, for example, veterans compensation cost $5.7 billion; means-tested pensions for disabled veterans (although not disabled as a result of wartime injury) produced expenditures of $1.1 billion; the bill for veterans hospitalization came to $2 billion; and the various veterans rehabilitation programs cost $0.4 billion.

E. The Private System

Not all disability expenditures arise from the public sector or from actions mandated by the government. A private system, interlocked with the public system, consists of private disability and health insurance and makes limited use of public and private rehabilitation programs. At the end of 1985, 28 million people had short-term disability protection that was provided by private companies; nearly 26 million people had some form of private long-term disability income protection, with nearly 75% of this coverage coming in the form of group policies. The typical long-term policy replaced about 60% of a person's pre-disability income and required the person to apply for Social Security benefits before receiving private benefits (Health Insurance Association of America, 1987, pp. 7–8; McNeil, 1986).

The linkages between the various parts of the private and public disability systems are far from straightforward and create many disincentives for the labor force participation of disabled persons. Many people buy insurance policies to cover the risks arising from specific events, such as an automobile accident or an airplane crash. But such policies do not preclude the person or the insurance company from utilizing the tort system to claim damages from a reckless driver or a negligent airline. The resulting system contains significant overlaps among the various insurance coverages and requires complicated rules to establish which program or party should make the "first payment" to the disabled person. Even with these rules, many possibilities exist for a disabled person to be "over-insured," and any recourse to the tort system typically involves the significant passage of time to conclude a case, with the effect of diminishing incentives for rehabilitation and labor force participation.

F.   Direct Employment Incentives

Each of these income maintenance–rehabilitation systems emphasizes income transfers, rather than the creation of jobs. Other laws and programs attempt to create direct incentives for the employment of the handicapped. These programs range from booster programs, such as the President's Committee on Employment of Persons with Disabilities, which publicizes the capabilities of handicapped persons, to more direct requirements, such as laws that mandate accessible workplaces on the part of federal contractors or reserve certain jobs for blind persons.

To understand these jobs creation programs, one might divide them into three groups. Some of the programs, such as a special provision in the minimum-wage law, modify federal or state labor standards in an effort to encourage the employment of the handicapped. Others, such as programs that allow blind persons to sell refreshments in federal buildings or require the federal government to purchase products from sheltered workshops, set aside portions of funds or reserve particular activities for handicapped persons. Still others combat prejudice on the part of employers in hiring workers or require modifications of the workplace.

This last group of programs, those dealing with civil rights and architectural barriers, may be the most important of all. Here we concentrate on Section 5 of the Rehabilitation Act of 1973. This act, passed without a great deal of congressional scrutiny, contains the following famous passage: "No otherwise qualified handicapped individual in the United States shall, solely by reason of his handicap, be excluded from participation in, be denied the benefits of, or be subjected to discrimination under any program or activity conducted by an Executive agency or by the United States Postal Service." Other subsections require affirmative action in federal employment and the achievement of accessibility in federal buildings through the creation of a board charged with ensuring compliance with the Architectural Barriers Act of 1968. Section 503 obligates any contractor entering into a contractual agreement with the federal government in excess of $2500 to take "affirmative action to employ and advance in employment persons with handicaps" (Scotch, 1984). Limited to the activities of the federal government, this act nonetheless constitutes America's most sweeping civil-rights statute on behalf of handicapped persons.

As this chapter was being written, congress was on the verge of passing the Americans with Disabilities Act of 1990. This legislation extends civil-rights protection to cover such areas as private employment and public accommodations. It brings the level of civil-rights protection for people with disabilities to parity with other minority groups.

This overview of disability programs makes it clear that civil rights has not yet become the major vehicle for solving the problems of disability. Instead, the American disability system consists of a Social Security track, complete with medical care and limited rehabilitation services, a public assistance track, also with medical care and rehabilitation services, a work injury track, special tracks for veterans, and a private-sector track. In addition, laws that alter minimum standards of employment, that set aside money or jobs, and that attempt to guarantee employment also characterize the American disability system. One cannot help but note that part of the system subsidizes retirement and encourages withdrawal from the labor force; another part explicitly seeks to encourage the entry of the handicapped into the labor force.

VI. THE DISINCENTIVE STUDIES

This description of the American disability system raises two major empirical issues. One concerns the effect of income transfers on the labor force participation of handicapped persons. The other involves the efficacy of the various measures, whether rehabilitation services or civil-rights statutes, designed to encourage the labor force participation of handicapped persons. Do these measures work, or do their costs outweigh their benefits?

First, let us consider what might be called the disincentive issue. Building on the labor–leisure trade-off, economists have long recognized the potential disincentive effects of transfer payments that are conditioned on the withdrawal of the beneficiary from the labor force. In particular, they have studied the effects of SSDI on labor force participation. Leonard (1986), in a masterful summary of these studies, notes that they agree on the direction but not the magnitude of the effect. Although we do not understand this issue as well as we do the effects of minimum wages or unions on labor supply, Leonard concludes that the studies have succeeded in "drawing attention to the labor supply effects of SSDI, demonstrating the link between the growth of the SSDI beneficiary rolls and the decline in labor force participation rates, and establishing some range within which the true labor supply effect of social security disability is likely to fall" (Leonard, 1986, p. 64).

The studies stem from an easily observed trend. The nonparticipation rate of males, aged 45–54, reached a low of 3.5% in the early 1950s, and then began to climb just as the SSDI program got underway (Parsons, 1984). The early studies of Gastwirth (1972), Swisher (1973), and Siskind (1975) made simple comparisons of the increases in the disability rolls and the decline in labor force participation. Hambor (1975) took economic factors into account, noting that the applicant rate increased with the unemployment rate. That suggested a degree of discretion in the labor force participation of disability insurance applicants that made the decision to seek disability benefits appear more like other labor supply decisions.

Using data from the National Longitudinal Surveys, Parsons (1980) estimated 1969 labor force participation rates of men who were 45–59 years old as a function of SSDI benefits, welfare benefits, wages, a mortality index, age, and unemployment. He took wages in 1966 as a proxy for expected labor force earnings. He also utilized mortality from 1969 to 1976 as a proxy for 1969 health status. A person who died during this period was assumed to be in poor health in 1969. He found that the elasticity of nonparticipation with respect to the replacement rate was 0.63 and that it varied greatly with the mortality index.

Parson's findings are disputed by Haveman and Wolfe (1984) and Haveman et al. (1984), who estimated a relatively inelastic labor supply response to disability benefits, although not specifically to SSDI benefits. Haveman and Wolfe used a 741-person subsample of 45- to 62-year-old men in the 1978 Michigan Panel Study of Income Dynamics. They focused on what caused labor force withdrawal rather than on the attractiveness of the SSDI program. They estimated a single grouped response to a set of disability-related transfers, including SSDI, SSI, veterans' disability benefits, other disability pensions, welfare, and help from relatives.

Haveman and Wolfe found an elasticity of labor force nonparticipation with respect to disability income that ranged from 0.0205 in a replication of Parson's specifications to 0.0056 with the addition of dependent benefits, other controls, selectivity corrections, and eligibility adjustments. Haveman et al. (1984) discovered an extremely nonlinear response with much larger elasticities among more disabled persons and those with lower earnings. We agree with Leonard that these results caution against the use of simple linear models to capture widely varying behavior.

In a 1979 study, Leonard used a sample of 1685 men aged 45–54 drawn from the 1972 Social Security Survey of Health and Work Characteristics merged with Social Security beneficiary records and earnings histories. The major econometric problem for the study was that a large proportion of the sample was out of the labor force and had no observable wage. Because of the nature of the available data, Leonard was forced to use specific health conditions as a proxy for impairment status, and these health conditions give no indication of severity. Despite these limitations in data, he found that the SSDI program had a large and significant effect in reducing labor supply: His estimate of the elasticity of labor supply in response to expected SSDI benefits was 0.35. A $180 increase in yearly benefits was discovered to increase the proportion of SSDI beneficiaries in the population by one percentage point. Leonard's work supports the hypothesis that a rise in SSDI benefits relative to the wage rate causes more men to apply and receive SSDI benefits and also causes their labor force participation rate to fall.

In an overall review of these and other studies, Leonard (1986) notes that, for all of their differences, the economic models of the labor force participation decision agree that expected income is an important variable. In practice, the studies differ in how expected incomes are imputed. We would add that these studies also demonstrate that the health condition of the person is an important variable, but the studies differ widely in how such a condition is measured. In short, disability transfer programs lead to some reduction in labor supply; how much is unclear. And, clearly, subjective factors, such as the perceived chances of obtaining benefits, play a role here. We know, for example, that disability benefits have been harder to get at some times than at others.

In WC, as in SSDI, the number of claimants bears a positive relation to the benefit level, but in WC, unlike SSDI, employers pay differential rates that may affect behavior. WC utilizes the concept of experience rating. Small employers pay a premium price (the manual rate) that reflects the expected accident and claims experience of all firms in the same line of business. Although nearly 85% of U.S. firms are manually rated, these firms employ less than 15% of those who work (Worrall and Butler, 1986). The remaining firms pay a premium that is based on a weighted average of their actual and expected loss experience. As premiums vary by firm size, so may safety incentives.

In WC, unlike SSDI, we must consider the effect of benefit levels on the provision of safety measures by employers, recognizing that firms may offer wage differentials to compensate for increased risk to workers. Smith (1979) has reviewed the literature. Arnould and Nichols (1983), Butler (1983), Dorsey (1983), and Dorsey and Walzer (1983) all find compensating differentials for risk bearing and a trade-off between the acceptance of WC benefits and wages.

A number of economists have examined the relationship between benefit levels, waiting periods, retroactive periods, and claims frequency. The research has been done for cross sections, time-series, and pooled cross-sectional time-series data at the level of the establishment, industry, or state. In a 1985 paper, for example, Worrall and Butler model the transition from a disabled to a non-disabled state as a function of wage, WC benefit, and other control variables. The principal finding is that the duration of disability varies directly with WC benefits and indirectly with the wage. Other research indicates that injury rates or claims frequency vary directly with WC benefits (Butler 1983; Butler and Worrall 1983; Chelius 1973, 1974, 1977, 1982, 1983; Ruser 1984; Worrall and Butler 1984; Worrall and Appel 1982).

In general, the findings from the WC experience echo those derived from an examination of the SSDI record. Applications and perhaps risk bearing and injuries are quite sensitive to changes in the level of benefits. There is also some evidence that the duration of nonwork spells associated with the receipt of WC benefits is a function of the level of those benefits. Not a great deal of research has been conducted on the impact of a "full" replacement rate, but one should keep in mind that a significant number of people who receive WC benefits also benefit from other programs.

VII. THE EFFICIENCY OF REHABILITATION

The efficiency of rehabilitation constitutes the second broad area of empirical studies that focus on the labor force participation of disabled persons. Here we focus on two aspects of the problem: the effectiveness of rehabilitation in general and the effectiveness of programs that attempt to rehabilitate beneficiaries of income maintenance programs, particularly WC.

Broadly defined, the rehabilitation process aids a person's recovery from the effects of an illness or injury and assists in a person's entry or reentry into the labor market. Both the public and private sectors provide rehabilitation. In the public sector, the VR program has emphasized the treatment of the severely disabled, a category that includes mental retardation and mental illness. Services include medical diagnosis and some treatment, education and training, counseling and guidance, and placement. Counselors employed by the state VR agencies provide the bulk of the counseling and guidance services and may arrange for education, training, or work evaluation services from vendors.

It is not easy to discern the market failure that would justify the public VR program. Traditionally, the program has justified its existence on the grounds that its benefits outweigh its costs. However, it has been reluctant to adopt modern evaluation techniques, and it has resisted any attempts to measure demand for its services by some sort of an experimental voucher system.

The problem of "preprogram dip" in earnings is more intense here than in the employment and training programs. Eligibility for VR depends on the existence of a physical or mental impairment that interferes with the person's labor market chances. The majority of clients who enter the program show zero wages at entry. The program defines a person who remains in a job for 60 days as a successful closure. Since average costs of services seldom exceed several thousand dollars and benefits are defined as the difference between the zero wages at entry and the positive earnings at closure projected over the person's working life, the program tends to display a favorable cost–benefit ratio.

Although program evaluations, initially crude, have become more sophisticated in recent years, they still suffer from the absence of a true control group to measure the treatment effects, of an outcome measure of long duration, and of a disability status measure that takes severity into account (Worrall, 1988). As a means around the first problem, Dean and Dolan (1988) have used status-30 persons, people admitted to the program who received no substantial services, perhaps because they dropped out or moved away, as a comparison group. For an outcome measure, they utilize earnings data for VR samples matched with records of the state employment service, thus allowing a longer period of follow-up than the traditional 60 days. This work shows a positive treatment impact for some groups given a particular array of services. Gibbs (1988) uses a hazard rate analysis to explore a different outcome variable. Instead of earnings, he looks at duration of work and nonwork spells and finds, using status-30 persons as a comparison group, some positive treatment effects.

As with so much of the work in the disability area, the measures of disability status tend to be crude, usually medical condition classifications. Dean and Millberg (1988) have experimented with using functional assessment measures to standardize for health condition.

In general, efforts to rehabilitate the beneficiaries of income maintenance programs pose different problems than those faced by the public VR programs. One might consider, for example, the many problems involved in the rehabilitation of WC clients. Which of the many compensation recipients should be selected to receive rehabilitation services? Which services should be offered? Who should authorize, provide and pay for the services?

Examples abound of various approaches to these problems. California makes rehabilitation a matter of right for the employee at the employee's request. That request could come at any time, including after the expiration of permanent partial benefits. In California, this provision, combined with the requirement that the employer/carrier is obligated to provide services once the plan has been approved, has led to a very costly system. Massachusetts has no provisions for a fixed number of days after which the case must be screened, but the employee, in indicated cases, must meet at least once with the rehabilitation personnel in the WC agency. New York maintains a voluntary system under which the carrier is supposed to screen cases for rehabilitation potential after a specified period, with little policing and no penalties for noncompliance.

States differ over the meaning of mandatory services. In California, the term means a plan where the provision of services is mandatory on the part of the carrier but the employee cannot be compelled to accept services. In Minnesota, Florida, and New Hampshire, by way of contrast, the employee may be penalized for noncooperation or refusal, although such penalties are difficult to enforce. Someone who does not want to receive rehabilitation services makes a problematic rehabilitation candidate.

The cost burden of rehabilitation differs by who performs the services. If the WC agency carries out evaluation and possibly supervises the delivery of services, the costs may well be met as part of the agency budget. That budget may be financed by separate state appropriation or by an assessment on all carriers and self-insurers in the state. If the VR program performs the services, the costs might be met by the regular VR agency budget, which is based on an 80% federal share and a 20% state share. However, the most common method of meeting rehabilitation expenses involves payment by the insurance carriers.

Placing the burden on insurance carriers follows directly from the theory on which WC is based. Under this theory, the worker waives the right to full recovery for all damages suffered. Instead, the worker receives compensation for a portion of wage losses, medical care designed to relieve the effects of the injury, and, presumably, rehabilitation services. Rehabilitation services thus become part of the compensation benefits and the worker has an entitlement only to benefits designed to restore his or her preinjury condition.

VIII. THE EFFECTIVENESS OF CIVIL-RIGHTS MEASURES

Civil-rights laws represent a different way to increase the labor force participation of handicapped persons. These statutes typically benefit people on the edge of the labor market who have not received a permanent entitlement to income maintenance benefits. Some argue that these people suffer the stigma of being handicapped and require special legal protection to overcome the forces of prejudice. Alternatively, such people might benefit from government-mandated accommodation of the work site to match their abilities.

Although these laws pose many analytical issues, the study of civil-rights statutes remains in its infancy. The very notion of submitting these laws to economic analysis strikes many as beside the point. Advocates argue that the proposals of civil-rights movements on behalf of blacks and women were not subjected to cost–benefit tests. Instead, Congress and the courts implicitly ruled that civil rights transcended costs. Put another way, no cost was too high to pay in return for securing racial or sexual equality. Advocates of rights for the handicapped make similar arguments. As one has written, "Economics cannot be the issue around which decisions turn. The Supreme Court has long ago said that civil rights cannot be abrogated simply because of cost factors" (Bowe, 1980).

Economists have nonetheless attempted to assess the costs and benefits of enforcing civil-rights laws. The Berkeley Planning Associates, for example, have analyzed the costs of making "reasonable accommodations" in order to employ disabled persons (Collignon, 1986). The term can be found in regulations that accompany Section 5 of the Rehabilitation Act of 1973, such as in the definition of a handicapped person as one "who is capable of performing a particular job, with reasonable accommodation to his handicap." The concept is elusive. Much of the law emphasizes the inherent productivity of handicapped people; the concept of reasonable accommodation implies a cost to making the handicapped worker as productive as his peers. To charge the handicapped person this cost by paying him or her less, however, invites a charge of wage discrimination, which is also against the law. But someone must bear the costs of accommodation.

Some factors mitigate the inherent dilemma. Fragmentary evidence indicates, for example, that expensive job modification is seldom required to accommodate handicapped workers. At times the required adjustment is relatively simple (O'Neill, 1976). One survey of 250 people in California with rheumatoid arthritis found that the ability to schedule one's own hours of work was a good indicator of whether a person would return to work (Yelin, 1979). In addition, the costs of accommodation can be used to offset other costs. If the firm has invested a lot of specific training in the worker and if the firm faces the alternative of high disability maintenance costs for the worker, it pays to invest in accommodation to the point where the marginal costs of accommodation equal the dollars saved in pension costs and the costs of training a new worker.

Stating these conditions is a much easier task than measuring the various costs and benefits. Collignon (1986) notes the paucity of hard data. There are no studies of reasonable accommodation in firms that are not federal contractors and hence not covered by Section 503. Such firms may be covered under state laws. All of the studies have examined the accommodation of workers already employed by the firm and not the accommodation of workers seeking entry to the firm. Furthermore, physical barriers in the workplace do not appear to be as significant as the worker's training and education in explaining a disabled person's success in the labor market, yet we would like to know more about the relative weights of these factors.

Another undeveloped area of inquiry concerns the costs of discrimination against persons with disabilities. Becker's notions of discrimination (1957) might usefully be extended to cover discrimination against the handicapped. The question becomes measuring an employer's taste for discrimination to determine how much he or she is willing to spend in order to have a labor force free of handicapped workers. Evidence does show that prejudice varies by the rate of impairment and that in general handicapped workers receive lower rates of return to education, experience, and health. Employers also appear to believe that disabled workers entail higher costs, because they are costly to supervise and less flexible in the jobs that they can do.

These findings imply that there would be benefits to eliminating discrimination. As Johnson (1986) notes, such an action would make for "more efficient use of labor, improved efficiency in the human capital market, and increase incentives for labor force participation by impaired workers." Nor, Johnson argues, can the market eliminate this prejudice, because much of the discrimination can be characterized as monopsonistic discrimination or as statistical discrimination.

IX. POLICY IMPLICATIONS

Where does this dense tangle of institutional and empirical detail leave us? Our overview of the field suggests that the economist would do better altering institutions at their margins rather than questioning the existence of those institutions. Furthermore, as our treatment of rehabilitation under WC suggests, we must be wary of making global generalizations. In short, institutions, by their very existence, constrain our behavior, and the institutions are extremely segmented, so that disability benefits in, say, Massachusetts are not the same as disability benefits in Illinois.

The situation resembles the ability of the economist to alter the minimum wage. Despite abundant studies of employment effects, minimum wages endure. At best, economists have succeeded in restraining the rise in minimum-wage rates and in pointing out the differences between the wish of high wages and the deed of accomplishing them. Similarly, the disincentive studies show us that rising disability benefit rates lower labor force participation rates, but the best we can hope for is that policymakers understand some of the costs of their actions when they raise rates.

Economists too often assume a degree of conceptual certainty that simply does not exist in the area of disability. The policy issues in vocational rehabilitation, for example, lie beyond simple calculations of costs and benefits. Because we know that the program will survive, the issue is not whether the program can justify itself but rather how it might operate more efficiently. Studies indicate that the program has an impact on some clients. Now these studies need to be extended to provide administrators with guidance on choosing clients and deciding the mix of services that would yield the most efficient outcomes.

Another promising line of reform lies in the relationship between income maintenance and rehabilitation. Here we might reconsider the relationship between VR and SSDI. The thrust of the VR programs and the rehabilitation efforts of the other agencies, whether SSA or state WC, is quite different. VR may give preference to whatever group Congress wishes to target, but essentially it is dealing with persons who are motivated enough to apply to the program. the objective of the VR program is to improve those persons and possibly to restore them to the maximum functioning capacity.

Most of the income maintenance programs have narrower objectives. They seek to save benefit dollars by providing services designed to restore beneficiaries to a work status. In the SSA program, the problem arises of identifying potential rehabilitees early enough. Once a person is on the rolls, that person has been disabled for at least six months and possibly for years. The applicant has been through a severe test in which the objective is to maximize impairment so as to qualify for benefits.

We think that the objective of this program may now appropriately be broadened to include rehabilitation. Surely one neglected area is the identification of persons who are potential rehabilitation beneficiaries before they even apply to the program. These persons have probably been receiving short-term benefits from an employer or state plan for some months before they apply to the SSDI program. In addition, a measure such as the proposed Social Security Work Incentives Act deserves consideration. This bill, already introduced in Congress, would allow workers to retain their Medicare benefits and some other benefits, even after they had returned to work. There might also be some tentative experiments with differential rates for disability insurance, depending on the employer's experience in keeping disabled people at work.

WC programs, which have the advantage of earlier identification than SSDI, have experimented with various methods to select rehabilitation candidates. States are natural laboratories of experiment, but with some exceptions (Gardner, 1985, 1988) they have taken little advantage of the opportunities to test the efficiency of the various systems. Some random-assignment studies are probably feasible in the state programs even if they are not acceptable in the VR programs.

Another variable of interest in the state WC programs concerns the method of paying benefits. Radically different incentives and disincentives stem from the interstate variations. Some states, such as New Jersey, pay permanent partial benefits (the costliest category of benefits) on an impairment basis. An award, once fixed, will not be changed if the worker goes back to his or her job. Such a system provides few disincentives for the worker to become rehabilitated once an award has been made. However, once the amount has been fixed, the employer has few incentives to encourage rehabilitation.

Other states fix benefits on the basis of loss of earnings or loss of earnings capacity. Here the employer has incentives to encourage rehabilitation if it means a reduction in benefits, but the employee has reasons to avoid any program that will reduce weekly benefit amounts. Granted, the programs have bewildering and complex ways to assess benefits; still, much can be said about the efficacy of these different incentive structures. As an example, Minnesota has begun to track its experiences under a fascinating system of differential benefits, designed with the incentive structure of both the employer and employee in mind.

Nor, in reforming our disability system, would we wish to dismiss the potential contributions of the private sector. Some firms have begun to experiment with a concept called disability management at the workplace, in which they make an effort to prevent their impaired workers from leaving the labor force. The evidence of these efforts is largely anecdotal, but some firms have discovered, in the time-honored manner of this literature, that hiring *their* handicapped employees is good business (Berkowitz and Berkowitz, 1989).

If the details of reform are sketchy, the general direction remains clear. We have developed a costly and reasonably adequate system of income benefits for disabled persons. We now need to give more thought to the adequacy of rehabilitation efforts, with the realization that rehabilitation, like any complex social goal, cannot be mandated into existence. We submit this examination of disability definitions, rates, and systems as proof.

REFERENCES

Arnould, Richard J. and Lem M. Nichols (1983), "Wage–Risk Premiums and Workers' Compensation: A Refinement of Estimates of Compensating Wage Differentials." *Journal of Political Economy* 91(2):332–340.

Becker, Gary (1957), *The Economics of Discrimination.* Chicago: University of Chicago Press, 1957.

Berkowitz, Edward D. (1987), *Disabled Policy: American Programs for the Handicapped.* New York: Cambridge University Press.

Berkowitz, Edward D. and Monroe Berkowitz (1989), "Incentives for Reducing the Costs of Disability." In Kenneth McLennan and Jack Meyer (eds.), *Care and Cost: Current Issues in Health Policy.* Boulder, CO: Westview Press, pp. 203–231.

Berkowitz, Monroe (1988), "Functioning Ability and Job Performance as Workers Age." In Michael E. Borus, Herbert S. Parnes, Steven H. Sandell, and Bert Seidman (eds.), *The Older Worker,* Industrial Relations Series, pp. 87–112.

Berkowitz, Monroe, Martin Horning, Stephen McConnell, Jeffrey Rubin, and John D. Worrall (1982), "An Economic Evaluation of the Beneficiary Rehabilitation Program." In Jeffrey Rubin (ed.), *Alternatives in Rehabilitating the Handicapped—A Policy Analysis.* New York: Human Services Press, pp. 1–87.

Boston Women's Health Book Collective (1984), *The New Our Bodies, Ourselves.* New York: Simon and Schuster, p. 7.

Bowe, Frank (1980), *Rehabilitating America: Toward Independence for Disabled and Elderly People*. New York: Harper and Row.

Butler, Richard J. (1983), "Wage and Injury Rate Response to Shifting levels of Workers' Compensation." In John D. Worrall (ed.), *Safety and the Work Force: Incentives and Disincentives in Workers' Compensation*. Ithaca, NY: ILR Press, pp. 61–86.

Butler, Richard J. and John D. Worrall (1983), "Workers' Compensation: Benefit and Injury Claim Results in the Seventies." *Review of Economics and Statistics* 65(4):580–589.

Chelius, James R. (1973), "An Empirical Analysis of Safety Regulation." In *Supplemental Studies for the National Commission on State Workmen's Compensation Laws*, Volume 3. Washington, DC: U.S. Government Printing Office, pp. 53–66.

———— (1974), "The Control of Industrial Accidents: Economic Theory and Empirical Evidence." *Law and Contemporary Problems* 38(Summer/Autumn 1974):700–729.

———— (1977), *Workplace Safety and Health*. Washington, DC: American Enterprise Institute.

———— (1982), "The Influence of Workers' Compensation on Safety Incentive." *Industrial and Labor Relations Review* 35:235–242.

———— (1983), "Workers' Compensation and the Incentive to Prevent Injuries." In John D. Worrall (ed.), *Safety and the Work Force: Incentives and Disincentives in Workers' Compensation*. Ithaca, NY: ILR Press, pp. 154–160.

Chelius, James R. and Robert S. Smith (1983), "Experience Rating and Injury Prevention." In John D. Worrall (ed.), *Safety and the Work Force: Incentives and Disincentives in Workers' Compensation*. Ithaca, NY: ILR Press, pp. 128–137.

Collignon, Frederick C. (1986), "The Role of Reasonable Accommodation in Employing Disabled Persons in Private Industry." In Monroe Berkowitz and M. Anne Hill (eds.), *Disability and the Labor Market*. Ithaca, NY: ILR Press, pp. 196–241.

Dean, David and Robert C. Dolan (1988), "Establishing a Mini-Data Link." In Monroe Berkowitz (ed.), *Measuring the Efficiency of Public Programs*. Philadelphia: Temple University Press, pp. 232–255.

Dean, David and William Millberg (1988), "Using Better Measures of Disability Status." In Monroe Berkowitz (ed.), *Measuring the Efficiency of Public Programs*. Philadelphia: Temple University Press, pp. 199–231.

Dorsey, Stuart (1983), "Employment Hazards and Fringe Benefits: Further Tests for Compensating Differentials." In John D. Worrall (ed.), *Safety and the Work Force: Incentives and Disincentives in Workers' Compensation*. Ithaca, NY: ILR Press, pp. 87–102.

Dorsey, Stuart and Norman Walzar (1983), "Compensating Differentials and Liability Rules." *Industrial and Labor Relations Review* 36(July):642–654.

Fries, James F. (1980), "Aging, Natural Death and the Compression of Morbidity." *The New England Journal of Medicine* 303(3):130–135.

Fries, James F. and L. Crapo (1981), *Vitality and Aging: Implications of the Rectangular Curve*. San Francisco: W. H. Freeman.

Gardner, John A. (1985), *Vocational Rehabilitation in Workers' Compensation: Issues and Evidence*. Cambridge, MA: Workers Compensation Research Institute.

———— (1988), *Vocational Rehabilitation in Florida Workers' Compensation: Rehabilitants, Services, Costs and Outcomes*. Cambridge, MA: Workers Compensation Research Institute.

Gastwirth, Joseph L. (1972), "On the Decline of Male Labor Force Participation." *Monthly Labor Review* 95(October):44–46.

Gibbs, W. Ernest (1988), "Changes in Duration of Employment and Unemployment Spells." In *Enhanced Understanding of the Economics of Disability—Final Report*, Grant No. G008300151. Washington, DC: National Institute of Disability and Rehabilitation Research.

Gruenberg, Ernest M. (1977), "The Failure of Success." *Milbank Memorial Fund Quarterly/Health and Society* 55(Winter):3–24.

Hambor, John C. (1975), "Unemployment and Disability: An Econometric Analysis with Time

Series Data." Staff Paper no. 20, U.S. Department of Health, Education and Welfare, Social Security Administration, Office of Research and Statistics, Washington, DC.

Haveman, Robert H. and Barbara L. Wolfe (1984), "The Decline in Male Labor Force Participation: Comment." *Journal of Political Economy* 92(3):532–541.

Haveman, Robert H., Barbara Wolfe, and Jennifer Warlick (1984), "Disability Transfers, Early Retirement and Retrenchment." In Henry Aaron and G. Burtless (eds.), *Retirement and Economic Behavior.* Washington, DC: Brookings Institution, pp. 65–93.

Haynes, R. Brian, David L. Sackett, D. Wayne Taylor, Edward S. Gibson, and Arnold L. Johnson (1978), "Increased Absenteeism from Work after Detection and Labeling of Hypertensive Patients." *The New England Journal of Medicine* 299(14):741–744.

Health Insurance Association of America (1987), *1986–1987 Source Book of Health Insurance Data.* Washington, DC: Health Insurance Association of America.

Johnson, William G. (1986), "The Rehabilitation Act and Discrimination Against Handicapped Workers: Does the Cure Fit the Disease?" In Monroe Berkowitz and M. Anne Hill (eds.), *Disability and the Labor Market.* Ithaca, NY: ILR Press, pp. 242–261.

Leonard, Jonathan (1979), "Social Security Disability Program and Labor Force Participation." Working paper 392, National Bureau of Economic Research, Cambridge, MA.

————— (1986), "Labor Supply Incentives and Disincentives for Disabled Persons." In Monroe Berkowitz and M. Anne Hill (eds.), *Disability and the Labor Market,* Ithaca, NY: ILR Press, pp. 64–94.

Manton, Kenneth G. (1982), "Changing Concepts of Morbidity and Mortality in the Elderly Population." *Milbank Memorial Fund Quarterly/Health and Society* 60(Spring):183–244.

Manton, Kenneth G. and Eric Stallard (1982), "Temporal Trends in U.S. Multiple Cause of Death Mortality Data: 1968–1977." *Demography* 19(November):527–547.

McNeil, John M. (1983), "Labor Force Status and Other Characteristics of Persons with a Work Disability: 1982." Current Population Reports, Special Studies, Series P-23, No. 127, Bureau of the Census, Washington, DC.

————— (1986), "Disability, Functional Limitation, and Health Insurance Coverage: 1984/1985: Data from the Survey of Income and Program Participation." Current Population Reports, Household Economic Studies, Series P-70, No. 8, Bureau of the Census, Washington, DC.

Newquist, Deborah (1984), "Trends in Disability and Health Among Middle-Aged and Older Persons." Unpublished paper, Andrus Gerontology Center, University of Southern California, Los Angeles.

O'Neill, David (1976), "Discrimination Against Handicapped Persons: The Costs, Benefits, and Inflationary Impact of Implementing Section 504 of the Rehabilitation Act of 1973 Covering Recipients of HEW Financial Assistance." Report to the Office for Civil Rights, Public Research Institute, Arlington, VA.

Parsons, Donald O. (1980), "The Decline in Male Labor Force Participation." *Journal of Political Economy* 88(1):117–134.

————— (1984), "Disability Insurance and Male Labor Force Participation: A Response to Haveman and Wolfe." *Journal of Political Economy* 92(3):542–549.

Robinson, Pauline K. (1986), "Age, Health and Performance." In James E. Birren, Pauline K. Robinson, and Judy E. Livingston (eds.), *Age, Health and Employment.* Englewood Cliffs, NJ: Prentice-Hall, pp. 63–77.

Ruser, John W. (1984), "Workers' Compensation Insurance, Experience Rating and Occupational Injuries." Mimeo, U.S. Bureau of Labor Statistics, Office of Research and Evaluation, Washington, DC.

Scotch, Richard (1984), *From Goodwill to Civil Rights.* Philadelphia: Temple University Press.

Siskind, Frederic B. (1975), "Labor Force Participation of Men, 25–54, by Race." *Monthly Labor Review* 98(July):40–42.

Smith, Robert S. (1979). "Compensating Differentials and Public Policy: A Review." *Industrial and Labor Relations Review* 32(3):339–352.

Social Security Administration (1985), *Social Security Bulletin Annual Statistical Supplement 1984–1985*. Washington, DC: U.S. Government Printing Office.

Swisher, Idella G. (1973), "The Disabled and the Decline in Men's Labor Force Participation." *Monthly Labor Review* 96(November):53.

U.S. Senate (1988), *Aging America: Trends and Projections, 1987–1989 Edition*. Washington, DC: U.S. Senate Special Committee on Aging, American Association of Retired Persons, Federal Council on Aging and U.S. Administration On Aging.

Virginia Department of Rehabilitation Services (1988), "Enhanced Understanding of the Economics of Disability—Final Report." Grant No. G008300151, National Institute of Disability and Rehabilitation Research, Washington, DC.

Wing, Steve and Kenneth G. Manton (1981), "A Multiple Cause of Death Analysis of Hypertension-Related Mortality in North Carolina, 1968–1977." *American Journal of Public Health* (July):823–830.

Worrall, John D. (1988), "Benefit and Cost Models." In Monroe Berkowitz (ed.), *Measuring the Efficiency of Public Programs*. Philadelphia: Temple University Press, pp. 45–62.

Worrall, John D. and David Appel (1982), "The Wage Replacement Rate and Benefit Utilization in Workers' Compensation Insurance." *Journal of Risk and Insurance* 49(3):361–371.

Worrall, John D. and Richard J. Butler (1984), "Heterogeneity Bias in the Estimation of the Determinants of Comp Loss Distributions." Paper presented at the 1984 American Risk and Insurance Association Meetings, August, Minneapolis, MN.

———— (1985), "Workers' Compensation: Benefits and Duration of Claims." In John D. Worral and David Appel (eds.), *Workers' Compensation: Benefits: Adequacy, Equity, and Efficiency*. Ithaca, NY: ILR Press, pp. 57–70.

———— (1986), "Some Lessons from the Workers' Compensation Program." In Monroe Berkowitz and M. Anne Hill (eds.), *Disability and the Labor Market*. Ithaca, NY: ILR Press, pp. 95–123.

Ycas, Martynas (1987), "Recent Trends in Health Near the Age of Retirement: New Findings from the Health Interview Survey." *Social Security Bulletin* 50(February):5–30.

Yelin, Edward (1979), "From Social Theory to Social Policy: Social Class and the Epidemiology of Disability among Persons with Rheumatoid Arthritis." Ph.D. Dissertation, Department of City and Regional Planning, University of California, Berkeley.

THE UNEMPLOYMENT EXPERIENCE OF THE WORKFORCE

Jonathan S. Leonard and Michael Horrigan

ABSTRACT

From 1969 until the current recovery, the trend has been for a greater proportion of the labor force to become unemployed, and for those who become unemployed to remain unemployed longer. Trend increases in unemployment appear fairly widespread across demographic and industry groups, and the increase cannot be attributed to greater proportions young or female in the labor force. Most of the unemployed are job losers, and this proportion has been increasing. The economy appears quite fluid, with roughly one in every nine jobs disappearing each year, and one in eight being newly created. An increasingly open economy, faster technological change, and increasingly competitive markets may all reduce job stability. Some evidence suggests that jobs have become less stable over time, and workers less mobile. Both factors would present a challenge for reducing unemployment.

I. INTRODUCTION

The current economic recovery appears to have broken a trend dating back to 1969 of rising unemployment rates at each stage of the business cycle. The

Research in Labor Economics, Volume 11, pages 201–221.
ISBN: 1-555938-080-2

current good news allows some breathing room to consider the sources and policy implications of the unsettling upward trend in the unemployment rate.

This paper reviews evidence of changes in labor supply, labor demand, and market function that might contribute to long-run increases in the unemployment rate. Section II reviews recent labor market trends. Section III explores the relationship of demographic shifts in the age, gender, race, and education of the labor force to unemployment, and also examines increases in the rate of job loss and in the duration of unemployment. The last section reviews a recently developing area of research on the volatility of labor demand, and discusses the labor market implications of job creation and destruction patterns in the U.S. economy.

II. SECULAR INCREASES IN AGGREGATE UNEMPLOYMENT RATES

Between 1969 and 1982, the civilian unemployment rate increased secularly. A comparison of the "low" unemployment rates reached in successive recoveries and the "high" unemployment rates in successive recessions indicates this upward drift. Comparing successive recoveries, the low unemployment rates reached during those periods were 3.4, 4.8, 5.7, and 7.4%, respectively. Comparing successive recessions, the high rates were 6.0, 8.9, and 10.7%, respectively (see Figure 1).[1]

The current economic recovery, the longest peacetime expansion in the post–World War II era, has posted a decline in civilian unemployment rates from 10.7% in 1982Q4 to 5.3% in 1988Q4 (see Figure 1). This latter rate lies below the low rate of 5.7% associated with the 1975–1980 recovery. Has the current recovery ended the general upward drift in unemployment rates? The answer must await the judgment of future cyclical turns in the economy. However, even if the next recession brings a return to the general upward trend, the current recovery will represent a significant break in the pattern.

What lies behind the trends in the overall unemployment rate? As the economy experienced secularly rising unemployment rates over the 1969–1982 period, what proportion of those increases can be explained by the shifting composition of the labor force? To what extent were the overall rising unemployment rates simply reflected in rising unemployment rates of various labor force groups? And finally, what has been the impact of the current recovery?

To answer these questions, comparisons are made of the respective low unemployment rates reached in the successive recoveries of the 1969–1988 period on the basis of the following stratifications of the unemployed: age, sex, educational attainment, reason for unemployment, industry affiliation of last job, and length of unemployment spell.[2] Similar comparisons are made of the respective high unemployment rates of successive recessions. Owing to the shortness of the minirecession and recovery between 1980 and 1981, the cyclical points associated with these periods are not included in the analysis.

Figure 1. Unemployment rate of all civilian workers, seasonally adjusted, 1948–1989.

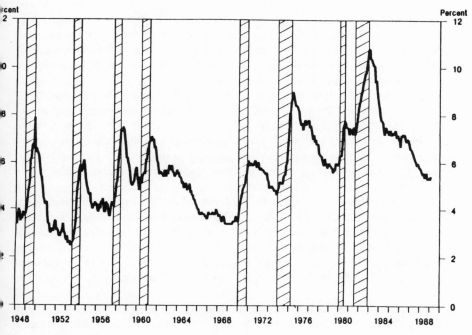

Note: Shaded areas represent recessions
Source: Bureau of Labor Statistics, February 3, 1989

III. SOURCES OF SECULAR INCREASES IN UNEMPLOYMENT RATES

This section uses a decomposition approach to estimate the degree to which changes in the demographic composition of the labor force have contributed to the secularly increasing unemployment rates between 1969 and 1982, and the effect of demographic factors in the current recovery.[3] Also considered in this section are the impacts of changes in the reasons for being unemployed, the industrial composition of unemployment, and the length of unemployment spells.[4]

A.   Demographic Factors

A division of the unemployed by age groups shows that, as expected, unemployment rates decline with age. The civilian labor force shares of individuals in the 16–24 age group peaked in the 1970s. The civilian labor force participation rates of this group increased over the entire three decades, although showing evidence of a slowdown in the 1980s. The civilian labor force share and the participation rates of the 25–34 age group reached plateaus in 1986 and 1987, respectively. As a result of the aging of the baby boom cohort, the labor force shares of the 35–44 age group declined until the mid-seventies and have been increasing since. The labor force participation rates of this group steadily increased over the entire 1960–1988 period.

Table 1 traces the contribution of age groups to the secularly rising unemployment rates between 1969 and 1982, and to the decline in overall rates in the current recovery. There are three noteworthy features to this table. First, between successive recoveries and successive recessions, it is the changing unemployment rates within age groups that explain the vast majority of changing overall rates. The contribution of changing labor force shares between different age groups is, with few exceptions, very small.

Second, between 1969Q1 and 1973Q2, when baby-boomers were entering the 16–19, and to a lesser extent, the 20–24 age groups, the increasing labor force shares of youth exerted upward pressure on overall unemployment rates. Though relatively small, the impact of changing labor force shares over this period is consistent with the fact that unemployment rates of teenagers tend to be substantially higher than for any other group, followed by the unemployment rates of the 20–24 age group.

Third, the decline in labor shares of teenagers between 1979Q2 and 1988Q4 and the demographic movement of the baby boom into prime age groups resulted in a natural rate of unemployment that is lower than it otherwise would have been over the period.

Table 1. Percentage Decomposition of the Total
Increase in Low and High Unemployment Rates
between Successive Recoveries, by Age[a]

	Contribution (%) due to		
Comparison dates	Changing unemployment rates	Changing weights	Interaction effects
Low rates			
1969Q1–1973Q3	79.5	14.3	6.3
1973Q3–1979Q2	91.8	8.0	0.3
1979Q2–1988Q4	−12.9	132.9	−19.9
High rates			
1971Q3–1975Q2	90.7	6.9	2.5
1975Q2–1982Q4	105.4	−8.4	3.0

Note: [a] Age groups are 16–19, 20–24, 25–34, 35–44, 45–54, 55–64, 65+.

A division of the unemployed into groups of teenagers, adult men, and adult women shows that the unemployment rate of teenagers is consistently higher than for either adult males or females. Further, until 1982, the unemployment rates of adult males were consistently lower than for adult females. Since 1982, equality between the sexes has been the norm. The labor force participation rates of adult men and women overall are also telling. In the post–World War II era, the participation rates have steadily declined for adult men and steadily increased for adult women. The pattern for adult women was particularly sharp over the 1969–1982 period. Another significant trend that has developed in the last two decades is the rising proportion of the population that is employed. The employment–population ratio, although sensitive to cyclical swings in the economy, has increased markedly since the 1973–1975 recession, especially in the current recovery.

The impact of changes in the unemployment rates and the labor force shares of men and women indicates the predominant role of changing unemployment rates within each group.[5] Consistent with the fact that labor force participation rates of females have increased substantially, the impact of changing labor force shares between men and women became slightly larger across the successive recoveries and the successive recessions of the 1969–1982 period. However, the magnitude of these effects is small. Changes in labor force shares by sex explain very little of the secularly rising unemployment rates over the period. A comparison of the declining unemployment rates between the two recovery periods, 1979Q2 and 1988Q4 yields a similar conclusion.

B.   Educational Attainment

A division of the population by level of educational attainment shows that the average level of educational attainment has increased steadily since 1969. Consistent with this increase has been the steadily falling proportion of the population with less than four years of high school, a stable proportion with exactly four years of high school, and steady increases in the proportions with one to three years of college and four years of college or more. The same trends hold true for a division of the labor force into educational attainment groups.

In addition, the unemployment rate of each educational attainment group has mirrored the behavior of overall rates, although the extent of secular increase over the 1969–1982 period was most pronounced in groups with educational attainment levels of less than high school and high school only.

What has been the impact of the upward trend in the educational attainment levels of the labor force? Ceteris paribus, an increase in educational attainment has the effect of putting downward pressure on unemployment rates. However, between 1969 and 1982, the magnitude of this effect is small, overshadowed by secularly increasing unemployment rates within each educational attainment group. While the degree to which unemployment rates trended up was most pronounced for those with less than a high school degree, the pattern for each educational attainment group reflected the movement of the overall unemployment rate.

As a result, a separate comparison of the successive recessions and the successive recoveries between 1969 and 1982 led to the conclusion that shifts in the educational attainment of the labor force did not have a pronounced impact on the trend in unemployment rates. The single most important factor was the behavior of unemployment rates within each educational attainment group. Again, a comparison of the 1975Q2–1980Q1 recovery with the current period does not change this conclusion.

C. Reasons for Unemployment

Individuals are divided into four broad categories of reasons for being unemployed: job loser, job leaver, reentrant to the labor force, and new entrant to the labor force. The job loser category is further divided into those on layoff and those who are not.

Job loss represents the largest single group in a division of the unemployed by reason for unemployment. Over the 1968–1988 period, job losers accounted for an average 47% of the unemployed. Over this same time period, those who lost their jobs for reasons other than layoff represented 69% of job losers, a sizable proportion, which also exhibited an increasing trend over the period.

The second largest group is reentrants, making up 28% of the unemployed on average over the last two decades. The other categories—job leavers and new entrants—are smaller in relative size, each representing approximately 13% of the unemployed. Across these groups, both categories of job losers tend to be strongly countercyclical, while job leavers are less variable but procyclical. Both new entrants and reentrants to the labor force are procyclical.

In assessing the contribution of reason for unemployment toward explaining secularly rising unemployment rates, it is not possible to use the decomposition approach employed above. This approach requires estimating the size of the labor force of each group, which, of course, is not possible for this particular stratification of the unemployed. Instead, the overall unemployment rate was expressed as the sum of ratios, where each ratio is the level of unemployment by reason, divided by the size of the overall labor force. A change in unemployment rates can then be expressed as the sum of changes in these ratios.

Applying this technique, the job loser category clearly dominated the upward drift in unemployment rates over the 1969–1982 period, and in proportions that are much greater than their representation among the unemployed. The next most significant group was reentrants to the labor force, especially through the mid- to late seventies. It has been suggested that the reentrant category is dominated by job losers (Clark and Summer, 1979). The extent to which this is true further strengthens the impact of job loss on the secular rise in unemployment over the period.

In addition, despite the decline in unemployment rates between 1979Q2 and 1988Q4, the comparison dates for the 1975–1980 recovery and the current period, the ratio of the number of job losers to the labor force increased while similar ratios for jobs leavers, new entrants, and reentrants posted declines.[6]

D. Industry Groups

The decomposition of industry unemployment rates suggests a cautious view of the claim that the shift between the goods-producing sector (especially manufacturing), and the service-producing sector was the cause of secularly rising unemployment rates over the 1969–1982 period. In each comparison over this period, the effect of changing labor force shares by industrial affiliation is insignificant. In contrast, a comparison of the current recovery with the 1975–1979 period does show a slightly greater effect of shifting labor force shares across industries. In all, labor force shifts across industries account at most 9% of the reduction in overall unemployment rates between 1979Q2 and 1988Q4.

To understand these results, it is particularly important to account for changes in both industry unemployment rates and the relative share of the civilian labor force within each industry. The patterns in manufacturing are a case in point. Over the 1969–1982 period, manufacturing's share of the labor force fell steadily over time from 36.9% in 1969Q3 to 27.8% in 1982Q4. By 1988Q4, this figure had fallen further to 24.1%. As well, over the 1969–1982 period, the unemployment rates within manufacturing were posting secular increases. These rates have fallen markedly in the current recovery—from a high of 14.2% in 1982Q4 to 5.2% in 1988Q4, matching the low reached during the 1975–1979 recovery.

The decline in the industry's relative share over the 1969–1982 period acts to diminish its percentage contribution to explaining secularly rising unemployment rates. However, the secularly rising unemployment rates within the industry act in the opposite direction. In other words, within manufacturing, unemployment rates increased secularly over the 1969–1982 period, although a smaller proportion of the civilian labor force was in manufacturing. Which effect dominated? As it turns out, the decline in manufacturing's labor force share did little to offset changes in manufacturing unemployment rates. One exception to this occurred in the comparison between 1975Q2 and 1982Q4, in which the declining labor force share nearly offset the rising unemployment rates in manufacturing between the two periods.

Turning to the service-producing sector, labor force shares in this sector have been rising since the early seventies. In particular, average civilian labor force shares in the finance and services industries have risen from 26.0% in 1969Q3 to 31.7% in 1982Q2. By 1988Q4 this figure had risen to 35.9%. As with the manufacturing sector, unemployment rates in the service-producing sector trended upward over the 1969–1982 period, falling during the current recovery to 4.4% in 1988Q4, below the low posted during the 1975–1979 recovery. Moreover, unemployment rates in the service-producing sector, especially in the finance and services industries, are consistently lower than overall non-agricultural unemployment rates. Over the 1969–1988 period, the average unemployment rate in the finance and services industries was 5.3%, compared to the 6.8% rate overall.

As with manufacturing, changing unemployment rates were of greater relative importance than changing labor force shares. One exception, also consistent with manufacturing, was the greater relative impact of labor force shares as compared to changing unemployment rates in the sector between 1975Q2 and 1982Q2.

When the shifts in labor force composition by industry are taken as a whole, however, their net impact on the secularly rising unemployment rates of the 1969–1982 period is not significant. Changes in unemployment rates within industry explain nearly all of the trend.

Finally, although the current recovery shows a slightly greater impact of shifting labor force shares than in any other comparison period (nearly 9%), changing unemployment rates still account for nearly 75% of the fall in unemployment rates between 1979Q2 and 1988Q4.

E.   Length of Unemployment

Although the divisions of the unemployed into the various groups considered thus far contribute to an understanding of unemployment, our knowledge is enhanced further if the dynamic flows in and out of unemployment over time are also examined. One way to capture these dynamic movements is to measure the average total length of time a newly unemployed individual can expect to remain unemployed.

Although estimates of duration vary, measures of average time spent unemployed are consistently found to be countercyclical. The official measure from the CPS typically ranges between 4 and 12 weeks, and has exhibited a strong secularly increasing pattern over the entire 1969–1988 period. This measure, however, captures the average age of unemployment spells among the currently unemployed as of the survey date. Studies of the average total time a currently unemployed individual remains unemployed report estimates in the range of 8 to 16 weeks (Akerlof and Main, 1980). The currently unemployed can be thought of as the remaining members of all prior newly unemployed groups. For any newly unemployed group, the average probability of exiting unemployment declines over the group's time in unemployment. As a result, the exit probabilities of the currently unemployed will tend to be lower on average than for the newly unemployed. Not surprisingly, studies examining the expected completed spell length of newly unemployed individuals find shorter average spell lengths, in the range of 1.5 to 3.5 months (Sider, 1985; Horrigan, 1987). In these latter studies, the countercyclical nature of duration is evident, but there is no indication of a secularly increasing pattern.

Measures of average spell length are summary statistics, and although informative, do not shed much light on the underlying distribution of spell lengths. In particular, across the entire 1969–1982 period, there was a dramatic secular increase in the proportion of individuals who are long-term unemployed (27 weeks or more). The current recovery has not reversed this upward drift. For example, the percentage of individuals in long-term unemployment spells in 1988Q4 (11.3%) was far above the previous low percentage value recorded in the 1975Q2–1980Q1 recovery (8.3%).[7] One explanation for this increase in the proportion of long-term unemployment spells that is not very likely is that it is due to changes in the provision of unemployment insurance. In the last decade, the proportion of unemployment insurance beneficiaries among the unemployed declined, benefits became taxable, and the system achieved a greater degree of experience rating. In addition, unemployment insurance benefits are rarely received after 27 weeks of unemployment.

As is generally the case, the composition of the long-term unemployed over the 1969–1988 period has differed considerably from the makeup of total unemployment. Membership in long-term unemployment is more likely to be comprised of prime-age and older males, job losers, and workers from cyclically sensitive industries such as manufacturing than are the unemployed as a whole.

The question of interest in this analysis is the extent to which the secular increase in the relative size of long-term unemployment has also changed the composition of the long-term unemployed. For example, has the degree to which job losers are overrepresented in long-term unemployment changed appreciably as the percentage of individuals in long-term spells has increased? The following general conclusions emerge: First, over the entire 1969–1988 period, two groups were represented disproportionately: 25–44-year-old males and job losers. However, even though these two groups make up a disproportionate share of long-term unemployment, their degree of overrepresentation has not changed over time.

Second, the industry composition of the long-term unemployed was also fairly neutral; that is, the burden of long-term unemployment, while always falling disproportionately on individuals from cyclically sensitive industries, did not shift noticeably between groups defined by industry affiliation. The one exception to this latter result is the relative shift that occurred within durable-goods industries in terms of their representation among the long-term unemployed. In particular, over the 1969–1988 period, manufacturing's share of the long-term group fell while that of construction and mining rose. Aside from these shifts, the remaining industry groups did not exhibit either a growing or falling trend.

The importance of these findings is underscored by the recent work of Summers (1986) and of Topel and Murphy (1987), who view the shift toward long-term unemployment as the main reason underlying the secular increase in unemployment between 1969 and 1982.[8] Despite a decline in the proportion of the unemployed receiving unemployment insurance benefits, unemployment spells have become longer. Increases in wage dispersion and increases in the proportion of working spouses, along with the unusual sectoral shocks of recent years, may have led displaced workers to search longer while unemployed.

F. Labor Supply—Summary Observations

In summary, this section has demonstrated that a division of the unemployed into groups on the basis of traditional supply side characteristics such as age, sex, and educational attainment levels does not provide much insight into the reasons underlying the secular increases in unemployment rates between 1969 and 1982. When compared to the recoveries between 1969 and 1982, however, the current recovery is marked by a significant impact of the changing labor force shares of different age groups, especially the declining share of teenagers. In general, the evidence suggests that the movement of the baby boom cohort into prime-age groups with their relatively lower rates of unemployment has tended to decrease the natural rate of unemployment. Similarly, declines in the labor force shares of individuals with less than four years of high school have served to make the overall unemployment rate lower than it would have been.

Among the various reasons for becoming unemployed, job loss among both sexes increasingly dominated the secularly rising unemployment rates between 1969 and 1982. However, despite the dramatic decrease in the labor force share of the manufacturing sector, and the relative increase in the service-producing sector, industry decomposition of the labor force suggests these shifts did not have a significant impact on the trend increase in unemployment rates.

Finally, across the 1969–1982 period, there was a dramatic increase in the proportion of individuals who are long-term unemployed. The current recovery has not reversed this upward drift. This shift toward long-term unemployment has largely been due to increased representation of 25–44-year-old males and job losers. However, the representation of these groups in long-term unemployment has mirrored their representation in the overall unemployment pool. As well, this shift has largely been neutral across industry groups; that is, no one industry has experienced disproportionate gains or losses in its share of total long-term unemployment.

IV. THE DEMAND FOR LABOR

If supply side factors explain very little of the secular increase in unemployment rates over the 1969–1982 period, then it remains to examine the demand side of the labor market for clues. Unemployment can be viewed as arising from insufficient aggregate demand, or from structural and frictional mismatches. One symptom of structural/frictional unemployment is that both the unemployment rate and the vacancy rate are high. People are looking for work at the same time that employers are looking for workers. Because of poor information, or geographic or skill mismatches, vacancies and unemployment coexist.

During the last two decades major structural shocks include the oil shocks of 1973 and 1978, and the trade shocks accompanying the exchange rate shifts of the early 1980s. Low-value-added sectors of U.S. manufacturing were particularly sensitive to the trade shocks. Structural changes in the regional distribution of U.S. employment growth also appears to have contributed to rising unemployment (Medoff, 1983). While structural shocks that create the need for labor reallocation across industry lines are more likely to result in unemployment, most employment fluctuation occurs within rather than across industries (Leonard, 1987, 1988). The resulting frictional unemployment may be increasing.

A. Job Creation and Destruction

The degree of structural/frictional unemployment in the United States may be far larger than commonly supposed. Leonard (1987) reports that in an average year at the beginning of the 1980s, one in every nine jobs was destroyed, while one in every eight was newly created. These substantial rates of job turnover change slightly over the business cycle, and were of comparable magnitude in most industries. The job gain rate is calculated as the net jobs added at growing establishments from one year to the next, divided by total employment in the initial year. Job loss is symmetrically defined, and ignores both employment fluctuations shorter in length than the period between observations and job loss that is offset within the establishment. For the manufacturing sector, Davis and Haltiwanger (1989) report that in an average quarter during the early 1980s, 6% of all jobs disappear, and 5% are created. From year to year, they report 8% job gain and 13% job loss rates. These are similar in magnitude to Leonard's findings for the population of private employers (including nonmanufacturing) in one state. However, Leonard does find evidence that more jobs are gained than lost, which is consistent with the history of net job creation in the United States.

Net job turnover is simply the sum of the rates of job gain and loss. It ranges from 20 to 33% in annual data, and is even higher across shorter time periods because of transient short-term fluctuations in employment. This suggests a much more turbulent labor market than is apparent from aggregate statistics of smooth and small net-employment changes. In other words, net-employment growth on the order of 3% is the result of much larger gross flows. Roughly 45% of all establishments grow by an average of 30%, 47% of all establishments shrink by on average 21%, and the remaining 8% of establishments maintain stable employment (Leonard, 1987). Employment levels are anything but stable at the typical establishment. Unemployment rates on the order of 6% then suggest a remarkably fluid and adaptable labor force in the face of the annual disappearance of 10–25% of all jobs.

The rates of job creation and destruction calculated from periodic counts of total establishment employment are of similar magnitude to annual rates of new hires and layoffs previously collected by the Bureau of Labor Statistics (BLS). Between one-third and three-quarters of the new hires and layoffs rates can be accounted for by job creation and destruction (Leonard, 1987). The job destruction rates are also comparable in magnitude to the flow from employment to nonemployment reported by individuals in the CPS (Leonard, 1987).

If all who desire stable long-term employment can find it, or are compensated for bearing the risk of unstable jobs, there is little room for government intervention. There are, however, a number of reasons to think this is not the case. Job turnover at the establishment level depends on the path of employment over time, but this is very difficult to predict (Leonard, 1987, 1988). There is tremendous heterogeneity in employment growth rates not only across different establishments, but also for the same establishment over time. It is difficult to segregate establishments into stable and unstable groupings. Small employers do tend to be more unstable, but their small size makes it less likely that they develop widespread reputations. There is only weak evidence that a compensating differential is paid for employment in unstable jobs (Abowd and Ashenfelter, 1981). The shock often expressed by workers displaced from jobs they believed to be permanent is evidence that unstable workers have very imperfect information on which jobs are stable and which are not.

The data on job destruction can be used to augment the sketchy data on job duration. If 6% of jobs disappear each quarter (Davis and Haltiwanger, 1989) in steady state with homogeneous jobs, then a job is expected to last just over four years. This refers not to a job–worker match, but to the existence of the job itself irrespective of who fills it. Jobs of such limited duration are likely frequently to fall short of the duration desired by workers. However, job loss is not evenly distributed. Newly created jobs in new firms suffer from high infant mortality rates. It is possible for high turnover rates to coexist with a high proportion of stable jobs, if turnover is concentrated in a few positions. While the data required to determine the concentration of turnover are currently unavailable, job turnover of roughly similar magnitude appears to be a pervasive phenomenon across industries, regions, size classes, and many countries (Leonard, 1986, 1987, 1988; Davis and Haltiwanger, 1989; OECD, 1988).

Job growth has a large transient component that is more pronounced in shorter time intervals. When measured on an annual basis, job loss rates appear to be in a narrow range from 11% (Leonard, 1987) to 13% (Davis and Haltiwanger, 1989). In steady state, this yields expected job durations of seven to nine years. At the other extreme, comparing employment levels five years apart, Dunne et al. (1987) report that the average job in manufacturing lasts about 20 years. This is almost certainly an overestimate because the short-duration jobs that are born and die between censuses are not counted at all, and because job loss is not counted if other employment shifts leave establishment size unchanged. Using data on individual workers, Hall (1982) reports that the expected median tenure of a worker in 1978 was about eight years (completed spell). It seems likely that the high rate of job destruction contributes to short-duration job–worker matches. While most workers eventually find their way into long-duration jobs, they typically first transit through a number of short-duration jobs, not all of which are mismatches. The rate of annual job loss is not trivial. It may account for a substantial part of the underlying rate of unemployment. This is often referred to as the "natural" rate of unemployment. Being considered natural, it is often thought of as an irreducible part of a normally functioning economy or, alternatively, not thought of at all. To illustrate, suppose the 6% quarterly job loss rate calculated by Davis and Haltiwanger applies in steady state to the whole economy and captures all job loss. (In reality it will miss short-duration jobs and job turnover that leaves establishment size unchanged.) This amounts to an annualized 24% rate of job loss. Suppose only half of this job loss results in any unemployment, and that a completed unemployment spell lasts three months. This yields an unemployment rate of 3%, or two-fifths of the 7.5% average unemployment rate during the 1980s.

A number of factors have led to speculation that the natural rate of unemployment is now lower than before. As we have already mentioned, the teenage proportion of the labor force has declined. In addition, unions represent a lower percentage of the workforce and have recently been less aggressive in pursuing wage gains. The U.S. economy has become more open to international competition, which along with the deregulation of some major industries increases competitive constraints on wages. The reorganization of large corporations, with a growing "informal" sector of arms length, part-time, or subcontracted workers to accommodate peak demands may also help lower the unemployment rate attainable before inflation accelerates. The next section asks whether these factors leading to a reduction in the natural rate may have been outweighed by the increasing instability of jobs.

B. Changes over Time

Is the underlying rate of unemployment higher today than in previous years because all jobs have become more unstable, perhaps because of faster technological change, a more open economy, or more competitive markets? The available historical data do not extend far enough back to give adequate perspective on this question. Based on quarterly data in the manufacturing sector, the annualized job turnover rate ranges from 33% (1979) to 53% (1982) (Davis and Haltiwanger, 1989). The annualized rate of job loss rises from 16% in 1979 to 33% in 1982, before falling to 21% in 1983, and so appears cyclical. Job gain rates also increase from 17% in 1979 to 25% in 1983 (Davis and Haltiwanger, 1989).

Using annual data on Wisconsin establishments, Leonard (1987) finds job turnover rates rising from 22% in 1979 to 34% in 1982, but again over too short a time period to discern a clear pattern. Job loss rates range from 7% in 1978 to 16% in 1982. Job gain rates range from 9% in 1981 to 18% in 1982. In a national sample of larger firms between 1978 and 1984, there is no strong evidence that the variance of establishment growth rates has increased over time (Leonard, 1988). While none of this evidence allows us to compare present conditions with those of the 1960s, it would be useful if such information were systematically collected so that we could tell whether increases in unemployment were due to a more challenging world (more unstable jobs), or to less success in meeting a constant challenge.

There is considerable evidence that the reallocation of labor across industries increases with (and may account for part of) the business cycle. Increases in the unemployment rate are associated with more uneven growth across industries (Lilien, 1982). In part this reflects the greater cyclical sensitivity of the manufacturing sector (Abraham and Katz, 1986). It may also indicate the transmission of shocks, such as the oil price increases of 1973 and 1978 through the manufacturing sector to the economy as a whole (Hamilton, 1988). In any event, much of the increase in unemployment during a recession is accounted for by the loss of manufacturing jobs. The evidence on cyclical changes in job turnover is sketchy and mixed. Leonard (1987) reports weak evidence that the variance of growth rates across establishments rises with the unemployment rate. Industries with the fastest growth rates also appear to have the most dispersed growth rates. For manufacturing plants, Davis and Haltiwanger (1989) report a contrasting result: the job turnover rate is lower when industry growth is greater. If true, this suggests that employment growth not only reduces unemployment directly, but also indirectly by reducing labor reallocation across plants within industry.

C. Job Stability by Industry

Shifts in labor demand derived from shifts in consumer demand, technological innovation, or trade or regulation changes have had different effects on trend growth rates across industry. The role such factors play in accounting for differences in job stability across industry is less clear. Job instability appears to be a pervasive phenomenon, with relatively minor differences across industries that yield few clues to suggest specific causes. Job instability is not limited to a few industries or regions, to the manufacturing sector, to unionized plants, to industries subject to rapid technological change, or even to nations with certain regulatory structures (Leonard, 1986, 1987, 1988; OECD, 1988).

Within manufacturing, average annual job turnover rates between 1980 and 1983 range from 14% in the paper industry to 27% in the lumber industry. Job loss rates range from 8% in tobacco and in paper, up to 17% in lumber. Job gain rates range from 4% in primary metals to 11% in apparel (Davis and Halti-wanger, 1989). It is notable that the most unstable industry, lumber, is also among the least affected by technological change, by import competition, or by shifts in consumer demand across differentiated products. Two industries com-monly viewed as undergoing rapid technological change, chemicals and elec-trical machinery, have job turnover rates that are respectively below and slightly above average (Davis and Haltiwanger, 1989). Similarly, exposure to recent upheavals in trade and exchange rate fluctuations do not strongly differentiate industry turnover patterns. Primary metals and transportation equipment, around which many trade battles have been fought, have job turnover rates one percent-age point below and above the mean, respectively. The instability of jobs in the apparel industry presents a stronger case for trade pressures, although it may simply reflect an industry of smaller plants dependent on changing tastes.

Certain industries, particularly in durable-goods manufacturing, are more sen-sitive to the business cycle. Their job turnover rates vary more over time. The highest time-series variances of job turnover are found in primary metals, non-electrical machinery, apparel, and lumber (Davis and Haltiwanger, 1989). Except for apparel, the outputs from these industries are all inputs into long-term invest-ments that are known to be sensitive to the interest rate. Apparel is unusual among this group. It has high and variable turnover rates, for reasons already mentioned.

Some evidence suggests that job loss within industry becomes more concen-trated in a few plants as industry- or economywide employment declines (Davis and Haltiwanger, 1989). A growing industry or economy tends to spread em-ployment growth more evenly across plants, reducing the variance of growth rates. The tendency of job losses to be concentrated in fewer plants during a downturn perhaps helps explain recent support for plant-closing legislation, even though plant closings account for no more than 15% of all jobs lost from quarter to quarter, or from 17 to 38% of annual job loss (Davis and Haltiwanger, 1989). The contribution of plant closings is smaller in quarterly than in annual data because transient employment changes play a larger role across shorter time periods.

The long-run employment trend in industrialized countries out of manufactur-ing and into services is well-known. This is expected to reduce cyclical unem-ployment because the service sector is generally less cyclically sensitive than is manufacturing. Indeed, job turnover rates do vary less over the business cycle in services than in manufacturing (Leonard, 1987). However, at any point in time, service sector jobs are less stable than those in manufacturing. The movement from manufacturing to services is a move to jobs that are more stable over the cycle, but less stable at any point in the cycle. This should make cyclical stabilization policies easier to pursue, but raise the difficulty of reducing steady-state rates of unemployment.

More flexible wages are commonly proposed as a means of reducing employment fluctuations in the face of volatile demand. Union plants are often thought to have wages that are not only too high, but also too rigid. Employment does appear to grow less rapidly, if at all, in union plants. However, apart from this trend, union jobs appear no more unstable over time than do similar non-union jobs (Leonard, 1985). This suggests either that the role of wage rigidity has been overemphasized or else that, rather than being a problem unique to the union sector, it is widespread among large plants irrespective of unionization.

The occupational mix within a plant affects both its growth and its stability. Within industry, employment growth rates are significantly faster in plants with a greater proportion of white-collar workers (Leonard, 1988). In part, this may reflect a U.S. comparative advantage in skill-intensive products. There is little reason to expect the United States to compete successfully in industries requiring neither physical nor human capital against countries well-endowed with unskilled labor. To compete successfully in capital-intensive industries will require continued investments in technological advance, education, and other capital improvements. The necessity of considering such investments is heightened in view of hints of a coming mismatch between the skills required by growing industries and those supplied by the next generation (U.S. Bureau of Labor Statistics, 1987). Already, returns to education are rising (Bound and Johnson, 1989). A growing share of the workforce will be composed of groups, such as Hispanics, that have typically had lower education levels than average. Investments in education will tend to reduce social divisiveness and improve future productivity (Leonard, 1989).

More skilled jobs also appear to be more stable. Employment levels fluctuate less over time in establishments with a higher proportion of white-collar workers (Leonard, 1988). In part because of the more durable bonds between workers and employers with joint investments in firm-specific skills, white-collar workers are less likely to be displaced (Oi, 1962).

D.   Data Needs

The types of unemployment discussed here point toward additional information that would help show where the problem of unemployment lies. Some information is already collected by the government for other purposes, and merely needs to be reorganized and made more accessible. Other information might only be available through additional data collection.

First, consider making fuller use of information that already sits deep within various federal and state bureaucracies. Start with an obscure, but perhaps for that very reason, typical example. Data on separations and accessions at the plant level can be useful in judging flows into and out of unemployment. In the past, such information was collected and published by the Department of Labor, but fell victim to budget restraints. Less well-known is that such data continues to be collected by another branch of the Department of Labor for a fragmentary but not insubstantial sample, as part of the department's mandated responsibilities to enforce the contract compliance program.

The studies by Davis and Haltiwanger (1989) and by Dunne et al. (1989) demonstrate innovative uses of the Longitudinal Establishment Data set recently put together by the Census Bureau at relatively modest additional cost from annual data already collected. By constructing a longitudinal file, plants can be followed over time, allowing measures of flows into and out of employment. Similar analyses have been performed using data collected by federal and state governments for other purposes. Job turnover among large employers can be calculated from Equal Employment Opportunity data (Leonard, 1986). Data collected by the states to administer the unemployment insurance program can also be used to measure job growth and turnover (Leonard, 1987).

These all represent creative ways of patching together a makeshift bridge over a gaping hole in U.S. data collection. While the government conducts, supports, and makes publicly available a number of very useful surveys of people (the Census of Population, the CPS, the National Longitudinal Survey, the Survey of Income and Program Participation), no such survey of employers is publicly available. A number of European governments appear much better informed in this regard. This one-sided data has subtly, but significantly, affected research and policy. For example, much of the debate over unemployment has been framed in terms of the characteristics of people: their education, experience, race, sex, and age. Until recently, relatively little evidence could be marshaled about the instability of jobs themselves, although such evidence may shift the ways we think about unemployment and our policies to combat it. Policies directed toward altering employers incentives or information, or improving employer–employee matches have had much less prominence than manpower training programs. A publicly available employer survey might usefully contribute to the analysis of employment problems by making information available on employment flows including accessions, separations, vacancies, vacancy durations, and applicant queues. Data on levels and changes of wages, benefits, and employment, as well as on tenure, industry, region, occupational mix, corporate structure, inventories, back-orders, geographic and industry scope of marketing, and production plans are all potentially useful. To give one example, vacancy data are routinely collected in the U.K., making it possible to differentiate cyclical from structural unemployment. In the United States, the chief source of data on vacancies is the Index of Help Wanted Advertising published by the Conference Board. Those concerned that the U.S. economy is currently below the natural rate of unemployment may be surprised to learn that the Index of Help Wanted Advertising has not yet increased (Abraham 1987). The collection of vacancy data may also provide a useful guide for government efforts to redirect the unemployed to sectors with many openings. The available data on net-employment growth by industry underestimates job openings because even in a declining industry, one-third of the establishments are growing, and even in industries where total employment is shrinking by at least 5%, gross job creation typically exceeds 7%. Ideally, a matched employer–employee survey would allow analysis of how changes in labor market opportunities affect unemployment and earnings over the working life.

ACKNOWLEDGMENTS

This project was funded under Purchase Order No. 99-9-4765-75-018-04 from the U.S. Department of Labor, Commission on Workforce Quality and Labor Market Efficiency. Opinions stated in this document do not necessarily represent the official position or policy of the U.S. Department of Labor, Commission on Workforce Quality and Labor Market Efficiency.

NOTES

1.   This analysis ignores the recovery and recession of 1980–1981 because of their extremely short duration.

2.   An analysis of the changes in unemployment by region of the country was also conducted. Owing to the fact that the data on regions are not strictly comparable, the results by region are reported in note 4, along with a discussion of the data used in the analysis.

3.   The formula for the decomposition approach is as follows: Let U_t be the level of civilian unemployment at time t and L_t the size of the civilian labor force at time t. For $i = (1, \ldots, N)$, let U_{it} be the level of civilian unemployment in group i at t and L_{it} the size of the civilian labor force in group i at t.

For exposition purposes, let $N = 2$ (for example, a stratification by sex). In this case, the aggregate unemployment rate equals:

$$U_t/L_t = (L_{1t}/L_t) * (U_{1t}/L_{1t}) + (L_{2t}/L_t) * (U_{2t}/L_{2t}).$$

This expression can be rewritten as:

$$UR_t = W_{1t} * UR_{1t} + W_{2t} * UR_{2t},$$

where UR_t is the aggregate unemployment rate at time t, W_{it} the civilian labor force share of group i at t, and UR_t the unemployment rate of group i at t.

Let the t' subscript be used to denote the value of these variables at time t'. The change in unemployment rates between time t and t' can be expressed as the sum of the following three terms:

$$(UR_{t'} - UR_t) = \sum_i UR_{it'} * (W_{it'} - W_{it})$$

$$+ \sum_i W_{it} * (UR_{it'} - UR_{it}) + \sum_i (W_{it'} - W_{it}) * (UR_{it'} - UR_{it}).$$

The first term measures the change in unemployment rates due to the changing labor force shares across groups, holding the unemployment rate of each group constant at its value in time t. The second term measures the change in unemployment rates due to changing group unemployment rates, holding the civilian labor force of each group constant at its value in time t. The final term is a measure of the covariance of the two effects of changing group labor force shares and changing group unemployment rates. It is often called the error term and is usually small in size. We report the error term in this paper.

4. A division of the unemployed by region of the country shows that changing unemployment rates within regions, rather than shifting labor force shares between regions, accounts for practically all of the changes in overall unemployment rates during the 1969–1988 period.

A potential problem with the data exists, however, owing to the fact that the population weights used in the data are inconsistent across the entire period. Data for 1969 are benchmarked to the 1960 decennial census; data for 1971, 1973, 1975, and 1979 are benchmarked to the 1970 census; and data for 1982 and 1988 are benchmarked to the 1980 census.

What is the effect of using inconsistent population weights? To gauge the potential bias, the following three statistics were calculated for each of the above-mentioned years using the pattern of census weights described above: the civilian noninstitutional population, civilian labor force, and civilian unemployment level. A comparison was then made between the value of these statistics with those derived for the same years using 1980 census weights.

As expected, the values of the statistics using inconsistent population weights underestimated the values derived using 1980 census weights. However, a comparison of ratio statistics derived from the levels—namely, the unemployment rate and the labor force participation rate—reduces the bias to zero. This latter finding is supportive of the efficacy of using these data.

5. A decomposition of the unemployed into age–sex groups was also conducted, although not reported in the tables. The results for this finer group stratification mirror the pattern found using a simple age decomposition.

6. Although not reported in Table 1, the analysis by reason for unemployment was repeated for male and female groups. Owing to the fact that such data are not seasonally adjusted, annual average values were used. Comparing low-unemployment-rate years in successive recoveries (1969, 1973, and 1979) as well as the high-rate ones in successive recessions (1971, 1975, and 1982), job losers of both sexes, reentrant women, and—to a lesser extent—new female entrants each posted significant increases in their contribution to secularly rising unemployment rates over the period.

7. The same pattern emerges for those unemployed 15 weeks or longer or 52 weeks or longer. As well, over the 1969–1988 period, the proportion of the unemployed in new spells declined secularly; the proportion in short-term spells remained flat, and medium-term spells increased their proportionate share slightly.

8. Topel and Murphy find that the "vast majority of the increase in unemployment is accounted for by an increase in the frequency of very long unemployment spells" (1987, p. 13). Similar to the conclusions reached in this paper, they also find that "the trend toward higher unemployment is not heavily concentrated in particular sectors of the economy. Unemployment has increased in all major industries, in all age and schooling groups, and in all major regions of the country" (1987, p. 12).

REFERENCES

Abowd, John and Orley Ashenfelter (1981), "Anticipated Unemployment, Temporary Layoffs, and Compensating Wage Differentials." In Sherwin Rosen (ed.), *Studies in Labor Markets*. Chicago: University of Chicago Press, pp. 141–170.

Abraham, Katharine (1987), "Help Wanted Advertising, Job Vacancies, and Unemployment." *Brookings Papers on Economic Activity* 1:207–248.

Abraham, Katherine and Lawrence Katz (1986), "Cyclical Unemployment: Sectoral Shifts or Aggregate Disturbances?" *Journal of Political Economy* 94(June):507–522.

Baily, Martin, ed. (1982), *Workers, Jobs, and Inflation*. Washington, DC: Brookings Institution Press.

Bound, John and George Johnson (1989), "Changes in the Structure of Wages During the 1980's: An

Evaluation of Alternative Explanations." NBER Working Paper #2983, NBER, Washington, DC.

Carlson, John and Michael Horrigan (1983), "Measures of Unemployment ration as Guides to Research and Policy." *American Economic Review* 73(December):1143–1150.

Clark, Kim and Lawrence Summers (1979), "Labor Market Dynamics and Unemployment: A Reconsideration." *Brookings Papers on Economic Activity* 1:13–60.

Darby, Michael, John Haltiwanger, and Mark Plant (1987), "The Ins and Outs of Unemployment: The Ins Win." NBER Working Paper #1997, NBER, Washington, DC.

Davis, Steven and John Haltiwanger (1989), "Gross Job Creation, Gross Job Destruction and Employment Reallocation." Unpublished manuscript, University of Chicago, and University of Maryland, College Park.

Dunne, Timothy, Mark Roberts, and Larry Samuelson (1987), "Plant Failure and Employment Growth in the U.S. Manufacturing Sector." Unpublished manuscript, Pennsylvania State University, University Park.

———— (1989), "Plant Turnover and Gross Employment Flows in the U.S. Manufacturing Sector." *Journal of Labor Economics* 7(January):48–71.

Hall, Robert (1982), "The Importance of Lifetime Jobs in the U.S. Economy." *American Economic Review* 72(September):716–724.

Hamilton, James D. (1988), "A Neoclassical Model of Unemployment and the Business Cycle." *Journal of Political Economy* 96(June):593–617.

Horrigan, Michael (1987), "Time Spent Unemployed: A New Look at Data from the CPS." *Monthly Labor Review* 110(July):3–15.

Leonard, Jonathan (1985), "On the Size Distribution of Establishments and Employment." NBER Working Paper #1951, NBER, Washington, DC.

———— (1986), "Employment Variation and Wage Rigidity: A comparison of Union and Non-Union Plants." Unpublished manuscript, University of California, Berkeley.

———— (1987), "In the Wrong Place at the Wrong Time: The Extent of Frictional and Structural Unemployment." In K. Lang and J. Leonard (eds.), *Unemployment and the Structure of Labor Markets*. Oxford: Basil Blackwell, pp. 141–163.

———— (1988), "Firm and Establishment Growth and Stability." Unpublished manuscript, University of California, Berkeley.

Lilien, David (1982), "Sectoral Shifts and Cyclical Unemployment." *Journal of Political Economy* 90(August):777–793.

Marston, Steven (1976), "Employment Instability and High Unemployment Rates." *Brookings Papers on Economic Activity* 1:169–203.

Medoff, James L. (1983), "U.S. Labor Markets: Imbalance, Wage Growth, and Productivity in the 1970s." *Brookings Papers on Economic Activity* 1:87–120.

Oi, Walter (1962), "Labor as a Quasi-Fixed Factor." *Journal of Political Economy* 70(December):538–555.

Organization for Economic Cooperation and Development (1988), *Employment Outlook*.

Perry, George (1972), "Unemployment Flows in the U.S. Labor Market." *Brookings Papers on Economic Activity* 2:245–292.

Podgursky, Michael (1984), "Sources of Secular Increases in the Unemployment Rate, 1968–82." *Monthly Labor Review* 107(July):19–25.

Sider, Hal (1985), "Unemployment Duration and Incidence: 1968–1982." *American Economic Review* 75(June):461–472.

Summers, Larry (1986), "Why Is Unemployment Rate So Very High Near Full Employment?" *Brookings Papers on Economic Activity* 2:339–396.

Topel, Robert and Kevin Murphy (1987), "The Evolution of Unemployment in the United States: 1968–1985." In Stanley Fischer (ed.), *NBER Macroeconomics Annual 1987*. Cambridge, MA: MIT Press.

U.S. Bureau of Labor Statistics (1987), "Projections 2000." *Monthly Labor Review* 110(September):1–63.

Warren, Robert (1977), "Technical Note: A Method to Measure Flow and Duration as Unemployment Rate Components." *Monthly Labor Review* 100(March):71–72.

UNEMPLOYMENT INSURANCE AND JOB SEARCH

James C. Cox and Ronald L. Oaxaca

I. INTRODUCTION

This paper examines the relationship between unemployment insurance (UI) benefits and the duration of unemployment. We review extant empirical evidence on the question of whether the receipt of UI benefits leads unemployed workers to prolong their spells of unemployment. Our objective is to examine representative studies of UI and worker job search responses with an eye toward eliciting implications for public policy and future research.

The current UI system was established by the Social Security Act of 1935 in response to the hardships imposed on the workforce by the Great Depression. Subject to minimum standards set by the federal government, the state governments administer the program and set their own requirements regarding eligibility and compensation. Funding for the program is derived from payroll taxes assessed against employers of covered workers. At the present time, well over 90% of wage and salary workers are covered by the UI system. Important eligibility requirements for covered workers who are unemployed include minimum earnings and employment over a base period preceding a spell of unemployment. In addition, states require a waiting period of one or two weeks before

Research in Labor Economics, Volume 11, pages 223–240.
Copyright © 1990 by JAI Press Inc.
ISBN: 1-555938-080-2

a claimant can begin receiving UI compensation. Within legislated minimum and maximum amounts, an unemployed worker's UI benefits are proportional to his or her previous earnings. The maximum duration of benefits is typically 26 weeks but can be higher in some cases. UI benefits have been subject to federal income taxes since 1978. Income maintenance and subsidization of job search are two objectives associated with the UI system. UI promotes income maintenance by providing a financial cushion for laid-off workers awaiting recall. UI assists workers on permanent layoff by financing job search; this is intended to promote better job matches than would be the case in the absence of the UI subsidy.

A disconcerting feature of empirical analysis of UI data is the wide range of estimated effects of policies and programs that abound in the literature. These disparate results stem from, among other things, differences in data sets, model specifications, time periods, and estimation techniques. One common finding in the studies reviewed below is a positive association between length of spells of unemployment and the receipt of UI benefits. However, this still leaves open the question of how to characterize the underlying behavior of unemployed workers. Two competing hypotheses have been suggested in the past: (1) UI benefits constitute a subsidy to leisure; and (2) UI benefits constitute a subsidy to job search. These competing hypotheses have implications for labor market efficiency and public policy.

Underlying the leisure subsidy argument is the basic static model of consumer choice of consumption and leisure (Moffitt and Nicholson, 1982). The income loss from a spell of unemployment overstates the value of the utility loss from reduced earnings. This is because of the value of the utility gain from the (forced) additional consumption of leisure. Hence, unemployment can have some value to workers because of the leisure consumption it makes possible. According to this view, UI benefits increase the attractiveness of unemployment by reducing the opportunity cost of leisure. Empirically, one would expect to find a positive association between UI and unemployment duration, and a clustering of unemployment terminations around the week of UI benefit exhaustion. In this framework, an increase in the potential maximum of UI benefit duration will have income and substitution effects for those who would otherwise have exhausted their entitlements. The consumption/leisure choice model predicts that, if leisure is a normal good, then the extension of potential duration of UI benefits will necessarily raise the duration of unemployment.

Job search theory holds that unemployed workers are searching for jobs in a manner that maximizes the present value of expected utility (expected income for a risk-neutral worker) from search (Mortensen, 1986). UI benefits serve to reduce the opportunity costs of the search process and can lead unemployed workers to search longer and hold out for better job offers. This model also predicts a positive association between UI benefits and the duration of unemployment as well as some clustering of unemployment terminations around the week of UI benefit exhaustion. Also, an extension of maximum-benefit duration is predicted to lead to a longer spell of unemployment. Empirically, the job search model is distinguished from the leisure subsidy model by the prediction that UI benefits will produce better job matches including higher postunemployment wages. Our review will examine the available empirical evidence of the effects of UI on unemployment duration in light of these two alternative models. The papers included in our review were selected to be representative of the approaches taken to understanding the link between UI and job search. Our selection criteria also included the prominence of particular papers in the literature and whether the studies were funded by the UI service of the U.S. Department of Labor.

The remainder of our paper is divided into three parts. Section II is a review and summary of nonexperimental empirical studies of the effects of the current UI program. Section III reviews completed and ongoing laboratory and field experiments on job search behavior and possible changes in the UI program. Section IV is a discussion of the research and program policy implications of what has been learned to date about the incentive effects of UI at the level of the individual worker.

II. REPRESENTATIVE NONEXPERIMENTAL STUDIES

Ehrenberg and Oaxaca (1976) estimated the effects of UI benefit payments on postunemployment wages, duration of unemployment, and time spent out of the labor force. This study used 1966–1971 data from the National Longitudinal Survey (NLS) on four gender/age cohorts: males 14–24 and 45–59, and females 14–24 and 30–44. Ehrenberg and Oaxaca specified their UI variable as a wage replacement fraction, i.e., the ratio of weekly UI benefits to preunemployment weekly wages. Here we confine our summary to the Ehrenberg and Oaxaca results pertaining to workers who completed their spells of unemployment by changing employers.

Ehrenberg and Oaxaca estimated the effects of raising the wage replacement fraction by 10 percentage points, from 0.4 to 0.5. If one takes a base wage replacement fraction of 0.5, this represents a 20% increase in UI weekly benefits. Such an increase was estimated by Ehrenberg and Oaxaca to raise the duration of unemployment (in weeks) by 0.2, 1.5, 0.5, and 0.3 for males 14–24, males 45–59, females 14–24, and females 30–44. The wage gain effects of this increase in UI benefits were estimated to be 7% for males 45–59 and 1.5% for females 30–44, respectively. Among the 14–24-year-olds, the wage replacement ratio had no statistically significant effects on wage gains. Finally, this increase in weekly UI benefits was estimated to reduce time spent out of the labor force by 0.8 weeks for females 14–24 and 0.7 weeks for females 30–44. This effect was not estimated for the older male group and was not statistically significant for the young males.

As far as the job search interpretation is concerned, the Ehrenberg and Oaxaca results are somewhat mixed. The lack of UI-induced wage gains for young workers is consistent with any of the following explanations: (a) job search among young people is simply unproductive; (b) young people use their subsidized spells of unemployment to search for jobs with better on-the-job training opportunities at the cost of initially lower postunemployment wages; and (c) UI is serving as a subsidy to leisure for young people. The Ehrenberg and Oaxaca study does not shed much light on which (if any) of these alternative explanations is correct. However, Ehrenberg and Oaxaca observe that the apparent substitution of unemployment for time out of the labor force by the young women is consistent with the leisure subsidy argument. In the two cases for older workers in which UI benefits were associated with wage gains, the magnitudes of these effects are implausibly large. The wage gain effects imply that an additional week of search induced by UI is associated with a 5% wage gain. One factor underlying these anomalous results could be that the NLS data used by Ehrenberg and Oaxaca did not permit any control for the effect of UI on search intensity.

Burgess and Kingston (1976) estimated the impact of the weekly benefit amount (WBA) on the duration of compensated employment using data from the 1969–1970 Service to Claimants (STC) experiment. The sample consisted of UI claimants who had not exhausted their benefits and who were deemed "job ready" but not "job attached." Since the design of the STC experiment was intended to test the effects of special job search assistance to UI claimants and not to test the effects of UI itself on search outcomes, we discuss the Burgess and Kingston results here rather than in Section III. The Burgess and Kingston estimates imply that an additional $10 of WBA raises subsequent annual earnings by $250. A problem here is that the duration of compensated weeks of unemployment was included as a control variable by Burgess and Kingston in their wage gain equations. According to search theory, wage gain and duration of search are jointly determined. Consequently, Welch (1977) applied a rough correction to the Burgess and Kingston estimates and came up with estimates that implied that the total effect of an additional $10 inWBA raises subsequent annual earnings by $180 to $200.

Another study by Burgess and Kingston (1981) used the STC data in estimating the effects of WBA on compensated weeks of unemployment after controlling for a worker's maximum duration of benefits. This study found that an additional $10 of WBA raises the duration of compensated unemployment by 0.15 weeks. Combining this effect with the Burgess and Kingston earlier wage gain estimates implies that an additional week of compensated unemployment raises annual earnings between $1200 and $1300. Burgess and Kingston estimated that an additional week of potential benefit duration raises compensated unemployment by 0.61 weeks. Some differences by demographic characteristics were evident from the Burgess and Kingston 1981 study. WBA effects on compensated unemployment tended to decrease with age while the potential duration effects on compensated unemployment tended to increase with age. Both the WBA and potential duration effects tended to be larger among nonwhites.

Classen (1977) sought to determine the effects of UI benefits on unemployment duration and earnings by taking advantage of the fact that legislated increases in maximum UI benefits took place in 1968. She used the Continuous Wage and Benefit History (CWBH) data set for 1960–1970. The duration variable was measured as weeks of UI benefits collected per successful claim, the UI variable was the WBA, and the earnings variable was high-quarter earnings in the year following a completed spell of unemployment. Using data for Arizona and Pennsylvania, Classen estimated that a $10 (1968 dollars) increase in WBA would cause an increase in benefit duration of 1.1 weeks in both states but have no significant effect on earnings in either state. Although the Classen and Ehrenberg and Oaxaca studies differ in many respects, they yield similar estimated overall effects of UI on duration. In addition to the lack of an earnings effect from UI, Classen's study cast further doubt on the productivity-enhancing effects of UI by failing to find any UI effect on the number of employers a worker had in the two-year period following a spell of unemployment. It was expected that if UI promoted better job matches, workers would have fewer employers following spells of insured unemployment.

Holen (1977) estimated the effects of UI benefits and potential weeks of eligibility on unemployment duration and subsequent wages using data from the STC experiment. Her results imply that a $10 (1969–1970 dollars) rise in WBA would raise compensated unemployment by about one week and quarterly earnings by $90. In other words, each additional week of UI-induced search raises quarterly earnings by $90. Holen conjectured that the wage gain effect reflected some combination of an extra week of search and increased search intensity. Her estimates also imply that extending the maximum potential eligibility period by one week would raise *compensated* weeks of unemployment duration by 0.8 weeks and quarterly earnings by $2.50. Holen investigated whether the extension of potential entitlement had any effect on search behavior. Her results suggested that the probability of short spells of unemployment was reduced and the distribution of total search duration was shifted toward longer spells of unemployment.

Hamermesh (1979) examined the entitlement effects of UI availability on labor supply and labor force participation among married women. The idea is that potential UI benefits make market work more attractive. Hamermesh drew a sample from the Panel Study of Income Dynamics for the period 1967–1971. His sample consisted of married white women between the ages of 30 and 54, who were married to the same husband from 1967 to 1972 and who resided in the same state from 1970 to 1972. For the entire sample, Hamermesh simulated the effects of a 20% increase in UI benefits. He estimated the resulting disincentive effects on total hours of work and the positive entitlement effects on labor supply and labor force participation. While the net effects are slightly negative, it is hard to escape the conclusion that they are *not* significantly different from zero.

Solon (1978) questioned the desirability of measuring the work disincentive effects of the UI system by looking only at the unemployment effects. If the UI system encourages labor force participation among those who would otherwise be out of the labor force, the estimated UI effects on unemployment would overstate the true disincentive effects as measured by *employment* effects. Solon used data for a sample of former UI claimants in the state of New York who had established benefit years over the period September 1972 to August 1973, and who had also exhausted their 26 weeks of *regular* UI benefit entitlement. He found a marginally statistically significant negative effect of extended UI benefit eligibility on subsequent weeks of employment. His results indicated that for every ten weeks of *extended* benefit eligibility, employment was reduced by one week. This effect was mainly confined to those who had received UI benefits in two of the previous five years (repeaters). Solon's estimates of work disincentives were smaller than what one would have inferred on the basis of unemployment effects because of the out-of-the labor force effects.

Fishe and Maddala (1980) estimated the effects of UI benefits on the duration of unemployment from a structural model of joint wage offer and reservation wage determination. They explicitly incorporated the assumption of finite search horizons among unemployed workers in contrast to the infinite-horizon specification implicitly or explicitly used by most researchers. Fishe and Maddala used a CWBH data set for a sample of workers in Florida who had been unemployed at some point between 1971 and 1975. The UI benefits variable in the Fishe and Maddala study is defined as the potential weekly benefit amount (PWBA) an unemployed worker is eligible for (equal to WBA for actual periods of compensation). Fishe and Maddala's results imply that a 20% rise in PWBA raises the weekly reservation wage by 2.8% of the average weekly wage and increases the duration of unemployment by 1.4 weeks. Furthermore, the exhaustion of UI benefits was estimated to drop the weekly reservation wage by 16.4% of the average weekly wage. Fishe and Maddala found that the number of weeks remaining until UI exhaustion was positively related to the reservation wage and was statistically significant. As each week passes without a job acceptance, the weekly reservation wage declines by 1.4%. This result was interpreted as evidence of a declining reservation wage over the search horizon. Fishe and Maddala treated the finite search horizon as a parameter that they estimated to be 40.9 weeks.

Moffitt and Nicholson (1982) examined the impact of changing the maximum duration of UI benefit eligibility on the duration of unemployment. The labor/ leisure choice (or leisure subsidy) model provided the theoretical underpinning for the employment (or labor supply) function in their study. A maximum-likelihood estimation procedure was used to incorporate the kink in the unemployed worker's budget line at the point of maximum UI benefit duration eligibility. Data for the study were drawn from a sample of workers who collected UI benefits under the Federal Supplemental Benefits (FSB) program. A negative estimated coefficient on the non-UI, nonwage income variable indicates that leisure is indeed a normal good. Moffitt and Nicholson estimated that increasing potential UI benefit duration by one week raises weeks unemployed by 0.1 weeks. This result implies that the 26-week extension of maximum duration of UI benefits triggered by the FSB program in response to the 1974–1975 recession increased unemployment duration by about 2.5 weeks. Moffitt and Nicholson also found that a 10% increase in the net wage replacement ratio would raise the duration of unemployment by 0.4 weeks for those with high probabilities of benefit exhaustion and by about 0.8 to 1 week for the typical claimant.

Feldstein and Poterba (1984) examined two major issues. The first is the existence of evidence that indicates that a significant proportion of unemployed workers hold unrealistically high and socially nonoptimal reservation wages. While one might question whether some of these individuals should be considered unemployed, they are nevertheless counted as unemployed according to the official definition of unemployment. The second issue is whether UI benefits exacerbate the problem of nonoptimal reservation wages by raising them further and hence prolonging unemployment.

Feldstein and Poterba used data obtained from a special supplement to the May 1976 *Current Population Survey* (CPS). Unemployed workers were asked to indicate the kind of work they were seeking and the lowest wage they would accept to do the specified work. From this group, Feldstein and Poterba selected a subsample of those unemployed who were receiving UI benefits. A reservation wage variable was constructed as the ratio of the reported reservation wage to the last wage received prior to the current spell of unemployment. Feldstein and Poterba constructed their UI variable as the ratio of WBA received to the previous wage adjusted for a constant marginal tax rate of 0.3.

Regression analysis by Feldstein and Poterba revealed that the UI wage replacement variable had a statistically significant positive effect on the reservation wage ratio for each of the groups of UI recipients in the sample ("job losers on layoff," "other job losers," and "job leavers"). Predictably, the UI effect was largest for "other job losers." For a worker in this latter category whose gross UI wage replacement ratio was 0.5 (0.7 after taxes), a 20% rise in WBA would increase the reservation wage by 6% of the previous wage. Feldstein and Poterba also found that the UI net wage replacement ratio had a positive statistically significant effect on the probability that an unemployed worker would have a reservation wage ratio in excess of 1.0. For the same worker as described above, a 20% increase in WBA would raise the probability that the reservation wage ratio exceeds 1.0 by 5 percentage points (31% of the "other job losers" sample had reservation wage ratios in excess of 1.0).

Moffitt (1985) attempted to deal with the problem of wide-ranging estimates of UI effects. Specifically, Moffitt focused on the effects of the maximum potential duration of benefits. His study adopted a uniform specification and estimation strategy across four selected data sets. The objective was to generate a narrower range of UI effects as well as to ascertain how much of the differences in estimates can be attributed to differences in data bases. The four data sets used were (1) CWBH (1978–1983), (2) the Employment Opportunity Pilot Project (EOPP) (1979–1981), (3) the Federal Supplemental Benefits (FSB) Follow-Up Survey (1975–1977), and (4) the Newton–Rosen data set (1974–1976). Moffitt's study yielded estimated effects of an additional week of potential duration of UI benefits that ranged from 0.17 to 0.45 additional weeks of unemployment for males and 0.10 to 0.37 additional weeks of unemployment for females. There was some hint that these effects were somewhat larger when the unemployment rate was higher. Moffitt also found that the effect of an additional week of potential duration on combined weeks of unemployment and out of the labor force was 0.52 weeks for males and 0.66 weeks for females. He found no strong evidence that increased potential duration had any effect on the labor supply of other members of a UI recipient's family. Finally, Moffitt failed to find any convincing evidence of an effect of potential duration on postunemployment earnings.

Katz and Meyer (1988) used hazard rate analysis to estimate the impact of potential duration and UI benefit level on the duration of compensated unemployment and on the timing of exits from unemployment. They used two data sources for their study: (1) a sample of heads of households from the Panel Study of Income Dynamics (PSID) over the period 1980–1981, and (2) a sample of males from the CWBH data for 1978–1983 supplemented by an additional CWBH data set covering the period 1979–1984. They found sharp spikes among UI recipients in the escape rates from unemployment at about the duration when UI benefits were exhausted (26 and 39 weeks). No such sharp pattern in escape rates was found for non UI recipients. Although the statistical significances of the potential duration and UI benefit level in the hazard models were marginal, the estimated effects were in the anticipated directions. Katz and Meyer's results imply that a one-week increase in potential duration would raise compensated duration by 0.16 to 0.20 weeks and that a 20% rise in UI for an individual with a replacement ratio of 0.5 would increase the length of a compensated spell of unemployment by 1.5 weeks.

III. FIELD AND LABORATORY EXPERIMENTS

Applied econometric studies of the effects of UI, such as those reviewed in Section II, establish statistical associations between UI benefits and unemployment duration, wage gains, and other variables of interest to policymakers. However, interpretations of these results in terms of search intensity, labor/ leisure substitutions, etc., require the use of theoretical models as maintained hypotheses. Many econometric studies of UI employ either a finite- or an infinite-horizon search model as a maintained hypothesis (Devine and Kiefer, 1988). Therefore, if the job search/job acceptance behavior of economic agents is *not* consistent with the search models, then the interpretations of the results of the applied research can be misleading. Hence, it is essential that search models be subjected to direct empirical testing to learn whether they can be falsified.

The literature contains some very ingenious studies that use econometric techniques designed to test search models with data from the historical record. Among these are Kiefer and Neumann (1979a,b), Warner et al. (1980), and Lancaster and Chesher (1983). However, the properties of search models pose inherent limitations on what can be learned with this approach. Consider some of the difficulties in attempting to use nonexperimental data to test job search theory. The models imply that the feasibility of recalling past wage offers, the length of the search horizon, and/or agent information about the distribution of wage offers are central determinants of an optimal search strategy. But possibilities of wage offer recall, the length of search horizons, and agent information on wage offer distributions are not observable in nonexperimental data sources. Hence such data are not very useful for learning whether job search models can be falsified by observations of job search behavior. In contrast, controlled experiments have some unique advantages for empirical evaluation of search models. The relative advantages of laboratory experiments and field experiments are somewhat different, and thus we will discuss both types.

Laboratory experiments designed to test finite-horizon search models were conducted by Cox and Oaxaca (1989a,b). In these experiments the researchers can control, and thereby observe, the possibility of recalling past wage offers, the length of the search horizon, and agent information about the wage offers distribution. Also under experimental control are theoretically hypothesized determinants of search behavior such as the discounting rate of interest and the cost or subsidy to search. Thus, such laboratory experiments are well-suited for learning whether people are capable of making choices in a dynamic, uncertain decision environment *as if* they were finding the optimal solutions to stochastic dynamic decision problems. This is the type of behavior that is modeled in job search theory and that is used as a maintained hypothesis in much econometric research on UI.

The Cox and Oaxaca (1989a) laboratory experiments were conducted with 60 subjects who participated in base line and various treatment trials. The experimental treatments consisted of variation of the rate of interest, the subsidy to search, the riskiness of the wage offers distribution, the probability of obtaining a job offer, and the length of the search horizon. The picture that emerges from these experiments is one of reasonably close agreement between the predictions of the risk-neutral search model and observed subject behavior. Overall, subjects terminated search exactly at the point predicted by the risk-neutral model in 77% of 600 trials. However, there was significant evidence of risk-averse behavior.

The risk-averse or risk-neutral (concave) model survived the experimental tests remarkably well. Fully 94% of the search terminations in 600 trials were consistent with this concave search model. The accuracy of the concave search model in predicting search behavior is supported by several parametric and nonparametric tests reported in the paper.

The theory of optimal job search focuses on reservation wages. But the typical message space of both naturally occurring labor markets and job search experiments includes admissible statements of job offer acceptance and rejection, not statements of (binding) reservation wages. Cox and Oaxaca (1989b) present the results of experiments designed for direct tests of the reservation wage property of a finite-horizon sequential search model. Since precommitment may frame the acceptance/rejection decision in an unfamiliar way, precommitment is introduced as an experimental treatment, with base line control, in order to test for any framing effects on search decisions. Overall, the results of the Cox and Oaxaca (1989b) precommitment experiments confirm the findings from the no-precommitment search experiments reported in Cox and Oaxaca (1989a). That is, the linear (risk-neutral) model and especially the concave (risk-neutral or risk-averse) search model are good predictors of both reservation wages and search terminations. Precommitment effects are initially present but they attenuate in subsequent experimental trials. The precommitment effect takes the form of earlier (than in base line) search terminations. The data base generated from the paired no-precommitment/precommitment experiments is also used to evaluate various econometric procedures for estimating reservation wages from job acceptance data.

There are six field experiments with the UI program that have either recently been completed or are currently at some stage of planning or implementation. The first of these was the completed Illinois reemployment bonus experiment. Further experiments with alternative bonus formulas are currently in progress in Washington. The completed New Jersey experiments involved several treatments that included combinations of reemployment bonuses, job search assistance, job training, and relocation assistance. The New Jersey experiments were targeted on structurally unemployed workers. Experiments currently in progress in Pennsylvania involve treatments that use alternative reemployment bonus formulas and job search assistance. Two other experiments that are currently in progress are the Washington and the Three State Self-Employment Demonstration Projects. These experiments involve treatments that consist of self-employment allowances and various support services to assist UI recipients who want to become self-employed. The Illinois and New Jersey experiments are the only ones for which results are currently available; hence we will focus our discussion on these two.

Results from the Illinois experiment are presented in Spiegelman and Woodbury (1987) and Woodbury and Spiegelman (1987). In this experiment, individuals in a selected subset of UI claimants were randomly assigned to one of two treatment groups or a control group. An individual who was assigned to the claimant treatment group was eligible for a $500 reemployment bonus if he or she returned to work with either his or her old employer or a new employer within 11 weeks of filing the UI claim and remained on that job for at least four months. If an employer hired an individual who was assigned to the employer treatment group then the employer was eligible for a $500 bonus if the worker met the 11-week and four-month filing and employment conditions. Bonus-qualifying jobs for both treatment groups had to provide at least 30 hours per week of employment.

The results of the Illinois experiment support the conclusion that reemployment bonuses can significantly affect the job-finding behavior of UI recipients. Individuals in the claimant treatment group had an average of 1.37 fewer weeks of unemployment than those in the control group during the first spell and 1.15 fewer weeks during the benefit year. The average differences between the employer treatment and control groups were 0.67 weeks in the first spell and 0.36 weeks during the benefit year. All of these figures except the 0.36 benefit year figure are significantly different from zero at the 5% significance level. Furthermore, the three significant reductions in weeks of unemployment also involve significant reductions in total UI benefits paid out, inclusive of the $500 bonuses. In addition, the lower average number of weeks of unemployment for the treatment groups does not appear to have been achieved at the cost of lower post-unemployment earnings.

Further analysis of data from the Illinois experiment is presented in Meyer (1988). He also discusses some ways in which the results of this field experiment might not be indicative of the effects of a permanent national reemployment bonus program. The Illinois experiment lasted only 17 weeks and was not publicized; hence it is unlikely that it induced firms to change their layoff and recall policies. However, if recalled workers were eligible for bonuses in a permanent program, this would provide a substantial subsidy to temporary layoffs. The responses by firms and workers to the incentive provided by this subsidy might lead to a substantial increase in UI claims. In contrast, if recalled workers were not eligible for bonuses (as in the New Jersey and Washington experiments) this would provide an incentive to break up employer/employee matches. Any response to this incentive by workers would increase UI claims and impose other costs on the economy. However, there could be an offsetting effect on firms in that they might reduce layoff frequency in order to avoid having their employees respond to the bonus incentive to join other firms.

Results from the New Jersey experiment are reported in Corson et al. (1988). In this experiment, individuals in a selected subset of UI claimants were randomly assigned to one of three treatment groups or a control group. The three experimental treatments were (1) job search assistance, (2) job search assistance combined with training or relocation assistance, and (3) job search assistance combined with a reemployment bonus. The eligibility screens that were used in selecting individuals for inclusion in the experiment were intended to select displaced workers (the target group). This was partially successful although other UI recipients were included. Not surprisingly, the experimental treatments were more effective for individuals not in the target group.

The reemployment bonus formula in the New Jersey experiment was different than the one used in the Illinois experiment that is described above. The New Jersey bonus formula offered individuals one-half of their remaining UI entitlement if they started work by the end of the second full week following the assessment/counseling interview. This implies that bonus eligibility began about the seventh week after an eligible claimant filed for UI. The amount that could be claimed during the first week of bonus eligibility averaged $1644. In subsequent weeks the bonus declined by about 10% of the original amount each week.

Data from the New Jersey experiment indicates that each of three experimental treatments significantly reduced both the number of weeks that claimants collected UI and the amount that they collected. Furthermore, the treatment with the reemployment bonus had the largest effect in reducing both weeks of UI duration and dollars of UI paid. The results also indicate that all three treatments increase both employment and earnings in the year following the UI claim. Thus the experimental treatments do not appear to have lowered reservation wages. Finally, various benefit–cost analyses are reported. They indicate that none of the treatments led to positive net benefits for the Labor Department. However, two of the treatments yielded positive net benefits for the government sector and, most importantly, all three of the treatments yielded positive net benefits to society as a whole and to claimants.

Although the results of the Illinois and New Jersey experiments appear to be favorable, Meyer (1988) explains why these results do not support policy conclusions. Both of these experiments were short-lived and were not widely advertised to workers and firms. Hence, it is reasonable to suppose that neither workers nor firms made strategic responses to *the existence* of the experimental treatments. However, the possibility of such strategic responses to a permanent program implies that the results of the experiments might not be a good predictor of the impacts of a permanent program.

Consider the possibility of strategic responses by workers to a permanent reemployment bonus program. The bonus formulas from the New Jersey and Illinois experiments provide good examples to illustrate the problem. The New Jersey bonus became available in the seventh week after a UI claim was filed. The average initial bonus of $1644 was about five-weeks' average wages. Thus, anyone who was planning to start a job after two weeks of UI could increase his or her income by waiting a few more weeks to become eligible for the bonus. In contrast, the Illinois bonus was available immediately after a UI claim was filed. Immediate availability of a bonus would provide an incentive for some people to file UI claims who otherwise might not file. The most obvious example of this would be someone who had a new job lined up upon termination of the previous job. With either type of strategic response, the larger number of benefit payments caused by added claimants might eliminate any cost savings of a bonus program. Therefore, the findings of positive net benefits for reemployment bonuses in the Illinois and New Jersey experiments do not support the prediction that a permanent bonus program of either type would yield positive net benefits.

Another question that was not addressed by the Illinois and New Jersey experiments is the possibility of displacement effects. That is, individuals in the experimental treatment groups who found jobs more quickly may have done so at the expense of others who took longer to find jobs. Any such displacement effects would detract from the calculated net benefits of the experimental treatments. The Pennsylvania experiment will attempt to examine this question by comparing the experiences of the control groups to similar groups in other labor markets. It remains to be seen whether this can be done effectively.

IV. IMPLICATIONS FOR RESEARCH AND POLICY

For all of the many differences in techniques, model specifications, time periods, and data sets that characterize empirical studies of UI effects on individual workers, it is remarkable that these studies all point to the same qualitative effect of UI benefits on work incentives: UI prolongs spells of unemployment and lowers employment among its recipients. Unfortunately, the magnitudes of these estimated effects vary more than one would like. Consider a 20% increase in WBA for a UI claimant with a wage replacement rate of 0.5. Based on the studies we reviewed, the estimated duration effect is substantially less than a week for females and young workers, more than a week for older males, exactly one week for all workers according to two studies, and 1.4 to 1.5 weeks according to two other studies. In the light of these findings a single best estimate at this point is that the duration effect is about a week. Another source of work disincentives is the maximum potential duration of UI benefits. Consider a one-week increase in the maximum potential duration of UI benefits. Four of the studies reviewed by us estimate that this increase would extend unemployment (or in one of the studies, reduce employment) by 0.1 weeks to 0.45 weeks. Two studies that found larger effects of 0.61 and 0.8 weeks used compensated weeks of unemployment, which may have overstated the effects on total weeks of unemployment. Given the preponderance of evidence for modest effects, a best guess at this point is that an additional week of potential duration increases a spell of unemployment by no more than 0.5 weeks. If one regards weeks of employment as a better measure of work disincentives, then the evidence thus far shows that at least extended benefits beyond the exhaustion of regular UI benefits has very small negative effects on employment.

The empirical evidence on the wage gain aspects of UI is not even in agreement on the existence of such an effect, let alone on its magnitude. This goes to the heart of the issue of whether the job search or the leisure subsidy hypothesis is the most appropriate for understanding the effects of UI on spells of unemployment. While some studies show a wage gain, others do not. At the present time one can find no compelling evidence in support of the proposition that UI increases wages because of better job matches and increased job stability. This does not necessarily mean that there are no such effects, but only that significant data problems prevent the research community from being able to test for their presence properly.

It should be appreciated that different estimated UI effects that merely reflect demographic differences are not necessarily a statistical problem. Different worker responses to UI can be anticipated when workers differ in their personal characteristics. This does, however, present a policy problem because of the political and legal difficulties in adopting UI legislation that treats potential UI recipients differently depending on their non–job-related personal characteristics.

What are the implications of previous research for the future UI research agenda? These implications fall into two categories: (a) appropriate data bases, and (b) research topics. Virtually all of the empirical evidence on UI to date is derived from nonexperimental sources. These include administrative records and household surveys. Few of the authors of these studies have been too inhibited to point out severe limitations of the data bases used by others (and sometimes even their own!). It seems clear that there is a consensus that using data based on only compensated spells of unemployment introduces unacceptable estimation biases when analyzing *total* duration of unemployment spells. But even with household survey data that yield information on completed spells of unemployment, there are too many important factors that go unobserved. These include the length of a worker's search horizon, the worker's discounting rate of interest, and a worker's search costs.

An essential concept of the search paradigm that provides the theoretical basis for most of the UI studies on individual worker behavior is the reservation wage. Yet this theoretical construct is not observed in the data. What about the question in the May 1976 CPS that asked unemployed workers to state the lowest wage they would accept for the kind of job they were seeking? We maintain that there is no basis for interpreting the answers to this question as corresponding to the theoretical notion of a reservation wage. In their actual job acceptance decisions, workers are in no sense bound by their answers to the reservation wage question. One might more plausibly argue that the answer to this question reflects a hoped-for or desired wage. Consistent with this view is the evidence found in Feldstein and Poterba (1984) that shows little or no decay in the ratio of stated reservation wages to the previous wage with the number of weeks the individual had been unemployed. Accordingly, we are not prepared to draw any policy conclusions from the magnitude of the estimated UI effect on the reported reservation wage in the Feldstein and Poterba study. This is an important issue because in the search paradigm it is the effect of UI on the reservation wage that produces the association between UI and the duration of unemployment. The absence of data on this variable could potentially be managed if one could observe all offers received by an unemployed worker instead of only the accepted offer. Unfortunately, traditional data sources do not provide information on all offers received.

One of the significant advantages of controlled experiments is that they can make some variables observable that would otherwise be unobservable. This is especially true of laboratory experiments in which such factors as the feasibility of recalling past wage offers, the length of the search horizon, and agent information about the distribution of wage offers are controllable and therefore observable. These theoretical determinants of job search behavior are inherently unobservable in nonexperimental data sources and difficult or impossible to observe in field experiment data sources. Although fewer variables are observable in field experiments than in laboratory experiments, the former have the obvious advantage of being conducted in an environment that is closer to the naturally occurring economy in which UI programs actually operate.

The UI research agenda of the future should include the topics described below.

The effects of UI on postunemployment earnings and on the quality of postunemployment job matches is still very much an open question. The answer to this question bears on how much we regard UI in its traditional role as income maintenance for workers on temporary layoff as opposed to its potential role for improving the efficiency of job search.

More research is needed to determine what effects UI has on search intensity. Changes in the UI system to provide monetary incentives to shorten the duration of UI claims may possibly work through some combination of lowering the reservation wage and increasing job search intensity. The fear some may have about the former is that poorer job matches may be encouraged.

If UI is found to raise postunemployment earnings through better job matches, then a cost–benefit analysis should be performed to determine whether the social gains offset the social costs of longer job searches.

The incentive effects of UI over the business cycle need to be examined more systematically. It seems reasonable to suppose that an additional dollar of UI benefits or an additional week of maximum potential duration will have different effects on search outcomes depending upon where the economy is in the business cycle.

Moffitt (1985) makes a convincing case for the value of improved modeling of the dynamics of the search process of unemployed workers as time-varying variables such as potential duration and the unemployment rate change during the search process. Changes in these factors can influence the efficacy of UI policy. This topic is related to the immediately preceding one.

More research is needed on the formal modeling and empirical testing of simultaneous search by firms for workers and search by workers for jobs. How does the UI system simultaneously affect both sides of the labor market?

Without awaiting the definitive work on the effects of UI on work incentives, there are some policy implications that can be raised at this point. If the UI system were found to produce better job matches, then why should there be a public subsidy to productive job search? A divergence between private and social gains could be one justification. The existence of imperfect capital markets might be a justification for a public subsidy. As argued in Classen (1977), such a justification need not require outright UI grants. Rather, one could make an argument that a subsidized unemployment loan program could address the problem of imperfect capital markets.

Policymakers are continually faced with the task of limiting the benefit costs of the UI programs. To the extent that the costs of the UI program are ultimately borne by employers and by workers in the covered sector, both parties have an interest in cost-effective UI plans. Aggregate benefit costs could be lowered by legislating reduced weekly benefit amounts and/or maximum weeks of UI entitlement. However, such measures would degrade the adequacy of UI benefits as an effective form of income maintenance during temporary spells of unemployment. Another cost-saving measure would be to tighten up on eligibility requirements in the nonmonetary determinations. This already occurs to some extent because claims deputies can give closer scrutiny to UI claims without the need for formal legislative changes.

The desire to reduce both the transfer payments of UI and its administrative costs can be accommodated by making the program function more like insurance rather than as income maintenance. The reemployment bonus payment plan is a step in this direction. There are of course the usual moral hazard problems to be concerned with. Furthermore, the results from completed UI bonus field experiments have not provided adequate evidence to support the conclusion that a permanent reemployment bonus program would be cost-effective.

Given the likelihood that the effects of the UI system are not invariant over the business cycle, it is unfortunate that the current UI system offers little flexibility in dealing with this issue. About the only automatic response is the Extended Benefits (EB) program, which is triggered by a state's insured unemployment rate reaching 6% for states with such provisions or a 5% rate that is at least 20% higher than the average for the corresponding period in the previous two years. One could imagine different UI payment schedules being triggered by a high unemployment rate. For example, consider a UI bonus plan in which a job acceptance bonus declines the longer a UI claimant goes without accepting a job. One possibility is that the UI bonus payment decreases at an increasing rate. This plan would provide the strongest incentives to accept an offer early in the spell of unemployment. This seems to be appropriate for periods of relatively low unemployment when the probabilities of receiving job offers are high. In periods of high unemployment the incentive for early job acceptance would be frustrated by the low probabilities of receiving job offers. During these periods it might be more effective to implement a UI bonus payment schedule that provided more incentive farther along in a worker's spell of unemployment. Such a plan would offer a UI bonus schedule that declined at a decreasing rate during a spell of insured unemployment.

We believe that such plans as we have discussed above are feasible and could meet the objective of adequate income maintenance assistance for the involuntarily unemployed without unacceptable work disincentives. They would be good candidates for inclusion in future field experiments.

Other future field experiments should be designed so as to not be subject to the major shortcoming of the present experiments that we discussed in detail in Section III. This shortcoming is that the results of the completed and in-progress experiments with reemployment bonuses, etc., may not be good predictors of the effects of a permanent policy because of differences in the feasibility of strategic responses by workers and firms. There is no low-cost solution to this experimental design problem. In order to incorporate in an experiment the same possibility for strategic responses that would exist with a permanent program the experiment must continue for a longer time period than has previously been tried with UI experiments. Of course, the incentive features of the experimental treatments would also need to be widely advertised.

ACKNOWLEDGMENTS

Financial support for this research was provided by the U.S. Department of Labor Commission on Workforce Quality and Labor Market Efficiency, and the National Science Foundation (grant number SES-8820552).

REFERENCES

Burgess, Paul L. and Jerry L. Kingston (1976), "The Impact of Unemployment Insurance Benefits on Reemployment Success." *Industrial and Labor Relations Review* 30(October):25–31.
———— (1981), "UI Benefit Effects on Compensated Unemployment." *Industrial Relations* 20(Fall):258–270.
Classen, Kathleen P. (1977), "The Effect of Unemployment Insurance on the Duration of Unemployment and Subsequent Earnings." *Industrial and Labor Relations Review* 30(July):438–444.
Corson, Walter et al. (1988), "The New Jersey Unemployment Insurance Reemployment Demonstration Project Impact and Benefit–Cost Report." Draft version prepared by Mathematica Policy Research, Inc, Princeton, NJ.
Cox, James C. and Ronald L. Oaxaca (1989a), "Laboratory Experiments with a Finite Horizon Job Search Model." *Journal of Risk and Uncertainty* 2(September):301–329.
———— (1989b), "Direct Tests of the Reservation Wage Property." Paper presented at the October 1989 meetings of the Economic Science Association, Tucson, AZ.
Devine, Theresa J. and Nicholas M. Kiefer (1990), *Empirical Labor Economics: The Search Approach.* New York: Oxford University Press.

Ehrenberg, Ronald G. and Ronald L. Oaxaca (1976), "Unemployment Insurance, Duration of Unemployment, and Subsequent Wage Gain." *American Economic Review* 66(December):754–766.

Feldstein, Martin and James Poterba (1984), "Unemployment Insurance and Reservation Wages." *Journal of Public Economics* 23(February/March):141–167.

Fishe, Raymond P. H. and G. S. Maddala (1980), "Effect of Unemployment Insurance on Duration of Unemployment: A Study Based on CWBH Data for Florida." Unemployment Insurance Occasional Paper 80-3, U.S. Department of Labor, Employment and Training Administration, Unemployment Insurance Service, Washington DC.

Hamermesh, Daniel S. (1979), "Entitlement Effects, Unemployment Insurance and Employment Decisions." *Economic Inquiry* 17(July):317–332.

Holen, Arlene (1977), "Effects of Unemployment Insurance Entitlement on Duration and Job Search Outcome." *Industrial and Labor Relations Review* 30(July):445–450.

Katz, Lawrence F. and Bruce D. Meyer (1988), "The Impact of the Potential Duration of Unemployment Benefits on the Duration of Unemployment." Working Paper #241, Industrial Relations Section, Princeton University, Princeton, NJ.

Kiefer, Nicholas M. and George R. Neumann (1979a), "An Empirical Job Search Model, with a Test of the Constant Reservation–Wage Hypothesis." *Journal of Political Economy* 87(February):89–107.

———— (1979b), "Estimation of Wage Offer Distributions and Reservation Wages." In Steven A. Lippman and John J. McCall (eds.), *Studies in the Economics of Search*. Amsterdam: North-Holland, pp. 171–189.

Lancaster, Tony and Andrew Chesher (1983), "An Econometric Analysis of Reservation Wages." *Econometrica* 51(November):1661–1676.

Meyer, Bruce D. (1988), "Implications of the Illinois Reemployment Bonus Experiments for Theories of Unemployment and Policy Design." Working Paper #242, Industrial Relations Section, Princeton University, Princeton, NJ.

Moffitt, Robert (1985), "The Effect of the Duration of Unemployment Benefits on Work Incentives: An Analysis of Four Data Sets." Unemployment Insurance Occasional Paper 84-4, U.S. Department of Labor, Employment and Training Administration, Unemployment Insurance Service, Washington DC.

Moffitt, Robert and Walter Nicholson (1982), "The Effect of Unemployment Insurance on Unemployment: The Case of Federal Supplemental Benefits." *Review of Economics and Statistics* 64(February):1–11.

Mortensen, Dale T. (1986), "Job Search and Labor Market Analysis." In Orley Ashenfelter and Richard Layard (eds.), *Handbook of Labor Economics*. New York: North-Holland, 1986.

Solon, Gary (1978), "Work Disincentives in Unemployment Insurance: A Brief Review of the Issue and Literature." Unemployment Insurance Technical Staff Paper 3, U.S. Department of Labor, Employment and Training Administration, Unemployment Insurance Service, Washington DC.

Spiegelman, Robert G. and Stephen A. Woodbury (1987), "The Illinois Unemployment Insurance Incentive Experiments." Final Report to the Illinois Department of Employment Security, W. E. Upjohn Institute, Kalamazoo, MI.

Warner, John T., Carl Poindexter, Jr., and Robert M. Fearn (1980), "Employer–Employee Interaction and the Duration of Unemployment." *Quarterly Journal of Economics* 94(March):211–233.

Welch, Finis (1977), "What Have We Learned from Empirical Studies of Unemployment Insurance?" *Industrial and Labor Relations Review* 30(July):451–461.

Woodbury, Stephen A. and Robert G. Spiegelman (1987), "Bonuses to Workers and Employers to Reduce Unemployment: Randomized Trials in Illinois." *American Economic Review* 77(September):513–530.

UNEMPLOYMENT INSURANCE FINANCING, SHORT-TIME COMPENSATION, AND LABOR DEMAND

Daniel S. Hamermesh

I. INTRODUCTION

The 54-year-old U.S. unemployment insurance (UI) program is a set of 53 separate programs loosely linked by federal requirements imposed through the tax structure that finances benefits and their administration. Unlike UI programs in nearly all other industrialized countries, benefits in the United States are almost entirely financed by taxes on employers, and those taxes are partly *experience rated*—taxes paid increase as benefits received by the employer's workers increase [see Edebalk and Wadensjö (1986) and Chinloy (1980)]. Since the mid-1970s knowledge of the likely impacts of those taxes on labor markets has burgeoned. It is thus especially timely to consider the effects of recent subtle, but sometimes major changes in the structure of UI taxes. This study presents a capsule summary of how UI is financed; demonstrates how UI financing can

Research in Labor Economics, Volume 11, pages 241–269.

affect the structure of employment, employment fluctuations, and the demand for workers and hours; and discusses various policy proposals.

II. THE UNEMPLOYMENT INSURANCE TAX SYSTEM

The general outline of UI financing in the United States is simple. Almost all UI benefits are financed by taxes on employers. Employers pay a small amount to the federal government to cover administrative and other costs. Employers' state UI tax liabilities can increase as more benefits have been paid to their laid-off workers and more benefits have been paid statewide compared to the state UI system's tax revenues.

An employer's state UI account can be thought of as a bathtub, with benefits running out of the tub and taxes pouring in. The rate of flow into the tub depends on how fast the water (benefit payments) flows out of the tub and on the water (tax) pressure statewide, which is higher when all tubs are low on water (funds). In some employers' tubs the benefits flow out so fast, and the spigot of taxes they must pay is relatively narrow, that the tub is always empty. At the opposite extreme, some other companies find that benefits flow out so slowly that the spigot of their taxes allows a sufficient inflow of taxes to keep the tub always full.

The details of financing are as follows. Under the Federal Unemployment Tax Act (FUTA) employers are liable to a tax of 6.2% on the wages of each employee, up to a ceiling (*tax base*) of $7000 per worker. Wages above this amount are not subject to federal tax. As long as the state UI tax system that finances benefits is constructed so that it is possible for an employer to pay at least a 5.4% tax rate, 5.4 percentage points of the FUTA tax is credited to that state's employers. The remaining 0.8 percentage points of the tax are retained by the federal government for use as grants to states for program administration, payment of long-term benefits, and loans to state UI systems.

Total FUTA tax collections (the 0.8 percentage points) in 1987 were $6.1 billion; but total state UI taxes in that year were $19.1 billion. While the FUTA tax is small, its impact on total UI taxes need not be. The reason is that the FUTA tax is the main lever used in federal legislation to influence state UI tax policy.

To qualify for the 5.4 percentage point credit on the FUTA tax, all states have adopted systems of at least partial experience rating. Over half of all employees are in states where experience rating is based on the *reserve ratio,* the excess of the employer's prior taxes minus prior benefits relative to the company's taxable wages (Topel, 1985). One-fourth are in states where experience rating is based on recent, usually three-year averages of the *benefit ratio,* benefits paid relative to taxable wages. These ratios essentially measure how well funded the employer's UI account is.

In the reserve ratio system, the typical tax structure can be described by

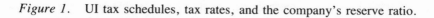

Figure 1. UI tax schedules, tax rates, and the company's reserve ratio.

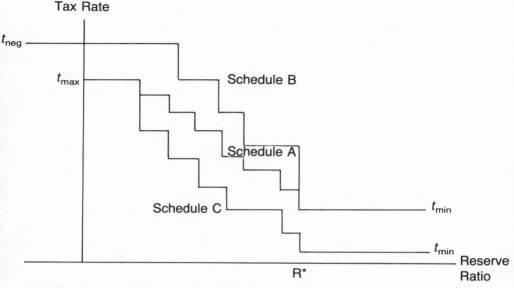

schedule A in Figure 1 (based on Brechling, 1981). (In a benefit ratio state the benefit ratio would be on the horizontal axis.) The tax rate cannot drop below a legislated minimum t_{min}, which is often zero in some states, even if reserves rise above some maximum reserve ratio R^*. As the company's reserve ratio drops, its tax rate rises in steps until it hits t_{max}, the highest tax rate on employers with positive reserves (positive balances). In some states an extra tax on *negative-balance employers*—those whose reserve accounts are in deficit—makes the highest tax rate t_{neg}.

Schedule A in Figure 1 is not permanent. An employer's tax rate also depends on the experience of the entire state UI fund. If the state fund is low—it has been paying out more than it has recently taken in—a higher tax schedule is imposed statewide. There is some *least-favorable* schedule, schedule B in Figure 1, that relates a firm's tax rate to its reserve ratio when the state fund is weakest. Obversely, if the state fund has been bringing in more taxes than have been paid out in benefits, lower schedules are imposed. There is some *most-favorable* schedule, schedule C, that employers face if the state fund is very flush. Notice that t_{min}, t_{max}, and t_{neg} can differ along the various schedules (though few states have both different minimum and maximum tax rates on their most- and least-favorable schedules).

A company whose reserve ratio is above R^* when the state is on schedule A cannot reduce its tax rate below the t_{min} now paid; and if the state were already on its most-favorable schedule, the tax rate could never be reduced. Unless t_{min}

= 0, these bounds on taxes mean that additional benefit payments will not raise the employer's tax bill; and lower benefit payments may not lower the tax bill. Additional benefits paid by an employer with a negative balance cannot raise the tax on a given schedule; and if the state is already on its least-favorable schedule, those benefits cannot raise taxes in the future if the employer continues to pay very high UI benefits. Also, negative-balance employers do not accrue any interest charges, and positive-balance employers are not credited with interest. The absence of interest charges means that other employers essentially provide interest-free loans out of their tax payments to finance benefits for employees of negative-balance firms.

State governments have made decisions that so-called *noncharged benefits*— those paid to voluntary quitters and selected other categories of recipients—will not be financed by taxes on the employer from whose company the worker was separated. The limits on tax rates, the absence of interest credits to employers with positive balances and of interest charges on those with negative balances, and the noncharging of some benefits mean that for some UI benefit payments the taxes are not experience rated—experience rating is said to be *ineffective*. All of these considerations imply that experience rating is incomplete—a firm's annual tax liability only partly reflects the actuarial present value of the benefits paid to its employees. The UI tax is only *partly experience rated*.

Over a period of time, taxes statewide must equal total payments of regular benefits; state UI systems must be self-financing. This consideration and the existence of noncharged and ineffectively charged benefits mean that the typical employer's UI tax liability is partly fixed per worker, partly increasing with past benefit payments. The typical employer's UI tax bill is

$$eB + T,$$

where B is total benefits paid to the firm's workers, T is a fixed amount that is large enough to keep the state fund in balance over a period of years, and e measures the effectiveness of experience rating—how many cents each extra dollar of benefits costs the typical employer (Feldstein, 1976). The measure e is crucial in analyzing many of the effects of UI on labor markets. If $e = 1$, experience rating would be complete; if $e = 0$, the UI tax would be independent of the firm's experience.

Table 1 presents information on the tax rate structures of the ten largest states for which comparable data are available for 1978 and 1988.[1] For each of the two years the table presents t_{max} and t_{min} on the most-favorable schedule (the lowest range of tax rates facing each employer) and on the least-favorable schedule (the highest range of tax rates). The tremendous diversity in the states' tax structures is made clear by these data. Interstate differences in the structure of tax rates can cause the effectiveness of experience rating to differ sharply among states.

Even more noticeable in Table 1 are the sharp increases in each state in the

Table 1.   State UI Tax Schedules, 1978 and 1988

| State | 1978 | | | | 1988 | | | |
| | Most favorable | | Least favorable | | Most favorable | | Least favorable | |
	t_{min}	t_{max}	t_{min}	t_{max}	t_{min}	t_{max}	t_{min}	t_{max}
California	0.00	3.30	0.40	3.90	0.30	5.40	1.30	5.40
Illinois	0.10	4.00	0.10	4.00	0.20	6.70	0.20	6.70
Indiana	0.02	2.80	2.70	3.30	0.02	5.40	1.30	5.40
Massachusetts	0.40	4.20	2.20	6.00	1.20	5.40	3.00	7.20
Michigan	0.30	6.90	0.30	6.90	0.00	8.00	1.00	10.00
New Jersey	0.40	4.30	1.20	6.20	0.30	5.40	1.20	7.00
New York	0.30	3.00	4.30	5.20	0.00	5.40	2.10	6.40
North Carolina	0.10	5.70	0.10	5.70	0.01	5.70	0.01	5.70
Ohio	0.00	3.60	0.60	4.30	0.00	5.20	0.30	7.30
Texas	0.10	4.00	0.10	4.80	0.00	6.00	0.00	6.00

Source: Comparison of State UI Laws, August 1978, September 1988.

range of rates between 1978 and 1988. The reason for the changes is clear: The Tax Equity and Fiscal Responsibility Act of 1982 (TEFRA) raised the creditable part of the FUTA tax rate from 2.7% to its current 5.4%, effective in 1985. This *federally imposed change meant that the potential for more complete experience rating has been much greater since the effective date of 1985.* Indeed, 8 states now have t_{max} above 7% on their most-favorable (lowest) schedules, and 16 have this on their least-favorable (highest) schedules. Moreover, many states have chosen to lower t_{min}; 12 states now have a t_{min} of zero on their most favorable schedule.

Along with the major changes in tax rate policy in the 1980s have come

Table 2.   The UI Tax Base, 1978 and 1988[a]

State	Base 1978	Base/AAW 1978	Base 1988	Base/AAW 1988
California	$6,000	0.475	$7,000	0.312
Florida	6,000	0.579	7,000	0.393
Illinois	6,000	0.445	9,000	0.403
Massachusetts	6,000	0.515	7,000	0.331
Michigan	6,000	0.399	9,500	0.394
New Jersey	6,200	0.476	12,000	0.525
New York	6,000	0.445	7,000	0.292
Ohio	6,000	0.451	8,000	0.377
Pennsylvania	6,000	0.493	8,000	0.401
Texas	6,000	0.500	8,000	0.377
All states	6,190	0.513	8,535	0.417

Note: [a]AAW, average annual wage.

important though less obvious changes in policy regarding the tax base. The tax base under FUTA was raised from $4200 to $6000 in 1978, and to $7000 in 1983. As Table 2 shows, an increasing number of states set the tax base above the federal minimum. State UI taxes are now applied to a tax base that exceeds $7000 in 37 of the 51 major jurisdictions (states and the District of Columbia). This has not prevented increases in taxable wages from driving the ratio of the base to the average annual wage (AAW) to the lowest it has been since the program's inception.[2] Federal policy consciously widened the range of experience-rated tax rates during the 1980s; it unconsciously reduced the fraction of wages to which those rates apply.

III.   EFFECTS OF UI TAXES ON THE LABOR MARKET

The labor market impact of UI taxes stems from two sources: (1) the incompleteness of experience rating—that $e < 1$; and (2) the limit on the tax base to an amount far less than the wage earned by most workers. The effects are felt in three broad areas: (1) the equilibrium industrial mix and the relative sizes of different industries, (2) the extent of employment fluctuations in an industry, and (3) the types of workers, their wages, and the length of their workweeks.

A.   Effects on Employment Structure

The incompleteness of experience rating causes taxes to exceed benefit payments in some firms and fall short in others. These differences are not random. In 1978, for example, agriculture–forestry–fisheries generated far more benefit payments than taxes in the 11 states examined by Becker (1981, Table 8). Construction generated more benefits than taxes in 10 of the 11 states, and mining did so in 9 of the 11. Incomplete experience rating produced the opposite result in several other major industries. In all 11 states, typical employers in finance–insurance–real estate paid taxes that exceed the benefits received by their workers. This was true in 10 of the 11 states in the transportation–communications–utilities industries, and in 9 of 11 in services and wholesale–retail trade. These systematic differences exist both within particular states and in the entire nation (see Munts and Asher, 1980). They were present in data covering a variety of states in the 1960s. Data for New Jersey in the mid-1970s show that a company paying t_{max} in one year is very likely to be paying that highest tax in succeeding years: the same employers consistently take more from the UI system than they put in (Marks, 1984). All these phenomena probably still exist, though the widening of tax rates in the mid-1980s almost certainly reduced the extent of the differences among industries. They represent a *cross subsidy* from those industries that pay taxes that exceed benefits to those where benefits paid fall short of taxes.

This subsidy lowers the cost of doing business in the subsidized industry. Because of it, employers can hire workers on more favorable terms, as workers are attracted to an industry that can offer them UI benefits financed by other employers; they can sell their products more cheaply; and/or they can make higher profits. Unless the entire impact comes in the form of higher profits, the subsidy raises output and employment in the subsidized industries above what they would otherwise be, and reduces them in the industries that are paying the subsidy. *The UI system subsidizes the expansion of high-unemployment industries through a net tax on more stable industries.* By causing an expansion of the demand for goods whose production creates more unemployment, incomplete experience rating makes the economy more prone to unemployment. Total employment economywide does not expand, though; the increase in the subsidized industries is offset by a drop in employment in industries that pay more in taxes than their workers receive in benefits.

Research on UI has pointed out the steady and continuing flow of subsidies toward certain industries, but has spent little time analyzing the size of their effects. There is substantial agreement that the cross subsidies do not affect profits, given the fairly competitive nature of American industry (McLure, 1977). Most of the impact is either on wages, and hence indirectly on product prices, or on prices directly. In either case the effect is to change the sizes of industries as customers switch to subsidized goods.

The few studies of this effect yield vastly different implications. The one study (Deere, 1988) that examines the impact of the subsidy on the relative sizes of industries across states finds that, in states where the subsidy is bigger, the least-stable industries are relatively larger. The implied effects are, indeed, huge. The only examination of the costs of the encouragement to excess production in the subsidized industries suggests that in construction, an industry that is heavily subsidized by the UI system, an amount equivalent to 0.25% of output is wasted (Topel, 1990). The directions of the likely impacts of the subsidy are clear, and we know that the result is the expansion of unstable industries and the contraction of stable industries. We just have very little evidence on the magnitudes of these effects.

B. Effects on Employment Fluctuations

Remember that for the typical firm $e < 1$—an extra dollar of benefits paid out to its employees raises its taxes by less than one dollar. Part of the cost of benefits is shared among all companies in the state UI system. How large is e? A study of nine states during 1971–1978 showed that benefits charged to employers with negative balances averaged around 20% of all benefit payments (Wandner and Crosslin, 1980). That study also found that noncharged benefits amounted to around 15% of the total, a result corroborated (Hibbard, 1980) by data for eight other states in the years 1971–1975. Yet another study (Becker, 1981, Table 8) demonstrated about the same extent of noncharging and a similar importance of benefits paid to employees of negative-balance employers for nine states in 1978. Data for 1983 for 12 states show that benefits charged to positive-balance employers and to negative-balance employers up to their tax contributions equaled 52% of all benefit payments (Office of the Inspector General, 1985). Finally, ignoring noncharged benefits, data for 19 reserve and benefit ratio states (Topel, 1984, Table 1) suggest that the cost to the typical employer of an extra dollar of UI benefits is only around 80 cents.

Taking all the evidence together, it seems fairly clear that e was between one-half and two-thirds during the 1960s and 1970s. Other data (Office of the Inspector General, 1985) suggest that e fell during the early 1970s. The substantial widening of the range of tax rates in 1985 probably raised e in the late 1980s. However, the continued existence of noncharged benefits, and the many firms whose benefit payments far exceed even 10% of their taxable payroll, means that the average extent of experience rating is still probably no more than 75%.

Incompletely experience-rated UI not only shifts resources to the subsidized, unstable industries, as Section IIIA showed; it also provides incentives for many companies to chose to lay off workers rather than spread work by reducing hours when product demand declines. This point has been well-known since the advent of UI:

> Though a compensation system might tend to cause employers to lay off or discharge work-men [sic] because provision had been made for their maintenance, rather than to permit them to share in the work available, this tendency can be checked by merit [experience] rating. (Millis and Montgomery, 1938, p. 176)

Recent theoretical work has formalized this observation and examined some of its ramifications (for example, Feldstein, 1976; Baily, 1977; Burdett and Hool, 1983; Burdett and Wright, 1988). Faced with a choice of whether to reduce hours or wages or to cut employment, the existence of incompletely experience-rated UI benefits gives employers an incentive to do the latter. By laying off the workers the employer can raise their incomes on average over the cycle, because more of them can collect b dollars of benefits during bad times, as compared to their incomes if wages were cut. By offering a wage–employment package that provides UI benefits during bad times, the employer can attract workers at a reduced wage, one lower than otherwise similar firms whose product demand does not vary or who do not choose to use the UI system. The employer is willing to offer this deal because its taxes do not rise one-for-one with each dollar of benefits paid—precisely because the degree of experience rating e is less than one.

This discussion suggests that (1) employers with substantial noncharged benefits, (2) negative-balance employers, (3) companies that are at t_{max}, and (4) firms whose reserve ratio exceeds R^* in states where $t_{min} > 0$, will all have an incentive to increase layoffs above what they would be if experience rating were complete or if there were no UI system. The incentive is greater where the product demand cycle that produces the layoffs is easily predicted, for employees are then more easily attracted to a company offering a slightly lower wage but the chance to receive substantial benefits during "UI vacations." This implies that seasonal and other temporary layoffs will be especially strongly affected by incomplete experience rating, as will permanent layoffs where business cycles are predictable. Other permanent layoffs, such as those stemming from increased foreign competition and other demand shocks, are not likely to be affected as much.

To some extent the heightened incentives to lay off workers are reduced by the existence of multiple tax schedules: Even though the benefits may not raise taxes this year, they may do so in future years as the state system shifts to a higher schedule (Brown, 1986; Wolcowitz, 1984). As Table 1 shows, though, in the late 1980s, and even on the least favorable schedule, the range of tax rates is often not very wide. There still exist incentives to expand layoffs, and thus to increase layoff unemployment.

Before 1987, when the Tax Reform Act of 1986 became effective, the incentive to lay off workers in bad times was even greater, because UI income was untaxed or only partly taxed. A dollar of benefits was worth more to the recipient than a dollar of (taxed) wages. This gave workers a still greater incentive to accept layoffs and gave their employers still lower costs, in the form of employees willing to work at lower wages than otherwise. Empirical studies of experience rating have not accounted for this, though most studies did that focused on incentives facing beneficiaries rather than employers.

In the last 12 years, substantial work has been done relating incomplete experience rating to employment fluctuations. We now know a fair amount about the size of its impacts on unemployment. More important, we know which characteristics of the UI tax structure produce most of these effects.

Table 3 summarizes the ten available studies of this effect. [Only one study was published before 1977; it and the state of knowledge about UI taxes generally up to that time are summarized by Hamermesh (1977).] The various studies have mainly attempted to discover the effects of the tax structure on the layoff rate or the rate of unemployment resulting from layoffs. They have tried to distinguish between effects on permanent and temporary layoffs, and to look for special effects on seasonal variation in employment. Both efforts are based on the observation that the largest effects of incomplete experience rating will be on those flows into unemployment that are most expected, and among those workers who are likely to retain an attachment to the employer who lays them off.

The studies differ greatly in method, type of data, and the structuring of the problem. In all studies, examining differences in the parameters of the states' UI tax systems allows the researcher to determine the impact of differences in experience rating. In some, though, the impact of state tax systems on individual

Table 3. Studies of Experience Rating and Unemployment

Study	Data	Results
Brechling (1981)	Reserve ratio states, 1962–1969, manufacturing industries	Higher t_{neg} sharply reduces layoff rate; smaller effect of lower t_{min}
Edebalk and Wadensjö (1986)	Sweden, 1954–1969	Sharp decline in temporary layoffs after introduction of partial experience rating
Halpin (1979)	Three small manufacturing industries, 1960–1974, 36–50 states	Reduced seasonal variability of employment where high tax base compared to wages; no consistent effects of other tax parameters
Halpin (1980)	41,000 individuals, 1976	Lesser chance of being on temporary layoff for (1) high tax base compared to wages; (2) smaller gap between t_{max} and tax rate needed to fund negative balances
Kaiser (1987)	Reserve ratio states, 1964–1969, manufacturing industries	Higher t_{neg} sharply reduces layoff rate; high tax base reduces layoff rate
Saffer (1982)	States, 1967–1975, data on industries	Larger gap between t_{neg} (or t_{max}) and t_{min} reduces layoff rate
Saffer (1983)	15,000 individuals, 1975	Lesser chance of being on temporary or permanent layoff if worker is in a state with a larger gap between t_{neg} (or t_{max}) and t_{min}
Topel (1983)	8000 individuals from 29 industries, 19 states, 1975	Lesser chance of temporary layoff, greater chance of returning to work with more complete experience rating; imperfect rating and not taxing benefits produced 30% of temporary layoff unemployment
Topel (1984)	34,000 individuals, from 29 industries, reserve and benefit ratio states, 1973–1976	Lesser chance of being on temporary layoff in states and industries where UI subsidy is smaller; smaller effect on permanent layoff unemployment
Topel (1985)	76,000 men, 1977–1981, reserve- and benefit- ratio states	Lesser chance of being on temporary layoff in states and industries where UI subsidy is smaller; smaller effect on permanent layoff and quit unemployment; perfect experience rating would reduce unemployment rate by 1.5 percentage points

experience may be muddied by the use of industry level data on turnover measures. In many studies the parameters of the tax systems are considered separately rather than as contributory factors to the degree of incompleteness of experience rating, which in turn can directly affect turnover. While all the studies advance our knowledge, these considerations suggest that Saffer (1983) and, especially, Topel (1983, 1984, 1985) are the most reliable.

While more research would be desirable, at this point it seems fairly safe to conclude that:

1. A higher t_{neg} or t_{max} reduces the layoff rate and the rate of layoff unemployment. This is so mainly for temporary layoffs and seasonal unemployment; the evidence for effects on permanent layoffs is more mixed. The effects are quite large. Topel (1990) did not explicitly measure the effect of UI taxes; but the study did bring together a variety of aspects of UI in an overall evaluation of the effect of incomplete experience rating that suggests that imposing complete experience rating would reduce unemployment by roughly 20%. This effect is probably too large to be believable: it is difficult to imagine that a program that taxes less than 1.5% of payroll can account for 1.5 percentage points of unemployment in the entire labor force. The result indicates, though, how important the impact of some aspects of incomplete experience rating can be.

2. Beyond this effect, little else can be concluded from the available research about the effects of tax rate policy. In particular, there is at best only sparse evidence that reducing t_{min} to zero has a discernible impact on layoff unemployment.

As Table 3 shows, empirical research has demonstrated that a higher tax base relative to taxable wages also reduces layoffs and seasonal unemployment. The reason to expect this is simple: For a particular set of tax rates, raising the tax base raises the tax liability of a negative-balance employer, or one at t_{max}, who lays off another worker. Raising the tax base is another way of increasing experience rating (see Brechling, 1977). Indeed, even though European UI systems are not experience rated, European employers rely less on temporary layoffs to meet drops in product demand. The reason may well be that, in Europe, UI taxes are essentially on a per-hour basis (because the ceilings are very high relative to wages) (Fitzroy and Hart, 1985).

C. Effects on the Employment Mix and on Worker Hours Substitution

Because it is not applied in equal proportions to all workers, the UI tax will induce firms to substitute workers whose labor is taxed less heavily for workers whose labor is taxed more heavily. A highly cyclical business in Pennsylvania that employs a worker earning $8000 can pay a tax of $736 on that worker's wages (a tax rate of 9.2% applied to the $8000 tax base). The same tax, $736, would be paid on the wages of a worker earning $40,000. In this case the low ceiling on the tax base raises the cost of employing the high-wage worker by

1.8%, so that the relative cost of employing the low-wage worker is increased by 7.4% (9.2 − 1.8). Assuming the workers' market wages reflect their skills and their value to the employer, the ceiling creates a powerful incentive to shift toward hiring higher-wage, more-skilled employees.

These incentives can create two effects. First, if the wages of low-skilled workers do not fall when the demand for their services is reduced, fewer of them will be employed. Second, if their wages can fall, they will. In either case the net income of the population of low-skilled workers in the state will be reduced.

Say all 100 workers in a Pennsylvania company earn $12,000 per annum working a 40-hour week, and the employer is already rated at t_{max} on the highest state tax schedule. On September 1 the employer realizes that product demand is booming and decides to expand output by 25%. Many factors will affect the choice between hiring 25 more workers and asking current employees to work overtime. An additional, potentially substantial one is that the employer must pay UI taxes of 9.2% of wages on each new worker, but would incur no extra UI tax liability on overtime hours of current workers (because the $8000 ceiling means the tax liability on them vanished on August 31 for the remainder of the calendar year). The limit on the tax base thus creates an incentive to use more hours and fewer workers.

No one has studied the effects of the UI tax itself on the mix of workers. The huge body of research on the impact of changes in relative labor costs on the skill mix of workers and the somewhat smaller set of research results on employers' ability to substitute hours for workers (Hamermesh, 1986; Hart, 1984) allow us to infer the probable impacts of the tax. Also, Hamermesh (1978) shows that greater UI coverage leads to greater reliance on employment reductions for a given drop in product demand. The evidence leads to the following conclusions:

1. Because the UI tax base is so close to the minimum wage (on an annual basis), it is unlikely that overtaxing low-wage employment can reduce the wage rates of low-skilled workers. Instead, it reduces the number employed. This effect is substantial, with each 1% increase in the relative cost of low-skilled workers lowering their employment by at least 1%. *The low limit on the tax base relative to taxable wages has reduced the number of jobs for low-skilled workers.*

2. We know that a rise in taxes that are assessed per worker leads employers to substitute extra hours per worker for employees, especially low-wage employees (Hart and Kawasaki, 1988; Wright and Loberg, 1987). We can conclude that *to some unknown extent the low tax base has increased employers' reliance on overtime and reduced employment, especially of low-skilled workers.*

IV. OPTIMAL EXPERIENCE RATING AND TAX BASE

There are two fundamentally different views of the appropriate extent of experience rating. Most public-finance economists would argue that experience rating should be structured to ensure that the UI system as a whole produces the same employment, unemployment, and industrial structure as would be produced in the absence of publicly provided UI. From this viewpoint, incomplete experience rating should be used to offset other taxes that produce distortions, such as other payroll taxes and income taxes (Boadway and Oswald, 1983). Under this view the UI tax should be used to increase the neutrality of the tax system, i.e., to minimize the distortions to the labor and other markets that taxes produce.

The alternative view, held by many specialists in UI and by some economists, is based on the nature of the employees' separation that generated the benefits that must be financed. Under this view one should attempt to distinguish between UI benefits that are due to the employer's actions and those that are beyond the employer's control, with only the former being charged to the employer. The latter, including perhaps benefits to voluntary quitters, long-duration claims, and cyclical increases in benefits, should be spread across the state (or even the national) UI system (Halpin, 1978; National Commission on Unemployment Compensation, 1980). This view does not necessarily conflict with the other; rather, its intellectual basis is entirely different. The evidence in Section IIIB shows that complete experience rating would essentially eliminate temporary layoff unemployment, and other evidence shows that most temporary layoffs return to their jobs. Proponents of this view should thus argue that taxes to finance all unemployment spells resulting from temporary layoffs should be fully experience rated.

UI tax policy should avoid increasing unemployment beyond what would occur in its absence if there were no social desire for publicly provided benefits. Yet the existence of that desire means that financing an optimal level of benefits may require an incompletely rated tax that increases unemployment and shifts resources toward certain industries. UI tax policy should not penalize employers for long-duration unemployment that is beyond their control. Yet long-duration unemployment can be lowered by reducing the number of workers becoming unemployed, and that can often be accomplished by increasing the extent of experience rating. These two considerations alone suggest there is no easy philosophical basis for choosing which implications of the two views to choose. As was recognized very early in the program:

> The degree of preference should be decided upon with due regard to the desire to further stabilization of employment on the one hand, and the safety of the fund and the desire to distribute the burden involved in carrying the cost with proper reference to ability to pay on the other (Millis and Montgomery, 1938, p. 167).

The choice of goals has implicitly been made for more than 50 years by the political process at the federal and state levels. Temporary benefit programs enacted by the federal government to provide for workers who have exhausted regular benefits have generally not been financed by experience-rated taxes.

(They have been financed out of general revenues or shared with state UI funds.) At the state level the philosophy underlying financing decisions is much less clear. Nonetheless, one can draw some inferences about the process that generates the tax structures by comparing interstate differences in taxes to differences in industrial and demographic characteristics. Experience rating is less complete where: (1) the distribution of employment is spread among more different industries; (2) unemployment is concentrated especially heavily in a few industries; and (3) the largest industry accounts for an unusually large share of unemployment (Adams, 1986; Maloney and McGregor, 1988).

All three results support the conclusion that the financing of state UI benefits is largely a matter of attempts by powerful, high-unemployment industries to use legislation to gain subsidies from other industries. This suggests that neither viewpoint is dominant in state UI policy, and that one must instead argue that the efficiency and equity considerations under either viewpoint should prevail over the outcomes currently generated by the political process at the state level. Such a choice in favor of increased experience rating was made, at least implicitly, in 1982 when the federal government effectively mandated the imposition of a minimum t_{max} of 5.4% for state systems starting in 1985.

There has been less discussion of the optimal tax base. The only full-blown argument is for setting the base at 50% of the average wage, in the belief that this will minimize voluntary turnover (Brechling, 1977). Given that most voluntary turnover takes place within a few jobs, since most workers are long-term employees, and given the importance of objectives other than minimizing voluntary turnover, this argument seems quite minor. Instead, optimal policy on the tax base should take into account its role in the experience rating of UI taxes and its effect on the types of workers hired and on employers' choices between workers and hours. From this viewpoint we have, by allowing the tax base to fall in relative terms, implicitly chosen to limit the effect on experience rating of the increased range of state tax UI rates; and we have increased the incentive the UI system provides employers to hire higher-wage workers, and to use more overtime rather than additional workers.

V. SHORT-TIME COMPENSATION, PARTIAL BENEFITS, AND UNEMPLOYMENT INSURANCE FINANCING

Short-time compensation (STC) is in general an adjunct to UI programs that allows the payment of benefits to workers who are only partly unemployed. In some programs in various industrialized countries, and in those in the United States, benefits are paid on a pro rata basis. Thus, for example, workers whose employer relies on a 20% hours reduction for all workers rather than laying off 20% of the work force will receive wages for 80% of the workweek and STC equal to 20% of their regular weekly benefit amount. One can view STC as an attempt to make UI neutral with respect to employers' decisions about meeting declining product demand by layoffs instead of reductions in hours.

Since the inception of the UI program most state systems have provided *partial UI benefits* to be paid when a worker is unemployed for at least several days per week. In most states payments are structured so that the worker and employer are severely discouraged from using them (Munts, 1970). Eleven states, compared to only six in 1978, have now made their partial benefits provisions more conducive to work sharing by specifying that benefits are reduced by only a fraction of each dollar of earnings. In most of them, though, the rates of reduction are quite high: With the exceptions of Alaska and Montana, the other states that structure partial benefits this way decrease them by at least 66 cents for each additional dollar earned.

Feeling a need to encourage work sharing, California in 1978 instituted its own STC program as part of the state UI system. Arizona and Oregon implemented STC programs in 1982, and in that year TEFRA required the secretary of labor to assist states in setting up STC programs. As of 1987, nine other states had implemented STC programs. Financial arrangements under the STC legislation differ sharply among the states. Arizona, California, and Oregon charge surtaxes to negative-balance or other high-unemployment companies whose workers receive STC, as do three other states. In six other state systems, though, STC payments are treated the same as regular UI benefits that are charged to the employer (Johnson, 1987).

Part of the legislation implementing federal assistance to states in setting up STC programs required that an evaluation of these programs be carried out. This was met by Kerachsky et al. (1986), who did a thorough evaluation of all aspects of STC programs in Arizona, California, and Oregon, based on a comparison of employers that used STC and otherwise similar employers that did not. In all states, total payments under STC were tiny fractions of all UI benefits. Thus in 1982, the biggest year of the Arizona program, STC was $2.4 million, only 1.4% of all benefits; in the same year in California, the corresponding figures were $18.6 million and 0.8% (Johnson, 1987). Clearly, STC could not have had much impact even in the states that implemented the program.

The results of Kerachsky et al. relevant to this discussion are

1. Workers in companies that used STC had more total hours of compensated time (by STC and regular benefits together) than did employees in otherwise identical firms.
2. Workers in firms that were more likely to use STC had higher than average benefit entitlements. Since weekly benefit amounts rise with wages (up to some maximum), this suggests that higher-wage employers were more likely to use STC.
3. The administrative cost per hour compensated was higher for STC than for regular benefits.

The first and third conclusions corroborated a detailed study of STC in California (unfortunately done without a control group).

The experience documented by Kerachsky et al. (1986) in Arizona, California, and Oregon is probably unusually favorable compared to STC in the other nine states that adopted it. In all three states, STC payments were more likely to be experience rated than regular UI benefits; in most other states, that is not so. This consideration suggests that the potential for the STC program to generate more compensated hours than would otherwise occur is greater even than that found in these three states. As I have argued (Hamermesh, 1978), and as Kerachsky et al's findings suggest, *STC not only leads to a greater reliance on work sharing relative to layoffs; it also produces a larger reduction in the total number of hours worked.*

A wider application of STC would probably reduce layoff unemployment and *spread work* among more people during slack times. However, it demonstrably *reduces the total amount of work* available, too, because it raises labor costs and thus reduces labor demand. There is not enough evidence to infer how large this effect is. Also, because STC is not completely experience rated, it increases the extent of cross subsidization implicit in the UI system. If no other characteristics of the UI system, including the tax structure, the tax base, and partial benefit formulas, can be altered, STC is a potentially effective tool if the only concern is work sharing. It is a costly one, though; and there are other means within the UI system of accomplishing the same goal with a less adverse impact on the labor market and lower administrative costs.

VI. POLICY ALTERNATIVES

Any policy for ameliorating the effects of UI on employment and wage outcomes must confront the necessity of maintaining fund solvency. UI has as its basic purpose maintaining living standards for unemployed workers, not improving labor market efficiency (Hamermesh, 1982). This means that, while some proposals might appeal to one's desire to reduce unemployment, the need to maintain confidence in the widely accepted UI program requires that desirable policies *both* reduce unemployment/increase labor market efficency *and* improve funding of the program without raising its budgetary cost. Most of the proposals are not new. However, the confluence of growth in the available evidence on the effects of UI financing and major changes in financing during the 1980s means that the discussion can be more confident and can take account of the changed conditions of the UI system.

Proposal 1:   Increase the FUTA Tax Base

The National Commission on Unemployment Compensation (1980, pp. 85–86) recommended raising the tax base to 65% of average annual taxable wages

Table 4.   The Impact of Tax Base Policies

State	1988 actual	Base = 2× (average benefit)	Base = 0.65 ×(AAW)	Uniform $14,000
California	$7,000	$17,264	$14,562	$14,000
Florida	7,000	20,800	11,583	14,000
Illinois	9,000	18,304	14,533	14,000
Massachusetts	7,000	24,544	13,758	14,000
Michigan	9,500	25,168	15,666	14,000
New Jersey	12,000	25,064	14,851	14,000
New York	7,000	18,720	15,605	14,000
Ohio	8,000	16,328	13,809	14,000
Pennsylvania	8,000	26,208	12,962	14,000
Texas	8,000	21,840	13,785	14,000
All states	$8,535	$19,443	$13,504	$14,000

(AAW) over a period of time. The FUTA base was originally the same as the tax base under Old Age and Survivors' Insurance; in 1989 that base was $48,000, while the FUTA base was $7000. Following the NCUC recommendation by increasing the FUTA base to 65% of AAW would, as columns (1) and (3) of Table 4 show, have raised the average tax base nationwide in 1988 by over 50%. A still more radical proposal, requiring that the base equal twice the average benefit (in light of the notion that UI replaces 50% of pretax earnings), would, as Table 4 shows, have resulted in a much larger increase, as would a uniform doubling of the FUTA base to $14,000. The simplest policy change, and the one I shall discuss, is that *the FUTA tax base in any year shall equal 65% of the national AAW two years earlier,* with the policy phased in over a two-year period.

Based on the theory and evidence presented here, the arguments for this policy are

1. The current low tax base means that we are using a tax on the employment of low-wage workers to finance the operation of state employment services (since the major use of FUTA revenues is as grants for administration of these services). Using a highly regressive tax to fund an institution that benefits the entire economy is unusual, and perhaps unique.

2. Forcing states to tax a larger share of total earnings would make experience rating more complete. It would clearly widen the fraction of charged benefits that are effectively experience rated. It would, as the evidence shows, lessen the incentives for employers to rely on temporary layoffs to meet reduced product demand, and would increase their reliance on work sharing instead.

3. In the short run, increasing the base would lead to a buildup of state UI reserves (see the appendix). This would occur when the reserves are nowhere nearly sufficient to meet requirements of a recession like that of 1974–1975 or 1981–1982.

4. The proposal would make the state UI systems more flexible, as fewer firms' tax liabilities would be limited by maximum tax rates. It would probably not result in higher taxes on employers after the initial period of phase-in. There is only weak evidence (see the appendix) that benefit amounts, which are the main proximate cause of higher state UI taxes, tend to increase when the base is raised.

The arguments against the proposal are

1. It might result in larger state programs, as legislators use the increased base to vote higher benefit formulas. At the least, it would mean a vast enlargement of FUTA revenues, as the higher base is combined with a very high FUTA tax rate of 0.8%.
2. This policy could produce a tax increase just at the time the economy is sliding into a recession.

The sharp increase in state maximum UI tax rates required by TEFRA has probably gone partway toward making experience rating more complete. The effects have, though, been partly offset by the continuing decline in the tax base relative to AAW. The higher tax rates on the smaller base have increased the regressivity of the tax and hurt labor market outcomes for low-skilled workers. To increase fund solvency and its ability to handle cyclical demands, and to reduce detrimental side effects on the labor market, *this proposal should be adopted*. However, to prevent a substantial enlargement of state bureaucracies and the buildup of very large loan funds, the 0.8% FUTA tax rate should be cut as the base rises. A policy like the following would index FUTA revenues without raising the share of FUTA taxes in employment costs, and would meet the goals outlined above:

Year	1990	1991	1992 and thereafter
Base as percentage of AAW	50	57.5	65
FUTA tax rate	0.65	0.6	0.5

Proposal 2:   Increase Maximum State UI Tax Rates

The National Commission on Unemployment Compensation (1980, p. 93) recommended raising state tax maxima so that "the vast majority of benefit payments are effectively charged." Presumably this implies an increase in the creditable component of the FUTA tax rate even beyond the 5.4% that became effective in 1985. Other than indicating that the maximum tax should increase if we wish to make experience rating more effective, no specific increase is implied by the evidence. The arguments for an increase are

1. Even with the increases in tax maxima documented in Table 1, there still are many negative-balance employers. This means that all the potentially detrimental effects on the labor market induced by incomplete experience rating still exist, though perhaps not to the same degree as before 1985.
2. The studies summarized in Table 3 show the especially strong impact of low state tax maxima on rates of temporary layoffs and the unemployment rate. Raising the creditable part of the FUTA tax still further would force states to raise their tax maxima still further, thus reducing incentives for layoffs and the cyclical instability of employment.
3. Increases in state tax maxima would in the short run increase UI tax revenues and help replenish depleted state UI reserves.

The arguments against the proposal are

1. The evidence on the effects of state tax maxima is based on the pre-1985 environment. It is not clear that the beneficial impacts of raising maxima still further will be so large, now that the system is probably more completely experience rated.
2. Raising tax maxima *in vacuo,* as was effectively done under TEFRA, makes UI taxes more regressive and increases employers' biases in favor of substituting hours for workers. By itself the proposal would reduce job opportunities and/or earnings for low-wage workers.

There is substantial evidence that some employers generate cost rates in excess of 10% year after year. The proposal would reduce cross subsidies to these employers; and the evidence clearly shows its impact in reducing layoffs. However, today's very low tax base relative to AAW means that by itself it would harm low-wage workers' labor market propects. *This proposal should be adopted, but only along with Proposal 1.*

Proposal 3: Require That Minimum State UI Tax Rates Be Zero

This has been proposed by many economists in the last 12 years, including this author and most of those cited in Table 3. The National Commission on Unemployment Compensation (1980, p. 93) recommended against it. The argument for it is

1. It would improve experience rating and reduce the detrimental effects of UI on the structure of employment and on employment fluctuations.

The arguments against it are

1. The evidence suggests that lower tax minima have small impacts on layoff rates. While the incentives exist, the responses are small.
2. In all states the cost of noncharged benefits is socialized. A zero minimum tax rate allows some employers to escape their share of these social costs.
3. There have never been even implicit federal standards for state tax minima. It is not worth creating this new area of federal interference in state programs.

Tax minima are already very close to zero: Even on the least-favorable tax schedules, 21 states had minimum rates below 1% in 1988; nearly all states had minimum rates below 1% on their most-favorable schedules. Given the apparently small changes in incentives that this proposal would produce and the absence of evidence that these incentives have any impact on employment fluctuations, the only argument in its favor seems minor compared to the arguments against it. *This proposal should not be adopted.*

Proposal 4:   Require Interest Charges and Payments on Employers' Accounts

Paying and charging interest on employers' accounts is another way to increase the experience rating of state systems. Interest at current short-term rates could be credited on positive balances and charged on negative balances. This would be similar to the crediting and charging of interest on states' balances with the federal UI trust funds. Arguments in favor are

1. The increase in experience rating would have all the desirable effects noted in Section III and discussed under Proposals 1–3.
2. Several studies (Bronars, 1985; Cottle and Macaulay, 1985) have demonstrated how this proposal could generate additional revenue for state systems.
3. The proposal is in accord with recommendations that most benefits be effectively charged to the employer.
4. The proposal accords with past practice that federal intervention in state programs operate through the tax system. It mirrors practices in existence since 1983 in the federal trust funds.

The negative arguments are

1. At a time of fairly low interest rates, the size of the incentives created is likely to be small, especially relative to the extra administrative costs imposed.

2.   There have never been federal standards for how states handle employers' reserves in state funds. It is not worth creating a new area of federal interference in state programs.

Despite the administrative costs, this proposal has merit. If short-term interest rates were 15%, as they were in 1980, it would provide powerful incentives to employers to avoid layoffs. The proposal is hardly a major extension of federal interference, since it does work through the tax system (although not through the FUTA tax rate itself). *It should be adopted.*

Proposal 5:   Require States to Limit Noncharged Benefits to a Small Fraction of Total Benefits

In some states noncharged benefits can account for 50% of all regular benefits. This implies that, no matter how wide the range of tax rates may be, half the benefits cannot be effectively experience rated. The arguments in favor of this proposal are

1.   The standard arguments regarding the necessity for increased experience rating. It accords with calls for greater effectiveness of rating.
2.   Discussion of this proposal would further a needed debate on the appropriate extent of experience rating in the UI system.

The counterarguments are

1.   This is a federal benefit standard and represents a substantial expansion of federal interference in state programs.
2.   The interference is in an area on which there is no general agreement (see Section IV). Why expand the federal role greatly if we do not know what the appropriate amount of noncharging is?

The lack of common agreement on the proper fraction of benefits to be charged, and the criteria for charging, suggest that *this proposal should not be adopted.* That conclusion is underscored by the implied change in the federal–state relationship that the proposal represents.

Proposal 6:   More Widespread Encouragement to Short-Time Compensation

Providing more federal technical assistance to states that institute STC programs, or even encouraging such programs through the FUTA tax, could induce employers to rely more on work sharing and less on layoffs. The arguments in favor of such assistance/encouragement are

1. Studies have demonstrated that STC does tilt employers' decisions toward hours reductions and away from layoffs. An expanded program would produce effects in the desired direction.
2. Other countries, particularly in Western Europe, have used expanded STC programs with apparent success.

The arguments against the program are

1. The major evaluation study demonstrates that STC is expensive to administer and that it raises total benefit costs.
2. Both in state programs here and in STC in other countries the utilization rate is tiny. It has not had a perceptible effect on unemployment rates.
3. By increasing benefit payments for incompletely experienced-rated employers, STC increases the extent of cross subsidization in the UI system.
4. Adopting Proposal 1 would produce a much greater increase in work sharing and a much larger decline in layoff unemployment without creating more federal interference in state programs and without generating new state bureaucracies.

STC has not been target efficient in the United States; and it probably generates negative side effects. Its goals can be attained more readily with less radical changes.

VII.   CONCLUSION

Legislated and administrative changes in the UI system during the 1980s probably reduced the program's detrimental effects on labor market efficiency. They did so without changing the nature of the federal–state relationship that makes the program so unusual. Regrettably, though, they hurt the labor market status of low-wage workers by greatly increasing the negative impact of UI taxes on the demand for their labor. This inequitable and socially dangerous side effect of an otherwise desirable idea can be reversed if the policy changes proposed here are adopted. Their adoption would in addition provide employers with increased incentives to spread work rather than lay off employees, resulting in smaller employment fluctuations and a lower unemployment rate.

APPENDIX:
A MODEL OF BENEFITS, TAXES, AND THE TAX BASE

To examine whether a higher tax base automatically leads to higher taxes and/or higher benefits as UI administrators and legislators try to spend an apparent revenue windfall, I estimated two models of taxes and benefits. The first consists of

$$TAXRAT_t = a_0 + \sum_0^4 a_{1i}BASTOT_{t-i} + \sum_1^4 a_{2i}BENTOT_{t-i}$$

$$+ \sum_1^4 a_{3i}TAXRAT_{t-i} + \epsilon_{1t}, \tag{1}$$

$$BENTOT_t = b_0 + \sum_0^4 b_{1i}IUR_{t-i} + \sum_1^4 b_{2i}BENTOT_{t-i}$$

$$+ \sum_1^4 b_{3i}TAXRAT_{t-i} + \epsilon_{2t}, \tag{2}$$

where TAXRAT is the ratio of state UI taxes to total payroll; BASTOT is the ratio of taxable to total payroll; BENTOT is the ratio of regular benefits paid to total payroll; and IUR is the covered unemployment rate. All variables are measured as percentages. Through Eq. (1) this model allows for a direct effect of a higher tax base on taxes. It allows for indirect effects through (2), as a higher base can raise taxes through the lagged effects of the higher TAXRAT feeding back through higher benefits onto future taxes. The model allows us to test for causality, in particular, to answer the crucial question whether the $b_{3i} = 0$, i.e., whether higher taxes lead to higher benefits.

The model does not allow for the possibility of a direct effect of a higher taxable base on benefit payments *independent of the effect of the base on benefits through its possible effect on the ratio of taxes to total payroll*. To do so, we respecify (2) as

$$BENTOT_t = b'_0 + \sum_0^4 b'_{1i}IUR_{t-i} + \sum_1^4 b'_{2i}BENTOT_{t-i} + \sum_1^4 b'_{3i}TAXRAT_{t-i}$$

$$+ \sum_0^4 b'_{4i}BASTOT_{t-i} + \epsilon'_{2t}. \tag{2}'$$

The VAR models (1) and (2), and (1) and (2)′, are estimated on annual data for the entire United States, with $t = 1950, \ldots, 1986$.

The results of the estimation are shown in Table A1.[3] The first thing to note is that benefits Granger-cause taxes, as should not be surprising. Taxes do not Granger-cause benefits: The F-statistics on the vectors of coefficients b_{3i} and b'_{3i} are not significantly different from zero even at the 90% level.

A test of the joint significance of b'_{3i} and b'_{4i} yields $F(9,17) = 1.91$, also not significantly different from zero at the 90% level. However, a test of the joint significance of the b'_{4i} alone yields $F(5,17) = 2.80$, different from zero at the 90% level of confidence (though not at the 95% level). There is only weak

Table A1. Estimates of a Model of UI Tax Rates and the UI
Tax Base, 1950–1986

| | Dependent Variable | | |
	Taxes/ total payroll	Benefits/ total payroll	Benefits/ total payroll
Base/AAW (current	1.5699		1.3936
value and four lags)	0.3226		−1.4336
	−1.4203		1.5467
	−0.1520		−0.4051
	−0.3377		−1.1385
Insured unemployment		0.3463	0.3499
rate (current value		−0.2712	−0.2761
and four lags)		0.0605	0.1000
		−0.1221	−0.0918
		−0.0099	−0.0101
Benefits/total payroll	0.2120	0.7582	0.7755
(four lags)	0.1860	−0.1523	−0.2667
	0.1078	0.3863	0.3280
	0.0963	0.0066	0.0299
Taxes/total payroll	0.3330	−0.0129	0.0235
(four lags)	−0.0289	−0.1232	−0.4203
	0.0602	0.2259	0.4351
	−0.0177	−0.1015	−0.0702
Adjusted R^2	0.968	0.981	0.987

F-statistics on vectors of lagged endogenous variables

	35.05*	0.56	2.02
	$F(4,23)$	$F(4,22)$	$F(4,17)$

Note: *Significant at the 99% level of confidence.

evidence that a higher base affects benefits. A higher base does, though, affect the ratio of taxes to total payroll, at least in the short run: The vector of coefficients a_{1i} is significantly different from zero [$F(5,23) = 6.92$] at all conventional levels. Interestingly, while the immediate direct effect of an increase in the base is huge ($\hat{a}_{10} = 1.57$), the long-run effect must be minute, for $\Sigma\hat{a}_{1i} = -0.018$). This implies that the steady-state impact of raising the tax base in model (1) and (2) will be essentially zero.

Reestimates of the models including time trends added little. None of the trend terms was significantly different from zero, and the changes in the a_{ji} and b_{ji} and in their sums were qualitatively unimportant. This and the very high values of the $\bar{R}^2$ for the equations suggest that the two models can be useful for simulating the effects of policy changes involving the tax base.

A number of simulations of such policies were carried out using the models. I concentrate here on policies that would have: (1) raised the tax base to 65% of taxable wages in 1978; and (2) raised it to 65% in equal increments over a three-year period. The year 1978 is chosen because the base was raised substantially

Table A2. Simulations of the Effects of Increasing the Tax Base

Year	Actual values			Simulation 1			Simulation 2		
	BASTOT	TAXRAT	BENTOT	BASTOT	TAXRAT	BENTOT	BASTOT	TAXRAT	BENTOT
				Model (1) and (2)					
1978	0.496	1.37	0.93	0.65	1.65	0.93	0.50	1.41	0.93
1979	0.474	1.42	0.94	0.65	1.77	0.92	0.55	1.49	0.93
1980	0.447	1.06	1.34	0.65	1.39	1.28	0.60	1.41	1.31
1981	0.423	1.02	1.17	0.65	1.27	1.15	0.65	1.43	1.16
1982	0.405	1.02	1.72	0.65	1.18	1.64	0.65	1.37	1.60
1983	0.431	1.20	1.43	0.65	1.25	1.33	0.65	1.35	1.32
1984	0.428	1.39	0.92	0.65	1.32	0.90	0.65	1.37	0.91
1985	0.415	1.29	0.95	0.65	1.23	0.97	0.65	1.25	0.97
1986	0.407	1.14	0.98	0.65	1.15	0.97	0.65	1.16	0.96
				Model (1) and (2')					
1978	0.496	1.37	0.93	0.65	1.63	1.17	0.50	1.40	0.96
1979	0.474	1.42	0.94	0.65	1.81	1.13	0.55	1.49	1.04
1980	0.447	1.06	1.34	0.65	1.49	1.60	0.60	1.43	1.51
1981	0.423	1.02	1.17	0.65	1.43	1.58	0.65	1.50	1.48
1982	0.405	1.02	1.72	0.65	1.43	2.04	0.65	1.51	1.99
1983	0.431	1.20	1.43	0.65	1.55	1.68	0.65	1.57	1.73
1984	0.428	1.39	0.92	0.65	1.65	1.22	0.65	1.66	1.30
1985	0.415	1.29	0.95	0.65	1.56	1.25	0.65	1.58	1.30
1986	0.407	1.14	0.98	0.65	1.46	1.22	0.65	1.50	1.25

then, and because choosing it allows sufficient time to infer the long-run effects of the policy change. Table A2 shows the actual values of BASTOT from 1978 to 1986 and their values under the two simulations. The first half of the table shows the results of simulating changes in system (1) and (2); the second half shows simulation results based on (1) and (2').

If we use (1) and (2), implicitly assuming—as standard statistical tests suggest is not unreasonable—that a higher base has no direct long-run effects on benefits, the results suggest that there are no indirect effects either. Moreover, while raising the tax base does raise TAXRAT in the short run, there is no long-run effect of a higher base on the rate of taxation. Unless something happens to raise benefit payments (in this model, higher insured unemployment), state funds reap a temporary windfall when the base is raised, but tax rates adjust downward within five years. At that point total taxes are unchanged from what they would have been if the base had not been altered, given the same rules on benefit payments and the same number of weeks claimed. The results are similar for the two simulations. The main difference is unsurprisingly that the phased increase in the base produces smaller effects each year but takes longer before the steady state is reached.

The conclusions change sharply if one simulates the effects in the system (1) and (2'). The direct effects of BASTOT in (2') are not significant, and their sum is -0.0369. But because the higher tax base has a large direct initial effect ($\hat{b}_{40} = 1.39$), the continuing substitution of 65% for the actual, lower values of BASTOT raises benefits, and hence the taxes that finance them (since the system is self-financing).

What can one conclude from this? The strongest evidence is that taxes are independent of the base in the long run, so that a higher base is eventually met by offsetting reductions in tax rates as employers move down experience-rated schedules. In the short run, a higher base does, though, raise taxes that finance regular state UI benefits. This suggests that an increase in the base should be imposed at a time when the effects of the short-run tax increase on business will be least onerous. The estimates indicate that a long-run increase in benefits is a possibility, though the results are only marginally significant. Even if they were significant, though, they ignore the decline in the insured unemployment rate that would occur, as a higher base produces more complete experience rating and thus reduces total benefit costs by reducing employment fluctuations. We may conclude that on net it is not apparent that increasing the base produces long-term increases in total UI taxes.

ACKNOWLEDGMENTS

The author thanks Lauri Bassi, David Crawford, Harry Holzer, and Michael Horrigan for helpful comments. This project was funded under Purchase Order No. 99-9-4767-75-020-04 from the U.S. Department of Labor, Commission on Workforce Quality and Labor

Market Efficiency. Opinions stated in this document do not necessarily represent the official position or policy of the U.S. Department of Labor, Commission on Workforce Quality and Labor Market Efficiency, or of the institutions with which the author is affiliated.

NOTES

1. The data used in Tables 1, 2, and 4 are from *Comparison of State Unemployment Insurance Laws,* revisions of August 1978 and September 1988. Additional data are from Employment and Training Administration, *ET Handbook No. 394* and the supplements to it.
2. Vroman (1987, Table 1.6). The weighted averages in Table 2 are based on covered employment in 1978 and 1985, respectively; the AAW for 1988 are based on extrapolations from 1985. For these reasons, and because the national averages are apparently not weighted averages, the data differ slightly from those used in the appendix.
3. The data are all taken from Employment and Training Administration, *ET Handbook No. 394* and the supplements to it.

REFERENCES

Adams, James (1986), "Equilibrium Taxation and Experience Rating in a Federal System of Unemployment Insurance." *Journal of Public Economics* 29:51–77.

Baily, Martin (1977), "On the Theory of Layoffs and Unemployment." *Econometrica* 45:1043–1064.

Becker, Joseph M. (1981), *Unemployment Insurance Financing.* Washington, DC: American Enterprise Institute.

Boadway, Robin and Andrew Oswald (1983), "Unemployment Insurance and Redistributive Taxation." *Journal of Public Economics* 20:193–210.

Brechling, Frank (1977), "The Incentive Effects of the U.S. Unemployment Insurance Tax." *Research in Labor Economics* 1:41–102.

——— (1981), "Layoffs and Unemployment Insurance." In S. Rosen (ed.), *Studies in Labor Markets.* Chicago: University of Chicago Press, pp. 187–202.

Bronars, Stephen (1985), "Fair Pricing of Unemployment Insurance Premiums." *Journal of Business* 58:27–47.

Brown, Eleanor (1986), "Unemployment Insurance Taxes and Cyclical Layoff Incentives." *Journal of Labor Economics* 4(January):50–65.

Burdett, Kenneth and Bryce Hool (1983), "Layoffs, Wages and Unemployment Insurance." *Journal of Public Economics* 21:325–357.

Burdett, Kenneth and Randall Wright (1988), "Optimal Firm Size, Taxes and Unemployment." CARESS Working Paper #88-05, University of Pennsylvania, Philadelphia.

Chinloy, Peter (1980), "Unemployment Insurance and Unemployment." Unpublished paper, University of British Columbia, Vancouver.

Cottle, Rex and Hugh Macaulay (1985), "Property Rights and Unemployment Insurance Reserves." *Policy Sciences* 18:127–139.

Deere, Donald (1988), "Unemployment Insurance and Unemployment." Unpublished paper, Texas A&M University, College Station.

Edebalk, Per Gunnar and Eskil Wadensjö (1986), "Temporary Layoff Compensation and Unemployment: The Case of Sweden." Unpublished paper, Swedish Institute for Social Research, Stockholm.

Feldstein, Martin (1976), "Temporary Layoffs in the Theory of Unemployment." *Journal of Political Economy* 84(October):937–957.

Fitzroy, Felix and Robert Hart (1985), "Hours, Layoffs and Unemployment Insurance Funding: Theory and Practice in an International Perspective." *Economic Journal* 95(September):700–713.

Halpin, Terrence (1978), "Three Essays on the Effects of Experience Rating in UI." Ph.D. Dissertation, Michigan State University, East Lansing.

——— (1979), "The Effect of Unemployment Insurance on Seasonal Fluctuations in Employment." *Industrial and Labor Relations Review* 32(April):352–362.

——— (1980), "Employment Stabilization." In National Commission on Unemployment Compensation, *Unemployment Compensation: Studies and Research,* Volume 2. Washington, DC: NCUC, pp. 415–424.

Hamermesh, Daniel (1977), *Jobless Pay and the Economy.* Baltimore: Johns Hopkins University Press.

——— (1978), "Unemployment Insurance, Short-Time Compensation and the Workweek." In National Commission for Manpower Policy, *Work Time and Employment.* Washington, DC: NCMP, pp. 231–264.

——— (1982), "Social Insurance and Consumption: An Empirical Inquiry." *American Economic Review* 72(March):101–113.

——— (1986), "The Demand for Labor in the Long Run." In O. Ashenfelter and R. Layard (eds.), *Handbook of Labor Economics.* Amsterdam: North-Holland, pp. 429–471.

Hart, Robert (1984), *The Economics of Non-Wage Labour Costs.* London: George Allen and Unwin.

Hart, Robert and Seiichi Kawasaki (1988), "Payroll Taxes and Factor Demand." *Research in Labor Economics* 9:257–285.

Hibbard, Russell (1980), "Solvency Measures and Experience Rating." In National Commission on Unemployment Compensation, *Unemployment Compensation: Studies and Research,* Volume 2. Washington, DC: NCUC, pp. 329–338.

Johnson, Esther (1987), "Short-Time Compensation: A Handbook of Source Material." Unemployment Insurance Service Occasional Paper 87-2, U.S. Department of Labor, Employment and Training Administration.

Kaiser, Carl (1987), "Layoffs, Average Hours, and Unemployment Insurance in U.S. Manufacturing Industries." *Quarterly Review of Economics and Business* 27(Winter):80–99.

Kerachsky, Stuart, Walter Nicholson, Edward Cavin, and Alan Hershey (1986), *An Evaluation of Short-Time Compensation Programs.* Unemployment Insurance Service Occasional Paper 86-4, U.S. Department of Labor, Employment and Training Administration.

Maloney, Michael and Rob Roy McGregor (1988), "Financing the Unemployment Insurance System and the Interest Group Theory of Government." *Public Choice* 56:249–258.

Marks, Denton (1984), "Incomplete Experience Rating in State Unemployment Insurance." *Monthly Labor Review* 107(November):45–49.

McLure, Charles (1977), "The Incidence of the Financing of Unemployment Insurance." *Industrial and Labor Relations Review* 30(July):469–479.

Millis, Harry and Royal Montgomery (1938), *Economics of Labor,* Volume 2, *Labor's Risks and Social Insurance.* New York: McGraw-Hill.

Munts, Raymond (1970), "Partial Benefit Schedules in Unemployment Insurance: Their Effect on Work Incentive." *Journal of Human Resources* 5(Spring):160–176.

Munts, Raymond and Ephraim Asher (1980), "Cross-Subsidies Among Industries from 1969 to 1978." In National Commission on Unemployment Compensation, *Unemployment Compensation: Studies and Research,* Volume 2. Washington, DC: NCUC, pp. 277–298.

National Commission on Unemployment Compensation (1980), *Unemployment Compensation: Final Report.* Washington, DC: NCUC.

Office of the Inspector General (1985), "Financing the Unemployment Insurance Program Has

Shifted from a System Based on Individual Employer's Responsibility Towards a Socialized System." Audit Report No. 03-3-203-03-315, U.S. Department of Labor, Washington, DC.

Saffer, Henry (1982), "Layoffs and Unemployment Insurance." *Journal of Public Economics* 19:121–129.

———— (1983), "The Effects of Unemployment Insurance on Temporary and Permanent Layoffs." *Review of Economics and Statistics* 65(November):647–652.

Topel, Robert (1983), "On Layoffs and Unemployment Insurance." *American Economic Review* 73(September):541–559.

———— (1984), "Experience Rating of Unemployment Insurance and the Incidence of Unemployment." *Journal of Law and Economics* 27(April):61–90.

———— (1985), "Unemployment and Unemployment Insurance." *Research in Labor Economics* 7:91–136.

———— (1990), "Financing Unemployment Insurance: History, Incentives and Reform." In W. Lee Hansen and James Byers (eds.), *Unemployment Insurance: The Second Half Century*. Madison, WI: University of Wisconsin Press, pp. 108–135.

Vroman, Wayne (1986), *The Funding Crisis in State Unemployment Insurance*. Kalamazoo, MI: W. E. Upjohn Institute for Employment Research.

Wandner, Stephen and Robert Crosslin (1980), "Measuring Experience Rating." In National Commission on Unemployment Compensation, *Unemployment Compensation: Studies and Research*, Volume 2. Washington, DC: NCUC, pp. 271–276.

Wolcowitz, Jeffrey (1984), "Dynamic Effects of the Unemployment Insurance Tax on Temporary Layoffs." *Journal of Public Economics* 25:35–51.

Wright, Randall and Janine Loberg (1987), "Unemployment Insurance, Taxes and Unemployment." *Canadian Journal of Economics* 20(February):36–54.

ECONOMIC ISSUES IN EMPLOYEE BENEFITS

Stephen A. Woodbury

For at least three reasons, employee benefits have become a central issue in employee compensation in recent years, and have become increasingly the subject of research and policy debate. First, employee benefits constitute a far greater proportion of total compensation today than at the end of World War II. This remans true even though, as will be seen, the growth of employee benefits as a proportion of compensation has slowed in the 1980s. Understanding the role of employee benefits—and the reasons for the growth or lack of growth of benefits—is clearly important to a general understanding of compensation and employment. Section I of this paper reviews research that attempts to provide such an understanding.

Second, the significance of the two private employee benefits on which dollar expenditures are largest—pensions and health insurance—has been enhanced by an increasing recognition that both are in part public goods. Both retirement income and health care in the United States are provided by a dual public–private system in which the private components play a pivotal role. A framework for evaluating policy toward private employee benefits is outlined in Section II.

Third, the public-good aspect of many employee benefits has led to debate over a constellation of related issues: the regulation of pensions, rapid increases

Research in Labor Economics, Volume 11, pages 271–296.
Copyright © 1990 by JAI Press Inc.
All rights of reproduction in any form reserved.
ISBN: 1-555938-080-2

in health care cost, health insurance for retirees, flexible-benefit plans, and emerging benefits such as dependent care. Section III offers a discussion of these further issues.

I. EMPLOYEE BENEFITS: TRENDS AND COVERAGE

What percentage of total labor cost is accounted for by employee benefits? How much have employee benefits grown during the last 25 years, and what are the reasons for the observed pattern of growth? Which industries incur high benefit costs, and what are the characteristics of workers who are covered and not covered by benefits? This section addresses the above questions.

A. Benefits in the Context of Total Labor Cost

Table 1 displays data on nonwage labor costs (including employee benefits) as a percentage of total labor cost for U.S. private domestic industries in 1965 (or 1966) and 1985. Nonwages are broken down into six groups, the most important of which for present purposes are statutory employee benefits (mainly social security, unemployment insurance, and workers' compensation), and voluntary employee benefits (mainly private pensions and health insurance).

Row (h) suggests that total nonwages have grown dramatically during the last

Table 1.   Nonwage Labor Costs as a Percentage of Total Labor Cost by Type of Cost, U.S. Private Domestic Industries, 1965 and 1985[a]

		National Income and Product Accounts		Chamber of Commerce	
	Type of Nonwage Labor Cost	*1966*	*1985*	*1965*	*1985*
(a)	Payments for time not worked	[b]		7.6	8.4
(b)	Benefits in kind	[b]		0.4	0.2
(c)	Other expenses of a social nature			1.5	1.6
(d)	Vocational training			0.1	0.2
(e)	Total employee benefits	9.16	16.0	10.3	17.0
(f)	Statutory employee benefits	4.9	7.9	4.5	7.9
(g)	Voluntary employee benefits	4.7	8.2	5.8	9.1
(h)	Total nonwage labor cost	9.6	16.0	19.8	27.4

Notes: [a] Data derived from U.S. Department of Commerce (1986, 1987) and U.S. Chamber of Commerce Research Center (various years).

[b] In the National Income and Product Accounts, payments for time not worked and benefits in kind are included as direct wage and salary payments. Other expenses of a social nature and vocational training have no counterpart in the Accounts.

20 years in the United States.[1] Defining nonwages as statutory and voluntary employee benefits, nonwages grew from just under 10% of total labor cost in 1966 to about 16% in the mid-1980s. Defining nonwages more broadly to include payments for days not worked, benefits in kind, other social expenses, and vocational training, nonwages grew from just under 20% of total labor cost in 1965 to over 27% in 1985.

Although row (h) of Table 1 shows that nonwages as a whole have grown significantly during the past 20 years, other rows of Table 1 reveal that not all components of nonwages have increased. Indeed, the main conclusion to be drawn from Table 1 is that the growth of nonwage labor costs during the 1965–1985 period can be attributed almost entirely to the growth of statutory and voluntary employee benefits [see rows (f) and (g)].

Table 2 shows more-detailed statistics on the mix of labor compensation in the United States during 1968–1986. The statistics are derived from the National Income and Product Accounts (U.S. Department of Commerce, 1986, 1987), and divide compensation into three parts—wages and salaries, statutory employee benefits, and voluntary employee benefits.

The figures showing annual percentage changes suggest that, over the past 20 years, the pattern of growth of statutory employee benefits has been more even than that of voluntary employee benefits. The data indicate that statutory benefits grew (as a proportion of total compensation) at an annual rate of 3.1% from 1968 to 1975, at an annual rate of 2.5% from 1975 to 1980, and at an annual rate of 1.6% from 1980 to 1986. In contrast, the growth of voluntary benefits slowed dramatically and plateaued during the 20-year period. The data show that voluntary benefits grew rapidly between 1968 and 1975 (at an annual rate of 5.9%), grew less rapidly during the late 1970s (at an annual rate of 3.1%), and *fell* at an annual rate of 1.2% between 1980 and 1986.

B. Industry Disaggregations and Estimates of Fixed Labor Cost

Table 3 displays total employee benefits as a percentage of total labor cost in five of the last 25 years, disaggregated by industry. The figures indicate much interindustry variation in the provision and incidence of benefits. Moreover, the pattern of interindustry variation changed over the 20-year period in question. In 1966, communications and utilities had the largest percentage of benefits (about 13–16%), whereas agriculture, services, the trade sector, and construction had the lowest (6–8%). By 1985, this pattern had changed somewhat: construction experienced an explosion of benefits, and benefits in finance, insurance, and real estate had lost ground in relative terms.

The division of total labor cost between fixed (per worker) costs and variable (per hour) costs is important to firms' decisions about whether to employ more workers or to increase hours per worker. Table 4 displays estimates of the percentage of total labor cost that is fixed rather than variable. A comparison of

Table 2. Total Compensation in Current Dollars and the Distribution of Compensation by Type, 1968–1986[a]

Year	Total compensation[b]	Percentage of total compensation paid as			Average annual rate of change in percentage paid as		
		Wages and salaries	Statutory employee benefits	Voluntary employee benefits	Wages and salaries	Statutory employee benefits	Voluntary employee benefits
1968	416,430	90.1	5.0	4.9			
1969	459,252	89.9	5.1	5.1			
1970	485,346	89.5	5.0	5.5			
1971	514,323	89.0	5.1	5.9	−0.60	3.1	5.9
1972	567,862	88.2	5.5	6.3			
1973	640,287	87.5	6.2	6.4			
1974	702,731	87.1	6.3	6.6			
1975	738,842	86.4	6.2	7.3			
1976	829,984	85.6	6.5	7.8			
1977	930,471	85.1	6.7	8.2	−0.44	2.5	3.1
1978	1,060,682	84.8	6.9	8.2			
1979	1,200,078	84.7	7.1	8.2			
1980	1,315,139	84.5	7.0	8.5			
1981	1,451,580	84.5	7.2	8.3			
1982	1,521,944	84.1	7.2	8.7			
1983	1,609,958	84.0	7.4	8.6	−0.02	1.6	−1.2
1984	1,775,291	84.1	7.7	8.2			
1985	1,899,965	84.3	7.7	7.9			
1986	2,006,269	84.4	7.7	7.9			

Notes: [a] All data are derived from U.S. Department of Commerce (1986, 1987).
[b] Current dollars in thousands; sum of wages and salaries, statutory employee benefits, and voluntary employee benefits.

274

Table 3. Total Employee Benefits as a Percentage
of Total Labor Cost in the United States by Industry,
1966, 1971, 1976, 1981, 1985[a]

Industry	1966	1971	1976	1981	1985
All private domestic	9.6	11.1	14.4	15.6	16.0
Agriculture	6.0	7.4	10.3	13.4	13.2
Mining	12.3	13.5	16.2	16.7	17.1
Construction	8.2	9.1	13.6	15.9	17.9
Manufacturing					
Durable	11.5	13.9	17.7	18.9	18.9
Nondurable	10.9	12.2	15.8	18.2	18.3
Transportation	10.2	11.7	16.4	16.5	18.6
Communications	15.7	20.6	21.8	22.1	22.3
Utilities	13.2	15.0	21.0	20.0	20.3
Trade					
Wholesale	7.6	9.2	11.7	12.8	13.6
Retail	7.6	8.7	11.1	12.3	13.4
Finance and insurance	11.0	12.4	16.5	15.9	15.9
Services	6.4	7.8	10.5	12.1	12.8

Note: [a] Total employee benefits are the sum of statutory and voluntary benefits.
Estimates derived from U.S. Department of Commerce (1986, 1987), Tables
6.4, 6.12, and 6.13.

Table 4. Estimates of Fixed Employee Benefits as
a Percentage of Total Labor Cost in the United States
by Industry, 1966, 1971, 1976, 1981, 1985[a]

Industry	1966	1971	1976	1981	1985
All private domestic	6.0	6.5	8.9	9.3	9.6
Agriculture	3.0	2.9	5.0	5.5	5.6
Mining	8.8	9.0	11.4	11.0	11.0
Construction	3.9	3.8	7.4	8.6	10.3
Manufacturing					
Durable	7.9	9.3	12.0	12.4	12.3
Nondurable	7.2	7.3	10.0	11.6	11.7
Transportation	5.2	6.2	9.2	8.7	9.9
Communications	12.5	17.0	17.2	16.9	16.7
Utilities	10.2	11.6	16.4	14.5	14.6
Trade					
Wholesale	3.9	4.9	6.4	6.7	7.7
Retail	4.2	3.9	5.1	5.6	6.7
Finance and insurance	8.1	8.8	12.3	11.0	10.8
Services	3.3	3.9	5.8	6.5	7.0

Note: [a] Estimates derived from U.S. Department of Commerce (1986, 1987). See
Hart et al. (1988, pp. 58–59) for details.

Table 5.   Fixed Employee Benefits and Skill Levels
in the United States by Industry, 1985[a]

Industry	Fixed benefits as percentage of total labor cost	Rank	Skill proxy	Rank
All private domestic	9.6	—	3.82	—
Agriculture	5.6	12	2.57	9
Mining	11.0	5	12.09	3
Construction	10.3	7	1.63	10
Manufacturing				
Durable	12.3	3	5.84	5
Nondurable	11.7	4	8.58	4
Transportation	9.9	8	5.82	8
Communications	16.7	1	21.05	2
Utilities	14.6	2	23.01	1
Trade				
Wholesale	7.7	9	2.63	8
Retail	6.7	11	1.43	11
Finance and insurance	10.8	6	3.74	7
Services	7.0	10	1.19	12

Note: [a] The skill proxy equals real capital consumption allowance per full-time equivalent employee (from U.S. Department of Commerce, 1986, 1987). The Spearman rank correlation coefficient between the fixed-benefits percentage and the skill proxy is 0.88.

Table 4 with Table 3 suggests that the growth of fixed benefits, both in aggregate and by industry, has been similar to that of benefits generally. Indeed, the growth of benefits in a given industry is mirror in the growth of fixed employee benefits in that industry with only two notable exceptions—construction and wholesale trade, where fixed labor costs grew significantly more than did employee benefits generally.

Table 5 attempts to show the relationship between fixed benefits and skill levels. The table repeats the 1985 data on fixed benefits from Table 4, and adds data on skill levels by industry, using real capital consumption allowance per full-time equivalent worker as a proxy for skill level (Long and Scott, 1982). The Spearman rank correlation coefficient between fixed labor costs and the skill proxy is 0.88, suggesting that industries that use highly skilled labor also face (or voluntarily take on) relatively high fixed benefits. Data not presented here suggest that fixed benefits are also related to average overtime hours in an industry (Hart et al., 1988), although the relationship is weaker than that between fixed benefits and skill.

C.   Benefit Coverage and Worker Characteristics

How are employee benefits distributed among individual workers? Given the public interest in retirement income and access to health care, it is important to understand the extent to which workers are covered in employer-provided pension and health insurance plans. Table 6 displays data on the distribution of employer-provided pensions and health insurance in 1988 among wage and salary workers (not in the military, not self-employed) who had positive earnings in 1987. The first row of the table shows that about 48% of these workers were included in an employer-provided pension plan, whereas 66% were included in a group health plan. Of those included in a group health plan, nearly two-fifths were in plans that were fully paid for by the employer. Finally, 43% of these workers were covered by both pension and group health plans.

Table 6.   Inclusion of Workers in Employer-Provided Pension and Group Health Insurance Plans, 1988[a]

Worker characteristics	Percentage included in pension plans	Percentage included in group health plan		Percentage included in both pension and health plan
		Total	Employer paid all	
All workers	48.1	66.1	25.2	42.9
Gender				
Male	52.6	73.4	28.1	48.9
Female	43.3	58.1	22.0	36.5
Age				
Under 25	14.5	37.7	11.8	12.9
25–34	46.6	70.6	27.1	42.4
35–64	59.9	72.8	28.3	53.1
Over 64	28.5	42.8	18.5	22.5
Ethnicity				
White non-Hispanic	48.6	66.5	26.1	43.4
Hispanic	36.2	58.5	19.7	31.6
Black	48.8	66.0	19.3	43.6
Other	51.1	65.2	22.9	44.9
Education (years)				
0–8	30.7	52.6	18.2	27.3
9–12	42.3	60.6	22.7	37.2
13 and over	56.6	71.0	28.7	51.2
Union coverage				
Covered	81.6	87.5	38.8	74.7
Not covered	40.0	60.9	21.9	35.3
Employment status				
Part-time	16.5	22.6	7.7	10.2
Full-time	55.1	75.6	29.0	50.1
Annual earnings				
$1–$10,000	14.0	28.7	7.5	9.7
$10,001–$20,000	45.0	68.2	25.5	38.9
$20,001–$30,000	65.2	82.9	33.5	59.0
$30,001 and over	74.9	89.7	37.1	70.8

(continued)

Table 6. (Continued)

Worker characteristics	Percentage included in pension plans	Percentage included in group health plan		Percentage included in both pension and health plan
		Total	Employer paid all	
Industry				
Agriculture	13.8	27.8	10.9	11.4
Mining/construction	40.1	60.7	23.7	34.3
Durable goods	63.2	85.8	37.5	60.0
Nondurable goods	56.7	80.5	27.8	53.4
Transport, communication, and public utilities	64.2	83.1	34.5	60.8
Wholesale trade	43.3	73.3	30.1	39.0
Retail trade	22.3	42.5	12.7	18.5
Finance, insurance, and real estate	53.5	72.5	24.4	47.5
Business services	28.8	56.3	21.6	24.7
Personal services	12.7	33.3	11.4	10.9
Entertainment services	22.7	44.8	17.7	20.2
Professional services	54.8	65.6	27.2	46.4
Public administration	83.1	83.4	26.9	75.1
Occupation				
Managerial	59.7	79.5	31.6	54.5
Professional/technical	64.1	77.3	29.8	57.8
Sales	27.3	54.9	18.1	27.3
Clerical	51.8	66.2	24.5	44.4
Craft	54.0	73.7	30.5	49.3
Operatives, except transport	51.0	77.1	29.1	47.9
Transport operatives	46.2	71.0	29.2	41.3
Laborers	34.0	54.8	19.9	29.8
Service and other	25.6	38.8	14.2	21.7
Household status				
Householder with relatives	58.9	79.1	30.0	54.7
Spouse of householder	47.4	56.3	20.6	37.7
Other relative of householder	20.2	40.1	14.0	18.1
Nonfamily householder or unrelated individual	46.2	71.4	30.4	43.2
Job tenure (years)				
Less than 1	14.2	37.2	14.7	11.7
1–5	37.6	62.1	22.8	32.7
More than 5	73.8	83.2	32.3	67.1
Employer size (workers)				
Fewer than 10	19.5	38.6	17.8	16.2
10–24	32.9	54.7	21.7	28.1
25–49	43.9	65.0	24.9	37.8
50–99	52.9	71.5	27.1	46.2
100–249	57.7	77.4	28.3	51.5
More than 249	73.8	85.9	30.5	68.6

Note: [a] Tabulations from the May 1988 Current Population Survey Employee Benefits Supplement. Sample includes wage and salary workers (not in the military, not self-employed) who had positive earnings in 1987. There are 20,826 workers in the sample.

Additional figures in Table 6 show that there is much variation among workers in pension and health insurance coverage: Female workers are less likely to be covered than male workers; young workers are less likely to be covered than old (except for those 65 and over); Hispanics are less likely to be covered than other groups; workers with lower educational attainment are less likely to be covered; nonunionized workers are less likely to be covered than unionized workers; part-time workers are less likely to be covered than full-time workers; the self-employed are less likely to be covered; and those with lower earnings are less likely to be covered than those with higher earnings. These coverage patterns hold for both pension and group health provision.

There are also sharp differences in pension and health insurance provision among industries. Public administration, transportation, communications, utilities, and manufacturing all have relatively high percentages of workers covered by both pension and group health plans. Agriculture, services (other than professional), and retail trade have relatively low percentages of covered workers. Industries that have relatively high pension coverage also tend to have relatively high health insurance coverage: the Spearman rank correlation coefficient between industry pension and group health coverage is 0.96.

The variation in employee benefit coverage across occupations is far less striking than the variation across industries. Sales workers, service workers, and laborers do have relatively low coverage by pension and group health plans. But the differential between the best- and worst-covered occupations is far smaller than that between the best- and worst-covered industries.

D. Explaining the Trends

The slowing growth of employee benefits (illustrated in Table 2) is an important change that demands explanation. To understand why benefit growth has slowed, we need to understand the reasons for the provision of voluntary employee benefits. These include (a) preferential treatment under the federal personal income tax code;[2] (b) rising real incomes; (c) economies of scale in the provision of pensions and health insurance (Mitchell and Andrews, 1981); (d) efforts to improve workers' productivity and reduce turnover by deferring payment of benefits (Logue, 1979; Lazear, 1981); (e) unionization (Freeman, 1981; Alpert, 1982); (f) changing demographic composition of the labor force; (g) workers' preferences and desires; (h) capital gains and losses to pension funds resulting from changing asset prices (Munnell, 1987); and (i) changing social norms. Good general discussions of these factors include Rice (1966a,b), Lester (1967), and Long and Scott (1982).

To what degree can each of these factors explain the pattern of growth of employee benefits? Both theoretical and empirical work suggest strongly that deferral of income reduces labor turnover and, by inference, improves productivity (Schiller and Weiss, 1979; Lazear, 1981; Wolf and Levy, 1984). But it is unclear that changes in the desired rate of turnover have been a driving force behind changes in the pattern of benefit provision. The only existing study of this question, by Mumy and Manson (1985), concludes that considerations of productivity and turnover were less potent explanators of pension growth in the 1970s than was the favorable tax treatment of pension contributions. Similarly, it is unclear that the "technology" of benefit provision has changed so that scale economies of benefit provision now exist where they did not before (Mitchell and Andrews, 1981).

Several studies have found evidence that unions and collective bargaining exert a positive independent effect on the provision of nonwage benefits (Freeman, 1981; Alpert, 1982; Rossiter and Taylor, 1982; Fosu, 1984; Mincer, 1983), so the stagnation of private-sector union growth since the 1950s makes unionism a possible source of slowing growth of benefit provision.

Other possible causes of changes in the growth of employee benefits are the changing composition and aging of the labor force, changes in the tax treatment of benefits, and changes in real incomes. Several early studies of employee benefit provision concentrated on the growth of pensions and health insurance, since until 1980 growth (not stagnation) was the pattern that required explanation. Although some studies give considerable weight to the role of changing real incomes (Alpert, 1983; Turner, 1987; Vroman and Anderson, 1984), most of these studies pointed to increases in the marginal tax rate on earned income as the main explanator of employee benefit growth (Atrostic, 1983; Holmer, 1984; Leibowitz, 1983; Long and Scott, 1982; Sloan and Adamache, 1986; Taylor and Wilensky, 1983; Woodbury, 1983). It would follow that the declining marginal tax rates of the 1980s played an important role in the slowing growth of employee benefits.

Three recent studies have focused specifically on the slowing growth of benefits within a framework that allows one to sort out which factors have been most important to changing trends in benefit provision. Woodbury and Huang (1988), using detailed industry data, and Hamermesh and Woodbury (1990), using data on college and university faculty, estimate models of the demand for employee benefits that indicate how responsive the employee benefit share of compensation is to changes in the marginal tax rate on wages, changes in real income, and other variables such as demographic characteristics of the workforce and establishment size. Both studies find (in accord with earlier findings) that employee benefits and wages are good substitutes for each other, so that when the marginal tax rate on wages goes up, workers demand a greater share of their compensation as benefits. Also, the studies find that the demand for employee benefits is income elastic, so that when real incomes rise, workers demand a greater share of their compensation as benefits.

The results of both studies suggest that changes in two variables—marginal tax rates on personal income and the level of real income—explain much of the growth of employee benefits up to the mid-1970s, the slowing growth that occurred between 1976 and 1981, and the decline that occurred into the late

1980s. In particular, both studies suggest that during the 1980s, reductions in marginal income tax rates and modest real income growth combined to dampen employee demand for benefits. Both studies attribute the decline in the share of compensation received as benefits during the 1980s to that dampened demand.

In a somewhat different vein, Woodbury and Bettinger (1991) examine the decline in the percentage of workers covered by pensions and health insurance that occurred during the 1980s. They find that two main factors—declining marginal tax rates and declining union coverage—are the most important explanators of the fall in benefit coverage.

II. A FRAMEWORK FOR EVALUATING EMPLOYEE BENEFITS POLICY

The growth of employee benefits in the years following World War II has been important to many aspects of economic behavior and policy. Considerable work has focused on the implications of the growth of benefits for employment costs, mobility, turnover, and the organization of production [see, for example, Hart (1984), Scott et al. (1989), and Hutchens (1989)]. Feldstein (1977) and Feldstein and Friedman (1977), among others, have argued that the growth of employee benefits represents misallocated resources and reduced economic welfare, because tax subsidies for employee benefits have led to greater than optimal provision of benefits. Chen (1981) and Munnell (1984) have noted that as the proportion of compensation paid as employee benefits grew, the proportion of all compensation paid as wages and taxed under the federal income tax declined.

What is the appropriate role of government policy regarding employee benefits? This section sets out some possible criteria for evaluating public policy toward employee benefits, treating them under three broad headings: (a) static economic efficiency, (b) capital accumulation and economic growth, and (c) equity and income distribution.

A. Static Economic Efficiency

Static economic efficiency has been often used as an argument for taxing employer contributions to pensions and health insurance. Indeed, the favorable tax treatment of employer contributions to voluntary employee benefit plans has been under attack since at least 1973, when Martin Feldstein argued that the exclusion of health insurance contributions from taxable income distorts the incentive to demand health insurance and ultimately to use the health care system. Feldstein (1973) and those who have followed him have made two points. First, they argue that the tax-favored status of health insurance is responsible for the rising cost of medical care: "The tax laws give an incentive to purchase more health insurance, and . . . health insurance encourages consumers to purchase more medical care than they would in the absence of health insurance" (Vogel, 1980, p. 220). Second, they have argued that a tax subsidy for health insurance is inefficient—the government could provide the same amount of health care directly, finance the health care through lump sum taxes, and have revenue left over that could be returned to taxpayers or used to buy other public goods or services.[3]

Mark Pauly (1986) has challenged those who advocate taxing health benefit contributions, arguing that the efficiency effects of removing the tax-favored status of health insurance are ambiguous because the health care market is imperfect. There are externalities associated with health care provision, and the market for health insurance is plagued by adverse selection. The theory of second best suggests that removing a distortion from such a market may not be welfare improving.

Another factor that could offset the alleged inefficiency of giving benefits favorable tax treatment is the flexibility the current system provides employers in structuring benefit plans. This flexibility may be desirable if it leads to a more efficient allocation of the labor force (better matches between workers and firms), or to greater work effort. Deferred benefits, such as pensions, have been theorized to be an efficient mechanism for inducing worker attachment, commitment, and accumulation of firm-specific human capital (Lazear, 1981; Shapiro and Stiglitz, 1984; Bell and Hart, 1988). Such considerations need to be evaluated and made part of any overall evaluation of employee benefit policy.

B. Capital Accumulation and Economic Growth

A policy's contribution to capital accumulation and long-run economic growth is a second consideration that requires evaluation. In the context of employee benefits, such questions bear mainly on policies that might influence pensions. In particular, controversy has surrounded the question of whether pensions result in net additions to saving, or merely replace saving that would occur in the absence of pension plans. Pensions would result in net additions to saving if pensions and private asset holdings were complements, which would be the case if pension eligibility led individuals to plan earlier and longer retirements (the additional assets would be needed to finance a longer retirement). Alternatively, pensions would simply substitute for private asset holdings if pension eligibility had no impact on an individual's retirement behavior (the pension assets would be used in place of other assets to finance a retirement of predetermined duration).

Pozo and Woodbury (1986) have reviewed the evidence on whether pensions result in net additions to asset accumulation, and offer additional evidence using the 1983 Survey of Consumer Finances (SCF). We find widely divergent results among the existing studies of pensions and saving, even among studies that use similar data. In our empirical work with the 1983 SCF, we find that estimates of the influence of pensions on private asset holdings are extremely sensitive to changes in specification of the estimating equation. In particular, an asset-holding model that excludes current household earnings yields estimates suggesting that pensions and asset holdings are complements and that households with greater pension wealth save more. But an asset-holding model that includes current household earnings yields the opposite result—that pensions and asset holdings are substitutes and that households with greater pension wealth save less. The fragility of these results suggests a need for improved data and estimating techniques in addressing questions about the influence of pensions on asset accumulation.

Individual Retirement Accounts (IRAs) have sparked similar concerns about saving behavior: Do (or did) IRAs simply substitute for saving that individuals would have engaged in anyway, or do they result in net increases in saving and private asset holdings? The evidence on this issue seems to support the notion that much IRA saving has represented new saving (Venti and Wise, 1987; Feenberg and Skinner, 1989).

C.   Equity and Income Distribution

How does the pattern of employee benefit coverage influence the distribution of income? This question has been considered by Smeeding (1983, especially Tables 6.6 and 6.7), who finds that, as a whole, voluntary employer contributions to pensions and to health and life insurance tend to make the distribution of income more unequal: High-wage workers receive a larger share of their total compensation as deferred income and insurance than do low-wage workers. Smeeding's findings are supported by the findings of Taylor and Wilensky (1983) and Chollet (1984) on health benefits, and of Andrews (1985) and Kotlikoff and Smith (1983) on pensions. But Smeeding also shows that it is important to decompose benefits into health and life insurance on the one hand, and pensions and other deferred compensation on the other. The reason is that health and life insurance benefits are roughly proportionately distributed, whereas deferred compensation is highly regressively distributed.

That voluntarily provided employee benefits seem to have a disequalizing influence on income distribution naturally raises questions about the desirability of exempting these benefits from federal payroll and personal income taxes. One response to such questions is that benefits such as pensions and health insurance are intended to insure workers against income loss resulting from old age and sickness. It is this "merit good" aspect of employee benefits that has been used to justify the favorable tax treatment that employer contributions to employee benefit plans receive. However, if a larger proportion of the total compensation of high-wage workers is received as nonwage benefits, as appears to be the case, then the exemption of those benefits from payroll and personal income taxes is clearly a regressive aspect of the U.S. tax system. That is, exemption of nonwage benefits violates the vertical equity precept that those with greater ability to pay for government services should do so. This concern has been the subject of an extensive study by the Congressional Budget Office (1987), which advocates reducing the tax advantages now associated with pensions.

In addition, tax exemption of employee benefits creates situations where horizontal inequities can arise. Consider two workers, each with total compensation (wages plus contributions to health insurance, life insurance, and pensions) of $20,000. Suppose also that they are both single and declare one exemption and the zero-bracket amount. If Mutt receives $17,000 in wages, whereas Jeff receives $18,500 in wages, then Jeff pays more taxes and faces a higher marginal tax rate than Mutt. This violates the principle of horizontal equity—that households equally situated should be taxed equally.

The "pure solution" to this problem, as Munnell (1984) has called it, is to include all employer contributions for employee benefits (and increases in accrued vested pension contributions) in taxable income. The pure solution is attractive both because it would mitigate inequities in the tax system and because it would raise federal revenues (or permit federal marginal income and payroll tax rates to be lowered). Munnell (1984, Table 2) estimates the revenue gain from such a comprehensive tax to be $64.3 billion, and suggests that the problems of implementing this approach would be minimal. Indeed, the problems that do exist pale beside the political opposition such a proposal would almost certainly meet. In view of the strong potential opposition to taxing employee benefit contributions, some workable alternative must be sought.

One alternative that has gained currency and that has been introduced in a variety of guises in legislative proposals is to limit the amount of the employer's contribution to both pensions and health insurance that is excluded from the worker's taxable income. There have been numerous discussions of such proposals (Adamache and Sloan, 1985; Chollet, 1984; Halperin, 1984; Katz and Mankiw, 1985; Korczyk, 1984; Steuerle and Hoffman, 1979; Sullivan and Gibson, 1983), and the Tax Reform Act of 1986 did tighten limits on certain forms of retirement saving (Congressional Budget Office, 1987). But recent attempts to limit the tax advantages given to health insurance (Section 89 of the Internal Revenue Code) never became effective because of employer opposition.

D.   Effects on Benefits of Changed Tax Policies

Much of the discussion in this section has focused on the tax treatment of employee benefits in a normative context. But what are the predicted effects of changes in tax policy on the provision of benefits? Woodbury and Huang (1991) have simulated the effects on benefits of four tax policy changes: (a) the 1986 tax reform; (b) treating all employer contributions to health insurance as taxable income; (c) a low tax cap on health insurance contributions, that is, treating annual contributions over $1125 (in 1982 dollars) as taxable income; and (d) treating all employer contributions to both pensions and health insurance as taxable income. Table 7 summarizes the simulations, showing how each of the policy changes would have altered real expenditures on compensation and compensation shares if they had been in effect during 1969–1982. All effects are shown in percentage terms, averaged over the 1969–1982 period.

The simulations suggest that the 1986 tax reform can be expected to produce significant increases in both real expenditures on health insurance and on the share of compensation taken as health insurance. These increases in health insurance occur in spite of the reduced incentive to receive compensation as health insurance that results from lower marginal tax rates on wages, and is attributable to the large positive income effects of the tax reform. Also, the tax reform can be expected to shift the mix of compensation away from pensions and toward health insurance. The latter prediction results from the finding that the demand for pensions is highly responsive to changes in marginal tax rates, so that reducing marginal tax rates reduces the share of compensation demanded as pensions.

The simulations suggest that treating all health insurance contributions as taxable income during the 1969–1982 period would have reduced real expenditures on employer-provided health insurance by over 22%. Similarly, a low tax cap on health insurance would have reduced expenditures on health insurance by nearly 14%. An apparent side effect of taxing health insurance contributions would be a reduction in real expenditures on wages and pensions. These de-

Table 7.   Summary of Effects of Tax Policy Changes
on Employee Benefit Provision: Average Percentatge
Changes under Tax Systems Existing 1969–1982[a]

Policy	Wages	Pensions	Health insurance
Effects of 1986 tax reform on			
Real expenditures	+9.4	+0.9	+10.4
Compensation shares	−0.3	−1.4	+7.7
Effects of taxing health insurance contributions on			
Real expenditures	−1.7	−5.8	−22.3
Compensation shares	+0.2	−4.7	+2.2
Effects of low tax cap on health insurance on			
Real expenditures	−0.4	−2.6	−13.9
Compensation shares	+0.1	−1.8	+0.7
Effects of taxing all benefits on			
Real expenditures	−0.8	−64.1	−27.9
Compensation shares	+3.0	−53.9	−2.4

Note: [a] The figures show how replacing the tax systems in effect during 1969–1982 with the specified tax policy changes would have changed real expenditures on each form of compensation and compensation shares. Changes are shown in annual percentage terms, averaged over the 14 years. See Woodbury and Huang (1991).

creases result because taxing health insurance would reduce real incomes, which would lead in turn to reductions in both wages and pensions. The decrease in pension provision should be considered in any public discussion of the merits of taxing health insurance, and ways of offsetting the decrease might be considered if it were viewed as undesirable.

Treating all employer contributions to pensions and health insurance as taxable income would dramatically reduce the provision of both pensions and health insurance. According to the simulations, taxing all employee benefits would have cut pension provision by 64% during the 1969–1982 period, and would have cut health insurance provision by 28%. Also, taxing all benefits would have caused a major shift in the mix of compensation away from pensions and health insurance and toward wages. These results suggest that reforming the tax system to include employer contributions as taxable income would be politically difficult, and could create strong pressure to increase Social Security benefits to compensate for the large decline in private pensions that would result.

Woodbury and Huang (1991) also simulated the distributional effects of the four policy changes they considered. Their findings suggest that the distributional effects of the 1986 tax reform are roughly proportional. Similarly, the distributional effects of taxing all health insurance contributions are not dramatic. But a low tax cap on health insurance contributions would significantly improve income equality, as would taxing all health insurance contributions.

III.   FURTHER ISSUES AND EMERGING BENEFITS

The discussion of public policy as it bears on employee benefits has to this point focused on the tax treatment of pensions and health insurance. In this section, I turn to a variety of additional issues concerning pensions, health insurance, the flexibility of benefits, and emerging benefits such as dependent care.[4]

A.   Pension Regulation and the Restructuring of Pension Plans

Congress appears to have had two purposes in legislating the Employee Retirement Income Security Act of 1974—ERISA (Public Law 93-406, 88 Stat., September 2, 1974). The first was to improve the information available to employees about their pensions by requiring reporting of financial and other information about pensions plans. The second was to improve the soundness of pensions plans by requiring them to meet vesting and funding standards, and by establishing plan termination insurance. Because complying with ERISA standards is costly to employers, there was speculation from the start that ERISA might lead to termination of the defined-benefit pension plans that ERISA was intended to regulate. This could imply the perverse effect of reduced coverage and lowered benefits for some workers (Ture, 1976; Stein, 1980).

But it was quickly noted by others that plan termination was not the only option available to employers who faced increased costs of defined-benefit pension plans as a result of ERISA. Employers could also convert from a defined-benefit to a defined-contribution plan and avoid the insurance, reporting, and disclosure costs of maintaining a plan covered by ERISA (Denzau and Hardin, 1983). Indeed, the movement from defined-benefit to defined-contribution plans—the so-called restructuring of pensions plans—has received increasing attention from pension practitioners.

From a social standpoint, it seems clear that the outcomes of interest are the total contributions made by employers to pension plans (whether defined-benefit or defined-contribution) and the benefits received by retirees. The question is whether plan restructuring is ultimately reflected in these outcomes. Taking this view, it is fairly straightforward to show that the impact of ERISA on total employer contributions to pension plans is ambiguous in theory—ERISA's impact may be either positive or negative (Woodbury, 1984). Accordingly, the impact of ERISA is really an empirical issue that must be settled by analysis of available data.

Unfortunately, there has been little empirical research on the effects of ERISA, that is, work that attempts to isolate the impact of ERISA apart from the other forces that act to alter the employer provision of pensions. Moreover, existing results are highly mixed. For example, an early study by Long and Scott (1982) suggested no effect of ERISA on pension contributions. But a later study (Woodbury, 1984) found that ERISA may have been responsible for as much as a one-percentage-point increase in the share of compensation received as pensions in the years immediately following its enactment. This would translate into a nearly 25% increase in pension contributions as a result of ERISA. Yet another study (Sloan and Adamache, 1986) concluded that ERISA significantly reduced the growth of pension contributions in the years following its enactment. It seems clear that high priority should be given to establishing more convincing evidence about whether and how ERISA has affected total employer contributions to pensions.

At least two other studies have examined the impact of ERISA on other outcomes. Cornwell et al. (1989) find that ERISA has had no discernible effect on involuntary separations from firms, that is, firms are no more or less likely than before ERISA to renege on their promises to pay pension benefits by terminating workers. Ippolito (1988) presents evidence that ERISA has had virtually none of the effects that might be expected on wages or employment and has failed to induce underfunded plans to increase their funding levels. But he also finds that ERISA has slightly increased the rate of defined-benefit plan terminations, and has increased the likelihood that newly created pensions plans would be defined-contribution plans.

Recently, much attention has been focused on the allegedly deleterious impacts of pension plan restructuring (Employee Benefits Research Institute,

1989b). In particular, restructuring has permitted many firms to recover the assets of defined-benefit pension plans that were actuarially overfunded, as well as to avoid the costs of complying with ERISA. Hence, corporate financial considerations (the availability of funds for investment and the attractiveness of a company as a takeover target) have come to dominate decisions about pension plan restructuring. These interests may be counter to the interests of workers, for whom benefits received in retirement are of paramount importance. Policies that balance these competing interests are difficult to make, given the paucity of knowledge about the impacts of current policy and of restructuring itself. Again, research on how policy and restructuring activities affect pension contributions and expected benefits is much needed.

B.   Health Care Cost Containment

Between 1982 and 1987, the cost of health insurance grew by 71%—more rapidly than any other component of consumption. During the same period, the cost of medical care generally increased by 35.6%, whereas the cost of all personal consumption items taken together grew by only 20.4% (U.S. Department of Commerce, 1988, Table 7.10).

A complete discussion of the reasons for the rapid increase in the cost of health care is well beyond the scope of this paper. Most observers attribute the increases to a constellation of factors acting simultaneously. On the supply side, they point to increasingly sophisticated technology and a market structure that is highly imperfect. On the demand side, they point to infusions of funds from public sources—mainly Medicare in recent years—as well as private sources. With respect to the increasing cost of health insurance in particular, they have pointed to health providers' practice of covering the cost of providing health care to uninsured and underinsured patients by charging higher rates to patients who are covered by private health insurance.

Employers have tried to stem the inflation of health insurance premiums in several ways (Employee Benefits Research Institute, 1989a). First, they have shifted the cost of health insurance and health care to their employees by requiring workers to contribute to the monthly insurance premium, increasing the deductible paid by the worker before the insurance pays, or increasing the copayment (payment by the worker) for each service received. Second, employers have made increasing use of so-called utilization review, under which the appropriateness of treatment is reviewed before treatment is administered. Third, they have moved away from traditional fee-for-service health insurance and toward health maintenance organizations (HMOs) and preferred provider organizations (PPOs).

There is little research on how well the various strategies of health care cost containment have worked, although the obvious judgment based on the recent record of dramatic increases in health insurance premiums and health care costs must be negative. As a result, it is not surprising that at least two of the country's largest employers—Ford Motor and Chrysler Corporation—have called for national health care financed by the federal government. These employers believe that a national plan would relieve them of the burden of paying for ever-increasing health insurance costs. There are, however, good reasons for questioning this presumption (Woodbury and Hogan, 1991).

How or whether the current debate over health care policy in the United States will resolve itself is a matter of speculation. Elsewhere in this paper, I argue that taxing employer contributions to health insurance would be a sensible way of improving the health care system. It would not address directly the problem of uninsured individuals or the resulting problem of health care providers shifting costs to privately insured patients. But it would contain the growth of health care costs, which is a prerequisite to improving access to health care. Other possible strategies, such as comprehensive national health care, are more far-reaching and less likely under a political system that tends toward incrementalism.

C.   Health Insurance Benefits for Retirees

In addition to facing rising costs of health insurance for current employees, employers who extend health insurance to their retired workers face the problem of financing health insurance for those retirees. U.S. Department of Labor statistics indicate that over three-quarters of full-time workers who are covered by the health insurance plans of medium and large firms (in the private sector) have health insurance coverage after retirement (U.S. Department of Labor, 1987, Table 29).

In general, employer-provided health insurance benefits for retired workers are the same as for current workers, although health insurance plans for retirees are usually integrated with Medicare. Integration with Medicare reduces the cost to employers of providing health insurance to retirees, but the existence of retiree health insurance during a period of rising health insurance costs poses a potentially serious problem for firms nevertheless. Specifically, retiree health benefits have been financed by companies on a pay-as-you-go basis, which suggests that as the population ages, these benefits will impose an increasing burden. Recent estimates suggest that the total unfunded liability of private employers for the future health insurance benefits of their workers (both current and retired) is $68.2 billion (Employee Benefits Research Institute, 1988). The Financial Accounting Standards Board has drafted rules under which companies would be required to treat the cost of health insurance promised to retirees as a liability in their balance sheets (Employee Benefits Research Institute, 1988).

D.   Flexible-Benefit Plans

Traditionally, employers have offered all workers within a given classification a fixed package of benefits. Often these benefits have consisted of a given number of paid holiday, vacation, and leave days, a pension plan, health insurance, and life insurance. Flexible-benefit plans—often called "cafeteria" plans—differ from this traditional arrangement by allowing workers to select from a menu of possible benefits the benefits that they most prefer (Employee Benefits Research Institute, 1985, Chapter 28).

Two advantages have been attributed to flexible-benefit plans. First, they may increase the value to some workers of the benefits that are provided by the employer in tax-favored form. Second, they may induce workers to become more aware of, and to gain a better understanding of, the benefits they receive.

To a researcher, perhaps the most striking aspect of flexible-benefit plans is that they have been so frequently mentioned in the press and in practical discussions of employee benefits, but that there exists virtually no substantive research or analysis of their use or effects. There can be little doubt that lack of data on flexible-benefit plans is an important reason for this gap in research on employee benefits.

Despite the lack of existing research, two points about flexible-benefit plans can be made. First, it has been noted frequently that the existence of flexible-benefit plans may lead to adverse selection, that is, to workers who are good risks (from the point of view of health insurance or life insurance, for example) opting out of a plan, leaving only bad risks. Models of adverse selection suggest that when good risks opt out of an insurance market, insurance premiums increase and ultimately the market fails. The only way to mitigate adverse selection in the context of flexible-benefit plans is to limit flexibility, for example, by placing insurance plans outside the basket of benefits among which workers may choose. But this thwarts the basic idea of the flexible-benefit plan.

The second point is that flexible benefits reduce the ability of policymakers to encourage provision and use of particular benefits. Instead, by designating a broad array of benefits as tax favored, flexible-benefit plans encourage provision and use of a rather arbitrary package of benefits. The flexibility inherent in flexible-benefit plans robs policymakers of the ability to direct resources toward particular benefits, directing resources instead toward a grab bag of activities and benefits.[5]

E. Dependent Care

The dramatic influx of women—especially married women—into the labor force since World War II has led to increasing attention being given to "the interaction of work and the family" (Norwood, 1988). In particular, the availability of child care (or, more generally, dependent care) has been an increasing concern in a labor market in which women with young children make up a substantial proportion of all workers.

Considerable research has been devoted to one or another aspect of dependent care (Friedman, 1989; Staines and Galinsky, 1989; Rodgers and Rodgers, 1989). There are several concerns, however, that are of special concern in the context of employee benefits. For example, Norwood (1988) has discussed the problems that the provision of child care and other nontraditional benefits raise for the measurement of total compensation. Hayghe (1988) reports the results of a recent Bureau of Labor Statistics special survey, which shows that only about 5% of all establishments with ten or more employees provide direct child care benefits (that is, day care or financial assistance). Moreover, "only 2 percent of the 442,000 establishments that reported no child care benefits or flexible work-schedule policies said they were 'considering' doing something in the future" (Hayghe, 1988, pp. 42–43). Robins (1988) has provided a survey of the existing federal programs that support or encourage child care.

IV. SUMMARY AND IMPLICATIONS FOR FUTURE RESEARCH

Perhaps the most important conclusions from this study are that the demand for increasing employee benefits and the growth of benefits as a share of compensation slowed during the 1970s and came to a halt in the mid-1980s (see Section I). Nevertheless, there are good reasons to believe that employee benefits will resume their growth in the future—in fact, there appears to have been a resumption of employee benefit growth during 1988 and 1989, spurred mainly by rising costs of health insurance. Whether benefits will again grow as rapidly as before 1974 is a matter of speculation, but two important determinants of the demand for benefits—personal incomes and marginal tax rates on income—are both likely to increase and create pressure for a higher percentage of compensation to be provided as benefits.

The possible resumption of employee benefit growth renews the importance of examining both the role of benefits in the economy and policies that are intended to influence benefit provision (see Section II). The static efficiency effects of employee benefits remain open to debate. Are benefits provided by employers because of the need to retain a high-quality workforce with specific skills? Or are benefits essentially a tax-favored form of compensation that results in an eroded tax base, a bloated health care sector, and an inequitable tax system? Likewise, the effect of benefits on capital accumulation and long-run growth remains an open issue. Do pensions contribute to saving and growth, or are they merely a tax-favored vehicle for high-income workers to provide for their retirements?

Questions about the role of employee benefits in the labor market are difficult to disentangle from the policy questions raised by benefits (Section III). The effects of pension regulation on pension contributions and the soundness of pension plans remains a matter of speculation. How employers are responding to sustained increases in the price of health insurance—the degree to which these increases are absorbed, shifted to workers, or passed on to consumers—remains an unanswered question. Moreover, there has been little work on how various policies that have been proposed to improve the health care system (that is, to reduce health care costs and increase access to health care) would influence the labor market and compensation (Woodbury and Hogan, 1991). Finally, research on the economics of flexible-benefit plans is almost nonexistent, and work on the economics of dependent care is in its infancy. The importance of such issues is unlikely to wane anytime soon, and good economic research into the various aspects of employee benefits should yield a high return.

ACKNOWLEDGMENTS

Work on this paper was supported in part by the U.S. Department of Labor, Commission on Workforce Quality and Labor Market Efficiency. The author wishes to thank Douglas R. Bettinger and Ellen Maloney for excellent assistance, and B. K. Atrostic, Laurie Bassi, Peter Cappelli, David Crawford, Olivia Mitchell, Daniel Slottje, and four anonymous reviewers for critical comments on earlier drafts.

NOTES

1. For details of the classification scheme used in Table 1, see Hart et al. (1988, pp. 47 ff.), from which this discussion is drawn.

2. It is important to distinguish between tax-exempt and tax-deferred benefits. Health insurance is a tax-exempt benefit because health contributions are not treated as taxable income under the federal personal income tax. Pension contributions are a tax-deferred benefit because, although pension contributions are not taxed when they are made, they *are* taxed when the employee receives the benefit in retirement. See, for example, Korczyk, 1984.

3. Similar arguments have been made about employer-provided pensions (Munnell, 1984, 1985, 1988). It has usually gone unmentioned that lump sum taxes are at best difficult to implement, and that efficient government provision of health care services (as of any good or service) entails myriad organizational problems.

4. Mandating of benefits, which is treated by Mitchell (in this volume), is not discussed here.

5. In addition, flexible-benefit plans may make it more difficult for employers to fashion a benefit package that enhances productivity and reduces mobility, the traditional role of pensions.

REFERENCES

Adamache, Killard W. and Frank A. Sloan (1985), "Fringe Benefits: To Tax or Not to Tax?" *National Tax Journal* 38(March):47–64.

Alpert, William T. (1982), "Unions and Private Wage Supplements." *Journal of Labor Research* 3(Spring):179–199.

———— (1983), "Manufacturing Workers' Private Wage Supplements: A Simultaneous Equations Approach." *Applied Economics* 15(June):363–378.

Andrews, Emily S. (1985), *The Changing Profile of Pensions in America*. Washington, DC: Employee Benefits Research Institute.

Atrostic, B. K. (1983), "Comment on Leibowitz." In Jack E. Triplett (ed.), *The Measurement of Labor Cost*. Chicago: University of Chicago Press and NBER, pp. 389–394.

Bell, David N. F. and Robert A. Hart (1988), "On-the-Job and For-the-Job Efficiency Labour

Payments." Discussion Paper No. 8806, Department of Political Economy, University of Glasgow.

Chen, Yung-Ping (1981), "The Growth of Fringe Benefits: Implications for Social Security." *Monthly Labor Review* 104(November):3–10.

Chollet, Deborah J. (1984), *Employer-Provided Health Benefits.* Washington, DC: Employee Benefit Research Institute.

Congressional Budget Office (1987), *Tax Policy for Pensions and Other Retirement Saving.* Washington, DC: Congress of the United States, Congressional Budget Office.

Cornwell, Christopher, Stuart Dorsey, and Nasser Mehrzad (1989), "Opportunistic Behavior by Firms in Implicit Pension Contracts." Paper presented at the Midwest Economics Association Annual Meeting, Cincinnati, Ohio, March 30–April 1.

Denzau, Arthur T. and Clifford M. Hardin (1983), "Company Retirement Plans Eight Years after ERISA." Formal Publication No. 55, Center for the Study of American Business, Washington University, St. Louis, MO.

Employee Benefits Research Institute (1985), *Fundamentals of Employee Benefits.* Washington, DC: Employee Benefits Research Institute.

———— (1988), "Issues and Trends in Retiree Health Insurance Benefits." *EBRI Issue Brief* 84(November):1–11.

———— (1989a), "Managing Health Care Costs and Quality." *EBRI Issue Brief* 87(February):1–14.

———— (1989b), "Pension Plan 'Surplus': Revert, Transfer, or Hold?" *EBRI Issue Brief* 88(March):1–22.

Feenberg, Daniel and Jonathan Skinner (1989), "Sources of IRA Savings." National Bureau of Economic Research Working Paper No. 2845, NBER, Cambridge, MA.

Feldstein, Martin (1973), "The Welfare Loss of Excess Health Insurance." *Journal of Political Economy* 81(March/April):251–280.

———— (1977), "The High Cost of Hospitals—And What to Do About It." *The Public Interest* 48(Summer):40–54.

Feldstein, Martin and Bernard Friedman (1977), "Tax Subsidies, and Rational Demand for Insurance, and the Health Care Crisis." *Journal of Public Economics* 7(April):155–178.

Fosu, Augustin Kwasi (1984), "Unions and Fringe Benefits: Additional Evidence." *Journal of Labor Research* 5(Summer):247–254.

Freeman, Richard B. (1981), "The Effects of Unionism on Fringe Benefits." *Industrial and Labor Relations Review* 34(July):489–509.

Friedman, Dana E. (1989), "Impact of Child Care on the Bottom Line." In Commission on Workforce Quality and Labor Market Efficiency, *Investing in People,* Volume 2. Washington, DC: U.S. Department of Labor, pp. 1425–1476.

Halperin, Daniel (1984), "Broadening the Tax Base—The Case of Fringe Benefits." *National Tax Journal* 37(September):271–281.

Hamermesh, Daniel S. and Stephen A. Woodbury (1990), "Taxes, Fringes, and Faculty." National Bureau of Economic Research Working Paper, NBER, Cambridge, MA.

Hart, Robert A. (1984), *The Economics of Non-Wage Labour Costs.* London: George Allen and Unwin.

Hart, Robert A., David N. F. Bell, Rudolf Frees, Seiichi Kawasaki, and Stephen A. Woodbury (1988), *Trends in Non-Wage Labor Costs and Their Effects on Employment.* Brussels and Luxembourg: Office for Official Publications of the European Communities.

Hayghe, Howard V. (1988), "Employers and Child Care: What Role Do They Play?" *Monthly Labor Review* 111(September):38–44.

Holmer, Martin (1984), "Tax Policy and the Demand for Health Insurance." *Journal of Health Economics* 3(December):203–221.

Hutchens, Robert M. (1989), "Seniority, Wages, and Productivity: A Turbulent Decade." *Journal of Economic Perspectives* 3(Fall):49–64.

Ippolito, Richard A. (1988), "A Study of the Regulatory Effect of the Employee Retirement Income Security Act." *Journal of Law and Economics* 31(April):85–125.

Katz, Avery and Gregory Mankiw (1985), "How Should Fringe Benefits Be Taxed?" *National Tax Journal* 38(March):37–46.

Korczyk, Sophie M. (1984), *Retirement Security and Tax Policy*. Washington, DC: Employee Benefits Research Institute.

Kotlikoff, Laurence J. and Daniel E. Smith (1983), *Pensions in the American Economy*. Chicago: University of Chicago Press.

Lazear, Edward P. (1981), "Agency, Earnings Profiles, Productivity, and Hours Restrictions." *American Economic Review* 71(September):606–620.

Leibowitz, Arlene (1983), "Fringe Benefits in Employee Compensation." In Jack E. Triplett (ed.), *The Measurement of Labor Costs*. Chicago: University of Chicago Press and NBER, pp. 371–389.

Lester, Richard A. (1967), "Benefits as a Preferred Form of Compensation." *Southern Economic Journal* 33(April):488–495.

Logue, Dennis E. (1979), *Legislative Influence on Corporate Pension Plans*. Washington, DC: American Enterprise Institute.

Long, James E. and Frank A. Scott (1982), "The Income Tax and Nonwage Compensation." *Review of Economics and Statistics* 64(May):211–219.

Mincer, Jacob (1983), "Union Effects: Wages, Turnover, and Job Training." In Ronald G. Ehrenberg (ed.), *New Approaches to Labor Unions, Research in Labor Economics, Supplement 2*. Greenwich, CT: JAI Press, pp. 217–252.

Mitchell, Olivia S. and Emily S. Andrews (1981), "Scale Economies in Private Multi-Employer Pension Systems." *Industrial and Labor Relations Review* 34(July):522–530.

Mumy, Gene E. and William D. Manson (1985), "The Relative Importance of Tax and Agency Incentives to Offer Pensions: A Test Using the Impact of ERISA." *Public Finance Quarterly* 13(October): 464–485.

Munnell, Alicia H. (1984), "Employee Benefits and the Tax Base." *New England Economic Review* (January):39–55.

———— (1985), "The Economic Effects of the Growth of Employer-Provided Fringe Benefits." In *Distribution and Economics of Employer-Provided Fringe Benefits*, Hearings before the Committee on Ways and Means, U.S. House of Representatives, September 17–18, 1984. Washington, DC: U.S. Government Printing Office, pp. 421–428.

———— (1988), "Public versus Private Provision of Retirement Income." *New England Economic Review* (May/June):51–58.

Munnell, Alicia H. with Nicole Ernsberger (1987), "Pension Contributions and the Stock Market." *New England Economic Review* (November/December):3–14.

Norwood, Janet L. (1988), "Measuring the Cost and Incidence of Employee Benefits." *Monthly Labor Review* 111(August):3–8.

Pauly, Mark V. (1986), "Taxation, Health Insurance, and Market Failure in the Medical Economy." *Journal of Economic Literature* 24(June):629–675.

Pozo, Susan and Stephen A. Woodbury (1986), "Pensions, Social Security, and Asset Accumulation." *Eastern Economic Journal* 12(July–September):273–281.

Rice, Robert G. (1966a), "An Analysis of Private Wage Supplements." Ph.D. Dissertation, Columbia University, New York.

———— (1966b), "Skill, Earnings, and the Growth of Wage Supplements." *American Economic Review* 56(May):583–593.

Robins, Philip K. (1988), "Federal Support of Child Care: Current Policies and a Proposed New System." *Focus* (Institute for Research on Poverty, University of Wisconsin) 11(Summer):1–9.

Rodgers, Fran S. and Charles Rodgers (1989), "Mixing Careers and Child Rearing." In Commission on Workforce Quality and Labor Market Efficiency, *Investing in People,* Volume 2. Washington, DC: U.S. Department of Labor, pp. 1645–1684.

Rossiter, Louis F. and Amy K. Taylor (1982), "Union Effects on the Provision of Health Insurance." *Industrial Relations* 21(Spring):167–177.

Schiller, Bradley R. and Randall D. Weiss (1979), "The Impact of Private Pensions on Firm Attachment." *Review of Economics and Statistics* 61(August):369–380.

Scott, Frank A., Mark C. Berger, and Dan A. Black (1989), "Effects of the Tax Treatment of Fringe Benefits on Labor Market Segmentation." *Industrial and Labor Relations Review* 42(January):216–229.

Shapiro, Carl and Joseph E. Stiglitz (1984), "Equilibrium Unemployment as a Worker Discipline Device." *American Economic Review* 74(June):433–444.

Sloan, Frank A. and Killard W. Adamache (1986), "Taxation and the Growth of Nonwage Compensation." *Public Finance Quarterly* 14(April):115–137.

Smeeding, Timothy M. (1983), "The Size Distribution of Wage and Nonwage Compensation: Employer Cost versus Employee Value." In Jack E. Triplett (ed.), *The Measurement of Labor Cost.* Chicago: University of Chicago Press and NBER, pp. 237–277.

Staines, Graham L. and Ellen Galinsky (1989), "Working Hours Flexibility." In Commission on Workforce Quality and Labor Market Efficiency, *Investing in People,* Volume 2. Washington, DC: U.S. Department of Labor, pp. 1609–1644.

Stein, Bruno (1980), *Social Security and Pensions in Transition.* New York: The Free Press.

Steuerle, Eugene and Ronald Hoffman (1979), "Tax Expenditures for Health Care." *National Tax Journal* 32(June):101–115.

Sullivan, Sean and Rosemary Gibson (1983), "Tax-Related Issues in Health Care Market Reform." In Jack A. Meyer (ed.), *Market Reforms in Health Care.* Washington, DC: American Enterprise Institute, pp. 185–197.

Taylor, Amy K. and Gail R. Wilensky (1983), "The Effect of Tax Policies on Expenditures for Private Health Insurance." In Jack A. Meyer (ed.) *Market Reforms in Health Care.* Washington, DC: American Enterprise Institute, pp. 163–184.

Ture, Norman B. with Barbara A. Fields (1976), *The Future of Private Pension Plans.* Washington, DC: American Enterprise Institute.

Turner, Robert W. (1987), "Are Taxes Responsible for the Growth in Fringe Benefits?" *National Tax Journal* 40(June):205–220.

U.S. Chamber Research Center (Annual), *Employee Benefits.* Washington, DC: U.S. Chamber of Commerce.

U.S. Department of Commerce, Bureau of Economic Analysis (1986), *The National Income and Product Accounts of the United States, 1929–82, Statistical Tables.* Washington, DC: USGPO.

——— (1987), *Survey of Current Business* 67(July).

——— (1988), *Survey of Current Business* 68(July).

U.S. Department of Labor (1987), *Employee Benefits in Medium and Large Firms, 1986.* Bureau of Labor Statistics Bulletin 2281. Washington, DC: USGPO.

Venti, Steven F. and David A. Wise (1987), "Have IRAs Increased U.S. Savings?: Evidence from the Consumer Expenditure Surveys." National Bureau of Economic Research Working Paper No. 2217, NBER, Cambridge, MA.

Vogel, Ronald J. (1980), "The Tax Treatment of Health Insurance Premiums as a Cause of Overinsurance." In Mark V. Pauly (ed.), *National Health Insurance.* Washington, DC: American Enterprise Institute, pp. 220–249.

Vroman, Susan and Gerard Anderson (1984), "The Effects of Income Taxation on the Demand for Employer-Provided Health Insurance." *Applied Economics* 16(February):33–43.

Wolf, Douglas A. and Frank Levy (1984), "Pension Coverage, Pension Vesting, and the Distribution of Job Tenures." In Henry J. Aaron and Gary Burtless (eds.), *Retirement and Economic Behavior*. Washington, DC: Brookings Institution, pp. 23–61.

Woodbury, Stephen A. (1983), "Substitution Between Wage and Nonwage Benefits." *American Economic Review* 73(March):166–182.

––––––– (1984), "ERISA and the Provision of Retirement Benefits." Paper presented at the Midwest Economics Association Annual Meeting, Chicago, Illinois, April 5–7.

Woodbury, Stephen A. and Douglas R. Bettinger (1991), "The Decline of Fringe Benefit Coverage in the 1980s." In Randall W. Eberts and Erica Groshen (eds.), *Issues in Contemporary Labor Economics and the Implications for Public Policy*. Armonk, NY: M. E. Sharpe.

Woodbury, Stephen A. and Andrew J. Hogan (1990), "Labor-Market Impacts of Policies to Expand Access to Health Care." In S. E. Berki, J. Goddeeris, and A. Hogan (eds.), *Improving Access to Health Care: What Can the States Do?* Kalamazoo, MI: W. E. Upjohn Institute for Employment Research.

Woodbury, Stephen A. and Wei-Jang Huang (1988), "The Slowing Growth of Fringe Benefits." Paper presented at the Eastern Economic Association Annual Convention, Boston, Massachusetts, March 10–12.

––––––– (1991), *The Tax Treatment of Fringe Benefits*. Kalamazoo, MI: W. E. Upjohn Institute for Employment Research.

THE EFFECTS OF MANDATING BENEFITS PACKAGES

The purpose of this paper is to evaluate the potential labor market consequences of government mandating of employee benefits. Both theoretical and empirical economic arguments for and against benefit mandating are presented and assessed. In view of the continuing policy debate over health care and parental leave, these two areas are the focus of special attention in the discussion below.

It should be stated at the outset that the paper's objective is to evaluate rather than to support or undermine policy proposals to mandate benefits for U.S. workers. First we examine the role of employee benefits in the U.S. labor market, seeking to explain why some firms and workers are less likely to have particular benefits, or have less generous benefits, as compared to others. Next, we discuss several rationales for mandating benefits, presenting the pros and cons from an economic policy viewpoint. Having established the policy context, the third part of the paper then outlines the likely effect of mandating benefits on key labor market outcomes. Available evidence from related literature is provided, and where possible special problems specific to small firms are emphasized. A final section summarizes and offers specific policy recommendations that should be considered when designing a mandatory benefits package. We also

Research in Labor Economics, Volume 11, pages 297–320.
Copyright © 1990 by JAI Press Inc.
All rights of reproduction in any form reserved.
ISBN: 1-555938-080-2

identify important remaining research questions for the benefits fields and describe the data necessary to address these.[1]

I. UNDERSTANDING WHY EMPLOYEE BENEFIT COVERAGE IS UNEVEN

Broadly defined, an employee benefit is any form of nonwage compensation. In this paper we narrow our focus to what is conventionally termed *voluntarily provided benefits,* which include payments in kind such as employer-provided group life, health, and disability insurance programs; deferred compensation, primarily in the form of company-sponsored pensions and other retirement savings vehicles; and more recent arrivals to the benefit scene such as subsidized child care arrangements, health spas, legal assistance in divorces and house closings, and flexible (cafeteria) benefits. All told, voluntarily provided benefits constitute 25–30% of private-sector payrolls (U.S. Chamber of Commerce, 1988). This category of benefits must be distinguished from *legally required benefits* mandated by law and funded through special payroll taxes (e.g., Social Security, workers' compensation, unemployment insurance); these latter comprise roughly 10% of private-sector compensation. Company contributions for both types of benefits have grown steadily over time until the last five years, when employer benefit outlays have moderated somewhat (Andrews, 1988; Woodbury, 1989).

There are marked differences in the distribution of voluntarily provided benefits across workers and firms. For instance, a unionized male worker with a long-term and full-time attachment to his job is far more likely to have life and health insurance coverage and a pension plan than a lower-wage female worker, a black employee, or a short-term or part-time worker. Researchers have also documented the fact that large firms tend to offer more nonwage benefits and a wider variety of such benefits than do small firms (Andrews, 1989; Frumkin, 1986; Bell and Marclay, 1987). For instance, over 80% of small as well as medium and large firms offer paid vacation time, but the prevalence of health and retirement coverage is much smaller among firms with fewer than 100 employees, as compared to larger firms (see Table 1).

This pervasive unevenness in benefit coverage is partly a reflection of worker and firm differences in their valuation of employee benefits. High-wage employees value benefits that permit them to shelter compensation from tax: for instance, if an employer picked up a $2000 health insurance premium, this health benefit is currently not taxable while the equivalent in cash income would be subject to federal, state, and Social Security tax.[2] Similarly, pension contributions and investment earnings on those contributions are tax-free until retirement, when the individual will be in a lower tax bracket. Hence one reason employee benefits are more prevalent among higher-paid workers is that they shield some compensation from higher marginal tax brackets.

There are additional reasons why workers value nonwage benefits in the

Table 1. Fraction of Full-Time Employees Participating in Company
Benefit Plans by Firm Size (1987)

	Employees participating (%) in benefit plan in	
Benefit plan	*Medium and large firms*	*Small firms*
Retirement/pension	91	43
Health insurance	96	75
Life insurance	96	59
Paid time off		
Vacations	99	81
Paid lunch break	10	19
Sick leave	67	26
Disability insurance (long term)	48	26
Other		
Educational assistance	76	23
Employee discounts	57	35
Child care	1	4

Note: Taken from Andrews (1988). Medium and large firms are those classified as having 100–250 employees, depending on the industry. Small firms are classified as those with fewer than 100 employees.

compensation package. Some employee benefits are designed to help workers accumulate funds that they might otherwise be tempted to spend (Thaler and Shefrin, 1981). Insurance costs are also lower among larger groups of people due to scale economies, administrative cost savings, and risk pooling, making group provision of benefits especially appealing (Mitchell and Andrews, 1981). Insurers prefer to work with groups formed for purposes other than the purchase of insurance to avoid unusual expenses due to adverse selection, so that employee groups have a special advantage in this regard (Beam and McFadden, 1988). One explanation for why union workers have employee benefits is that labor unions appear more responsive to older and stable employees' demands (Freeman, 1981). Putting all these factors together, it seems clear that part of the unevenness in benefit coverage across the working population is due to a concentration of worker demand among high-wage and unionized employees in large firms. Conversely, demand for benefits has been the lowest among low-wage workers, for whom the tax shield is worth less and for whom the need for cash compensation is greatest.[3]

Another reason that benefit coverage is not universal in the U.S. labor market is that companies differ in the way they perceive the value of employee benefits. Some employers are indifferent as to whether they devote a given sum to wages, say $1000, or allocate the same sum of $1000 to nonwage benefits: in both cases the expenditure is treated as labor cost and deductible as a business expense. On the other hand, Mumy (1985) finds that some companies perceive benefit expenditures as being worth "more" since contributions reduce payroll taxes such as Social Security and workers' compensation payments. In addition, firms also use benefit packages to achieve certain employment objectives: deferred compensation attracts stable workers, pensions are structured to induce early retirement, health insurance plans are tailored to attract and retain certain types of workers, and child care subsidies may be offered to reduce absenteeism and turnover (Gustman and Steinmeier, 1989; Mitchell, 1982; Sindelar, 1982; EBRI 1989). Firms also structure stock ownership and profit-sharing benefit plans to induce more productivity and serve as a work incentive tool (U.S. General Accounting Office, 1986). More complex analyses have also identified the fact that corporations alter their benefit plans so as to enhance their balance sheets and meet overall corporate goals (Bulow, 1982; Ippolito, 1986).

In overview then, surveys confirm that benefits and wages appear in different mixes from one firm to the next. Labor market research contends that this is the result of differences in employees' demands for benefits, interacting with employers' differential willingness to provide benefits of various kinds. Dollars devoted to benefits come at the expense of dollars that could have gone to wages, though the exact degree of substitutability between the various forms of compensation will vary from one workplace to another.

II.   MANDATING EMPLOYEE BENEFITS:
THE POLICY CONTEXT

The uneven distribution of employee benefits in the U.S. labor market has for many years generated controversy among labor analysts. Some argue that no intervention in the market is justified, believing that cross-sectional benefit differences are simply the natural outgrowth of differences in firms', workers', and labor unions' valuation of nonwage compensation (Becker, 1988). Others take issue with this conclusion, suggesting instead that the government should influence or even dictate which benefits should be provided as well as who should receive them.[4] In this section we examine several rationales for and against government intervention in the employee benefit arena, with the goal being an assessment of the issues that must be considered in making sensible government policy.

To clarify arguments, we organize the discussion around two questions: (1) When, if at all, should the government intervene in firms' and workers' election of nonwage compensation such as health or life insurance, pension, or other benefits? (2) What are the pros and cons of having the government mandate that firms provide nonwage benefits, on the assumption that there is a rationale for government intervention? Each question is taken up in turn.

A.   Should Government Intervene in Firm's and Workers' Election
of Nonwage Benefits?

Analysts of different political and economic persuasions arrive at very different conclusions about the need for government involvement in benefits provision. We begin by evaluating various rationales offered to justify government intervention in the nonwage benefits area, and then go on to do the same for arguments against the proposition.

One motivation for government involvement in the benefits area is paternalism. Supporters identify a list of "merit goods" or "minimum labor standards" and contend that all should be covered by these; the next step is to argue that the government must require that these be provided "even if the members of the society do not demand them" (Rosen, 1985, p. 64). Inevitably there is disagreement about which items should and do fall into the merit good category. One merit good about which there is relatively little debate at present in the United States is public education, which the government requires (virtually) all school-age children to consume. However, in the benefits context there is far more disagreement. If health is identified as a merit good, it then follows that health care insurance is a benefit to which the government must guarantee access. On the other hand, good health is an elusive concept and insurance is expensive. Furthermore, calling something a merit good "is not really a justification for [public] support—it merely invests a bit of terminology to designate the desire to do so" (Baumol and Baumol, cited by Rosen, 1985, p. 65). In short, the merit good argument does not stand on economic grounds as a rationale for a government benefit mandate. On the other hand analysts recognize that there are other philosophical and perhaps ethical reasons to support (or to oppose) the proposal.

A different justification for government intervention in the provision of benefits stems from information problems. Specifically, when workers and/or firms are poorly informed of the important advantages vs. costs of nonwage benefits, they will demand suboptimal levels of such benefits as compared to what would be socially efficient. This may arise, for instance, when people fail to buy health insurance because they are not aware of possibly catastrophic medical costs or cannot accurately judge the long-term consequences of not having the insurance coverage. A similar case might be made for family or child care benefits: prior to having children, most people are probably unaware of their future demand for parental leave and high-quality child care. Another example arises from the fact that even highly educated workers misestimate their expected life spans (Hamermesh, 1979); as a consequence they will tend to make incorrect retirement savings plans. In such cases, the most clear-cut role for government is to rectify the information gaps where possible by publicizing relevant risks and costs (Mitchell, 1988). In unusual cases when information problems are not easily corrected, the government may perceive a need to require benefit coverage directly. Interestingly, no research has yet shown that this is a serious problem in the health care or family leave area.

A third rationale for government intervention in the benefits arena is externalities. For example, government intervention in the unemployment insurance (UI) area is often rationalized on grounds that UI is necessary to force firms to internalize costs of layoff, which produce negative spillovers for the economy at large (Ehrenberg and Schumann, 1982). In the medical-care area, similar spillovers may occur. When someone stays in the hospital longer or consumes more medical care than medically necessary simply because health insurance picks up most of the tab, that individual is imposing higher medical-care costs on others. A related problem arises because the medically indigent are frequently subsidized by taxpayers and private insurers (Pauly, 1988). Here the externalities are negative, since indigent people's demand for health care is met by hospitals and medical practitioners who then must raise prices for those having health insurance coverage. Recently supporters of parental leave bills have offered similar justifications for their proposals: for instance Democratic Connecticut Senator Christopher Dodd recently argued that insufficient maternal leave imposes costs on society later in the form of greater need for remedial education (Bureau of National Affairs, 1989). In such instances an appropriate role for government may be to alter incentives so that individual decisions about how much to demand and supply incorporate spillover effects on others.

A fourth rationale for government intervention in the benefits area is that sometimes private markets are unable to provide insurance coverage very effectively or cheaply. For instance, adverse selection makes it prohibitively expensive for the chronically ill to obtain low-cost health insurance on their own. However, if risks of poor health could be pooled over a large enough group, and if people agreed to precommit to such insurance before their adult health status was fully known, the risk spreading so achieved should lower costs for all. It has been argued that the government is needed to create such risk pools for insurance purposes because it has more information than do individuals, or because the government can benefit from scale economies of large-scale operation.[5] In both instances, government operation might be cheaper than private-sector initiatives. This may also characterize the market for nursing home insurance: insurers only recently have begun to offer long-term care policies, partly because the older population has not fully recognized the high risk and high costs of such care. Here the argument is that the government may be able to redistribute and/or internalize risks in ways that the private sector cannot. Similarly, small firms seeking to purchase health care insurance often find that obtaining health coverage for a handful of employees is prohibitively expensive, or else simply not possible if the work group is too small. This is because of insurers' fear that risks cannot be adequately pooled over small groups, particularly if there is the possibility for adverse selection on the part of prospective employees. Here again, the argument is that the government can intervene when private markets fail to provide needed insurance.

A final motivation for government involvement in the benefits area is equity. Current tax law shelters benefits from income and payroll taxes, which comprise a relative high share of high-income workers' compensation. In most cases company contributions to health and disability insurance plans are not taxed at all, while employer contributions to pension plans are taxed only after retirement (generally at lower rates). Some who favoring benefit mandating claim that this is necessary to restore progressivity to the tax system; for instance, benefits non-discrimination requirements were justified in Congress on grounds that plans qualifying for tax-exempt status would have to provide benefits irrespective of employees' pay levels (Beam and McFadden, 1988). Many economists contend that equity and efficiency would be better served by taxing all forms of compensation similarly (Munnell, 1989), though real-world policymakers may not have the political leeway to achieve a "first-best" solution to efficiency and equity concerns.

B. Should Government Mandate That Firms Provide Nonwage Benefits?

Assuming that government intervention can be justified on the grounds just discussed, the question remains as to who can most efficiently and fairly provide these benefits to the relevant population. In other words, one must judge whether the advantages of mandating that employers provide these benefits outweigh the costs of having them do so, or whether some other entity might do it more effectively and in a less costly way.

Arguments in Favor of Employer Provision

Some analysts would contend that requiring firms to provide a specific benefits package permits tailoring of the offerings to employees' and firms' needs, while still taking advantage of cost savings due to group benefit purchase (Mitchell and Andrews, 1981). In contrast, if a government agency were to offer similar benefits, standardization could limit the adaptation of benefits to specific employee and firm circumstances (Summers, 1988). An additional factor is that employers may also have better information than governmental agencies regarding workers' risks, insurance costs, and benefits; this might make employer-provided plans cheaper as a result of lesser moral hazard.

Several additional arguments have been offered in support of requiring that employers offer mandated benefits. First, some political pragmatists argue that at present there is no more direct way to extend benefit coverage to uncovered employees, in view of current budget deficits. A second rationale recognizes that some benefits are already offered voluntarily in the labor market, and it may be that requiring employers to offer a mandatory benefits package could be less disruptive than would a government tax/transfer program requiring the same general set of benefits. This is because at least the most immediate impact of a mandate would be limited to workplaces where such benefits are not currently offered. In addition, several commentators have noted that the political appeal of a mandate rests on the assumption that putting the burden on company shoulders both preserves the benefits providers market, and also keeps "big government" from growing even larger than it already is (Pauly, 1988; Quayle, 1987). Offsetting this effect is the possibility that, for some, labor supply might actually increase under a mandated-benefits approach. Empirical evidence on this latter point appears in the next section.

Criticisms of Employer Provision

Though the arguments in favor of requiring that employers provide benefits are numerous, there are also some important criticisms of such proposals that policymakers must confront. Some analysts argue that any government intervention is per se coercive and thus must be discouraged; others highlight government enforcement and administration costs. Opponents of the mandated benefits idea have also emphasized equity problems with the proposals: that is, people who do not currently hold jobs would not be helped by mandated employee benefits, for the most part.[6] Certain employers would also be more affected than others: in particular, small firms currently offer fewer nonwage benefits, appear the most constrained by minimum-wage laws, and probably face more competitive constraints than their larger counterparts (U.S. Small Business Administration, various years). In addition small firms hire more women than do larger companies, so that some worry that the incidence of mandating benefits might fall most heavily on groups others wish to protect (Becker, 1988; Smith, 1988).

Objections raised on efficiency grounds are also worrisome. Mandating benefits raises labor costs for firms without benefits, with eventual negative consequences for wages and employment levels. Affected employers, seeking to pass on the increased labor costs to their workers, will reduce wages (or wage growth) to offset new benefit costs. In some instances all that is required is that employers rearrange the components of compensation moving away from cash toward more benefits, and on net when this can be done in a costless manner there will be relatively little impact on employment, product prices, and profitability. It should be noted that even in this instance, some employees' well-being will decline when they would have preferred to receive cash wages over the additional benefits they are forced to consume with the benefit mandate. In other instances, employers will find it impossible to increase benefits by reducing cash pay, especially where pay rates are constrained by the legal minimum wage. In these cases, requiring higher benefits pushes up labor costs, which in turn introduces incentives for affected firms to alter their overall employment levels, curtailing labor usage and eventually reducing production and raising consumer prices.

C.   Fixed- versus Variable-Cost Benefits Packages

The precise manner in which employers respond depends on how a given policy mandate is structured. One way to frame a benefit mandate is to require that all employees be provided with the same benefit package irrespective of whether that employee works part- or full-time. In this case, benefit takes on *fixed-costs* characteristics; that is, the employer must bear the same benefits cost irrespective of how many hours that employee actually works. Fixed-cost bene-fits of this type increase low-wage workers' compensation relatively more than highly paid employees, so employers will tend to substitute away from low-skilled toward high-skilled labor (Hamermesh, 1988). In addition, those affected will utilize more hours per worker, and probably fewer total worker hours overall (Ehrenberg, 1971; Hart, 1984). How much the total number of employees varies depends on firms' ability to substitute labor for capital and is not theoretically determinable.

The fixed-cost approach to mandated benefits is not merely a hypothetical notion: in fact, several mandatory health insurance bills discussed in Congress over the last few years take exactly this form. Many of the plans required that a specified set of health care items be provided: for example, one stipulated that employers offer health insurance coverage for physician and hospital services, prenatal and maternity care, limited mental health services, and catastrophic coverage, limiting worker out-of-pocket expenses to $3000. These specific cov-erage requirements were to be combined with government-set deductibles, copayment rates, and exclusion restrictions. Another example of a fixed-cost viewpoint was found in many of the parental-leave bills before Congress in 1988 and 1989. These bills typically would entitle employees to ten weeks leave during which health benefit coverage must continue, and this benefit was seen as a per-worker entitlement rather than accruing according to hours worked.

An alternative method of structuring a mandated benefit proposes a *variable-cost* approach, tying benefit entitlements to hours of work rather than having them accrue on a flat per-worker basis. Those who tout this idea note that a mandated-benefits program where benefits are tied to the number of hours worked would probably cost employers and society as a whole less, than would regulation mandating that all employees must be provided with a common set of benefits (Bell and Hart, 1988; Summers, 1988). This prediction assumes that a tax increase would be required to pay for the plan, which in turn would induce an across-the board reduction in labor supply. In contrast, under the mandating approach, only the subset of newly covered workers would be immediately affected.

Again, the variable-cost approach is not merely hypothetical: a variant of it was proposed by President Carter's Commission on Pension Policy when this body sought to design a mandatory pension proposal over a decade ago. The plan called for a minimum of 3% of each worker's pay to be deposited into a defined contribution pension plan (or something producing equivalent retirement income if it were a defined benefit plan).

In analyzing the likely effect of this and other variable-cost mandate proposals, it must be recognized that some portion of the benefit cost increase must be passed on to workers in the form of lower wages. In addition, to the extent that cost increases due to mandated benefits could not be fully passed on to workers in the form of lower wages, some employment would probably be lost. On the other hand, the additional undesirable distributional consequences inherent in a fixed-cost benefit would not apply. From this perspective then, the variable-cost method of assigning mandated benefits has a somewhat greater appeal on equity grounds.[7] An example recently appeared in an article about Brazil's decision to mandate maternity leave of four months for all employees. As a consequence of this action, many women were "told they would not be hired because they were pregnant and others . . . were warned they would lose their job in case of pregnancy . . . many employers had already signaled that they want to replace young women with men" (Simons, 1988).

D.   Allowing Small Firms to Remain Exempt or Provide Reduced Coverage

It becomes more difficult to predict the likely labor market consequences of mandating either per-worker or variable benefits when portions of the workforce are exempted from the benefit mandate. In point of fact, however, real-world proposals usually have a partial coverage feature because part-timers and/or workers in small firms are often exempted (or may be covered by a somewhat less generous package). Hamermesh (1988) finds that limiting a benefit mandate to a subsector of the economy produces strong incentives for firms to contract out employment, hire temporaries, and otherwise replace "protected" with "unprotected" workers. This could be a particular problem for the health insurance bills currently under consideration, which propose to cover only people employed 17.5 hours a week or more. In a parallel manner the proposed parental leave bills before Congress are structured to include only firms with more than 35–50 employees.

E.   Possible Labor Supply Responses

Not only does partial coverage affect demand for labor of different types— labor supply too may be influenced. While establishing the size of the effect is primarily an empirical question to be addressed below, it is worth speculating about the likely direction of the expected changes. Some predict that women may be less likely to leave their jobs due to childbearing or might seek paid employment during childbearing years if paid maternity leave were mandated. On the other hand, quit rates and absenteeism patterns may change for those newly covered by benefits, and in comparison to workers in the uncovered sector. In general, theoretical analysts conclude that it is probably impossible to predict the complete effect of a benefit mandate when these real-world and interesting extensions are incorporated (Hart, 1984). Empirical evidence is needed to explore whether these different effects are sizable.

F. Are Other Policy Goals Thwarted?

A final caution raised about mandating benefit plans is that this policy alters labor costs across workers of different types, which may unexpectedly undermine other public policy goals. For instance, employers required to offer a standard health insurance package or parental-leave policy might find it more expensive to employ women workers (Becker, 1988; Cook, 1989). This cost differential could induce some firms to substitute men for women in employment. Similar selection problems could arise for low-income workers where health problems may be perceived to be more likely. In contrast, a publicly funded and operated program that provided the same benefits would spread benefit costs across gender, health status, age, and other factors, removing employers' incentives to become more selective in hiring and retention of now more costly workers.

G. Overview

In conclusion, there are many reasons to both favor and oppose proposals to have the government intervene further in the employee benefits area, and the rationales differ from case to case. In the case of health insurance, three arguments for government intervention are emphasized in the literature: some people are uninsurable in the private market; some people have insufficient income to buy private health insurance; and externalities in the medical-care market appear to justify regulation. In contrast, two arguments are frequently offered to justify mandating parental leave: some say it is a merit good, which all should receive, while others emphasize possible externalities (e.g., some say children who do not "bond" after childbirth may cause social problems later). When it comes to pension provision, generally the argument is formulated as one where government action is required because improvident workers undersave or workers overconsume due to insufficient information about their retirement needs. Despite these philosophical differences motivating those who favor mandating benefits of one kind or other, all in favor of the policy seem united in a pragmatic stance. That is, they unite in the belief that large-scale government provision of new benefits is unlikely in the current budget environment and look to employers to begin to fill the gap. Those who oppose benefit mandating do so for very different reasons. Some analysts are philosophically opposed, preferring as little government intervention in the labor market as possible. Yet others point out that employment-linked benefit proposals still leave unprotected several million uninsured people who are not in the labor force, and whose family members are also without coverage (Chollet, 1987a).

III. EVIDENCE ON THE LABOR MARKET CONSEQUENCES OF MANDATING EMPLOYEE BENEFITS

Having identified the key policy arguments for and against government mandating of employee benefits packages, we now move to an examination of empirical evidence on the likely labor market consequences of mandated benefits. Rather than delving into specific legislative proposals, we take a more general approach and refer the interested reader to others' reviews of specific recent benefit proposals. [See, for instance Morgan (1987), Meyer (1988), Rix (1987), U.S. Congress (1987), U.S. General Accounting Office (1987; 1988).]

The discussion proceeds in two parts. First comes a review of evidence on the likely impact of mandated benefits on compensation and employment. We focus on what the empirical literature has to say on overall hours and employment level adjustments, and the length of time such adjustments might be expected to take. Also noted are differential adjustment patterns across sectors of the economy. Next, the discussion turns to an assessment of evidence on workers' likely responses to mandated benefits. Here we focus on changes in labor supply, turnover behavior, and sorting patterns of workers across the labor market.

A.   Consequences for Compensation Patterns and Employment

The first empirical question we investigate in the mandated-benefit context is as follows: If the government mandates a new benefit, what effect will this have on other elements of the compensation package? One literature that might be thought helpful in answering this question examines trade-offs between different forms of compensation in the workplace. Nevertheless the studies in this genre are often seriously limited by data and estimation problems. A careful study of the public sector found a one-for-one trade-off between wages and employer-provided benefits (Ehrenberg and Smith, 1979). Taken literally, these results imply that mandating an employee benefit package costing 10% would depress affected workers' pay by the same amount. However, private-sector studies of wage/benefit trade-offs tend to find no evidence in support of the compensating-differentials theory, and indeed most often report a positive relationship between wage levels and benefits (Mitchell and Pozzebon, 1987; Smith and Ehrenberg, 1983). The jury is still out on whether these generally negative results prove that the theory is wrong or that error-ridden data simply cannot be relied on to test the hypothesis.

Other forms of adjustment in the compensation package besides employment loss can occur. For instance a 1957 survey in New York state showed that raising retail stores' labor costs for low-wage workers reduced a number of employee benefits including rest and meal breaks, year-end bonuses, paid vacations, sick leave, store discount privileges, premium pay, and other compensation (Wessels,

1980). Precise response magnitudes for this type of trade-off have not yet been pinpointed, however.

A second line of inquiry on benefit/pay trade-offs takes a different tack, comparing benefit patterns in states that currently mandate particular benefits with those in states that do not. One such study is that of Trzcinski (1988), who examines whether private-sector workers are paid differently in states that mandated paid maternity leave policies as compared to states that do not. Her results do not paint a consistent picture. In states that treat maternity leave as a special medical disability, she finds that hourly wages for women in small firms are depressed by 0–7%, and benefit coverage rates are lower by 0–11%. The upper-bound responses seem unbelievably large.[8] She also concludes that women's pay is apparently not depressed in states that treat pregnancy and childbirth leave like other disability leaves. (Men's pay was not depressed in any of her results.) The author does not offer an explanation for the differential impact by type of benefit plan, but it may be that different funding methods under the two policies contribute to observed differences. When pregnancy leave is formulated as a special disability program with readily identifiable premiums tied to the number of women in a workplace, the funding method will highlight additional costs of hiring women and exert downward pressure on women's compensation and employment. In contrast, treating maternity leave as one of many covered events in an overall disability policy induces more risk pooling and probably more cross subsidization in premiums.[9]

In overview then, theoretical research on the pay/benefits trade-off indicates that mandating benefits will reduce compensation for some groups of workers in the long run. Nevertheless the empirical evidence suggests that the full costs of mandated benefits may not be immediately passed on to private-sector workers via reductions in their wages and benefits. In this event, mandating benefits increases employers' labor costs.

Following this line of argument, the next question to be addressed is, If mandating a new benefit raises labor costs, what happens to labor demand? The empirical labor economics literature is of some help in assessing likely response magnitudes. Research shows that there will probably be "only slight substitution away from workers and toward hours, *holding total worker-hours constant*" (emphasis added, Hamermesh, 1988, p. 24; see also Ehrenberg and Schumann, 1982). However, overall labor demand in covered firms will decline if there is not a one-for-one trade-off between increased benefits and reduced wages. In general, the literature suggests that when labor costs rise by 10%, overall labor demand will fall by 1–5%, with most of the adjustment taking place within one year (Hamermesh, 1988; Hart et al., 1988). Hence the econometric evidence implies that mandating benefits will certainly reduce employment in covered firms, though the exact magnitude depends on the cost increase embedded in any given benefit proposal.

As we have noted above, mandating benefits is likely to alter *relative* labor costs in addition to overall labor costs. Consider, for instance, the effect of dramatic changes in relative labor costs predicted in a recent assessment of a proposed mandatory health insurance bill (U.S. Congress, 1988). The bill would boost minimum-wage workers' total compensation by 15–20% as a result of imposing the mandatory health insurance plan, but would have virtually no effect on higher-wage employees' cash income (most in the highly paid group were asserted to be already covered by a plan meeting the minimum standards). A consequence of changing relative wages in this way would be to induce employers to substitute away from low-wage employees toward more highly skilled labor and capital. Substitution is likely to be most feasible among lesser-skilled employees, many of whom are minimum-wage earners. Indeed, recent estimates show that teenagers, women, and part-time employees comprise, respectively, 36, 65, and 66% of all minimum-wage workers (Stout, 1988). These workers also tend to be concentrated in small firms and are the least likely to have employee benefits (U.S. Small Business Administration, various years).

Studies in a related genre have also noted that low-wage employers may not be able to pass on increased benefit costs when their employees are already at the minimum-wage floor. The likely impact in this instance would be reduced employment. From econometric analyses of the minimum wage, we know that that raising pay by 10% among minimum-wage workers is associated with 0.5–3% decline in youth employment (see Brown, 1988; Mitchell, 1982; Mitchell and Mikalauskas, 1988), so similar outcomes might be anticipated if benefit mandates of this magnitude were implemented.

Other researchers have simulated the disemployment consequences of pay increases using simulation models. While the models can be criticized on grounds of not representing the real world in important ways, they do tend to suggest similar response magnitudes as those unveiled in more conventional econometric studies. For example, Anderson's simulation exercise (1987) points to 160,000 workers losing their jobs as a result of mandating a 3% defined-benefit pension; in subsequent years he finds the job loss rate would taper to some 60,000 employees. Anderson also contends that over half of the job loss would be concentrated in firms with fewer than 25 employees, and an additional 20% in firms with between 25 and 99 workers. Others have evaluated employment effects of benefit mandates without relying on specific simulation models. Extrapolating from some of their other work, Karen Davis and Edward Gramlich both testified on November 4, 1987, before the Senate Committee on Labor and Human Resources that a mandated health insurance plan that raised low-wage workers pay by 15% would induce job losses for around 100,000 workers. In each of these cases cited, the figures represent more-or-less educated guesses since the assessments are only loosely linked to econometrically robust models estimated with appropriate data. Nevertheless, the fact remains that policy researchers clearly do not believe that job losses would be zero as a result of a mandated benefits plan. Whether disemployment effects are judged to be large or small depends, of course, on the observer: as (then Senator) Quayle stated, "We may talk in terms of 100,000 jobs as not being a lot, but if you take 100,000 jobs of minority teenagers, that population has suffered enough" (Quayle, 1987).

For reasons of political feasibility, mandated-benefits proposals such as the health benefits or parental-leave policies described above often exempt some portion of the labor market from coverage, on the argument that cost increases are simply too great for some employees and firms to bear. For this reason, small businesses are frequently allowed to avoid participating or in some cases the benefits they must offer are permitted to be less comprehensive than those required of larger firms. Along the same lines, some reform bills suggest that benefits need not be provided to part-time employees at all, or in lesser amounts. Unfortunately in practice the definition of a small firm or a part-time employee appears to change from one version of a bill to the next without much attention to how benefit costs and disemployment patterns might vary. The end result, though, is the same: these exemptions have the effect of mandating benefit coverage across only portions of the labor market.

B.   Consequences for Labor Supply

Thus far the discussion has emphasized employers' likely responses to increases in labor costs due to mandated benefits. However there is a reasonable chance that workers also might alter their behavior if firms are required to provide health insurance, family leave coverage, or other benefits. Several different dimensions of labor supply response should be considered, though they are rarely (if ever) brought up in policy evaluations.

Increases in absenteeism may be one undesirable effect of devoting a larger fraction of compensation to benefits. This is particularly true when benefit entitlements accrue on a per-worker fixed-cost basis and the value of the entitlement is not affected by a few additional absences from work. Research shows, for instance, that being eligible for sick leave increases workers' absenteeism rates (Allen, 1981; Ehrenberg et al., 1989; Winkler, 1980). Hence cost estimates of proposed family and medical-leave plans that assume constant worker absenteeism are probably too optimistic: allowing workers to take a given number of family and medical leave days per year will probably increase absenteeism and should be included in cost forecasts. A similar prediction follows for mandated health benefits, though here the effect is more subtle. Increasing workers' total income by imposing a mandated health plan makes workers better off if wage cuts do not fully offset the new benefit. This produces an income effect inducing them to work less, without materially altering the cost of not working (wages foregone). The end result will be more absenteeism (Ehrenberg and Smith, 1988). On the other hand programs that tie benefit accrual to work time, using a variable-benefit format, would have fewer incentives in this direction.

A different labor supply response to mandated benefits must also be examined:

turnover. Benefits are frequently structured in such a way to discourage quits and tie workers to their jobs; for instance, vesting and other rules make it costly to leave an employer if a worker is covered by a pension (Mitchell, 1982), while waiting periods and exclusion rules probably have a similar effect in the area of health insurance. Changing jobs would become much easier and probably more prevalent if health coverage were made mandatory and if, as some of the proposals were formulated, waiting periods and exclusions for preexisting conditions were prohibited. However a rise in turnover brings with it higher search, recruitment, and training costs, which in turn reduces net labor productivity and output. In other words, an overall decline in output and labor productivity would be a worrisome possibility if mandated benefits prohibited employers from using benefits to discourage job changing, now permitted in existing benefit plans.

Studies show that such partial coverage patterns will induce movements of workers from covered-sector jobs to jobs without mandated benefits. Specifically, evidence from the United States and several European countries indicate that increases in nonwage costs among first-tier workers contributed to more employment in the uncovered second tier, including temporary help, part-timers, and subcontracted workers (Ehrenberg et al., 1988; Hamermesh, 1988; Mangum et al., 1985). Expansion of the uncovered sector is troubling in light of the fact that one important motivation for mandating benefits is to reach workers currently lacking such coverage. As yet there are no hard estimates of the likely growth in the uncovered sector given an increase in labor costs in the covered sector, which probably explains why policy studies to date have not accounted for these in any scientific way. What seems clear, however, is that workers in the second-tier sector are significantly less likely to be covered by employee benefits of all kinds (Williams, 1989). Hence the possibility remains that mandating benefits might not increase benefit coverage among low-wage workers, if this combination of effects is large enough.

There is yet a different way that mandated benefits can and will affect labor supply. Specifically, the chance to qualify for benefit coverage will induce some people to enter the labor force and to remain employed beyond the point they might have otherwise. This is especially probable for new mothers receiving continuation of health care coverage and job reinstatement under the family and medical-leave plan, who might have left their jobs (or perhaps been discharged) prior to the reform. While response magnitudes to these particular bills are not known, results from other benefits programs are informative. One study pertinent to this issue demonstrated that raising UI payments by 20% increased the fraction of women working by about 1% and women's work hours grew by about 12%. The latter is an entitlement effect: women worked longer so as to meet the minimum income level for unemployment program coverage (Hamermesh, 1979). A related study by Ehrenberg et al. (1988) also concluded that "supply side responses exceed demand responses" when part-time compensation was raised in the United States over time. In consequence, it must be concluded that coverage-induced increases in labor supply are very likely among groups of people who previously were not offered benefit coverage. Designers of mandated-benefits packages must recognize such downward pressure on pay attributable to the supply side responses since, as we showed above, these tend to be low-wage, low-skilled workers.

A final labor supply response to mandated benefits worthy of consideration here is an issue that arises because workers and firms differ in their valuation of benefits packages. If the government mandates that a fixed-cost benefit be provided to a portion of the labor force, yet workers differ in the way they value it, those valuing the benefit least will tend to move to jobs exempted from the mandate. Evidence of this is offered by Scott et al. (1989, p. 228), who warn that "enactment of this legislation would increase the amount of labor market segmentation faced by low-income workers." Unfortunately likely response magnitudes cannot be computed from the numbers given in that study.

Despite the importance of supply side responses, few policy analysts have recognized them when discussing the potential consequences of mandating benefits. This is certainly an area where more research would be valuable. Inevitably, those interested in labor market efficiency must be troubled by the finding that mandated benefits probably increase absenteeism and turnover. Those focusing on equity would, in addition, be concerned about likely increases in labor supply due to mandated benefits, which have the beneficial effect of tying low-wage workers to the market more closely, but also may drive down this group's wages. In addition, it appears that mandating a fixed-cost benefit would probably have the largest supply side effects, while allocating benefits on a variable per-hour-worked basis might well have smaller labor supply consequences.

IV. CONCLUSIONS AND POLICY OPTIONS

A. Conclusions

This paper identifies and, where possible, quantifies potential labor market consequences of government mandates of employee benefits. Policy analysts should consider two questions when contemplating mandated benefits: (1) What relative importance should be attached to those who gain under the mandate vs. those who lose? (2) Could feasible alternative policies have more beneficial outcomes? Existing policy research suggests the following conclusions:

1. Mandating benefits will increase benefit coverage and generosity for numerous workers and their families. Nevertheless, many people lacking insurance coverage will not be helped by this type of mandated employee benefit program.
2. Even when mandating benefits does improve benefit provision, there will be offsetting effects. These include wage and other benefit cuts, reduced

work hours, reduced employment, and possibly output reductions in covered sectors. Employer bias against "expensive to insure" workers may also result, producing labor market sorting and segmentation.

3. Most workers currently without benefit coverage are employees of small firms, women, and part-time and minimum-wage workers. Nevertheless, most mandated-benefit proposals exclude or reduce coverage for these workers to alleviate the financial burden on small firms.

B. Policy Options

While a full discussion of each of these concerns in the present context goes beyond the purview of this paper, it should be emphasized that deciding whether or not to mandate a given benefit or set of benefits requires the analyst to evaluate and weigh increases in well-being afforded to workers (and their families) that would be newly covered by such a mandated benefit, with the pay and the employment cuts borne by the less fortunate. In addition it must be asked what other feasible alternative policy scenarios might be if Congress did not mandate benefits. An option popular with some would be to keep the status quo, letting the market generate its continuing uneven pattern of voluntarily provided benefits. Others concerned about gaps in insurance coverage instead advocate a greatly expanded government role in the health and pension field supported by taxes and providing benefits for the population at large.[10] Alternatively, Congress might take a middle road by offering incentives such as tax subsidies for employers who expand benefit coverage, without directly mandating additional specific benefits. While this last approach has the virtue of encouraging insurance coverage among employees, it would not help those without jobs. It does seem that proposals that cost the Treasury will be sternly regarded in this era of "no new taxes."

Given that mandating employer-provided benefits remains a viable option after having done this broader analysis, it remains true that mandates raise labor costs and produce job losses that will probably be concentrated among low-wage workers in smaller firms. However, there may be ways to design a mandated benefit so as to reduce these negative effects somewhat. We have argued above that the variable-cost approach—requiring that benefits accrue at a percentage rate per worker-hour—has the advantage of reducing the bias against low-wage employees currently without coverage. In contrast, the fixed-cost approach such as that inherent in most current health and family leave proposals makes low-wage workers and the firms that employ them proportionately much more vulnerable to the negative consequences of cost increases. On the other hand, some critics would suggest that a variable-cost approach in the health insurance area would not insure all workers' access to basic and major medical insurance at affordable rates. Similarly, variable-cost pension contributions would not ensure high levels of retirement income for part-time or part-week workers, and along the same lines, pro-rated family leaves would not ensure that all employees get ample paid time off with infants or sick children. Hence those concerned with providing a basic level of social insurance might judge the fixed-cost approach preferable even with its greater potential for more severe disemployment effects among particular sectors of the economy.

Based on the analysis above, the following options are worth considering:

1. While mandating benefits using a fixed-cost structure is viewed positively by some, it raises labor costs most for low-wage workers, inducing substitution away from them toward more skilled employees. Fixed-cost benefits also reduce flexibility in designing benefit packages and are not responsive to worker and firm differences in the demand for benefits. In contrast, a variable-cost format where benefits accrue according to hours worked somewhat mitigates these drawbacks.

2. Many firms claim they require tax incentives to help them provide benefit coverage. If tax incentives become necessary for political reasons, they should be paired with a cap on the overall fraction of payroll that can be used for tax-shielded employee benefit contributions. This would make the tax and the benefit system more equitable as a whole.

3. If government decides to mandate more employee benefits, a gradual approach should be taken. Each element of a target mandated-benefit package should be ranked in a priority list and justified on both efficiency and equity grounds. Subsequently, after the labor market consequences of one such benefit are evaluated, additional benefit mandates might be considered.

4. A separate approach should be designed to meet the needs of those not covered by employer-provided benefit programs.

C.   Remaining Research Questions

Several questions should be addressed in future research if policy analysis is to be useful in guiding decisions on mandatory employee benefits packages. We need to know more about why workers differ in their demand for benefits, and why some firms supply benefits of particular types and levels of coverage, while others do not. Only armed with this information will it be possible to understand why voluntarily provided benefits are so unevenly distributed across the labor market.

More research should also be done on the labor market impact of state level regulations regarding the form and content of benefits. Additional analysis would also be useful on different ways to structure benefits, following up on the variable- vs. the fixed-cost format. Last but not least, more research is required on the extent to which the low-wage population regards public sources of insurance as a good substitute for private/employer-provided benefits.

To understand these and other important questions in the benefits arena, the research community needs new and improved data sets containing information on both workers and their employers, as well as details on their wage and benefit compensation packages. In addition, longitudinal surveys on worker consumption of and perceptions of insurance would be most valuable.

ACKNOWLEDGMENTS

The paper was funded under Purchase Order No. 99-9-4757-75-009-04 from the U.S. Department of Labor, Commission on Workforce Quality and Labor Market Efficiency. Opinions stated in this document do not necessarily represent the official position or policy of the U.S. Department of Labor, Commission on Workforce Quality and Labor Market Efficiency. Without implicating them, I would like to thank the following people for helpful comments: Emily Andrews, Deborah Chollet, Ronald Ehrenberg, Gary Fields, Daniel Hamermesh, Robert A. Hart, Michael Horrigan, Katherine Montalto, and Robert S. Smith.

NOTES

1.   Space constraints preclude a discussion of benefits offered to inactive workers, such as retiree health insurance benefits.

2.   This is true as long as the employer-provided plans meet nondiscrimination requirements; see Beam and McFadden (1988).

3.   Some of the demand for insurance programs among low-wage workers may be met by social insurance programs. However, many low-income individuals are ineligible for Medicaid, and those out of the labor force cannot receive Social Security; see Chollet (1987b).

4.   A succinct summary of these arguments appears in McArdle (1988); that same conference volume also reports additional perspectives on mandating health and pension benefits.

5.   Kotlikoff et al. (1982) examine many of these arguments in the pension context. See also Kotlikoff (1987).

6.   The size of the uncovered population depends on the benefit in question. See Chollet (1987b), Andrews (1989), and EBRI (1988).

7.   Of course, in practice, mandated-benefit proposals often have both variable and fixed elements.

8.   The author's upper-bound wage responses seem improbably large assuming that a four-month maternity leave for a woman having two children would probably cost an employer no more than 3% of her lifetime earnings if the woman remained with that employer 20 years (the effect would be far smaller if discounting were taken into effect). Shorter completed-tenure spells would raise the estimate somewhat, but over time women are becoming more committed to the labor force and to their jobs (Mitchell, 1986).

9.   The fact that funding policies matter in the mandated-benefit context is also emphasized in some interesting work by Jensen and Gabel (1988) and Jensen et al. (1987). They find growing self-insurance of employer-provided health benefits plans; one explanation is that firms self-insure to avoid state mandates of coverage for specific services including alcoholism, drug and mental health treatment, and chiropractors when they self-insure. An additional explanation for this pattern is that self-insured firms are not required to participate in state risk pools covering people who cannot buy insurance on their own.

10. A nationally funded and operated health plan would reduce incentives to select against "expensive" employees, and would reduce labor market segmentation due to employee sorting. Specific suggestions to expand the role of Medicaid for the medically needy uninsured population are discussed and evaluated by Chollet (1987b) and Meyer (1988).

REFERENCES

Allen, S. F. (1981), "Compensation, Safely and Absenteeism: Evidence from the Paper Industry." *Industrial and Labor Relations Review* 33(January):207–218.

Anderson, J. (1987), "Effects of Mandatory Pensions on Firms, Workers and the Economy." In Dallas Salisbury (ed.), *Government Mandating of Employee Benefits*. Washington, DC: Employee Benefit Research Institute.

Andrews, E. S. (1988), "An Overview of the Employee Benefit System." Employee Benefit Research Institute, Paper presented at the National Research Council, November, Washington, DC.

———— (1989), *Pension Policy and Small Employers: At What Price Coverage?* Washington, DC: Employee Benefit Research Institute.

Beam, B. T., Jr., and J. J. McFadden (1988), *Employee Benefits*, 2nd edition. Homewood, IL: Irwin.

Becker, G. S. (1988), "If It Smells Like a Tax and Bites Like a Tax . . . ." *Business Week* (August 22).

Bell, D. N. F. and R. A. Hart (1988), "On-the-job and For-the-job Efficiency Labour Payments." Discussion Papers in Economics No. 8806, University of Glasgow.

Bell, D. and W. Marclay (1987), "Trends in Retirement Eligibility and Pension Benefits." *Monthly Labor Review* (April):18–25.

Brown, C. (1988), "Minimum Wage Laws: Are They Overrated?" *Journal of Economic Perspectives* 2(Summer):133–145.

Bulow, J. (1982), "What Are Corporate Pension Liabilities?" *Quarterly Journal of Economics* (August):435–552.

Bureau of National Affairs (1989), *Daily Labor Reporter* 21(February 2).

Chollet, D. (1987a), "A Profile of the Nonelderly Population Without Health Insurance." In Dallas Salisbury (ed.), *Government Mandating of Employee Benefits*. Washington, DC: Employee Benefit Research Institute.

———— (1987b), "Public Policy Options to Expand Health Insurance Among the Nonelderly Population." In Dallas Salisbury (ed.), *Government Mandating of Employee Benefits*. Washington, DC: Employee Benefit Research Institute.

Cook, A. H. (1989), "Public Policies to Help Dual Earner Families Meet the Demands of the Work World." *Industrial and Labor Relations Review* 42(January):201–215.

EBRI (1988), "Dependent Care: Meeting the Needs of a Dynamic Work Force." Issue Brief, Employee Benefit Research Institute, Washington, DC.

Ehrenberg, R. G. (1971), *Fringe Benefits and Overtime Behavior*. Lexington, MA: Lexington Books.

Ehrenberg, R. G. and P. J. Schumann (1982), *Longer Hours or More Jobs?* Ithaca, NY: ILR Press.

Ehrenberg, R. G. and R. S. Smith (1979), "Who Pays for Pensions in the State and Local Sector: Workers or Employers?" *IRRA 32nd Annual Proceedings*. Madison, WI: IRRA.

———— (1988), *Modern Labor Economics*, 3rd edition. Glenview, IL: Scott, Foresman.

Ehrenberg, R. G., P. Rosenberg, and J. Li. (1988), "Part-Time Employment in the United States." In R. A. Hart (ed.), *Employment, Unemployment, and Labor Utilization*. Boston: Unwin Hyman.

Ehrenberg, R. G., R. A. Ehrenberg, D. I. Rees, and E. L. Ehrenberg (1989), "School District Leave Policies, Teacher Absenteeism, and Student Achievement." Unpublished paper, Dept. of Labor Economics, Cornell University, Ithaca, NY.

Freeman, R. (1981), "The Effect of Unionism on Fringe Benefits." *Industrial and Labor Relations Review* 34(July):489–509.

Frumkin, R. (1986), "Health Insurance Trends in Cost Control and Coverage." *Monthly Labor Review* (September):3–8.

Gustman, A. L. and T. L. Steinmeier (1989), "An Analysis of Pension Benefit Formulas, Pension Wealth, and Incentives from Pensions." In R. Ehrenberg (ed.), *Research in Labor Economics*. Greenwich, CT: JAI Press, pp. 53–106.

Hamermesh, D. S. (1979), "Entitlement Effects, Unemployment Insurance and Employment Decisions." *Economic Inquiry* 17(July):317–332.

——— (1988), "The Demand for Workers and Hours and the Effects of Job Security Policies: Theories and Evidence." In R. A. Hart (ed.), *Employment, Unemployment and Labor Utilization*. Boston: Unwin Hyman.

Hart, R. A. (1984), *The Economics of Non-Wage Labour Costs*. London: George Allen and Unwin.

Hart, R. A., D. N. F. Bell, R. Frees, S. Kawasaki, and S. A. Woodbury (1988), *Trends in Non-Wage Labour Costs and Their Effects on Employment*. Commission of the European Communities, Programme for Research and Actions on the Development of the Labour Market. Luxembourg: Office for Official Publications of the European Communities.

Ippolito, R. (1986), *Pensions, Economics, and Public Policy*. Homewood, IL: Dow Jones–Irwin.

Jensen, G. A. and J. R. Gabel (1988), "The Erosion of Purchased Health Insurance." *Inquiry* 25(Fall):328–343.

Jensen, G. A., M. A. Morrisey, and J. W. Marcus (1987), "Cost Sharing and the Changing Pattern of Employer Sponsored Health Benefits." *Milbank Quarterly* 65(4):521–550.

Kotlikoff, L. (1987), "Justifying Public Provision of Social Security." *Journal of Policy Analysis and Management* 6(4):674–689.

Kotlikoff, L., A. Spivak, and L. Summers (1982), "The Adequacy of Savings." *American Economic Review* 72(5):1056–1069.

Mangum, G., D. Mayall, and K. Nelson (1985), "The Temporary Help Industry: A Response to the Dual Internal Labor Market." *Industrial and Labor Relations Review* 38:599–611.

McArdle, F. (1987), "The Pressure for New Legislated Mandates." In Dallas Salisbury (ed.), *Government Mandating of Employee Benefits*. Washington, DC: Employee Benefit Research Institute.

Meyer, J. (1988), "Mandated Benefits for Employees: A Policy Analysis." Report Prepared for the National Chamber Foundation, Washington, DC.

Mitchell, O. S. (1982), "Fringe Benefits and Labor Mobility." *Journal of Human Resources* 17(Spring):286–298.

——— (1982), "The Labor Market Impact of Federal Regulation: OSHA, ERISA, EEO, and Minimum Wage." In T. Kochan, D. Mitchell, and L. Dyer (eds.), *Industrial Relations Research in the 1970's: Review and Appraisal*. Madison, WI: Industrial Relations Research Association.

——— (1986), "How Does Job Tenure Vary with Sex and Age?" Department of Labor Economics Working Paper, Cornell University, Ithaca, NY.

——— (1988), "Worker Knowledge of Pension Provisions." *Journal of Labor Economics* 6(January):21–39.

Mitchell, O. S. and E. S. Andrews (1981), "Scale Economics in Multiemployer Pension Plans." *Industrial and Labor Relations Review* 34(July):522–530.

Mitchell, O. S. and A. Mikalauskas (1988), "The Impact of Government Regulation on the Labor Market." In D. Salisbury (ed.), *Government Mandating of Employee Benefits*. Washington, DC: Employee Benefit Research Institute.

Mitchell, O. S. and S. Pozzebon (1987), "Wages, Pensions and the Wage-Pension Tradeoff." Department of Labor Economics Working Paper, Cornell University, Ithaca, NY.

Morgan, G. G. (1987), "Parental Leave and the Child Care Issues." In Dallas Salisbury (ed.),

Government Mandating of Employee Benefits. Washington, DC: Employee Benefit Research Institute.

Mumy, G. E. (1985), "The Role of Taxes and Social Security in Determining the Structure of Wages and Pensions." *Journal of Political Economy* 93(June):574–585.

Munnell, A. (1989), "It's Time to Tax Employee Benefits." *New England Economic Review* (July–August):49–63.

Pauly, M. V. (1988), "The Incidence of Health Insurance: Is Everyone Out of Step but Economists?" Paper presented at the Industrial Relations Research Association Meetings, New York.

Quayle, Sen. D. (1987), Hearings on S.1265 before the Committee on Labor and Human Resources, U.S. Senate, November 4.

Rix, S. (1987), "Mandated Benefits and the Work/Family Dilemma." In Dallas Salisbury (ed.), *Government Mandating of Employee Benefits.* Washington, DC: Employee Benefit Research Institute.

Rosen, H. S. (1985), *Public Finance.* Homewood, IL: Irwin.

Scott, F. A., M. C. Berger, and D. A. Black (1988), "Effects of the Tax Treatment of Fringe Benefits on Labor Market Segmentation." *Industrial and Labor Relations Review* 42(January):216–229.

Simons, M. (1988), "Brazil Women Find Fertility May Cost Jobs." *The New York Times,* December 12.

Sindelar, J. (1982), "Differential Use of Medical Care by Sex." *Journal of Political Economy* 90(October):1003–1019.

Smith, R. S. (1988), "Comparable Worth: Limited Coverage and the Exacerbation of Inequality." *Industrial and Labor Relations Review* 41(January):227–238.

Smith, R. S. and R. Ehrenberg (1983), "Estimating Wage-Fringe Tradeoffs: Some Data Problems." In J. Triplett (ed.), *The Measurement of Labor Cost.* Chicago: University of Chicago Press.

Stout, H. (1988), "Propping Up Payments at the Bottom." *The New York Times,* January 24.

Summers, L. H. (1988), "Some Simple Economics of Mandated Benefits." *American Economic Review Papers and Proceedings.*

Thaler, R. and H. M. Shefrin (1981), "Pensions, Savings and Temptation." Graduate School of Business Working Paper No. 81-26, Cornell University, Ithaca, NY.

Trzcinski, E. (1988a), "Incidence and Determinants of Maternity Leave Coverage." Unpublished paper, University of Connecticut, Department of Economics.

———— (1988b), "Wages and Employment Effects of Mandated Leave Policies." Unpublished paper, University of Connecticut, Department of Economics.

U.S. Chamber of Commerce (1988), *Employee Benefits 1987.* Washington, DC: U.S. Chamber of Commerce.

U.S. Congress, Senate Committee on Labor and Human Resources (1987), *Hearings: Minimum Health Benefits for All Workers Act of 1987: Part II.* Washington, DC: U.S. Government Printing Office.

———— (1988), *Background Information on S.1265,* May 11.

U.S. General Accounting Office (1986), *Employee Stock Ownership Plans.* Washington, DC: U.S. Government Printing Office.

———— (1987), *Parental Leave: Estimated Costs of HR 925, The Family and Medical Leave Act of 1987.* Washington, DC: U.S. Government Printing Office.

———— (1988), *Parental Leave: Estimated Costs of the Revised Parental and Medical Leave Act.* Washington, DC: U.S. Government Printing Office.

U.S. Small Business Administration (Various years), *The State of Small Business: A Report to the President.* Washington, DC: U.S. Government Printing Office.

Wessels, W. J. (1980), "The Effect of Minimum Wages in the Presence of Fringe Benefits: An Expanded Model." *Economic Inquiry* 18(April):293–313.

Williams, H. B. (1989), "What Temporary Workers Earn: Findings from New BLS Survey." *Monthly Labor Review* (March):3–6.

Winkler, D. (1980), "The Effects of Sick Leave Policy on Teacher Absenteeism." *Industrial and Labor Relations Review* 33(January):232–240.

Woodbury, S. A. (1989), "Current Developments in Employee Benefits." Paper Prepared for the Commission on Workforce Quality and Labor Market Efficiency, March.

Research in Labor Economics

Edited by **Ronald G. Ehrenberg,** *New York State School of Industrial and Labor Relations, Cornell University*

REVIEWS: " ... an interesting new 'journal' in labor economics".
— *Journal of the American Statistical Association*

" ... the volume consists primarily of previously unpublished work by some of the leading figures in analytical labor economics. For this reason alone, it is worth perusal and anyone interested in the field ... If the editor can continue to find papers as high in quality as those published in this volume, the need for a publication like RLE will have demonstrated itself ..."
— *Industrial and Labor Relations Review*

"The collection of papers presented in the volume is good and presents potentially new directions for future research in labor market phenomena."
— *Southern Economic Journal*

Volume 5, 1982, 368 pp. $63.50
ISBN 0-89232-312-4

Supplement 2 - New Approaches to Labor Unions
Proceedings of a Conference on New Aproaches to Labor Unions, Blacksburg, Va., 1981
1983, 353 pp. $63.50
ISBN 0-89232-265-9

Edited by **Joseph Reid,** *Virginia Polytechnic Institute and State University*

JAI PRESS

Wayne Vroman, The Urban Institution. **Unemployment and Unemployment Insurance,** *Robert Topel, University of Chicago.* **The Impact of AFDC on Family Structure and Living Arrangements,** *David T. Ellwood, Harvard University and Mary Jo Bane, New York State Department of Social Services.* **Does the Labor Market Care? A Survey of the Evidence for the U.S.,** *Thomas J. Kniesner and Arthur H. Goldsmith, University of North Carolina, Chapel Hill.* **Military Manpower Research: An Introduction,** *Robert H. Baldwin, Thomas V. Daula, and D. Alton Smith, U.S. Military Academy, West Point.* **Estimating Enlistment Models for the U.S. Army,** *Thomas V. Daula and D. Alton, Smith, U.S. Military Academy, West Point.* **Army Recruit Attrition and Force Manning Costs: Methodology and Analyses,** *Robert H. Baldwin and Thomas V. Daula, U.S. Military Academy, West Point.* **Modeling the Retention Behavior of First-Term Military Personnel: Methodological Issues and a Proposed Specification,** *Robert H. Baldwin and Thomas V. Daula, U.S. Military Academy, West Point.*

Volume 8, 1986, 2 Volume Set
Part A-235 pp.   Part B-231 pp. $127.00
ISBN 0-89232-653-0

JAI PRESS